EXILES AND PIONEERS

Exiles and Pioneers analyzes the removal and postremoval histories of Shawnee, Delaware, Wyandot, and Potawatomi Indians. The book argues that the experience of these eastern Indians from the late 1700s to the 1860s was, at its core, a struggle over geographic and political places within the expanding United States. As American expansion limited the geographic scope of Indian lands, the extension of American territories and authority raised important questions about the political status of these Indians as individuals as well as nations within the growing republic. More specifically, the national narrative, and even the prominent images of Indian removal, cast the eastern Indians as exiles who were constantly pushed beyond the edges of American settlement. This study proposes that ineffective federal policies and ongoing debates within Indian communities also cast some of these eastern Indians as pioneers, unwilling trailblazers in the development of the United States.

John P. Bowes is an Assistant Professor in Native American History at Eastern Kentucky University. Dr. Bowes received a B.A. in history from Yale University and completed both his M.A. and Ph.D. in history at the University of California at Los Angeles. After receiving his doctorate, and prior to starting at Eastern Kentucky University, he spent two years as the Andrew W. Mellon Postdoctoral Fellow in Native American Studies at Dartmouth College.

Studies in North American Indian History

Editors

Frederick Hoxie, University of Illinois, Urbana-Champaign
Neal Salisbury, Smith College

This series is designed to exemplify new approaches to the Native American past. In recent years, scholars have begun to appreciate the extent to which Indians, whose cultural roots extended back for thousands of years, shaped the North American landscape as encountered by successive waves of immigrants. In addition, because Native Americans continually adapted their cultural traditions to the realities of the Euro-American presence, their history adds a thread of non-Western experience to the tapestry of American culture. Cambridge Studies in North American Indian History brings outstanding examples of this new scholarship to a broad audience. Books in the series link Native Americans to broad themes in American history and place the Indian experience in the context of social and economic change over time.

Also in the series:

RICHARD WHITE   *The Middle Ground: Indians, Empires, and Republics in the Great Lakes Regions, 1650–1815*

SIDNEY L. HARRING   *Crow Dog's Case: American Indian Sovereignty, Tribal Law, and United States Law in the Nineteenth Century*

COLIN G. CALLOWAY   *The American Revolution in Indian Country: Crisis and Diversity in Native American Communities*

FREDERICK E. HOXIE   *Parading through History: The Making of the Crow Nation in America, 1805–1935*

JEAN M. O'BRIEN   *Dispossession by Degrees: Indian Land and Identity in Natick, Massachusetts, 1650–1790*

CLAUDIO SAUNT   *A New Order of Things: Property, Power, and the Transformation of the Creek Indians, 1733–1816*

JEFFREY OSTLER   *The Plains Sioux and U.S. Colonialism from Lewis and Clark to Wounded Knee*

DAVID J. SILVERMAN   *Faith and Boundaries: Colonists, Christianity, and the Community Among the Wampanoag Indians of Martha's Vineyard, 1600–1871*

Exiles and Pioneers

Eastern Indians in the Trans-Mississippi West

JOHN P. BOWES

Eastern Kentucky University

THANKS FOR THE
GREAT INTRO AND DISCUSSION.
John Bowes

CAMBRIDGE
UNIVERSITY PRESS

CAMBRIDGE UNIVERSITY PRESS

Cambridge, New York, Melbourne, Madrid, Cape Town, Singapore, São Paulo, Delhi

Cambridge University Press
32 Avenue of the Americas, New York, NY 10013-2473, USA

www.cambridge.org
Information on this title: www.cambridge.org/9780521857550

First published 2007

Printed in the United States of America

A catalog record for this publication is available from the British Library.

Library of Congress Cataloging in Publication Data

Bowes, John P., 1973–
Exiles and pioneers : eastern Indians in the Trans-Mississippi West / John P. Bowes.
p.   cm. – (Studies in North American Indian history)
Includes bibliographical references and index.
ISBN 978-0-521-85755-0 (hardback) – ISBN 978-0-521-67419-5 (pbk.)
1. Indians of North America – Relocation.   2. Indians of North America –
Government relations.   3. Indians of North America – Land tenure.
4. Forced migration – Middle Atlantic States.   5. Forced migration – Northwest,
Old.   6. Middle Atlantic States – History.   7. Northwest, Old – History.
I. Title.   II. Series.
E98.R4B68   2007
973.04'973 – dc22   2006101962

ISBN   978-0-521-85755-0 hardback
ISBN   978-0-521-67419-5 paperback

To Mom and Dad

Contents

Acknowledgments

In January 2003 two people sat me down and presented an honest analysis of the dissertation draft I had recently written. I had high hopes for completing this project in time to file that May and receive my doctorate in June. Because that meeting took place nearly three years ago, I fail to remember every word that was uttered. I do know that a general discussion of additional research and revisions took place. In the end, however, one phrase from that conversation will always remind me of that day. That phrase contained two words – "mind numbing."

There is no need to identify the person who described my work in such a manner. But I would be remiss if I did not begin these acknowledgments by thanking Melissa Meyer and Steve Aron, first for their honesty in January 2003 and second for their guidance both during and after my years at UCLA. My dissertation and this book would not be if not for their able and astute advising. Melissa was the first professor I met at UCLA, and her intellectual and emotional support from day one made my graduate school experience worthwhile. She committed to me and I will always be in her debt. I am honored to have her as a mentor and fortunate to be her friend. Steve helped me formulate my ideas and refine my argument. But most important, he fostered a community among graduate students with similar interests. The discussions of WHEAT dissertation chapters at his house – assisted by good food, beer, and humor – taught me how to critique and be critiqued. Together, Melissa and Steve taught me to be a scholar.

It was my good fortune to find another supportive community right out of graduate school. Words will never quite capture the importance of the two years I spent as the Andrew W. Mellon Postdoctoral Fellow in Native American Studies at Dartmouth College. It made me a better historian and a better person. Colin Calloway kept his door open at all times and willingly read chapter after chapter of my ongoing revisions. He is a true mentor in every sense of the word. Darren Ranco made sure that I enjoyed my time in Hanover and kept me honest in my scholarship. Mishuana Goeman, my partner on the third floor, made sure that I read as much native literature as possible in my two years and constantly amazed me with the breadth of her knowledge. I could not ask for more from colleagues and friends. Vera Palmer, Dale Turner, Sergei Kan, Dan Runnels, and Linda Welch also brightened my days at Dartmouth. Thank you as well to Ed Miller and other members of the History Department who made me feel welcome. The two years passed by too quickly.

My work over the past eight years could not have been accomplished without the assistance of a number of places and people. First and most important, the UCLA History Department awarded me enough funding over the course of my graduate career to concentrate on my academics. A research grant from the UCLA Institute of American Cultures provided the financial support for my three-month stay in Kansas and Oklahoma. That excursion introduced me to a number of incredible institutions. I am forever indebted to the friendly librarians and archivists at the Kansas State Historical Society, the Kansas Collections at the University of Kansas, the Western History Collections at the University of Oklahoma, and the Oklahoma State Historical Society. I also thank Corey Hoover and Josh Clough, who made my time in both states all the more enjoyable. Thank you also to the fine people at the Missouri Historical Society in St. Louis and to Binh Tranh for housing me during my time in his town. The librarians, particularly those who manage inter-library loans, at UCLA and Dartmouth College will forever have my gratitude. But, for their support, the Leslie Humanities Center at Dartmouth and the Andrew W. Mellon Foundation deserve my utmost thanks. The two years of my fellowship allowed me the time and resources to turn my dissertation into a book. Thank you.

Countless additional people have contributed to this historical exercise. I have benefited from curious and critical questions at conferences, at job talks, and during informal conversations. To those unnamed individuals and groups, I thank you. As for those who shall be named, they are as follows. My fellow members of WHEAT – Lissa Wadewitz, Samantha Holtkamp, Lawrence Culver, Cindy Culver Prescott, Mike Bottoms, and Arthur Rolston – I appreciate your patience, insight, and friendship. Nick Rosenthal has been a good friend and I have benefited both from his comments on my work as well as his willingness to share his own writing with me. Tom Appleton's editorial expertise assisted me in my final revisions. And the insightful critiques of Fred Hoxie, Neal Salisbury, and the anonymous readers for Cambridge University Press made sure that this final product was as sharp and enlightening as possible. Thank you as well to Eric Crahan for all his work behind the scenes. Of course, what errors and/or mind-numbing prose are still in the manuscript remain my sole responsibility and all of the above individuals are free of blame.

Without the assistance of these scholars and friends, the substance of this book would not be here. Without the friendship and love of the people named below, I would not be here. The importance of my friends has been immeasurable long before I started this project and I must thank those who were with me from the beginning of my journey. To Mike Skonieczny, Ted Dowling, Bill Woods, Jason McBean, and Tyler Leshney I owe my sanity and good humor. One individual should not be so lucky to have such men in his life. To Grant Davis, Jane Davis, and Hannah Flynn, I thank you for making southern California a hospitable place for a New England boy. To Ryan Abraham, thank you for your friendship during my years in Los Angeles – this is the "paper" I have been working on for all this time.

My family has supported me at every point in my life and it is hard to thank them properly. Suzy, Katie, Chris, Michael, and Brendan have made my life, and the world for that matter, better. My parents, Jay and Taffy Bowes, have always been my biggest fans. Their confidence in me has helped me throughout my entire life and I love them more than words can say. I have told my wife, Sarah, many times that she should have read the acknowledgments of several history books before she agreed to marry me. It is early yet, and I have already taken her from the friendly confines of Hermosa Beach, California, to Derry, New Hampshire, and Lexington, Kentucky. And I am sure our adventure has only just begun. She is the love of my life and I am a better man because of her.

Abbreviations

ARCIA	*Annual Report of the Commissioner of Indian Affairs*
ASPIA	Walter Lowrie and Matthew St. Clair Clarke, Eds., *American State Papers, Documents, Legislative and Executive, of the Congress of the United States (1789–1815), Class II, Indian Affairs* (Washington, DC, 1832).
CFP	*Chouteau Family Papers*, Missouri Historical Society, St. Louis, MO
CIA	Commissioner of Indian Affairs
FBP	*Francis Barker Papers*, Kansas State Historical Society, Topeka, KS
IMP	*Isaac McCoy Papers*, Kansas State Historical Society, Topeka, KS
IMSC	Indian Mission Schools History Collection, 1837–1879, Kansas State Historical Society, Topeka, KS
Indian Affairs	Charles Kappler, compiler and editor, *Indian Affairs: Laws and Treaties* (7 volumes, Washington, DC, 1904).
JBA	James B. Abbott Papers, Kansas State Historical Society, Topeka, KS
JGP	John G. Pratt Papers, Kansas State Historical Society, Topeka, KS
JMP	Jotham Meeker Papers, Kansas State Historical Society, Topeka, KS
JTP	Nellie Armstrong Robertson and Dorothy Riker, comps. and eds., *John Tipton Papers* (3 volumes, Indianapolis, 1942).
KSHS	Kansas State Historical Society, Topeka, KS
MHS	Missouri Historical Society, St. Louis, MO

OIA-LR	Record Group 75 M234. Letters Received by the Office of Indian Affairs, 1824–1881. National Archives and Records Administration, Washington, DC. To reduce the length of the footnotes, roll number as opposed to name indicates the individual Superintendencies and Agencies.
OIA-TR	Record Group 75 T494. Documents Relating to the Negotiation of Ratified and Unratified Treaties with Various Indian Tribes, 1801–1869.
OSHS	Oklahoma State Historical Society, Oklahoma City, OK
RCA	*Richard Calmit Adams Papers*, Kansas Collection, Kenneth Spencer Research Library, University of Kansas, Lawrence, KS
RGP	*Richard Graham Papers*, Missouri Historical Society, St. Louis, MO
RSP	*Robert Simerwell Papers*, Kansas State Historical Society, Topeka, KS
SIA	Superintendent of Indian Affairs
TFP	*Thomas Forsyth Papers*, Missouri Historical Society, St. Louis, MO
TP	Clarence Edward Carter and John Porter Bloom, Eds., *The Territorial Papers of the United States* (28 volumes, Washington, DC, 1934–1975)
WNP	*Wyandot Nation Papers*, Kansas Collection, Kenneth Spencer Research Library, University of Kansas, Lawrence, KS

Introduction

Miss Mary McKee was 73 years old in 1911, and one of only a few Wyandot speakers on the Anderdon reserve in southwestern Ontario. In June of that year, she told anthropologist Marius Barbeau a number of stories, one of which summarized the relationship between Euro-Americans and Indians. She told the story in English. "In the beginning the white man came to speak to the Indian, who was sitting on the end of a log. 'Sit over!' said the white man. So the Indian allowed the stranger to sit on the log. But the other fellow kept on pushing him and repeating, 'Sit over! Sit over!' until the Indian found himself at the other end of the log. And then the white man said, 'Now all this log is mine!'" It was at once an uncomplicated, brief, and powerful narrative.[1]

What also strikes me about Mary McKee's story is how it contrasts with the documents I have spent hours reading over the past decade. Take, for example, a letter written in April 1850 by six Shawnee men. Charles Fish, Paschal Fish, James Captain, John Fish, Crane, and William Rogers wrote to Commissioner of Indian Affairs Orlando Brown from their homes south of the Kansas River just west of the Missouri border. Their seven-page missive detailed a number of complaints against the Methodists living and working on their reserve. Among other misdeeds, the missionaries had bribed and corrupted members of the Shawnee Council and neglected the children who attended their manual labor school. "The truth cannot be concealed," the six Shawnees proclaimed, "they [the Methodists] have departed from their legitimate office and have become 'money changers.'" But this accusation did not complete the list of grievances. The missionaries had also sided with proslavery forces in the recent split

---

[1] C. M. Barbeau, *Huron and Wyandot Mythology, with an appendix containing earlier published records* (Ottawa, 1915), xi, 287.

of the Methodist Episcopal Church. They then proceeded to harass those Shawnees who supported the antislavery Methodists and would not allow a northern preacher on the reserve. Charles Fish and his partners had a simple question for Commissioner Brown: "Shall we who live on free soil enjoy less liberty than the citizens of a slave state?"[2]

In some respects, it is not fair to compare McKee's story and the Shawnee letter. They come from different contexts and serve divergent purposes. One was a brief tale – McKee even told Barbeau that it was a saying, implying that "sit over" was a punch line to a cruel joke. The Shawnee letter, on the other hand, was written for a specific audience and was not intended for public consumption. Yet, the juxtaposition of these native voices and perspectives helps illuminate neglected aspects of the removal and postremoval experiences of eastern Indians. McKee's tale has a clear moral: white greed forced Indians from their land until they lived on a small fraction of their former territory. The visual imagery of McKee's Indian moving farther and farther down the log applies neatly to removal, where expansion and American policy forced tens of thousands of eastern Indians to relocate west of the Mississippi River. The 1850 letter, however, has a much more complicated context that involves not only a contest for power between two Shawnee factions, but also a national conflict over slavery and expansion in the western territories. More important, the letter and its contents present a more nuanced perspective of the relationship between Americans and Indians during the removal and postremoval era. Mary McKee's story provides the broad brushstrokes of a recognizable tale. The Shawnee letter opens a window into an unfamiliar story that is framed by familiar events – Indian actors whose lives were intertwined with the seminal events of American expansion in the nineteenth century.

Multilayered relationships in eastern Kansas influenced those six Shawnee men. An internal power struggle with a faction of Ohio Shawnees partially explains the written attack against the Methodists. But the choice of words is also telling. Charles Fish and his compatriots charged the missionaries with abandoning their religious principles and becoming "money changers." The very use of the phrase, perhaps a reference to the men Jesus threw out of the temple in a familiar Biblical event, highlights the background of at least two of the Shawnees. Both Charles and his brother Paschal attended mission schools in their youth, and while Charles translated for missionaries in the 1840s, Paschal often preached

---

[2] Shawnee Indians to Orlando Brown, April 22, 1850, OIA-LR, roll 303.

at the services. Finally, in their references to slavery these men displayed a clear understanding of past legislation and contemporary politics. They knew the Missouri Compromise prohibited slavery in their region and wanted it known that both missionaries and Shawnee leaders were in direct violation of that legislation.

The presence of the Shawnees in Kansas as well as their active engagement with Christianity and contemporary political issues were not anomalies. Shawnees and their Indian neighbors in the Great Lakes region did not simply vanish in the mid-nineteenth century. Their histories continued after notable events like the War of 1812, the Black Hawk War, and the Potawatomi Trail of Death. Military defeat and the Indian Removal Act served as points of transition, not as benchmarks of their demise. In short, the Mississippi River was not a contemporary version of the River Styx, with the ferryman collecting annuities as the Indians' payment for a one-way trip to the West. Indeed, the letter sent by six Shawnee men to Commissioner Brown in 1850 is only one thread from a diverse tapestry.[3]

But the thousands of native men, women, and children who left their homes and crossed the Mississippi were more than survivors. Not surprisingly, and as evidenced by the words of the Fish brothers and their colleagues, eastern Indians in the West had a very active interest in the events and people who influenced their lives. Midcentury disputes over slavery were viewed from a national perspective and through local contexts among the Wyandots and Shawnees. In their respective councils, Delawares and Potawatomis debated the difficulties associated with land ownership in the West and negotiated around the demands of railroads. They were American Indians who did not live in isolation from events that comprise the narrative of American history.

Exiles and Pioneers focuses on Shawnees, Delawares, Wyandots, and Potawatomis during a period of American expansion and evolving federal policy. It has at its foundation a simple premise – the history of these Indian communities in the nineteenth century encompasses a contest over

---

[3] One can find the story of Black Hawk in a number of sources. One place to start is Donald Jackson (Ed.), *Black Hawk: An Autobiography* (Urbana, IL, 1964). Within the context of Great Lakes history, a helpful summary of the conflict is in Helen Hornbeck Tanner (Ed.), *Atlas of Great Lakes Indian History* (Norman, OK, 1987), 151–154. A more recent account is Kerry A. Trask, *Black Hawk: The Battle for the Heart of America* (New York, 2006). For reports on the Potawatomi Trail of Death, see Irving McKee, *The Trail of Death: Letters of Benjamin Marie Petit* (Indianapolis, 1941); "Journal of an Emigrating Party of Pottawattomie Indians, 1838," *Indiana Magazine of History*, XXI(December 1925): 315–336. The events of the Trail are discussed in more detail in Chapter 2 of this book.

geographic and political place. Negotiations over and resistance to removal as well as the later struggles over land in Kansas decided the physical location of American Indians in the United States. But removal from the Great Lakes and subsequent relocations from Kansas tell only part of the history. In the 1850s and 1860s, the western expansion of the United States, through the creation of territories and states, made the standing of Indians in American politics an important element of policy discussions and diplomatic negotiations. Here, in the course of debates over allotment and citizenship, Indians as well as federal and state officials battled over the political status of native communities and individuals. Were they to become the citizen farmers once promoted by Thomas Jefferson or would they continue to exist as tribal communities separated from the American populace? Was it even that simple a proposition?

The federal government did not dominate the battle for physical space. In fact, during the removal era and the decades that followed, the enforcement of federal Indian policies remained ineffective. But such shortcomings proved a double-edged sword to eastern Indians. Although the absence of federal authority allowed for the persistence of native autonomy, it also provided traders, settlers, speculators, and local officials countless opportunities to promote their agendas at the expense of both federal policies and Indian interests. As a result, local power struggles rivaled and often exceeded federal legislation in importance. Rather than being a demonstration of the federal government's strength, therefore, the history of Indian removal and postremoval encompasses the prolonged battle for influence on both sides of the Mississippi River. From the late 1700s onward, Indian residents of the trans-Mississippi West exploited the weaknesses in U.S. Indian policy to maintain a measure of autonomy even as they suffered from the inability and unwillingness of the American government to protect Indian welfare.

From the early 1850s to the late 1860s, negotiations for Indian lands west of the Mississippi introduced allotment, discussed Indian citizenship, and resulted in near complete dispossession. Removal cast the Indians as exiles, a population that needed to move beyond the boundaries of the established nation until they could assume a place in American society. Yet, relocation also made the eastern Indians pioneers. On the prairie grasslands and along the thinly wooded waterways west of the Missouri state line, eastern Indians broke ground and struggled to adapt to a new environment. With the organization of Kansas Territory and Kansas' subsequent statehood, these border Indian communities faced both a choice and a challenge. The choice was clearly defined. They could leave lands they had only recently settled and move south to Indian Territory, or they could take their land in severalty and attempt to coexist with the white men and women who quickly populated the region. The challenge was more intricate. Having made their decision, Shawnees, Wyandots, Delawares, and Potawatomis had to struggle with the consequences. Internal power struggles often placed members of those four communities in opposition in debates over their future in the West. Meanwhile, the interference of state and federal officials further complicated the choice between citizenship and relocation as well as its consequences. But it was the pervasive dispossession in 1860s Kansas that provided the most significant obstacle and highlighted the underlying problem. In the end, the combination of those internal and external obstacles usually made the choice between relocation and citizenship irrelevant.

This process of Indian exile in the 1850s and 1860s built on the legacies and policies of the seven previous decades. Powerful and intrusive forces of American expansion transformed the lives of eastern Indians in the nineteenth century, and in the end, the Shawnees, Delawares, Wyandots, and Potawatomis lost most of their struggles over geography. Successive periods of land loss and relocation left most with small reserves, hundreds of miles from where they had lived decades earlier. Even the property rights granted by allotment provided little protection from settlers and speculators, and few Indians who sought to live as equals beside their Kansas neighbors met success. White pioneers populated Kansas before, during, and after the Civil War and Indians were once again cast as exiles. But native communities persisted. Although the struggles surrounding allotment and citizenship advanced dispossession in Kansas, that same process created the political structures and legal relationships that grounded the existence of numerous Shawnee, Delaware, Wyandot, and Potawatomi polities in the decades that followed.

The origins of this argument, and this book for that matter, are rooted in most of the usual places – graduate student naiveté, prior scholarship, archival research, conference presentations, classroom discussions, and continuous revisions. An article written by David Edmunds supplied the initial inspiration. By looking at the Potawatomis as pioneers in a different version of the western frontier, Edmunds highlighted a neglected period of movement, encounter, and experience. As eastern Indians confronted life in the West, they had new challenges before them, ones comparable to those faced by the European and American emigrants so prominent in

this country's national narrative. My appreciation for the western movements of eastern Indians was further enhanced by comments I received
one Sunday morning years ago at a conference in Tucson. As an attentive
crowd of three early risers looked on, Peter Iverson delivered a thought-
ful and thought-provoking critique of my presentation on Indian removal
in the Great Lakes. In one of his most helpful comments, Dr. Iverson
described Indian history as "a map in motion," an idea that directed my
attention to the larger context of Indian removal. Fortunately, or unfortunately, depending on one's perspective, my argument is also infused with
a dash of conceit nurtured by numerous graduate seminars in which I
had learned to dissect assigned readings. Bolstered by intellectual pride, I
set aside more than five hundred pages of complexity and nuance to take
issue with a single sentence from Richard White's influential study, *The
Middle Ground*. I focused my indignation on page 523, where "the Americans arrived and dictated," once the British left the *pays d'en haut* after
the War of 1812. Although I no longer see this phrase as a call to arms,
it makes sense that my first chapter begins with Tenskwatawa's stories,
drawn from the same source White used in the conclusion of his work. The
words within this book are, in some respects, a conversation with these
three phrases and, therefore, reflect the responses I have crafted over the
past several years to the conclusions that these scholars and others have
drawn from them.[4]

But this study does more than converse with the work of three historians. *Exiles and Pioneers* aims to rescue the Shawnees, Delawares,
Wyandots, and Potawatomis from the periphery of several prevailing narratives. The War of 1812 most often serves as the endpoint for discussions
of Indian activity in the southern Great Lakes region. Rather than retreating to the margins of history after the end of the War of 1812, however,
Indians from the Old Northwest remained vital participants in the territorial expansion and policy development of the American state in the
mid-nineteenth century. Autonomous migrations and ongoing diplomatic
relations provide pictures of native networks that did not disappear. This
narrative extension of Great Lakes Indian history subsequently opens the
door to another perspective on the removal era. Images of the Cherokees
on the Trail of Tears have epitomized both the removal experience and

---

4 R. David Edmunds, "Indians as Pioneers: Potawatomis on the Frontier," *The Chronicles
of Oklahoma*, 65(Winter 1987–1988), 340–353; Richard White, *The Middle Ground:
Indians Empires, and Republics in the Great Lakes Region, 1650–1815* (New York,
1991), 523.

the final defeat of Indians residing east of the Mississippi. But although numerous parallels exist between events in the Southeast and Great Lakes, the Cherokee experience is not necessarily representative of removal among the Shawnees, Delawares, Wyandots, and Potawatomis. Finally, slavery conflicts, American settlement, and railroad promotion have usually assumed center stage in the histories of both Kansas and the United States. Yet, struggles over slavery and the organization of Kansas Territory as well as enlistments in the Union Army likewise illustrate experiences that Indians shared with an expanding American nation.[5]

Those interested in the political, commercial, and social interactions between Indians and Europeans during the colonial era have primarily focused on events in the Ohio Valley. Drawn by the vibrant and violent episodes of the Seven Years' War and the American Revolution, historians focus on native confederacies and alliances with British, French, and American governments. The figures of Pontiac and Tecumseh have achieved particular notoriety because of their prominence in the resistance to colonization and external authorities. Such studies, intent on developments in the eighteenth century, have often pushed forward into the nineteenth century only because the War of 1812 serves as a tidy ending for the varied attempts of eastern Indians to battle Euro-American expansion between the Appalachian Mountains and the Mississippi River. Recent works have illustrated the complexities of these interactions more substantially than those in the past. Few can now question the fact that Indians throughout the Great Lakes region in the eighteenth century lived with an understanding of and an ability to influence imperial diplomacy. But even those histories that have brought greater sophistication to this narrative have used the year 1815 as a grand conclusion. The American

---

[5] Only Grant Foreman has broadly examined the removal and postremoval history of eastern Indians from the Southeast and the Great Lakes. See his *Indian Removal: The Emigration of the Five Tribes of Civilized Indians* (Norman, OK, 1932); *Advancing the Frontier, 1830–1860* (Norman, OK, 1933); *The Last Trek of the Indians* (Chicago, 1946). A number of other scholars have focused their efforts on Cherokee removal and the following list is only a sample of that larger historiography. See Thurman Wilkins, *Cherokee Tragedy: The Ridge Family and the Decimation of a People* (Norman, OK, 1988); William L. Anderson (Ed.), *Cherokee Removal: Before and After* (Athens, GA, 1991); Theda Perdue and Michael Green (Eds.), *The Cherokee Removal: A Brief History with Documents* (New York, 1995); John Ehle, *Trail of Tears: The Rise and Fall of the Cherokee Nation* (New York, 1997); Vicki Rozema, *Voices From the Trail of Tears* (Winston-Salem, NC, 2003). Even the examinations of removal policy primarily discuss the Cherokees and other southeastern Indians. The most notable examples include: Ronald N. Satz, *American Indian Policy in the Jacksonian Era* (Norman, OK, 2002); Anthony F. C. Wallace, *The Long, Bitter Trail: Andrew Jackson and the Indians* (New York, 1993).

victory in that conflict serves as the beginning of the end, the death knell for the native presence.[6]

Individual tribal histories have only partially corrected this shortcoming. Acknowledgments of physical and cultural persistence, rejections of a simple accommodation or resistance modality, and recognition of individual and tribal agency have strengthened the historiography in general. However, although most histories follow the tribal experience after the War of 1812, the emphasis remains on events of earlier time periods. Certain groups have received extensive attention while others have remained a part of the supporting cast. The Shawnees serve as the model for the Old Northwest. Numerous books have focused on Tecumseh, Tenskwatawa, and the Shawnee-driven confederacy in the late eighteenth and early nineteenth centuries. Once Tecumseh dies and Tenskwatawa loses authority, however, the Shawnees appear to vanish. Their role in the narrative comes to a decisive end. Although a recent study by Steve Warren provides a much-needed analysis of Shawnee political developments through 1870, his work and its chronology remain the exception rather than the norm.[7]

---

[6] For histories focused on struggles of the eighteenth century, see Randolph C. Downes, *Council Fires on the Upper Ohio: A Narrative of Indian Affairs in the Upper Ohio Valley until 1795* (Pittsburgh, 1940); Michael McConnell, *A Country Between: The Upper Ohio Valley and Its Peoples, 1724–1774* (Lincoln, NE, 1992); Colin G. Calloway, *The American Revolution in Indian Country: Crisis and Diversity in Native American Communities* (New York, 1995). For works that illustrate my latter point, see Colin G. Calloway, *Crown and Calumet: British-Indian Relations, 1783–1815* (Norman, 1987); White, *The Middle Ground*; Gregory Evans Dowd, *A Spirited Resistance: The North American Struggle for Unity, 1745–1815* (Baltimore, 1992). Other works that highlight the complicated nature of relationships in the region during this period include Eric Hinderaker, *Elusive Empires: Constructing Colonialism in the Ohio Valley, 1673–1800* (New York, 1997); R. David Edmunds, *The Shawnee Prophet* (Lincoln, NE, 1983); Susan Sleeper-Smith, *Indian Women and French Men: Rethinking Cultural Encounter in the Western Great Lakes* (Amherst, 2001); Patrick Griffin, "Reconsidering the Ideological Origins of Indian Removal: The Case of the Big Bottom 'Massacre,'" in Andrew R. L. Cayton and Stuart D. Hobbs (Eds.), *The Center of a Great Empire: The Ohio Country in the Early Republic* (Athens, OH, 2005), 11–35.

[7] The historiographies encompassing the histories of the Cherokee, Iroquois, and Sioux Indians are the best examples of this trend. Tribal histories consulted for this project include: C. A. Weslager, *The Delaware Indian Westward Migration: With the Texts of Two Manuscripts (1821–1822) Responding to General Lewis Cass's Inquiries About Lenape Culture and Language* (Wallingford, PA, 1978); C. A. Weslager, *The Delaware Indians: A History* (New Brunswick, NJ, 1972); James A. Clifton, *The Prairie People: Continuity and Change in Potawatomi Indian Culture 1665–1965* (Lawrence, 1977); R. David Edmunds, *The Potawatomis: Keepers of the Fire* (Norman, 1978); Robert Emmett Smith, Jr., "The Wyandot Indians, 1843–1876" (Ph.D. Dissertation, Oklahoma State University, 1973). Histories on the Shawnee Indians are largely based in their experience up to the War of 1812. See Jerry E. Clark, *The Shawnee* (Lexington, 1993); R. David Edmunds, *The*

This emphasis on the Old Northwest and the military confederacies in the Ohio Valley has also created a misleading chronology. The seemingly instinctive narrative shift from the defeat of Tecumseh and Tenskwatawa to the Cherokee struggles against Georgia implies that removal only followed military defeat and was an imposition of the federal government through legislation. It is here that Iverson's description of the "map in motion" fits so well. Shawnees, Delawares, Potawatomis, and Wyandots were only four of the many native communities who migrated into, out of, and within the Great Lakes region in the eighteenth and nineteenth centuries. And although analytical concepts, such as the middle ground, have highlighted intricate aspects of diplomacy, warfare, and coexistence, the maps that accompany such sophisticated arguments capture only a moment in time. Even the *Atlas of Great Lakes Indian History*, a work that performs a tremendous service to scholars of the titular region, presents freeze-framed locations of Indian settlements in different eras. A single map cannot adequately capture the relocations of individuals, families, and bands as they moved in response to the seasons, their relationship with each other, or their need to be closer to or farther from Euro-American settlements. Most important, this historical map in motion provides a broader chronological context for discussions of removal.[8]

The military defeats of the 1810s and the Indian Removal Act of 1830 did not spark migrations in otherwise sedentary native populations, a point illustrated by the experiences of Shawnees and Delawares in the decades prior to the passage of removal legislation. As of the late eighteenth century, the Shawnee population included some of the most well-traveled native communities on the entire continent. Former Shawnee villages could be found throughout the eastern United States from north to south. The Lenni Lenape, or Delaware Indians as English colonists called them, were also late arrivals to the Ohio Valley, having first encountered Europeans along the Atlantic Coast. Prior to taking up residence along the White River in Indiana in the late eighteenth and early nineteenth centuries, the main Delaware villages had gradually moved west

---

Shawnee Prophet (Lincoln, 1983); John Sugden, *Blue Jacket: Warrior of the Shawnees* (Lincoln, 2000). Two exceptions (beyond Warren) to this trend are neither recent nor comprehensive. See Grant Harrington, *The Shawnees in Kansas* (Kansas City, KS, 1937); Henry Harvey, *History of the Shawnee Indians, From the Year 1681 to 1854, Inclusive* (New York, reprinted in 1971). As noted, Steve Warren's work marks an important step in the right direction. See his *The Shawnees and Their Neighbors, 1795–1870* (Urbana, 2005).

[8] Tanner, *Atlas of Great Lakes Indian History*.

through Pennsylvania, retreating in response to the advance of colonial settlement. Shawnees and Delawares also made some of the most substantial migrations west of the Mississippi in the years prior to removal legislation. Indeed, by 1830, the majority of Shawnees lived west of that river.[9]

At its foundation, Indian removal is a narrative about power and geographic relocation. Although the changing power relations of this historical era cannot be ignored and are difficult to dispute, an examination of movement provides a new perspective. Only by analyzing this larger history will a new understanding emerge regarding the continuities and discontinuities in westward relocations and power relations. The first two chapters treat removal within that expansive context. In Chapter 1, competing visions and uses of the Mississippi River from the late eighteenth to the early nineteenth century offer insights into both colonial rivalries and the nature of Indian migrations. From the 1760s to the 1820s the Spanish, British, and Americans fought to define the Mississippi River as a political boundary and tried to control the movements of peoples in the region. Despite these efforts, both Shawnees and Delawares consistently viewed the Mississippi as a corridor while simultaneously depending on networks of kinship and commerce to support their departures from the conflict-ridden Ohio Valley. Chapter 2 analyzes the enactment of Indian removal through the experiences of multiple Potawatomi bands from the southern Great Lakes as well as the relocation of a multiethnic emigrant party from Wisconsin Territory. After the passage of the Indian Removal Act, U.S. treaty commissioners made every effort to obtain Indian lands and arrange for the relocation of the Potawatomis and their neighbors from the region. But the dispersed nature of federal authority allowed for both the manipulation of the process by local officials and traders and the continuation of native kinship networks that still supported Indian movements.

Removal to the western territories instigated changes in the eastern Indians' way of life. The journey had displaced them from familiar lands

---

[9] James H. Howard, *Shawnee!: The Ceremonialism of a Native Indian Tribe and Its Cultural Background* (Athens, OH, 1981), 6–16; Vernon Kinietz and Erminie W. Voegelin (Eds.), *Shawnese Traditions: C. C. Trowbridge's Account* (Ann Arbor, June 1939), 55–57, 60–63; Charles Callender, "Shawnee," in William C. Sturtevant (Ed.), *Handbook of North American Indians* (17 volumes, Washington, DC, 1978), XV, 630–631; Jerry Eugene Clark, "Shawnee Indian Migration: A System Analysis" (Ph.D. Dissertation, University of Kentucky, 1974); Dark Rain Thom, *Kohkumthena's Grandchildren: The Shawnee* (Indianapolis, 1994), 235–246; Ives Goddard, "Delaware," in Sturtevant, *Handbook of North American Indians*, XV, 213–239; Weslager, *The Delaware Indian Westward Migration*.

and forced them to find a way to live in a new environment. But how dramatic was that change? Where were the continuities and discontinuities in the fabric of their lives? In short, when did the removed and emigrant Indians from the Great Lakes become border Indians living in eastern Kansas?

It is neither a simple question nor a simple answer, if only because so many different individuals and communities took part in the process. Chapter 3 grounds the discussion by addressing the day-to-day existence on the border. For the Shawnees and Delawares who first moved west of the Mississippi in the late eighteenth century, the relocation to eastern Kansas was less transformative than for the Potawatomis forced west at gunpoint in the late 1830s. All encountered environments – climate, timber resources, and vegetation – that were dissimilar from their previous homes. It is often difficult to access their ordinary lives and the ways that relocation affected daily survival. But it is clear that their adjustments reflected both the particular nature of life on the Missouri state line from the 1830s to the 1850s and the persistence of traditional subsistence patterns.

Adaptations in daily life were paralleled by negotiations not only among the vast numbers of relocated Indians and the western tribes they had displaced, but also with the threat of impending American expansion. In Chapter 4, continuity and discontinuity remain important ideas as border Indian leaders fashioned their responses to the tendrils of American settlement that crossed the border shortly after relocation and with increasing strength in the early 1850s. The eastern Indians turned first to diplomacy and looked for ways to adapt customary practices to their new realities. They made numerous attempts to reestablish former alliances. But every council participant recognized the need to balance the desire for unified resistance to American expansion with the specific interests of their respective communities. And even as the relit council fires illustrated the perseverance of inter-Indian diplomacy west of the Mississippi, the failure of those confederacies revealed the unwillingness of many to cede any power over their lands and negotiations on the border.

Chapter 5 uses Joseph Parks and William Walker to exemplify the dramatic and intertwined changes in the religious and political lives of the Shawnees and Wyandots on the Kansas River. Although they were not emblematic of the average resident of their respective reserves, each man reflected the alterations in leadership that occurred throughout the border Indian communities. From the late eighteenth century to the mid-1850s, men like Parks and Walker ascended to positions of power by taking

advantage of the intertwined disruptions in the religious and political lives
of the Shawnees and Wyandots. This process of political change began
prior to removal, and it came to fruition in the 1840s and 1850s.

From the very beginning of my research, world-systems theory, with its
use of societal cores, peripheries, and regions of refuge, has provided a
useful, although at times limited, framework for my analysis. In its initial
formation from the work of Immanuel Wallerstein, this theory concen-
trates on the ways that core regions incorporate peripheries primarily
through economics. In subsequent articles, Thomas D. Hall uses several
examples to argue that peripheral societies do not simply submit to the
core's attempts at absorption, but, rather, shape the process of incorporation. Critiques of world-systems theory as well as new research has led
Hall and others to revise their ideas, and a theory once focused on economics is now a perspective or a paradigm that includes discussions of
political and cultural interactions in addition to economics.[10]

Although this ongoing evolution of the world-systems perspective
reflects constructive responses to its critics, its framework remains incomplete and cannot account for events in eastern Kansas in the 1850s and
1860s. Specifically, the central tenets of world-systems continue to emphasize the incorporation of peripheries and the extent to which native societies are able to resist absorption into the core. Although this line of
questioning takes native agency into account, it fails to address more
intricate negotiations. Indeed, the various struggles between Indians and
non-Indians in the nineteenth-century trans-Mississippi West embody
what Hall refers to as "contested frontiers" with two "competing world-
systems." This is particularly evident in the complex struggles in eastern Kansas after the organization of Kansas Territory. In the 1850s, the
Wyandot elite worked hard to bring their community into the American

---

[10] For early formations of world-systems theory, see Immanuel Wallerstein, *The Modern
World-System II: Mercantilism and the Consolidation of the European World Economy,
1600–1750* (New York, 1980); Thomas D. Hall, "Incorporation in the World-System:
Toward a Critique," *American Sociological Review,* 51(June, 1986): 390–402; Thomas
D. Hall, "Peripheries, Regions of Refuge, and Nonstate Societies: Toward A Theory
of Reactive Social Change," *Social Science Quarterly,* 64(1983): 582–597. For a brief
overview of world-systems as well as an extensive bibliography of recent work in the
field, see Thomas Hall, "World-Systems Analysis: A Small Sample from a Large Uni-
verse," in Thomas D. Hall (Ed.), *A World-Systems Reader: New Perspectives on Gender,
Urbanism, Cultures, Indigenous Peoples, and Ecology* (Lanham, MD, 2000), 3–28. For
a discussion of how altered perspectives have affected the treatment of native peoples
in world-systems, see Thomas D. Hall, "Frontiers, Ethnogenesis, and World-Systems:
Rethinking the Theories," in Thomas D. Hall (Ed.), *A World-Systems Reader,* 237–270.

nation even as more conservative leaders struggled to maintain a sovereign tribal government. Similar factions within the Shawnees battled in the 1860s to preserve a national identity even as they accepted the concepts of individual land ownership. Both situations illustrate characteristics of world-systems but blur the more straightforward relationships that ground this paradigm.[11]

In the 1850s and 1860s, American expansion collided full-force with a treaty-proscribed Indian Country west of the Missouri border. For the better part of two decades, Kansas Territory served as both the stage for critical events in the national progression toward civil war and the focal point for dispossession and removal of the border Indians. Kansas entered the Union as a free state in 1861 and, by the early 1870s, was mostly free of an Indian population. But the history of those events is as much about the process as it is about the fact that dispossession occurred. Over the course of nearly 20 years, the leaders of border Indian communities made crucial decisions regarding land ownership and tribal status. Although ultimately more complex, the choice was seen as one between living with American expansion and accepting yet another relocation. The Indians in Kansas could choose to be exiles or pioneers.[12]

---

[11] For two critiques of world-systems theory, see Melissa L. Meyer, *The White Earth Tragedy: Ethnicity and Dispossession at a Minnesota Anishinaabe Reservation, 1889–1920* (Lincoln, 1994), 2–4; Brian C. Hosmer, *American Indians in the Marketplace: Persistence and Innovation Among the Menominees and Metlakatlans, 1870–1920* (Lawrence, 1999), 9–13; Hall, "Frontiers, Ethnogenesis, and World-Systems," 253.

[12] For American Indian history in Kansas, only a few works address the period covered by my study. See Craig Miner and William E. Unrau, *The End of Indian Kansas: A Study of Cultural Revolution, 1854–1871* (Lawrence, reprinted in 1990); Joseph B. Herring, *The Enduring Indians of Kansas: A Century and a Half of Acculturation* (Lawrence, 1990); Dorothy V. Jones, "A Preface to the Settlement of Kansas," *Kansas Historical Quarterly,* 29(Summer 1963): 122–136; Anna Heloise Abel, "Indian Reservations in Kansas and the Extinguishment of their Title," *Transactions of the Kansas State Historical Society,* 8(1903–1904): 72–109; Bert Anson, "Variations of the Indian Conflict: The Effects of the Emigrant Indian Removal Policy, 1830–1854," *Missouri Historical Review,* 59(October 1964): 64–89. The period prior to 1854 is largely neglected, except through individual tribal histories. Some relatively recent articles prove to be chronological exceptions, although they all focus on the Shawnees. See Kevin Abing, "A Holy Battleground: Methodist, Baptist, and Quaker Missionaries Among Shawnee Indians, 1830–1844," *Kansas History,* 21(1998): 118–137; Kevin Abing, "Before Bleeding Kansas: Christian Missionaries, Slavery, and the Shawnee Indians in Pre-Territorial Kansas, 1844–1854," *Kansas History,* 24(2001): 54–70; Stephen Warren, "The Baptists, the Methodists, and the Shawnees: Conflicting Cultures in Indian Territory, 1833–1834," *Kansas History,* 17(1994): 148–161; see also Louise Barry (Ed.), *The Beginning of the West: Annals of the Kansas Gateway to the American West, 1540–1854.* Although it is not a narrative

Chapters 6 and 7 expand on the complications inherent in that process. Chapter 6 details how Delaware leaders turned to allotment when it became apparent that neither the federal nor the territorial government had an interest in protecting Indian lands. Their Wyandot neighbors pushed for allotment and citizenship before 1854, hoping to establish themselves securely and even possibly to profit from the waves of American settlement. In each case, a powerful minority made these decisions. Under opposition and protest from members of their communities, men who believed they would benefit from allotment and the growth of American settlements decided the fate of their people.

In the end, however, the absence of federal authority and the intrusions of local interests made the choice between being an exile and being a pioneer an empty one. Although it was a story similar to that of the Wyandots and Delawares, the story of the Shawnees and Potawatomis detailed in Chapter 7 focuses not only on the power relations that structured the decisions made by the Ohio Shawnee Council and the Potawatomi Business Committee but also on the aftermath of their decisions. In each case, the leadership that benefited from the intertwined relationship between wealth and power worked hard to create a secure existence alongside the American citizens who flooded the region. But, in the years after the Civil War, even those who had once believed in their ability to remain in Kansas signed treaties arranging for relocation to Indian Territory.

This book ends at the point where most Potawatomis, Delawares, Wyandots, and Shawnees left Kansas and established new homes in Indian Territory or elsewhere. Although the Epilogue references the presence of federally recognized bands and nations in the twenty-first century, the intent is not simply to stress survival or persistence. Instead, the histories presented in the following pages emphasize the importance of events in the mid-nineteenth century to the future of these native communities. Not only did the Potawatomis, Delawares, Wyandots, and Shawnees still exist once they crossed the Mississippi River from the 1780s to the 1840s, but they also established new lives on the border. Residents of Kansas during a critical juncture in U.S. history, these Indians were active participants in the regional history of trade, land rushes, slavery, and the Civil War.

Indeed, in many respects, this history does not deviate far from the standard discussions of nineteenth-century U.S. history. There is nothing new in stories about westward movement and the struggle to work the land. The evils of land speculation fit well in many tales of American

history, Barry's book is an invaluable source for events in the region from the 1820s to 1854.

pioneering and the connections between the Kansas Territory and slavery require no further emphasis. Shawnee women who sold off portions of their allotment in the 1860s because they needed money while their husbands fought in the Civil War could have found empathy in contemporary northern and southern communities. And the legal battles against unjust taxation might live comfortably in just about any century. In short, the Potawatomis, Wyandots, Delawares, and Shawnees discussed in *Exiles and Pioneers* fit neatly within the national narrative that has so often left them behind or on the margins.

From the 1780s to the 1870s, these border Indian communities negotiated, debated, and fought for their geographic and political place in an American nation envisioned and created by settlers, businessmen, politicians, and bureaucrats. Although dispossession limited the struggles over geography in the years that followed, the battles over political place had only just begun and the epilogue of this historical study therefore hints at hidden ambitions. Distinct Potawatomi, Shawnee, Delaware, and Wyandot bands located throughout the United States continue to negotiate their sovereignty in relation to local, state, and federal governments. And although so much has changed over the years, the foundations of those contests have not. More than those of any other historical period, developments of the mid-nineteenth century created the framework for the legal and political battles of these four communities in the decades and centuries that have followed. That they continue to promote their distinct interests is a testament to the strength and experience of the Potawatomis, Delawares, Wyandots, and Shawnees respectively. That they still have to fight these battles is a testament to the influence of events described in the following pages.

PART ONE

FROM THE GREAT LAKES TO
THE PRAIRIE PLAINS

THE USE OF THE INDIAN REMOVAL ACT AS A PROMINENT TURNING point in American Indian history requires a framework of conflict, revitalization, and power. Bloody contests of the late colonial and early national period dominate discussions of the Great Lakes region prior to 1830. Imperial battles, pan-Indian resistance, and backcountry raids tore apart the homes and the lives of native residents. Hand in hand with the native resistance to the endless physical and cultural assaults came the resurgent spiritual and revitalization movements led by Pontiac, Handsome Lake, and Tenskwatawa. At the same time, in both obvious and subtle ways, the balance of power in Indian relations first with Europeans and then with Americans began to shift. With the rise of the American republic came a decline in the ability of Indians to negotiate from a position of strength. The viability of the middle ground seemed to have fallen with the death of Tecumseh and the decline of the Indian Confederacy. This created an interdependent relationship that allows for little wiggle room in historical interpretation. Removal serves as the logical endpoint to failed attempts by Indians to resist invasion through militant and cultural means.

But 1830 and the Indian Removal Act need not be such preeminent benchmarks. In the first place, their usefulness as narrative turning points relies on a rejection of the perspectives and histories of the Indian peoples targeted by the removal policies. By 1830, most Shawnees and Delawares had long ago departed their homes in the Ohio Valley, and their concerns and homes rested on the banks of the Missouri and Kansas rivers. Many of these emigrants had taken advantage of imperial rivalries and moved west of the Mississippi River in the late eighteenth century. For these communities, therefore, 1803 might serve as a more critical year. The transfer of the Louisiana Territory from Spain to the United States signaled the dawn of a new era because the waters of the Mississippi no longer separated Shawnee and Delaware settlements from the reach of U.S. policies. Even the relocations that occurred after 1830 reflected a more intricate combination of causes and effects than those envisioned by federal officials who wrote the Indian Removal Act. Most important, the removals of Indians from the Great Lakes region in the 1830s often illustrated the continued presence and relevance of native kinship networks even as they indicated the strength and influence of local settlers and traders. The Potawatomi Trail of Death in the fall of 1838 proved that the absence of complete federal authority did not eliminate the harsh realities of removal. But the migration of a multiethnic party of Stockbridge, Delawares, and Munsees one year later revealed that forced relocation was only one thread in a more expansive narrative.

The power imbalance at the center of this story is impossible to ignore. By the late 1840s, thousands of Indians lived on reserves west of the Mississippi instead of in their homes on the Wabash, St. Joseph, and other rivers throughout the Great Lakes region. Their experiences illustrated the impact of federal policy and the brute force of colonial expansion. But this history of removal also exists within a larger narrative of migration and within the natives' understanding of the world around them; and that is an important distinction.

I

Border and Corridor

Shawnees, Delawares, and the Mississippi River

In the mid-1820s, in Detroit, Charles C. Trowbridge, the personal secretary and assistant to Governor of Michigan Territory Lewis Cass, spoke with Tenskwatawa, also known as the Shawnee Prophet, and Black Hoof, who was an elderly headman of the Ohio Shawnees. In separate interviews, the young secretary requested specific information regarding Shawnee family relations, government structures, and religious practices. Almost a decade removed from the defeat of the Indian confederacy inspired by his own visions and organized by his brother Tecumseh, the Shawnee Prophet was very willing to talk. He and his small band of followers lived in exile near Fort Malden, Ontario, and the Prophet now saw an opportunity to regain influence by renewing relations with American officials. Black Hoof, an 80-year-old veteran of conflicts against the Americans before, during, and after the Revolution, similarly sought to strengthen his position by presenting his perspective on Shawnee origins and governance.[1]

Both men spoke of migrations from the centuries of Shawnee history. Asked about the "sacred fire" maintained by the Shawnees, Tenskwatawa referred to his ancestors' first movements. "When the Shawnees first crossed the sea," the Prophet began, "the Great Spirit told them to go to Shawnee river, which was the center of this Island....From there he told

---

[1] Vernon Kinietz and Erminie W. Voegelin (Eds.), *Shawnese Traditions: C. C. Trowbridge's Account* (Ann Arbor, 1939). For a brief background of Trowbridge, see C. A. Weslager, *The Delaware Indian Westward Migration: With the Texts of Two Manuscripts (1821–1822) Responding to General Lewis Cass's Inquiries about Lenape Culture and Language* (Wallingford, PA, 1978), 159–160. For two analyses of Trowbridge's interviews with Tenskwatawa and Black Hoof, see Richard White, *The Middle Ground: Indians, Empires, and Republics in the Great Lakes Region, 1650–1815* (New York, 1991), 519–523; Stephen Warren, *The Shawnees and Their Neighbors, 1795–1870* (Urbana, 2005), 13–17.

them that they would go to Weeyukewaa wee Theepee, Mad River . . . and
thence to the Mississippi, where they would remain a short time, and
where they would discover something coming towards them (the whites),
which would make them very poor and miserable." Black Hoof presented
a slightly different version but also addressed some of the more recent
Shawnee migrations. In the elderly headman's description, the confederated tribes of Shawnees fought their way from the Mississippi River to
the eastern seaboard, where they encountered the Delawares just prior
to the arrival of the Quakers. The Shawnees stayed in that area for only
a short period of time, kept moving, and did not form a permanent settlement until they reached the mouth of the Scioto River in present-day
Ohio. Although some Shawnees later moved south and settled among the
Creek Indians, others crossed the Mississippi River and settled in Spanish
territory. According to the Shawnee headman, the approximately three
hundred Indians living west of the Mississippi, the four hundred living
at Wapakoneta, and the small numbers of the Prophet's party constituted
the Shawnee nation.[2]

Trowbridge's interviews with these two prominent Shawnees were more
than just cultural research. They also represented the clash between the
native traditions of movement and the American government's plans for
the lands east of the Mississippi River. Tenskwatawa and Black Hoof
spoke of migrations that crisscrossed the continent. Over the previous
centuries, individuals, families, and bands had moved by choice and
necessity, depending on the circumstances. But Trowbridge spoke with
the two Shawnee leaders to capture ethnographic information about a
people viewed by Americans as defeated and in decline. At both the state
and national level, proponents of Indian removal agitated for an established policy that would clear the eastern lands of native residents. Even
as Tenskwatawa and Black Hoof talked about the movements of the past
and the settlements of the present, American officials prepared to erase
the native presence from the eastern woodlands.[3]

---

[2] Kinietz and Voegelin (Eds.), *Shawnese Traditions*, 55–57, 60–63. Black Hoof's estimation
   of the Shawnee population west of the Mississippi was much lower than the actual
   number of nearly two thousand. A more comprehensive account of seventeenth- and
   eighteenth-century Shawnee migrations can be found in James H. Howard, *Shawnee!:
   The Ceremonialism of a Native Indian Tribe and Its Cultural Background* (Athens, OH,
   1981), 6–16; Jerry Eugene Clark, "Shawnee Indian Migration: A System Analysis" (Ph.D.
   Dissertation, University of Kentucky, 1974).

[3] Shawnee accounts of migrations were not unique. See "Account of some of the Traditions, Manners, and Customs of the Lenee Lenaupaa or Delaware Indians," in C. A.
   Weslager, *The Delaware Indians: A History* (New Brunswick, NJ, 1972), 473–476; Daniel

The contest between these competing visions revolved around the Mississippi River. To Americans, the Mississippi was a border. In the past, it had been an imperial instrument that delineated French, Spanish, and British territories. Even after the Louisiana Purchase, it geographically and figuratively divided the settled eastern states from the untamed western territories. Soon, federal officials hoped, the river would fulfill Thomas Jefferson's vision and separate American settlers and civilization from the savagery of an Indian Country populated by western and relocated eastern tribes. To Indians, however, the Mississippi was a corridor that supported intertwining kinship, commercial, and migratory networks. During and after the colonial era, the river carried people and trade goods, just like all the other waterways coursing through the Great Lakes region. And although aware that this liquid boundary often restricted Euro-American movements, the eastern Indians did not submit to similar limitations.

Native use of the Mississippi River as a corridor persisted despite efforts by the United States to impose its political and figurative meaning – a circumstance reflected most clearly in the diverse migrations of Shawnee and Delaware bands from the American Revolution to the late 1820s. America's status as the primary colonizing power in the trans-Mississippi West heralded the decline of the middle ground in the region once described by the French as the *pays d'en haut*. However, nominal American authority did not eliminate relationships that had long supported diplomacy and migration. Nor did American ideas about the Mississippi River force eastern Indians to view it as a border created and controlled by American policies. Instead, bands of Shawnees and Delawares worked within familiar frameworks to arrange for both their migration to and settlement in the western territories. American expansion into the Ohio Valley served as a catalyst for these migrations and simultaneously provoked calls among American citizens for the relocation of all native residents. The federal government also negotiated treaties that foreshadowed the Indian-removal legislation to come. But into the late 1820s, it was the Indians' conception of the Mississippi, not the machinations of local or federal officials, which underscored their movements to and from the West.[4]

G. Brinton, *The Lenape and their Legends: With the Complete Text and Symbols of the Walam Olum* (New York, 1969), 122–126; Robert Emmett Smith, Jr., "The Wyandot Indians, 1843–1876" (Ph.D. Dissertation, Oklahoma State University, 1973), 8–15; James A. Clifton, *The Prairie People: Continuity and Change in Potawatomi Indian Culture, 1665–1965* (Lawrence, KS, 1977), 35–41, 66–68, 158–161.

4 For the history of European and Indian interactions that defined this middle ground in the Great Lakes region, see White, *The Middle Ground*.

The Mississippi River served diverse purposes during the colonial period. Tenskwatawa referred to it as a destination, a marker in the course of Shawnee migrations, and the point of first contact with white men. From the perspective of Spanish, French, and English officials, the Mississippi River both delineated the boundaries between colonial interests and carried the produce of the fur trade. Although this wide waterway, at times, presented a formidable natural obstacle to travelers on either side, it also allowed traders and missionaries to journey from the Great Lakes to New Orleans with only a few portages required. The river connected as much as it divided, and Indians on both sides used it as a causeway and a boundary, depending on their needs. For the Shawnees and Delawares who journeyed west in the late eighteenth century, the Mississippi River served as both an avenue to Spanish Territory and a buffer against the American expansion that drove them from the Old Northwest.

The Shawnees had a longer history in the Ohio Valley than did the Delawares. Though some disagreement exists over specific precontact locations, most Shawnees resided north of the Ohio River by the mid-seventeenth century. The residents of these scattered settlements shared a common language and historical relationship, but they did not form a united polity. Five semiautonomous divisions – Chillicothe, Maykujay, Thawegila, Piqua, and Kispokotha – structured Shawnee relations. Although each division had its distinct leadership, the principal Shawnee headman originated from either the Chillicothe or the Thawegila division. Under this loose confederation, however, Shawnee governance was grounded in kin and village relations, not in the proclamations of a single leader. Their migrations illustrated this dispersed autonomy. Conflict with the Iroquois in the 1660s drove them from their lands, and the Shawnees began a cycle of dispersal and regrouping that lasted into the 1800s. The dawn of a new century found Shawnee bands along the Ohio, Savannah, Susquehannah, and Illinois rivers, locations that, for the most part, served as temporary homes. A coalescence of these disparate communities occurred gradually in the first decades of the eighteenth century as Shawnees migrated either to settlements along the Susquehannah in Pennsylvania or to villages among the Upper Creeks on the Chattahoochee River in southern Georgia. Trade, conflict, and treaties influenced the movements of both the northern and southern Shawnee communities in the years that followed. Although game population decline and Iroquois land cessions pushed the northern groups westward from Pennsylvania, clashes with the Chickasaws and alliances with the Creeks guided

Shawnee settlement further south. And when the Iroquois ceded large chunks of Shawnee and Delaware lands in the Treaty of Fort Stanwix in 1768, the Ohio River became, on paper at least, the southern boundary for the northern Shawnees.[5]

The Delawares arrived in the Ohio Valley from the Delaware River Valley via Pennsylvania, a gradual migration that played out over two centuries. The designation of Delaware for those who called themselves Lenape has generally applied to those Indians who spoke two different dialects, Unami and Munsee, though, like the Shawnees, these groups never formed a clear political unit. They lived close to the centers of colonization along the mid-Atlantic Coast during the first decades of contact and, therefore, encountered Dutch, Swedish, and British settlers earlier than the Shawnees did. Trade relations flourished, but the increasing European populations led to tension and violence in the mid-1600s. By the early 1700s, Delaware settlements were concentrated in the Susquehannah Valley in eastern Pennsylvania. Over the next several decades, the Quaker invasion eroded Indian land ownership, most notoriously in the Walking Purchase of 1737. In this infamous arrangement, the Englishmen turned a boundary agreement into a colonial-era adventure race and claimed a total of 60 miles when the Indians intended to cede no more than 25 miles. When the French and British once again moved toward war in the 1750s, many Delawares relocated to avoid conflict, leaving the Allegheny and Beaver valleys behind for the somewhat more secure environs along the Muskingum and Scioto rivers to the west.[6]

[5] Charles Callender, "Shawnee," in William C. Sturtevant (Ed.), *Handbook of North American Indians* (17 vols., Washington, DC, 1978), XV, 630–631; Warren, *The Shawnees and Their Neighbors*, 14–17; Henry Harvey, *History of the Shawnee Indians, From the Year 1681 to 1854, Inclusive* (New York, 1971), 81–85; Helen Hornbeck Tanner (Ed.), *Atlas of Great Lakes History* (Norman, 1987), 39–45, 57–67; John R. Swanton, "Early History of the Creek Indians and Their Neighbors," *Smithsonian Institution Bureau of American Ethnology*, Bulletin 73 (Washington, DC, 1922), 317–320. For a larger discussion of Indian movements and imperial warfare in the Ohio Valley, see Michael N. McConnell, *A Country Between: The Upper Ohio Valley and Its Peoples, 1724–1774* (Lincoln, 1992). For the conflicts between colonists and the Shawnees in Kentucky, see Stephen Aron, *How The West Was Lost: The Transformation of Kentucky from Daniel Boone to Henry Clay* (Baltimore, 1996).

[6] This synopsis of Delaware migrations does not do justice to the complexities, and those interested in more information regarding many of these events should read, in addition to Weslager's books, James H. Merrell, *Into the Woods: Negotiators on the Pennsylvania Frontier* (New York, 1999); and Herbert C. Kraft, *The Lenape: Archaeology, History, and Ethnography* (Newark, NJ, 1986), 218–239. Eric Hinderaker argues that the commercial

Although these western movements brought some Delaware bands together, geography and religion prevented full political unity. By the 1760s, most of the southern Unami Delawares, and many of the northern Unamis, resided either along the Allegheny or the Muskingum and were organized into the Wolf, Turkey, and Turtle social and political divisions. But several Delaware bands continued to reside throughout the mid-Atlantic region. Living either independently, or with the Iroquois or the Mahicans, these Delawares attempted to hold onto lands in New Jersey and New York, while others migrated farther north to British Canada. In many of these regions, communities of Indians who were living separately from their relatives had adopted a Christian lifestyle. These Delawares and Munsees had primarily joined with the Moravians and, as a result, inhabited distinct settlements that kept them away from their kin who remained faithful to customary practices.[7]

The American Revolution inflamed frontier residents and wreaked havoc in Indian settlements, setting off another series of migrations in the 1770s and 1780s. Repeated clashes between Shawnees and backcountry settlers and militia led to a significant rupture within the Indians' extended Ohio community in the war's early years. Members of the Chillicothe had responded to the European invasion with violence while the Thawegilas advocated peaceful resolutions. Their difference of opinion turned into a more decisive split in the battles with Anglo invaders in the mid-1770s, which included Lord Dunmore's War. As the prospects for peace between settlers and Indians appeared slight, Kikuskawlowa, a Thawegila headman, led his followers to live among the Creeks. In the years that followed, most Piquas and Kispokothas also separated from their relatives who chose to stay in Ohio. Rather than moving to live among the Creeks, however, these emigrants made their way west, and, by 1790, the majority of these emigrants had finally settled west of the Mississippi River. Even Kikuskawlowa's people eventually left the Creeks, and although some returned to Ohio, most reunited with the Piquas and Kispokothas in Spanish Louisiana.[8]

---

framework established by trade among the Indians, French, and British in the eighteenth century had a significant influence on Indian movements during the period. See *Elusive Empires: Constructing Colonialism in the Ohio Valley, 1673–1800* (New York, 1997), 51–54. For the Walking Purchase, see Weslager, *The Delaware Indians*, 188–191.

[7] Ives Goddard, "Delaware," in Sturtevant, *Handbook of North American Indians* (17 vols., Washington, DC, 1978), XV, 213–239.

[8] For the backcountry violence during the American Revolution, see Colin G. Calloway, *The American Revolution in Indian Country: Crisis and Diversity in Native American*

The western migration occurred gradually and encompassed a series of negotiations. It began with a yearlong trip to St. Louis, the seat of government for the administrators of Spanish Louisiana. The length of the journey, and the members of the party at its conclusion, indicate that significant discussions occurred among a number of eastern Indian communities prior to their arrival in the Spanish territory. At journey's end, in March 1782, a delegation of forty Indians from the Shawnees, Delawares, Chickasaws, and Cherokees spoke with the Spanish lieutenant governor, Don Francesco Cruzat. The native delegates first presented Cruzat with four strands of wampum made with white and blue beads, a sign of their commitment to peace. During the course of the discussions that followed, the delegates declared their desire to live under the protection of the Spanish. Conscious of both propriety and the importance of strong diplomatic relations with these visitors, especially the Cherokees and Chickasaws, Cruzat offered presents to his guests. Although the exact numbers remain unclear, small bands of both Shawnees and Delawares soon established settlements west of the Mississippi.[9]

A larger influx of emigrants from both native communities arrived later in the decade, facilitated, in part, by two men who capitalized on both the Spaniards' desire to encourage Indian immigration to Upper Louisiana and their personal connections to the Indians. The Spanish wanted friendly native settlers to establish themselves between Spanish citizens and the more hostile western tribes like the Osages. Indian allies would also augment the limited Spanish presence on their northern frontier. Louis Lorimier and Colonel George Morgan took advantage of these needs. The Franco-Shawnee trader Lorimier negotiated with the Governor-General Don Francisco Luis Hector, the Baron de Carondelet, and secured for the Shawnees title to a sizeable land grant in 1793. This 25-mile square tract, located south of St. Louis near Cape Girardeau, became the home for hundreds of emigrant Shawnees until 1825. Morgan worked in a similar fashion to encourage Delaware migration.

Communities (New York, 1995); Thomas Wildcat Alford, *Civilization*, as told to Florence Drake (Norman, 1936), 200–203; Howard, *Shawnee!*, 14–17, 24–26. No set nomenclature is established for these political and social divisions within the Shawnees. Throughout this book, I use the spellings from Warren, *The Shawnees and Their Neighbors*.

[9] Francesco Cruzat to Estevan Miro, March 19, 1782, in Louis Houck (Ed.), *The Spanish Regime in Missouri* (2 vols., Chicago, 1909), I, 209–210; Louis Houck, *A History of Missouri from the Earliest Explorations and Settlements Until the Admission of the State Into the Union* (3 vols., New York, 1971), I, 208; Rodney Staab, "Settlements of the Missouri Shawnee, 1793–1825," *Papers of the Thirtieth Algonquian Conference* (1999): 351–373.

A former Indian agent in western Pennsylvania, Morgan crossed the Mississippi in 1789 with the understanding that he would receive the rights to land south of Cape Girardeau from Spanish authorities. On this piece of land, he intended to build a settlement for Indians and whites. Lorimier and Morgan's efforts increased emigrant Indian populations west of the Mississippi, and by the early 1790s approximately six hundred Delawares and nearly twelve hundred Shawnees resided on Spanish lands.[10]

The Shawnees and Delawares did not follow Lorimier and Morgan simply because the two men asked. In each man, the Indians recognized a potentially influential mediator who could help strengthen relations with the Spanish. Both Lorimier and Morgan had substantial connections to the respective Indian bands and personal reasons for moving west. Born to a French father and a Shawnee mother, Lorimier ran a trading post in the Ohio Valley before the Revolution. His business connected him to neighboring Indian communities and he also forged stronger bonds by marrying the Franco-Shawnee woman Charlotte Pemanpieh Bougainville. For business purposes, kinship ties, or both, Lorimier supported the British during the American Revolution. Regardless of the motivation, this decision made his presence untenable east of the Mississippi, especially once George Rogers Clark's militia exacted their revenge for his Anglophonic stance by torching Lorimier's trading post in the early 1780s. Morgan, on the other hand, was a former Indian agent connected by marriage to a Philadelphia trading company. Among other reasons, his dream of New Madrid grew from his years as an Indian agent in western Pennsylvania for the new American government. During his tenure, Morgan developed an especially strong relationship with the Delaware headman named White Eyes, and his diplomatic efforts on the Delawares' behalf had led them to call him "Tamanend," the name of a highly respected former chief. When the revolutionary government built forts on Indian lands and mistreated

[10] Charles E. Mix to A. H. H. Stuart, June 21, 1851, vol. 1, *RCA*; Lynn Morrow, "Trader William Gillis and Delaware Migration in Southern Missouri," *Missouri Historical Review*, 75 (January 1981): 147–167; Tanis Thorne, *The Many Hands of My Relations: French and Indians on the Lower Missouri* (Columbia, MO, 1996), 80–81; Stephen Aron, *American Confluence: The Missouri Frontier from Borderland to Border State* (Bloomington, 2006), 81–84. The spelling of Lorimier varies within the documents and articles, and for the sake of uniformity I have chosen to use the spelling found in the Spanish documents in Abraham P. Nasatir (Ed.), *Before Lewis and Clark: Documents Illustrating the History of Missouri, 1785–1804* (2 vols., St. Louis, 1952). For Morgan's plan for the settlement near New Madrid, see George Morgan to Don Diego De Gardoqui, August 20, 1789, in Houck, *The Spanish Regime in Missouri*, I, 287–308.

their Indian allies in 1779, Morgan resigned his post. Spanish Louisiana offered both opportunity and security that no longer existed in western Pennsylvania.[11]

Neither Lorimier nor Morgan had to work hard to sell the benefits of a region that promised a release from the violence and settler invasion that consumed the Ohio Valley in the last decades of the eighteenth century. The end of British rule eliminated the Proclamation Line of 1763 and its restrictions on settlement west of the Appalachian Mountains. Not long after the new nation obtained its independence, its citizens flooded the Ohio Valley and made conflicts with the native inhabitants almost inevitable. One of the more notable population explosions occurred just south of the Ohio River in present-day Kentucky, where the numbers of non-Indians increased from three hundred in 1775 to approximately 73,000 fifteen years later. In the 1780s, particularly following the passage of the Northwest Ordinance in 1787, American settlers gradually crossed the Ohio River and began to intrude on territories deemed protected by the Fort Stanwix Treaty of 1768. These American settlers met significant resistance from a strong confederation of Ohio Indian tribes.[12]

Beginning in the late 1760s, Shawnee leaders in Ohio brought the northern Indians together both to declare their independence from the Six Nations of the Iroquois and to organize resistance to the non-Indian invasion. This alliance soon included Cherokees and Creeks, who met the northern tribes in council on the Scioto River in 1769. Both ongoing conflicts and persistent inter-Indian diplomacy marked the 1780s, as the eastern Indians sought to hold a firm line against American settlement. By the early 1790s, the strong multitribal confederation was based at the

---

[11] Grant Harrington, *The Shawnees in Kansas* (Kansas City, KS, 1937); Charles E. Mix, Acting CIA, to A. H. H. Stuart, June 21, 1851, vol. 1, *RCA*, Morrow, "Trader William Gillis," 149–150; Thorne, *The Many Hands of My Relations*, 80–81; Houck, *The History of Missouri*, II, 170–176; Lynn Morrow, "New Madrid and Its Hinterland: 1783–1826," *Missouri Historical Society Bulletin*, 36(July 1980): 241–250; Weslager, *The Delaware Indians*, 295–300. The name "Tamanend" appears with numerous alternate spellings in various colonial documents. Tamany is the most familiar to readers largely because of Tammany Hall in nineteenth-century New York politics. Weslager briefly traces the connection on pages 167–270; Paul Chrisler Phillips, *The Fur Trade, Vol. II* (Norman, 1961), 225–227; Randolph C. Downes, *Council Fires on the Upper Ohio: A Narrative of Indian Affairs in the Upper Ohio Valley until 1795* (Pittsburgh, 1940), 220–221.

[12] *Indian Affairs*, II, 39–45; Tanner, *Atlas of Great Lakes Indian History*, 68–73, 84–91; Calloway, *The American Revolution in Indian Country*, 158–181. For the broader impact of events in Indian Country after 1763, see Colin G. Calloway, *The Scratch of a Pen: 1763 and the Transformation of North America* (New York, 2006); Calloway, *The American Revolution in Indian Country*.

Glaize, where they prepared to fight the soldiers sent by George Washington's administration. Despite early successes in 1790 and 1791 against two different American armies led by Generals Josiah Harmar and Arthur St. Clair, respectively, however, the Indians could not proclaim victory. Many Shawnees and Delawares had already begun to leave Ohio and the Americans became more determined to impose order on the region. In 1794, an army of two thousand regulars and one thousand militiamen under General Anthony Wayne defeated the Indian confederates at the Battle of Fallen Timbers, aided, in large part, by the withdrawal of British support. This setback brought the Miami war chief Little Turtle and other Indian leaders to the negotiating table. The resulting Treaty of Greenville, signed in the summer of 1795, declared peace, designated land cessions, and delineated boundaries between American settlements and remaining Indian lands. For the Indians present at Greenville, the accord also signaled the retreat of their fair-weather British allies from the Ohio Valley even as it solidified the American presence. One Delaware stated as much in the fall of 1794. "You goad us into war while you sit quietly on our hands," he charged. "You have betrayed us thus for many years. Therefore we will go away and leave the fighting to you."[13]

By crossing the Mississippi, whether independently, or under the auspices of Lorimier and Morgan's negotiations, the Shawnees and Delawares distanced themselves from this violence. More important, they used a political boundary to evade the Americans who flaunted their new independence with a vengeance in the Ohio Valley. The Indian delegates to St. Louis in 1782 had stated their intention to separate "completely from the affiliations they had previously had," and declared their desire to establish a firm peace with the Spaniards. These Indians still viewed the Mississippi River as a corridor, but they now saw the opportunity to benefit from its concurrent status as a border between imperial nations. Under U.S. policy, the Shawnees and Delawares dealt with invasion. Their negotiations

---

[13] Tanner, *Atlas of Great Lakes Indian History*, 68–73, 84–91. For more information on the Scioto Councils, the battles of the 1790s, and the Treaty of Greenville, see Gregory Evans Dowd, *A Spirited Resistance: The North American Struggle for Unity, 1745–1815* (Baltimore, 1992), 42–44, 103–115; White, *The Middle Ground*, 433–468; Helen Hornbeck Tanner, "The Glaize in 1792: A Composite Indian Community," *Ethnohistory*, 25(Winter 1978): 15–39. For an analysis of this off-and-on British–Indian alliance, see Colin G. Calloway, *Crown and Calumet: British-Indian Relations, 1783–1815* (Norman, 1987). The Delaware Indian is quoted in Linda Sabathy-Judd (Ed. and Transl.), *Moravians in Upper Canada: The Diary of the Indian Mission of Fairfield on the Thames, 1792–1813* (Toronto, 1999), 66–67.

with the Spanish as well as their trust in Lorimier and Morgan resulted in land grants and the protection of an administration that showed signs of favoring Indian interests as opposed to ignoring them.[14]

The commercial center of St. Louis also factored into the Indians' decision to settle in Spanish Louisiana. This trading community on the western banks of the Mississippi had its origins in the imperial contests of the mid-eighteenth century. The paper transfer of Louisiana Territory from the French to the Spanish after the Seven Years' War nominally removed the French presence, but it did not dramatically alter the daily realities at the focal points of trade. French fur traders had operated in the region for years, and the founding of St. Louis in 1763 anchored their presence in the decades that followed. In one of his final acts, the last governor of French Louisiana, Jean Jacques Blaise D'Abbadie, granted an exclusive trade monopoly for the Missouri River and the western bank of the Mississippi to a trading firm headed by Gilbert Antoine Maxent and Pierre Laclède. Both men were veterans of the Illinois Country trade. But it was Laclède, joined by his 14-year-old stepson Auguste Chouteau, who led the first expedition to establish a trading post upriver.[15]

Laclède, Chouteau, and thirty employees left New Orleans in early August and journeyed north against the Mississippi's current for three long months. It was a grueling voyage, and they traveled upriver at the same time that the 1763 Treaty of Paris transferred the eastern banks of the Mississippi River to the English. Preexisting posts were inadequate for their proposed trading operations. Fort Chartres would soon be abandoned, and the tiny mining and farming settlement of Ste. Genevieve lay too far south of the Missouri River. Eager to find a suitable location, despite the obstacles presented by the winter weather Laclède spent much of December scouring the western banks of the Mississippi. When he first gazed upon the spot where the city of St. Louis now stands, the French trader did not hesitate. "Besides the beauty of the site," Auguste Chouteau observed, "he [Laclède] found there all the advantages that one could desire to found a settlement which might become very considerable hereafter." Its elevation would keep it safe from flooding even as the location

[14] Francesco Cruzat to Estevan Miro, March 19, 1782, in Houck, *The Spanish Regime in Missouri*, I, 209–210.

[15] William E. Foley and C. David Rice, *The First Chouteaus: River Barons of Early St. Louis* (Chicago, 1983), 4–15; Jay Gitlin, "Constructing the House of Chouteau: Saint Louis," *Common-Place*, 3 (July 2003), found at http://www.common-place.org/vol-03/no-04/st-louis/. (Accessed May 24, 2006); Thorne, *The Many Hands of My Relations*, 68–72.

provided easy access to the Mississippi, Missouri, and Illinois rivers. St. Louis quickly became a magnet for settlers, traders, and Indians in need of provisions. When the French abandoned their military outposts in the Illinois Country in July 1764, Laclède convinced many of the French-speaking refugees to move to St. Louis. Although the Spanish revoked Laclede's monopoly soon after assuming power, during the remaining decades of the eighteenth century and well into the nineteenth century, the trading network built by Laclède, Chouteau, and their descendants attracted Indian peoples from both sides of the Mississippi to work and trade in the vicinity. Small bands of Osages, Sauks, and Mesquakies often visited to barter foodstuffs for material goods. The Missouris, who had the distinction of being the first Indian visitors to St. Louis in the spring of 1764, did more than just procure provisions. Several women and children, in exchange for vermillion, awls, and verdigris, dug the cellar for Chouteau's house.[16]

The Shawnees and Delawares in the West were partners in this Mississippian merchant community. Indeed, the presence of emigrant Indian communities contributed to the growth of outlying settlements at New Madrid, Ste. Genevieve, and Cape Girardeau. Well-worn paths soon connected Indian villages to the four main Spanish towns, and by the end of the eighteenth century, the flow of skins and other goods contributed to a thriving market. François and Joseph Lesieur, brothers and French-Canadian fur traders, set up trading posts in the southeastern corner of present-day Missouri in 1783 under the direction of Gabriel Cerré, a French merchant based in St. Louis. Cerré intended to profit from the Delaware and Shawnee hunters who traveled the well-forested lands that provided forage for deer, and buffalo and elk populations. The Lesieurs' business performed well until the arrival of Morgan and other American settlers undermined their chances of monopolizing the local trade. Yet, while the French-Canadian brothers saw their profits decrease, the Delawares and Shawnees capitalized on the growing regional trade network. Delawares and Shawnees living near New Madrid sold bear and deer skins year round and bartered honey and bear's oil in the spring.

[16] Foley and Rice, *The First Chouteaus*, 4–15; Thorne, *The Many Hands of My Relations*, 68–72; "Narrative of the Settlement of St. Louis," in John Francis McDermott, (Ed.), *The Early Histories of St. Louis* (St. Louis, 1952), 45–59; Arrell M. Gibson, *The Kickapoos: Lords of the Middle Border* (Norman, 1963), 32. For a description of Indians who received presents from and traded with the Spanish at St. Louis, see Report of Francesco Cruzat, November 15, 1777, in Houck, *The Spanish Regime in Missouri*, I, 141–148.

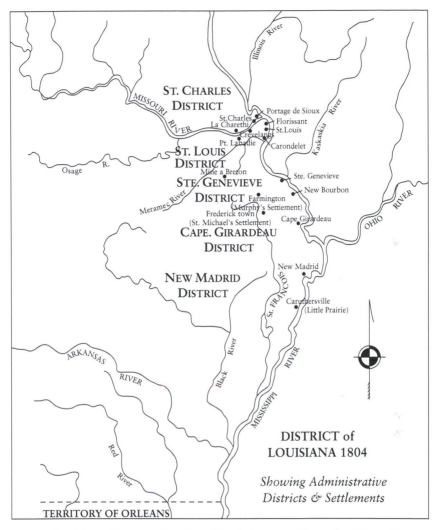

MAP 1. Louisiana Territory in 1804. Based on a map from the Osage County Historical Society.

Their reach extended beyond the nearest markets, and they also made biannual trading expeditions to the northern towns.[17]

---

[17] Morrow, "New Madrid and Its Hinterland," 241–250; Houck, *The History of Missouri,* I, 211–212, 231–232. For a discussion of these Indian trails and a map of the known trails in Missouri, see ibid., 223–231; Donald Holliday, "All Roadbeds in Southern Missouri Surveyed by Osage Indians," *OzarksWatch,* 7 (Fall 1993/Winter 1994): 1–2.

The Shawnees and Delawares who lived north of New Madrid relied on both agriculture and local trade. Shawnee residents of Rogerstown on the Meramec River southwest of St. Louis had adopted more established agricultural practices, so their business involved fewer skins. But they frequently sold cattle in St. Louis. Farther south, two Shawnee villages and one Delaware village were located in the vicinity of Apple Creek on the route between Cape Girardeau and Ste. Genevieve. The Shawnee settlements, according to the French traveler Nicolas de Finiels, "were more systematically and solidly constructed than the usual Indian villages." Cleared fields and fences in these Shawnee settlements reflected their agricultural lifestyle, and the Indians opened their homes to Finiels, especially when they discovered that he spoke English. "During the evening they entertained me with several dances and games with which they pass the time not consumed in hunting or agriculture," the Frenchman recorded. The Delawares showed no similar desire to expand their agricultural habits and continued to rely on hunting and smaller gardens for their subsistence. Residents of all three villages, however, traded often with Lorimier, whose local warehouses, according to Finiels, "are always stocked with Indian trade goods."[18]

The same characteristics that made this western region attractive to the Shawnees and Delawares made it a crossroads for colonial conflict. St. Louis stood at the intersection of European interests in the late eighteenth century, largely because its geographic advantages made it a natural trading center. Despite the transfer of jurisdiction in 1763, the town remained under the direction of a French administrator, Louis de Bellerive St. Ange, until the summer of 1767. In deference to the influential cohort of French traders, and in recognition of its own weakness, the new Spanish regime relied heavily on the preexisting relations between the traders and local Indians. But this extension of the Spanish presence gave birth to an increased rivalry with the British. Numerous Indian communities took advantage of this competition as British traders operating out of Detroit, Michilimackinac, and Prairie du Chien lured the furs that would otherwise go to New Orleans via St. Louis. Spanish administrators in St. Louis responded by ignoring budgetary constraints, favoring their Indian trading partners with gifts and medals, and restricting both the presence

---

[18] Houck, *The History of Missouri*, I, 211–212, 231–232; Nicolas de Finiels, *An Account of Upper Louisiana*, edited by Carl J. Ekberg and William E. Foley, translated by Carl J. Ekberg (Columbia, MO, 1989), 34–36, 118–119; Staab, "Settlements of the Missouri Shawnee," 354–362.

of unlicensed foreigners and the sale of alcohol to Indians. On their part, Indian traders worked the proper angles to secure the best prices for their furs. By the 1770s, established traders like Auguste Chouteau and his younger brother Pierre even sent their employees to the Indian villages.[19]

The willingness and ability of Indians to work both sides of the Mississippi River forced traders and local administrators to ignore international boundaries and hostilities. Spanish and British officials may have characterized the fur trade as a competition between two European powers, but veteran traders depended on their Indian suppliers and did not allow artificial borders to undermine business. This was particularly noticeable once the Spanish declared war on England in June 1779. A British force of a reported three hundred regular soldiers and nine hundred Indian allies attacked a fortified St. Louis on May 26, 1780, only to be repelled by several hundred Spanish militiamen under the command of Don Fernando de Leyba. Although this conflict heightened regional tensions considerably, commercial activity during this time proved telling. British blockades of interior waterways compelled St. Louis merchants to obtain necessities from British merchants on the eastern banks of the Mississippi in Cahokia. The tacit sanction of this behavior by Spanish authorities revealed not only their desire to maintain the Indian trade, but also the influence of the Indians' use of the Mississippi River. At war's end, though Spanish administrators tried repeatedly to orient trade through New Orleans, St. Louis merchants sent the bulk of their furs north.[20]

By crossing the Mississippi, therefore, the Shawnees and Delawares could not avoid colonial intrigues and instead exchanged American policies for Spanish agendas. The Spanish administration welcomed other Europeans willing to live under Spanish rule in Louisiana, and in 1796, thirty Kentucky families settled in Cape Girardeau under this system. But a more immediate problem grew from Spanish plans for an Indian buffer zone. During its fourty-year rule, Spain never made an effort to establish its presence in Louisiana like it had in the Caribbean and Mesoamerica. The first Spanish Lieutenant Governor did not even assume his post in St. Louis until almost seven years after the official transfer of title. Subsequent Spanish administrators not only struggled to regulate trade conflicts

---

[19] Foley and Rice, *The First Chouteaus*, 16–30; A. P. Nasatir, "The Anglo-Spanish Frontier on the Upper Mississippi 1786–1796, " *Iowa Journal of History and Politics,* 29(1931): 155–232.

[20] Nasatir, "The Anglo-Spanish Frontier," 160–166; Foley and Rice, *The First Chouteaus,* 26–30, 37–41; Houck, *A History of Missouri,* I, 304–310; Aron, *American Confluence,* 84–87.

with the British but also strained to gain the upper hand with the Osage Indians. The Osages resented the presence of settlers along the Mississippi and fought to control European access from the Arkansas River to the Missouri River. A mutual interest in trade made the Osages and the Chouteaus logical allies, and Auguste and his brother Pierre developed strong ties as early as the 1770s. The Spanish relied heavily on the ability and influence of these prominent Frenchmen who had almost unparalleled connections to and knowledge of the Osages by the late eighteenth century. But even the Chouteaus' influence did not end the raids. Throughout the 1780s, parties of both the Big and Little Osages harassed and stole property from the Ste. Genevieve settlements, especially when Spanish gifts proved unsatisfactory. Under these circumstances, the Spanish viewed the Shawnees and Delawares as an additional measure of security. Despite this physical buffer, however, both Indians and settlers lost property and lives to Osage attacks well into the 1790s.[21]

When the mere presence of the emigrant Indians failed to curtail the Osages, Spanish authorities took a different approach. In August 1793, the new Lieutenant Governor Don Zenon Trudeau attempted to organize a Spanish–Indian military expedition to attack the Osage villages. Trudeau, who had some initial success negotiating with the Osages, realized that to maintain his credibility with the settlers in Upper Louisiana, he needed to take more decisive action. He turned to the Shawnees and Delawares. But though these Indians had suffered from Osage incursions, they refused to serve as Trudeau's pawns. They had moved west with the understanding that the Spanish would protect their land, property, and interests, and refused to answer Trudeau's call unconditionally. Instead, they manipulated Spanish insecurities regarding the northern frontier of their colonial dominion. At one point, a Shawnee delegation even threatened to reconcile with the United States and leave Louisiana if the Spanish did not take stronger measures against the Osages. Trudeau and other Spanish administrators also discovered that the emigrant

[21] Finiels, *An Account of Upper Louisiana*, 36. The Spanish administration especially sought out French Canadians, in part because of their Catholicism. See Bernardo de Galvez to Sr. Don Joseph de Galvez, January 27, 1778, in Houck, *The Spanish Regime in Missouri*, I, 152–153; Aron, *American Confluence*, 87–102; Foley and Rice, *The First Chouteaus*, 20–21, 45–58; Willard H. Rollings, *The Osage: An Ethnohistorical Study of Hegemony on the Prairie-Plains* (Columbia, MO, 1992), 130–178. Although no documents mention marriages between either of the Chouteau brothers and Osage women, scholars have used tribal oral histories to support statements that both men maintained such relationships as part of their trade with the Osages. See John J. Mathews, *The Osages: Children of the Middle Waters* (Norman, 1961), 285.

Shawnees and Delawares would not fight without proper compensation. The "savages . . . are too enlightened and interested [mercenary]," an exasperated Trudeau reported to his superior Carondelet, "for one to be able to make them act without a large and great expenditure which it would be necessary to renew as often as one would want them employed." It is clear that the Shawnees and Delawares had a choice when it came to working with Spanish authorities and did not have to submit to the wishes of Trudeau and other officials. Yet, the emigrant Indian communities discovered early on that shelter from American expansion did not equal immunity from other colonial agendas.[22]

Although the waters of the Mississippi did not isolate the Shawnees and Delawares from European policies, it granted them refuge from the American invasion that had devastated the Ohio Valley. The documented migrations of the Shawnees and Delawares also suggest the possibility of numerous other undocumented river crossings, especially because both groups often maintained contact with relatives and allies who remained behind. Small and large parties of Peorias, Kickapoos, Ottawas, and Potawatomis resided throughout the Louisiana Territory by the late 1700s. And like those who arrived before them, these emigrants often settled within range of established villages and familiar traders with whom they engaged in a considerable exchange in furs – primarily deer, but also beaver and other pelts. Kinship and trade grounded the migrations of most eastern Indians in the late eighteenth century as they profited from both native and European visions of the Mississippi River.[23]

---

[22] Foley and Rice, *The First Chouteaus*, 50–51; Rollings, *The Osage*, 186–188; Gilbert C. Din and A. P. Nasatir, *The Imperial Osages: Spanish Indian Diplomacy in the Mississippi Valley* (Norman, 1983), 51–58, 149–153; Carl J. Ekberg, *Colonial Ste. Genevieve: An Adventure on the Mississippi Frontier* (Gerald, MO, 1985), 97–98. For more information on the details of this rivalry between the Spanish and English in this region, see Nasatir, "The Anglo-Spanish Frontier," 155–232; Trudeau to Carondelet, September 28, 1793, in Nasatir, *Before Lewis and Clark*, I, 197–203.

[23] Trudeau to Gayoso de Lemos, December 20, 1797, in Nasatir, *Before Lewis and Clark*, II, 525–529; Rollings, *The Osage*, 185–187. For other pre-1803 Indian emigrant parties, see John Mack Faragher, "'More Motley than Mackinaw': From Ethnic Mixing to Ethnic Cleansing on the Frontier of the Lower Missouri, 1783–1833," in Andrew R. L. Cayton and Fredrika J. Teute (Eds.), *Contact Points: American Frontiers from the Mohawk Valley to the Mississippi, 1750–1830* (Chapel Hill, 1998), 304–326; Mary M. Lembcke and Dorris Valley (Eds.), *The Peorias: A History of the Peoria Indian Tribe of Oklahoma* (Miami, OK, 1991), 24, 41–44; Ekberg, *Colonial Ste. Genevieve*, 112–114; Houck, *A History of Missouri*, I, 208–210; Grant Foreman (Ed.), "Glimpses of the Past: Notes of Auguste Chouteau on Boundaries of Various Indian Nations," *Missouri Historical Society*, 7(October–December 1940): 119–140.

Imperial struggles at the turn of the century ended the Spanish era in Louisiana. In 1803, President Thomas Jefferson's administration negotiated the Louisiana Purchase, and the western Shawnees and Delawares once again faced the prospects of a settler invasion. But as an adolescent American government attempted to extend its authority in Indian affairs from the Atlantic coast to the western banks of the Mississippi, its policies had an uneven impact. In St. Louis and its surroundings, the same commercial relationships that provided a structure for Spanish policies and Indian migrations in the eighteenth century provided the foundation for American administration and continued Indian relocations in the years after the Louisiana Purchase. This very fact made the transition of colonial authority slightly less traumatic for the Indians in the West than it could have been. As did the Spanish before them, American officials found that they could not impose a new order on St. Louis and its residents. This meant that well into the nineteenth century, St. Louis under American authority had a similar look to St. Louis under Spanish authority. In short, the Louisiana Purchase may have changed the flag over the city, but the actions of diplomats and politicians created few intrusive changes in the daily lives of people on the ground.[24]

In the first stages of its gradual expansion across the Mississippi, the U.S. government could not dismiss the frameworks and people that supported this diverse and far-reaching commercial enterprise. Just as the Spanish depended on Auguste Chouteau in the 1770s to negotiate with the Osages, Jefferson named Pierre Chouteau to administer Indian affairs in upper Louisiana in 1804. Three years later, Pierre received a demotion when the appointment of William Clark to the general superintendency of Indian affairs restricted the Frenchman's jurisdiction to only the Osages. But even this change did not eliminate government–trader connections. Clark, only recently returned from his journey to the Pacific with Meriwether Lewis, was one of the founding fathers of the Missouri Fur Company in 1809. In this venture, the new general superintendent united his economic interests with a number of prominent traders and businessmen, including Manuel Lisa, Pierre Chouteau Sr., Auguste Chouteau Jr., and Pierre Menard. Although this partnership officially dissolved in the summer of 1814, due in large part to the problems presented by the War of 1812, Clark continued to operate within the mercantile community. The

---

[24] For a broader examination of the Louisiana Purchase within the context of American history, see Jon Kukla, *A Wilderness So Immense: The Louisiana Purchase and the Destiny of America* (New York, 2003).

French-Canadian Pierre Menard also worked in both worlds. He ran a trading post in Kaskaskia even as he served both as the interpreter for the government in its dealings with the Kaskaskias and Piankeshaws in southern Illinois and as a subagent for the Illinois Indians. Menard's roots reached even deeper into the local community, however. His marriage to Angelique Saucier in 1806 made him Pierre Chouteau Jr.'s brother-in-law, and his daughter Berenice subsequently married Chouteau's half-brother, François. As if the employment of Chouteau, Clark, and Menard did not do enough to facilitate its administration in the West, the U.S. government even tapped Louis Lorimier for the position of Indian agent for the Shawnees and Delawares. The then-territorial governor James Wilkinson recommended the trader for the post, and Lorimier mediated Indian–American relations from 1805 until his death in 1812.[25]

The increase in settlement that accompanied this transition to American authority had a more significant impact in the first several decades than did the transfer of political power. In 1805, the approximate population of non-Indians in the region totaled 10,120. Of that number, just less than half were Americans and nearly 3,800 were French. The end of the War of 1812 sparked a wave of western expansion and in 1820, when Missouri entered the Union, the state claimed a population of almost 70,000. More than half of that number arrived after 1814, and as many as thirty to fifty wagons crossed the Mississippi daily. These emigrants from Kentucky, Virginia, and Tennessee spread throughout the region, grabbed plots of land, and established townships. Because of this dispersal, St. Louis grew in size, although, by 1821, it still contained only 5,600 citizens. French and Indian settlements did not disappear in this onslaught, though the Indian settlements struggled to endure. Traders thrived in the expanding market, and the French influence persisted with them. Indeed, French was still the predominant language in Ste. Genevieve in 1816.[26]

The picture was less hopeful for the Shawnees and Delawares. Illegal squatting on Indian lands, especially after 1815, proved especially problematic. William Clark made feeble attempts to enforce federal policy

---

[25] Foreman, "Glimpses of the Past," 119; Jerome O. Steffen, *William Clark: Jeffersonian Man on the Frontier* (Norman, 1977), 72–85; Aron, *American Confluence*, 121–124; Governor Edwards to the Secretary of War, December 1, 1815, in *TP, XVII*, 254; Richard E. Oglesby, "Pierre Menard," in LeRoy R. Hafen, (Ed.), *French Fur Traders and Voyageurs in the American West* (Spokane, 1995), 217–228. For the expansive Chouteau family tree, see Mary Cunningham and Jeanne C. Blythe, *The Founding Family of St. Louis* (St. Louis, 1977); Faragher, "More Motley Than Mackinaw," 307.

[26] Houck, *A History of Missouri, III*, 140–166; Aron, *American Confluence*, 158–164.

and to protect Indian property, but the waves of American settlers in the region refused to abide by these regulations. Increasing criticism of Clark's protection of Indian rights helped defeat his gubernatorial ambitions in the 1820 elections. This loss simply confirmed the prevailing trend among Missourians favoring American expansion in the region. In the late 1810s, individual Shawnees in and around Rogerstown fought squatters both physically and legally in an effort to keep their lands. Wapapilethe and the Apple Creek Shawnees objected that the white settlers who harassed them did not steal for aggrandizement but "to make us abandon our land and take it for themselves." Further south, J. Hardeman Walker's plantation replaced a Delaware settlement near New Madrid by 1818. Although not the case for all, Shawnees and Delawares throughout Missouri moved to the interior or south to the Arkansas River valley as the white settlements multiplied.[27]

This expansion of American settlement into Missouri Territory did more than encroach on Shawnee and Delaware villages, foster national tensions over slavery, and lead to the Missouri Compromise in 1820. It also highlighted the demise of the Mississippi River as a political boundary and its persistence as a figurative one. The Louisiana Purchase removed the Mississippi from political considerations in 1803 and the ascension of Missouri Territory confirmed the western extension of the United States. Even with this change, however, the emblematic Mississippi remained an important factor in Indian affairs. Like many politicians past and present, Thomas Jefferson often said in private what he could not state in public. In an 1803 letter written to William Henry Harrison, then the Governor of Indiana Territory, the President outlined his Indian policy in stark terms. The Indians "will in time either incorporate with us as citizens of the United States, or remove beyond the Mississippi," Jefferson explained. More than twenty years later, Secretary of War John C. Calhoun prepared a report for President James Monroe that included the names and numbers of Indians "remaining within the limits of the different States and Territories." Calhoun also assessed the "appropriation necessary to commence the work of moving the Indians beyond the Mississippi." Thomas

---

[27] Faragher, "More Motley Than Mackinaw," 316–323; Landon Y. Jones, *William Clark and the Shaping of the West* (New York, 2004), 235–255; Aron, *American Confluence*, 156–158, 183–184. For the locations of different Shawnee and Delaware villages, see Houck, *A History of Missouri, I*, 216–220; Staab, "Settlements of the Missouri Shawnee," 351–373. Quotation from Stephen Warren, "Between Villages and Nations: The Emergence of Shawnee Nationalism, 1800–1870" (Ph.D. Dissertation, Indiana University, 2000), 122.

Jefferson was still alive when Calhoun submitted this report, and despite the presence of nearly one hundred thousand non-Indians within the limits of state of Missouri, so was his vision of the Mississippi River as the boundary between American civilization and Indian savagery.[28]

Both Jefferson and Calhoun described the Mississippi River as the demarcation point between American settlement and Indian lands as part of the growing emphasis on Indian removal. Yet, the promotion and initial enactment of a removal agenda in the first three decades of the nineteenth century built on rather than supplanted the ongoing westward migrations of Delawares, Shawnees, and other eastern Indians. Therefore, though a treaty arranged for the relocation of the Indiana Delawares to Missouri in the late 1810s, a separate emigration of Ohio Shawnees only a few years later occurred as part of an expansive inter-Indian diplomatic framework. Just as the rhetoric did not match the reality when it came to the Mississippi River as a boundary, the first attempts of government-sponsored removal could not replace the kinship and commercial networks that had long supported Indian migrations.

The War of 1812 and the defeat of the Indian confederacy under Tenskwatawa and Tecumseh drastically shifted relations among the Indians, American settlers, and American government in the Old Northwest. Simply put, a sea of humanity engulfed the Ohio Valley. The non-Indian population of the state of Ohio alone rose from 230,000 in 1810 to approximately 940,000, twenty years later. In those same two decades, both Indiana and Illinois gained statehood, with populations totaling 343,000 and 157,000, respectively, by 1830. As the number of settlers increased and the British presence decreased, American officials used treaties and councils to encourage Indian residents to give up claims to their lands and move west of the Mississippi. Local settlers and politicians applied similar pressure to Indian inhabitants who no longer had the option of substantial British support. Warfare had nominally secured the American government as the local authority and appeared to terminate the middle ground diplomacy that had structured relations in the region for so many years. Delaware and Shawnee leaders recognized the changing

---

[28] Jefferson letter quoted in Francis Paul Prucha (Ed.), *Documents of United States Indian Policy* (Lincoln, 1990), 23; John C. Calhoun to the President of the United States, January 24, 1825, in *ASPIA*, 542–544. For Jefferson's vision for Indian affairs, see Anthony F. C. Wallace, *Jefferson and the Indians: The Tragic Fate of the First Americans* (Cambridge, MA, 1999), 13–20, 221–226.

environment around them and adapted to the growing settlements both outside of and within their lands.[29]

Most eastern Delawares lived in Indiana Territory by the 1810s. Shortly after the Treaty of Greenville in 1795, Indians living along the Wabash River drainage invited the Delawares and others to move west and settle as their neighbors. Though it remains unclear whether the Miamis, Potawatomis, or Piankeshaws extended this invitation, by the early 1800s Delaware bands had established from nine to eleven villages along the White River. Chief William Anderson, or Kikthawenund, Buckongahelas, Hockingpomska, and Tetepachksit were among the leaders who relocated to these lands and built towns. Buckongahelas and Kikthawenund had always preached the need for the Delawares to hold tight to their customs. But Tetepachksit did not necessarily agree and informed the Moravian missionaries then at the Fairfield settlement in Canada that the Delawares wanted to hear the gospel. As a result, during their time on the White River the Delawares dealt repeatedly with federal agents and missionaries who promoted a sedentary, agricultural lifestyle. Over the next decade, even as many continued to resist these attempts, the Delawares suffered from the growing invasion of squatters as well as the widespread and devastating trade in alcohol. And although the Delaware Council decided not to support Tecumseh and Tenskwatawa, their neutrality did not help them after the war. In 1818, the Delawares signed a treaty at St. Mary's, Ohio that ceded their entire claim to lands in Indiana in exchange for land west of the Mississippi. Given three years to prepare for the relocation, Kikthawenund, Captain Killbuck, and others reluctantly agreed to follow their relatives who had made the journey nearly three decades earlier.[30]

Although the bulk of the Delaware community traveled west in the fall of 1820, they did not travel together, and the trip through Indiana and southern Illinois proved grueling as the weather grew colder and the Indians entered more unfamiliar territory. Because U.S. officials did little to organize the removal at its origin, few records exist to document

---

[29] For approximations of population numbers among non-Indians, see Tanner, *Atlas of Great Lakes Indian History*, 96, 122; White, *The Middle Ground*, 469–523. As mentioned in the introduction, although I agree that the War of 1812 had a tremendous impact, I disagree with White's conclusion that the American government established its authority in the Great Lakes region so quickly.

[30] Weslager, *The Delaware Indians*, 329–355; Lawrence Henry Gipson (Ed.), *The Moravian Indian Mission on White River* (Indianapolis, 1938), 12–19, 108–110, 606–611; *Indian Affairs*, II, 39–45, 170–171.

the journey and it is difficult to know how many died along the approximately three hundred-mile route that took the Delawares from their villages along the White River to Kaskaskia, Illinois. But in October and November 1820, more than thirteen hundred Delawares and their fifteen hundred horses crossed the Mississippi. Pierre Menard, the Indian agent at Kaskaskia, paid for ferry passages and worked with a number of local traders to provision the Delawares on both sides of the river with flour, beef, corn, salt, and other necessities. After the sometimes harrowing crossing and the long journey that preceded it, most of the Delawares settled in temporary encampments on the Current River in eastern Missouri. Disease continued to slow their progress, and several contingents stayed near Kaskaskia to recover horses stolen before the river crossing.[31]

This westward movement meant not only relocation but also reunion. Of the over thirteen hundred Delawares who relocated from Indiana to Missouri, approximately eight hundred did so under Kikthawenund, a leader who had grown in stature since the death of Buckongahelas in 1805. Although not all left their eastern lands with Kikthawenund's band in 1820, by the following year the Delawares no longer resided in Indiana in substantial numbers. Meanwhile, the descendants of the Cape Girardeau Delawares had shifted farther west in the years after the War of 1812. Some relocated to northern Arkansas Territory, some to northeastern Oklahoma with the western Cherokees, and others to the Jack's Fork River Valley in present-day Shannon County, Missouri. When Kikthawenund and his band crossed the Mississippi, they settled first on the Jack's Fork River and then moved west to the James River, south of Springfield, Missouri. In this new settlement at James River, the Indiana Delawares and the Missouri Delawares under Captain Paterson or Meshayquowha united as one community. Kikthawenund became the principal chief of this band and Meshayquowha served as the second chief. Combined, these Delaware towns in the southwestern corner of Missouri may have contained as many as twenty-five hundred men, women, and children.[32]

New and familiar names in the trading community matched these Delaware movements. Louis Lorimier Jr., who had inherited his father's

---

[31] "Abstracts of disbursements made by Pierre Menard, subagent at Kaskaskia, in the quarter ending the 31st of December, 1820, under the directions of William Clark, Governor of Michigan Territory," in *ASPIA*, 302–303; Weslager, *The Delaware Indians*, 359–362; Grant Foreman, *The Last Trek of the Indians* (Chicago, 1946), 41–43.

[32] Weslager, *The Delaware Indian Westward Migration*, 209–217; John G. Pratt to Thomas Murphy, February 14, 1868, OIA-LR, roll 635; Morrow, "Trader William Gilliss," 147–167.

business, built a trading house on the Swan River just east of the James River village. Another trader, William Gilliss, bought this post in 1822, and over the next several years he profited from the furs brought in by the growing Delaware population. Gilliss had first dealt with the Delawares as a trader operating out of Kaskaskia in the late 1810s, and had quickly connected to the lucrative Indian trade in Ste. Genevieve and St. Louis. Specifically, he joined with the firm established by Pierre Menard and his business partner François Vallé. Gilliss also made a more personal connection with the Delawares, marrying a woman named Wawautiqua in 1820. When the Indians migrated westward, Gilliss moved with them. He soon set up another post west of the James River in the midst of the Delaware settlements. This operation included multiple buildings, including the residence where he lived with his second Delaware wife, Poquas, whom he married in 1822. Neither the Delawares nor Gillis remained on the James River for long. Kikthawenund complained about the quality of lands chosen for the Delawares in Missouri, and he negotiated another treaty with the United States in 1829. Shortly thereafter, the Delawares moved to present-day eastern Kansas, a small contingent arriving in 1829 and a larger party under Kikthawenund moving in 1830. Gilliss promptly bought land in Jackson County, Missouri, on the western border of the state. From there, he carried on a profitable trade with the Delawares and other emigrant Indians.[33]

Although it foreshadowed future removal policy, the Delaware experience did not set the tone for Indian movements in the decade before the Indian Removal Act. Instead, because the Delawares also moved within a commercial and kinship framework, the westward journey had closer connections to other Indian migrations of the same time period. The actions of Ohio Shawnee leaders and bands in the 1820s showed the strength and persistence of the native frameworks similar to those that supplemented the Delaware movements of the same period. Based on their previous migrations and participation in multitribal alliances, the Shawnees were particularly well-placed to operate within a vast diplomatic network. Their negotiations in the 1820s bridged the Mississippi River and renewed bonds between northern and southern native communities.

The series of inter-Indian councils that led to these nineteenth century Shawnee relocations began in the West and reached back across the Mississippi River. In 1810, following several years of disputes within the

---

[33] Weslager, *The Delaware Westward Migration*, 209–217; Morrow, "Trader William Gilliss," 148–159.

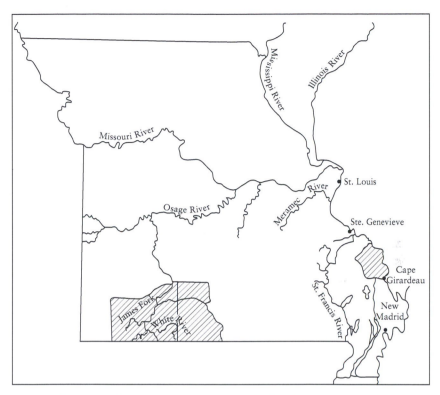

MAP 2. Shawnee and Delaware Land Cessions in the Missouri, 1825–1832. Based on Map 38 in Charles C. Royce (Comp.), *Indian Land Cessions in the United States.*

Cherokee nation over land cessions and removal, a party of approximately one thousand Cherokees moved west and settled on the Arkansas River. As had other Indian emigrants, the Cherokees often fought the Osages over hunting territories in the region. Together, the conflicts with the Osages and the growth of white settlement in Missouri served as a catalyst for defensive and diplomatic alliances among the Cherokees and the other eastern Indians, especially the Delawares and Shawnees. By the early 1820s this western alliance consisted of Cherokees, Delawares, Shawnees, Weas, Peorias, Kickapoos, and Piankeshaws.[34]

These diplomatic ventures expanded eastward as the desire for a confederacy connected to discussions of removal among the Ohio Shawnees. An Ohio Seneca-Shawnee named Captain Lewis, or Quitewepea, instigated

---

[34] Dowd, *A Spirited Resistance*, 161–166; Warren, *The Shawnees and Their Neighbors*, 73–96.

this trans-Mississippi mediation following a treaty signed in 1817. The treaty reduced the Shawnee holdings to lands around Wapakoneta, Hog Creek, and Lewistown. Although the same accord also granted him an individual reservation, Lewis became an advocate for removal, and a personal visit to the Indians west of the Mississippi in 1820 only strengthened his beliefs. As he traveled throughout southern Missouri and northern Arkansas Territory, he spoke to the Shawnees and other Indian residents in the region and admired the lands on which they lived. The specific conversations between Lewis and his various hosts were not recorded. But it is clear that his agenda intertwined with that of Indian leaders hoping to establish a confederation of eastern Indians in the West. Upon his return to Ohio, Captain Lewis made a decision. He would actively promote the appeal of the western territories. For the next several years he preached this message to the Ohio Shawnees.[35]

The negotiations instigated and facilitated by Lewis encompassed western and eastern Indians as well as agents of the U.S. government. The first council convened early in 1823 on Crooked Creek in northern Arkansas and included representatives from the Shawnees, Delawares, Weas, Kickapoos, Piankeshaws, Peorias, and Western Cherokees. These discussions focused primarily on making it possible for new migrants to settle on lands neighboring the Cherokees in Arkansas Territory. Following initial deliberations, the respective delegations exchanged strands of wampum to demonstrate their commitment. The next council was scheduled to take place on the other side of the Mississippi in Lewistown. But when the death of a beloved leader caused the Cherokees to miss this meeting, negotiations faltered. According to Lewis, "ill disposed persons" were to blame for the Cherokees' failure to arrive. Then, on January 7, 1824, Superintendent of Indian Affairs William Clark and a delegation of Cherokee, Shawnee, and Seneca Indians finally met in St. Louis. Each party assured the others that the process would move forward despite the initial problems. An unnamed Cherokee speaker expressed both a commitment to the process and the "future happiness of the red people," through the relocation of eastern Indians. Lewis then reiterated his position and answered those who sought to sabotage the process. "The Cherokees are at last arrived," he declared to the Senecas present, "you see that all I had communicated to you is the truth, and all this wampum confirms what I have told you."[36]

---

[35] R. David Edmunds, *The Shawnee Prophet* (Lincoln, 1985), 169–172; Warren, *The Shawnees and Their Neighbors*, 129–139; *Indian Affairs*, II, 145–155.

[36] Council Notes, January 7, 1824, OIA-LR, roll 747; Edmunds, *The Shawnee Prophet*, 169–172; Warren, *The Shawnees and Their Neighbors*, 129–139.

Over the months that followed, Lewis and other Indian diplomats tried to strengthen their negotiations with American material support. In the fall of 1824, the Shawnees, Delawares, Kickapoos, Peorias, Piankeshaws, and Miamis solicited the services of the Western Cherokee chief, Tekatoke, to accompany their delegates to Washington to help negotiate with President Monroe. They wanted the resources of the American government to facilitate the planned relocation. Only a few months later, a party of Cherokees sat down with Clark in St. Louis to discuss this possibility. The Cherokee representatives presented the Superintendent with a large amount of wampum they had received from the various eastern tribes. They discussed the occupation of "a Country convenient to each other for the purpose of union," reported subagent William Alexander, "and support of regulations calculated to govern the whole and promote the culture of the earth and a tendency to civilization." The Cherokee delegates then displayed strands of wampum they had received from the Six Nations, the Shawnees of Ohio, the Nottoways, the Wyandots, the Miamis of Ohio, the Delawares, the Potawatomis, and many others for a total of nineteen different delegations. As a testament to the reach of these councils, the Cherokees also presented messages from eighteen Indian villages between Arkansas Territory and New Mexico signaling their willingness to welcome the eastern emigrants as neighbors.[37]

Strings, strands, and belts of wampum played a crucial role in these repeated efforts to sustain the far-reaching alliance. Though these material exchanges may have appeared secondary to the non-Indian witnesses, the wampum underscored the persistence of native diplomacy. The Shawnees and other eastern Indian groups relied on preexisting patterns of relations to prepare for relocation and turned to the government merely for assistance. But the wampum solidified and communicated these discussions and agreements beyond the American government's control and understanding. Most American agents were familiar with the strands of beaded shells or beads in the 1820s. Yet few, if any, would have seen those same objects as anything more than expected elements of Indian councils that had lost meaning and influence over the years.

Wampum as an instrument of communication and exchange played a prominent role in inter-Indian relations, as well as in the diplomatic and economic interactions between Indians and Europeans throughout the colonial period. Belts, strings, necklaces, and bracelets were made using material obtained from shells along the eastern seaboard, and most

---

[37] Declaration of Cherokee Indians, vol. 1, *RCA*; William Alexander to William Clark, January 6, 1825, OIA-LR, roll 747.

studies of wampum's ceremonial and diplomatic purposes have focused on the Indian tribes and confederacies of the northeast. But although the location of the raw materials for the manufacture of wampum may have led to its widespread use among northeastern peoples, its importance spread beyond that geographic region.[38]

These woven arrangements of the cylindrical beads served many purposes within eastern Indian societies. The Shawnees sometimes used strings of wampum as payment to the relatives of an individual who had been murdered. Records of the Colonial era relate that the Iroquois Confederacy often demanded wampum as tribute from subjugated coastal Indians. Wampum belts and strings also grounded condolence ceremonies, marriage proposals, and, among some eastern confederacies, the elections of chiefs. The woven beads also served diplomatic purposes. Eastern Indian groups, with the Six Nations the most prominent, used wampum belts as historical accounts that recorded formal agreements, including alliances and other declarations of friendship. Strings of wampum had a slightly different connotation, and most often served as representations and remembrances of oral exchanges or as mnemonic devices. Although Indian messengers used words to communicate messages to the receiver of the wampum, the color of the shells and the design of the belt also indicated whether those words signaled war or peace. In the various contexts, then, wampum organized future plans as much as it recorded historical events.[39]

---

[38] Two analyses of wampum's functions within northeastern Indian communities are provided by Frank G. Speck, "The Functions of Wampum among the Eastern Algonkian," *Memoirs of the American Anthropological Association*, VI(1919): 3–71, and Robert M. Leavitt and David A. Francis (Eds.), *The Wampum Records: Wabanaki Traditional Laws* (Fredericton, 1990). For some insights into the larger colonial context of wampum use among the Iroquois, see Daniel K. Richter, *The Ordeal of the Longhouse: The Peoples of the Iroquois League in the Era of European Colonization* (Chapel Hill, 1992), 47–49, 138–141, 214–217.

[39] Howard, *Shawnee!*, 112. For more general overviews of the uses and manufacture of wampum, as well as more specific commentaries on its use by the Iroquois, see Wilbur R. Jacobs, "Wampum, the Protocol of Indian Diplomacy," *The William and Mary Quarterly*, VI(October 1949): 596–604; Willard Walker, "Wabanaki Wampum Protocol," in William Cowan (Ed.), *Papers of the Algonquian Conference*, no. 15 (1984): 107–122; Michael K. Foster, "Another Look at the Function of Wampum in Iroquois-White Councils," in Francis Jennings (Ed.), *The History and Culture of Iroquois Diplomacy: An Interdisciplinary Guide to the Treaties of the Six Nations and Their League* (Syracuse, 1985), 99–114. Foster in particular argues that the Indians did not simply use wampum to record the past but to organize or structure future relations. For an example of how the Delaware leader Netawatwes instructed his messengers in the use of wampum strings in 1773, see Earl P. Olmstead, *David Zeisberger: A Life among the Indians* (Kent, OH, 1997), 351–353.

Most important to the negotiations of the 1820s, however, the meaning and uses of wampum had changed over the years depending on the parties involved. Over the period of colonial encounter, wampum had become less useful in European–Indian relations because of the European dependence on the written word. Early colonists noted the ornamental, commercial, and symbolic uses of wampum among the Indians. Because of its multiple uses and its popularity, the Dutch even created a wampum exchange rate for the fur trade, and both British and French officials incorporated wampum belts in their dealings with the Iroquois. But by the late eighteenth century, some Indians, realizing the Europeans' reliance on paper documents for recording treaties and other transactions, did not rely on wampum to seal diplomatic negotiations. Europeans relied on the written word, and the histories contained within the beaded belts did not hold much weight in the world of paper documents. For their part, British and American officials viewed wampum as a symbolic tool in diplomacy, but neither trusted nor recognized its validity as either historical record or legal contract. Therefore, although the councils between Europeans and Indians in the 1600s and 1700s usually incorporated exchanges of wampum, by the 1800s, the belts of woven beads seemingly lost their effectiveness in diplomatic negotiations with Americans.[40]

In inter-Indian councils, however, wampum remained crucial well into the mid-nineteenth century. The negotiation for relocation in the 1820s among the eastern Indians alone reflects its practical and symbolic importance. The nineteen different eastern bands that sent wampum to the Cherokees all used white shell beads presented as belts or, as the record states, bunches. Blue beads only appeared in the wampum patterns in the presentations of the Creeks and Choctaws. Although there are no detailed descriptions of these latter belts, the blue beads very well may have been used within a belt of white in a design that narrated the past relations or negotiations among these southeastern tribes. The use of beaded belts as symbol extended even to the western tribes that sent their welcoming message through the Cherokees. Eighteen villages signaled their willingness to accept the emigrant settlements by delivering to the Cherokees

[40] For exchange rates set by the Dutch, see Weslager, *The Delaware Indians,* 129. Other discussions of the use of wampum in exchange or as currency can be found in J. S. Slotkin and Karl Schmitt, "Studies of Wampum," *American Anthropologist,* 51(1949): 223–236. For examples of Indians discontinuing the use of wampum in negotiations with Euro-Americans, see Weslager, *The Delaware Indians,* 309–310 and Jacobs, "Wampum," 601–602.

a "string of white beeds encircled and curiously connected, attached to
a piece of Tobacco." William Alexander did not describe these objects
delivered by the western villages as wampum, yet his observations point
to the similarities in their design. Whether their beaded communications
could be specifically termed "wampum" or not, the use of white beads
by these western Indians indicated a desire for peace and friendship, and
the inclusion of tobacco also could be seen as a welcoming gesture, an
invitation to sit down and to share a pipe.[41]

But even the use of wampum could not save the attempt to foster both
a large-scale relocation and the formation of a western Indian confederacy. Dissent within the Ohio Shawnee community consumed Captain
Lewis's plans. Lewis was confident that the Shawnees would support him
in the council planned for the spring of 1825, and asked Secretary of War
Calhoun "to commission some person to be there and to have full power
to make an exchange with us for other Land west of the Mississippi."
Instead, both Black Hoof and the Shawnee Prophet undermined the process, although each man had vastly different reasons for doing so. Ever
since the Treaty of Greenville, Black Hoof had decided that the Shawnees
needed to work with the United States. He petitioned the government
to send missionaries who would teach his people to become farmers like
the whites who poured into their country. Despite the growing difficulties
with Ohio settlers after the War of 1812, he refused to support removal.
Consequently, Black Hoof actively worked against Lewis both in and out
of the Shawnee councils. Tenskwatawa was more of an enigmatic figure. He fled to Ontario after the Battle of the Thames in 1813 to avoid
any punishment by American authorities and for the next several years
regrouped and attempted to recapture his position of influence. By the
mid-1820s, however, the British no longer wanted him as an ally and
the Americans no longer considered him a threat. Lewis Cass, Governor of Michigan Territory and Superintendent of Indian Affairs, even
hoped to use Tenskwatawa to assist U.S. efforts to move the Shawnees
who remained in Ohio. To fulfill his part of this bargain, Tenskwatawa
traveled with Cass to a council at Wapakoneta in May 1825. Intent
on arguing for removal, the Prophet discovered that Black Hoof had
established a hard line against any relocation west of the Mississippi.
Believing that there was greater feeling against Lewis than the idea of
removal, Tenskwatawa switched his stance and sided with Black Hoof.

---

[41] Council with William Clark, January 6, 1825, OIA-LR, roll 747. For pipes and tobacco
used in combination with wampum, see Olmstead, *David Zeisberger*, 351–353.

The maneuver left Lewis standing alone, and few joined him when he departed months later.[42]

With the elimination of Captain Lewis from the Shawnee settlements and councils, Cass's plan to use Tenskwatawa to promote removal regained its footing. The end result of these machinations, however, revealed more shortcomings than strengths in the government's abilities and resources. The Shawnee Prophet abandoned Black Hoof's position as soon as Captain Lewis had left and eventually convinced more than two hundred Shawnees to leave Ohio. At the same time, the federal government prepared for these removals by negotiating a treaty with the Shawnees in Missouri. At a council held in Washington in November 1825, the Missouri Shawnees ceded the land grant given them by Spain and agreed to move to lands farther west along the Kansas River. This treaty provided for both the Missouri and Ohio Shawnee bands, and over the next several years, hundreds of Shawnees took advantage of its terms.[43]

The first western emigration to follow the 1825 treaty encountered distinct problems. In September 1826, a party of approximately two hundred and three Shawnees and twenty-four Senecas left their homes in Ohio. The two men assigned to guide this party, Joseph Parks and William Broderick, blazed a difficult trail through Indiana and Illinois. Other than the initial provisions provided by the government, the emigrants received supplies only at William Conner's trading post on the White River and Vincennes on the Indiana-Illinois border. But the real disaster struck when Broderick abandoned the journey at the Embarrass River and Parks did the same at the Little Wabash River in southeastern Illinois. "They left us at these places," reported Tenskwatawa, "stating that Johnson told them that they must not exceed a certain number of days and that if on that time they did not get here [Kaskaskia] – they must turn back – or they would not get pay." As a result, the Shawnees who arrived in Kaskaskia in December were in extremely poor condition, as both they and their horses suffered from starvation. On the recommendation of Pierre Menard, the emigrants encamped east of the Mississippi until spring, at which time federal officials investigated the circumstances of their journey and arrival. From all appearances, Clark had little idea that the emigrants had left

---

[42] John Lewis to Secretary of War Calhoun, February 28, 1825, OIA-LR, roll 300; R. David Edmunds, "'A Watchful Safeguard to Our Habitations': Black Hoof and the Loyal Shawnees," in Cayton and Teute, *Contact Points*, 162–199; *Indian Affairs*, II, 262–264; Edmunds, *The Shawnee Prophet*, 168–183.

[43] Major Richard Graham to William Clark, SIA, April 4, 1827, OIA-LR, roll 749.

Ohio under government supervision. More familiar with the independent movements of Indian parties, Clark sent agent Richard Graham to ask the Shawnees why they had traveled to the Mississippi. Graham uncovered the truth behind their migration and came away amazed at the lack of organization. He also seemed surprised to hear that fifty-five Shawnees had migrated the previous year and that the over two hundred Indians in Kaskaskia expected another fifty to join them in Illinois at any point. Frustrated by the entire situation, Graham lamented that some "regular arrangements for the transportation and subsistence of Emigrating Indians are not made on their journey. The sufferings . . . will no doubt have a considerable effect upon those who remain behind in preventing their emigration." He specifically wondered whether or not such an experience might hinder the removal of Black Hoof and the one hundred and seventy-eight Shawnees still living at Wapakoneta.[44]

Following his arduous experience, Tenskwatawa provided some perspective on government-sponsored Indian removals in the late 1820s. "We have taken that advice [to remove] and listened to what our Great Father said to us," he explained. "That is the reason that you see us here, because we are following his advice." But the government appeared to have little to offer but guidance without material support. U.S. officials had not fulfilled the promises made in Washington and Ohio and had left the Shawnees to fend for themselves. "It is true he [Indian agent John Johnston] gave us some clothes," the Prophet stated, "but we were obliged to sell them on the way to get something to eat. We gave a shirt, a Blanket for anything to eat." The litany of problems grew longer as Tenskwatwa detailed the losses sustained by the Shawnees for their willingness to work with the American government. "You see us here before you, in great want," he concluded, "ask you to take pity on us, and wish to know if we will be paid for those things we left behind us and our Improvements."[45]

Tenskwatawa's party shows up as a brief note in the journal Superintendent of Indian Affairs William Clark and his clerks maintained in his St. Louis office from 1826 to 1831. Most entries in the journal document

---

[44] Memo of a talk made by the Shawnees Emigrating from Ohio, April 2, 1827, OIA-LR, roll 300; Shawnee Indians to Secretary of War, April 3, 1827, OIA-LR, roll 300; Major Richard Graham to William Clark, April 4, 1827, OIA-LR, roll 749; Edmunds, *The Shawnee Prophet*, 174–183; John Lauritz Larson and David G. Vanderstel, "Agent of Empire: William Conner on the Indiana Frontier, 1800–1855," *Indiana Magazine of History*, 80(December 1984): 301–328.

[45] Memo of a talk made by the Shawnees Emigrating from Ohio, April 2, 1827, OIA-LR, roll 300.

weather patterns and steamboat schedules. But Clark and his clerks also recorded the comings and goings of the people who passed through the city's environs. As the Superintendent of Indian Affairs for the St. Louis Superintendency, Clark was the most powerful representative of the President within the western territories. Consequently, he often met with Indian residents of the region on official business to discuss their complaints and to present them with gifts. Emigrant bands also used the city to rest, trade, or decide on a final destination. On the dates of August 6 and 7 in 1827, the entry begins, "125 Shawnees (Emigrating from Ohio) arrive." The short and colorless description never even hints at the struggle that preceded the arrival of Tenskwatawa and the Shawnees who traveled with him. Instead, it gives rise to questions about the stories hidden behind equally bland entries.[46]

Despite its shortcomings, this journal has significance not only for discussions of Indian movements in the 1820s but also for those of prior decades. Most emigrant Indian parties that passed through St. Louis at this time were small and autonomous. On June 29, 1826, for example, "30 Emigrating Kickapoos arrived from the East of the Mississippi." And from June 12 to June 17 in the year 1827, "six Shawnees from Kaskaskia arrived and departed after a day, ten Weas and Miamis arrived and left after emigrating from the Wabash, eight Kickapoos came and went, and on the day the Kickapoos left, eleven Delawares appeared." This did not demonstrate government direction of removal. Indeed, though the demographic explosion in the Ohio Valley and federal policies played their part in these relocations, geography, kinship, and the commercial history of the region also had a say in the Indians' journeys through St. Louis. Just as important, Clark's journal reveals the movements of Indians headed in the opposite direction. In some instances, the Indians who departed on steamboats for Kaskaskia and Louisville may have only been visiting family or friends. But in September 1827, two families of Shawnee Indians renounced their intention of removing west and left from St. Louis for their former lands.[47]

Assuming this journal contains a representative record of Indian movements through the region, fewer Indians traveled east than west in the early nineteenth century. This trend was a logical outgrowth of American

[46] Louis Barry (Ed.), "William Clark's Diary, May 1826-February 1831," *Kansas Historical Quarterly,* 16(February 1948): 1–36; (May 1948): 136–174; (August 1948): 274–305; (November 1948): 384–410. The notation for the arrival of Tenskwatawa's party is on page 32 in the February volume.

[47] Barry, "William Clark's Diary, May 1826–February 1831."

expansion into the Ohio Valley and, as a result, not surprising. But more important than the numbers involved are the attitudes those movements reflect. Well into the 1820s, St. Louis remained a hub for the varied and independent movements that marked the relationships and networks in the trans-Mississippi West. And despite all literal and figurative references to the contrary, Shawnees, Delawares, and others continued to view the Mississippi as a path that could lead them to their kin in the West or their former homes in the East. Neither the political nor the figurative application of the Mississippi River had power over those who consistently viewed it as a corridor and not a border.

2

Potawatomis, Delawares, and Indian Removal in the Great Lakes

In November 1839, Levi Konkapot piloted a boat down the Mississippi River toward St. Louis. Robert Konkapot, Levi's father, and other members of their family sat in the vessel and watched the riverbank glide by as they rode with the current. Although he was a young man no older than twenty-five, Levi knew the Mississippi well, as he had, for several years, worked as a boatman in the trade that used the waterways connecting Green Bay to the interior of the United States. This time, however, he used his expertise for a different purpose. Instead of merchandise, his boat carried people and their belongings. More specifically, Levi was employed by John Newcom to pilot the sixty-nine-person-strong Emigrant Party of Stockbridge Indians to St. Louis. From there, they boarded a steamboat that took them to their new home on a section of the Delaware reserve. In a treaty that was signed only months earlier in Wisconsin Territory, these Stockbridges had ceded their claims to the reserve just north and east of Lake Winnebago and prepared for a new life in the West. Rather than wait for Senate ratification and thus delay their relocation, the Stockbridges appointed one of their own men, Newcom, to conduct their journey.[1]

Levi controlled only one of many vessels in this water-borne convoy. The other boats trailed behind, beneficiaries of the path Konkapot cut through the water. Although these trailing vessels included at least ten Stockbridges, most of the passengers were Munsees and Delawares. The latter Indians, 105 in number, hailed originally from the settlement of New Fairfield in Upper Canada, and also intended to settle along the

---

[1] Robert Konkapot et al. to Hon. T. H. Crawford, July 30, 1841, OIA-LR, roll 301; *Indian Affairs*, *II*, 529–531; To the Congress of the United States of America from Gideon Williams and Jacob Moonhouse, January 8, 1858, Indian Files – Wyandot, Box 6, KSHS.

Kansas River. Although these Indians were not participants in the 1839 treaty, Gideon Williams and his fellow Canadian Indians had lived near the Stockbridges on the shores of Lake Winnebago for nearly two years. They now took advantage of the Stockbridge emigration and followed the course set by Newcom and Konkapot. For the Delawares and Munsees, more than just a new home awaited them west of the Missouri border. They would also be reunited with nearly eighty former residents of New Fairfield, emigrants who had traveled straight from Canada to Kansas and bypassed the two-year hiatus in Wisconsin Territory.[2]

This relocation of fewer than two hundred people had an import beyond its size because of both national and local contexts. In the late 1830s, the plight of the Cherokee Nation placed forced removals at the forefront of federal Indian affairs. Residents of the Great Lakes had also witnessed and participated in local versions of the Trail of Tears. As summer turned to fall in 1838, approximately eight hundred Potawatomis marched at gunpoint for more than 660 miles from the Yellow River in northern Indiana to the Osage River just west of the Missouri border. The combined efforts of state officials and local citizens drove the Indians from their villages near Twin Lakes, and many Potawatomis did not survive the agonizing two months spent on this Trail of Death. In this environment of forced removal, the water journey of the Stockbridges, Delawares, and Munsees stood out because of the very absence of explicit coercion. Just as important, the diversity within this group from Wisconsin reflected the intricate foundations of the journey. The Emigrant Party of Stockbridges chose to relocate because they believed that increased American settlement and the constant pressure of federal officials made it the right choice for the future of their people. However, the simultaneous movement of the Delawares and Munsees suggested that more than demographics and politics were responsible. Indeed, this emigration had equally significant ties to the kinship networks that continued to support Indian relationships and relocations in the 1830s and 1840s.[3]

---

[2] Robert Konkapot et al. to Hon. T. H. Crawford, July 30, 1841, OIA-LR, roll 301; Muster Roll of a company of Stockbridge Indians emigrated within the Fort Leavenworth agency from the Territory of Wisconsin, January 31, 1840, OIA-LR, roll 301; Muster Roll of a company of Delaware and Munsee Indians emigrated to the Fort Leavenworth agency in November 1839, in company with the Stockbridges from the Territory of Wisconsin, January 31, 1840, OIA-LR, roll 301; Richard Cummins to T. Hartley Crawford, February 12, 1839, OIA-LR, roll 301.

[3] James W. Oberly, *A Nation of Statesmen: The Political Culture of the Stockbridge-Munsee Mohicans, 1815–1972* (Norman, OK, 2005), 55–69.

The relentless advance of American settlement both produced and enforced the Indian Removal Act of 1830. A population explosion in the Ohio Valley after 1815 as well as growing sentiments in favor of removal made it extremely difficult for eastern Indians to remain in the states and territories carved out of the Old Northwest in the early nineteenth century. Because of the strength and influence of these regional and dramatic changes, the removals of thousands of Indians from the northern lands often depended more on the power of local interests than the legislative dictates of the federal government. Instead of movements orchestrated from Washington, D.C., the Indians' relocation largely depended on ill-conceived or fraudulent negotiations among state officials, traders, and the Indians themselves.

As the Potawatomi Trail of Death illustrated, the relative weakness of federal power did not necessarily lessen the severity of the impact of removal. Yet not all Indians moved west at the end of a bayonet. In the early 1830s, several Potawatomi bands chose to leave Illinois and Indiana because they felt threatened by the hostile environment in the region. The emigration of Canadian Munsees and Delawares at the end of the decade reflected a similar desire to leave behind white settlers. But the extended and complicated nature of this relocation also marked the persistence of native frameworks for migration. Enactment and enforcement of official removal policy in the 1830s created an inhospitable climate for Indians in the Great Lakes region. Although these conditions led to forced relocations as harsh as any seen in other sections of the country, the dispersed nature of federal authority also meant that the threads of preexisting kinship networks continued to influence and support the movements of Indian bands into the 1840s.

Congress attached a simple and straightforward subtitle to the 1830 Indian Removal Act: "An Act to provide for an exchange of lands with the Indians residing in any of the states or territories, and for their removal west of the river Mississippi." The act authorized the president and his representatives to negotiate treaties, set apart western lands, and prepare for the removal of any Indian tribe that "chose" to leave their eastern homes. This bill and its agenda reflected ideas formulated during the presidency of Thomas Jefferson and not simply the mindset of the current president, Andrew Jackson. Jefferson's Indian policy evolved during the course of his two terms in the early 1800s. Although he consistently pushed for civilization and assimilation, the Louisiana Purchase had made available other options for handling eastern Indians who resisted his policies. Relocation to the "open lands" west of the Mississippi became a defining element of Indian affairs for the next several decades. When President James Monroe declared to the Senate as he left office in 1825 that, "the removal of the Indian tribes from the lands which they now occupy ... is of very high importance to our Union," he merely echoed the sentiments of a predecessor. And although Indian removal became the official policy during his first term, Jackson's suggestion that the U.S. government set aside "an ample district west of the Mississippi" for eastern Indians who chose to relocate was more derivative than innovative.[4]

Removal legislation also continued in the tradition of federal authority in Indian policy set by earlier bills such as the Trade and Intercourse Act. That 1790 legislation and its subsequent revised editions attempted to create a distinct hierarchy in which federal control of Indian trade and treaties trumped both the interests and jurisdictions of state and local governments. However, just as there had been difficulty with the enforcement of the numerous versions of the Trade and Intercourse Act, there were also problems with removal. The relatively succinct and straightforward wording of the 1830 bill expressed that the American government intended to establish a simple course of action. But there was a big difference between the passage and enactment of legislation in the southern Great Lakes region. In the 1830s, particularly among the Potawatomis, federal policy played a far more diminished role than did the actions of local interests. On a practical level, the bill's implementation depended largely on local individuals, agendas, and power relations that frustrated as much as they facilitated the U.S. government's goals. Self-interested traders, missionaries, state officials, and Indians rarely acted according to the dictates of scripts written in the nation's capital.[5]

From the turn of the century to the 1830s, the United States depended on state and territorial officials, federal treaty commissioners, and Indian agents to deal with Indian affairs in the Old Northwest. For the first two decades of the nineteenth century, Indian Territorial Governor William

---

[4] For the development of Jefferson's policy, see Anthony F. C. Wallace, *Jefferson and the Indians: The Tragic Fate of the First Americans* (Cambridge, MA, 1999), 206–240. The text of the Removal Act as well as the quotations from Monroe and Jackson in Francis Paul Prucha (Ed.), *Documents of United States Indian Policy* (Lincoln, 1990), 39, 47, 52–53.

[5] For an overview of the Trade and Intercourse Acts see Francis Paul Prucha, *The Great Father: The United States Government and the American Indians* (2 vols., Lincoln, 1984), I, 89–114. Prucha deals with this topic even more extensively in a prior work, *American Indian Policy in the Formative Years: The Indian Trade and Intercourse Acts* (Cambridge, MA, 1962).

Henry Harrison oversaw Indian affairs in the region. During his tenure, he secured both a substantial land cession through the Fort Wayne Treaty in 1809, and he commanded the army that defeated the Indian forces led by Tenskwatawa at the Battle of Tippecanoe two years later. All told, Harrison negotiated eleven of the twelve different treaties signed in Indiana Territory from 1800 to 1810. Less than a year after Harrison departed his post for other ventures in 1812, Lewis Cass became the Governor of Michigan Territory, an office he held for the next eighteen years. As Governor and Superintendent of Indian Affairs, Cass complemented the efforts of his St. Louis-based colleague, William Clark. And from 1831 to 1836, Cass supervised all removal efforts from his position of Secretary of War under Andrew Jackson. Yet despite the hands-on involvement of these three officials in the negotiation of removal treaties, Indian agents bore the logistical brunt of Indian policy. Consequently, the process of removal on the ground did not always unfold in the manner prescribed by treaty commissioners and officials like Cass and Clark.[6]

Fortunately for federal employees posted in the southern Great Lakes, one of the strongest supporters of Indian removal worked as a missionary in southern Michigan and northern Indiana. Although many eastern reformers viewed removal as a reversal of ongoing efforts to civilize and assimilate native communities, Reverend Isaac McCoy did everything in his power to move the Indians west. McCoy was a Baptist missionary appointed to work among the Kickapoo and Miami Indians in northern Indiana in 1817. He opened the Carey Mission School among the Potawatomis in southern Michigan in 1822 and the Thomas Mission among the Ottawas in 1826. Along with his colleague Robert Simerwell, McCoy criticized the "ruinous habit of dealing out spirits" to the Indians and condemned the negative influences of white settlers. Convinced that the vices of civilization were destroying the Indians with whom he worked, McCoy took up the cause of removal and by the mid-1820s worked for the federal government. Until his death in 1846, McCoy tirelessly

---

[6] Robert M. Owens, "William Henry Harrison's Indiana: Paternalism and Patriotism on the Frontier, 1795–1812" (Ph.D. Dissertation, University of Illinois at Urbana-Champaign, 2003), 231–299; *Indian Affairs, II*, 64–105. Cass urged Congress to create the position of Commissioner of Indian Affairs to ease the strain in the War Department. The Commissioner, however, was based in Washington and dependent on the agents in the field. See Ronald Satz, *American Indian Policy in the Jacksonian Era* (Lincoln, 1975), 152–168. For Clark's involvement with removal and Cass, see Jerome O. Steffen, *William Clark: Jeffersonian Man on the Frontier* (Norman, OK, 1977), 129–150.

promoted both the removal of eastern Indians to the West and the organization of a separate Indian Territory.[7]

Although McCoy's support for removal made him friends in the federal government, it often placed him in opposition to those who had economic interests in the development and implementation of Indian policy. More than any other segment of the population, the region's prosperous merchant community had the ability to disrupt the government's agenda. Through intermarriage and regular business transactions, fur traders had developed connections to eastern Indian groups long before any government authority. By the nineteenth century, a significant percentage of these men could also claim descent from European–Indian relationships formed during the height of the trade. As a result of these intricate kinship connections, their economic influence remained strong despite the increased presence of the United States and its representatives. This combination of economic interest and kinship ties gave these individuals a particular advantage in treaty negotiations, and traders either supported or defied commissioners based on the manner in which the treaty arranged for debt payment and land allotment.[8]

Traders were far from a minor component of the removal process and had especially strong links to the Potawatomis. Even as different companies struggled over access to and control of the fur trade in the nineteenth century, the foundation of that economy remained the same – mixed descent individuals married into local Indian communities. By the 1830s, both the American Fur Company and the brothers William and George Ewing had a strong presence in the region. John Jacob Astor established his business in the early 1800s and relied on the abilities of his employees in the field, both men and women, who had grown up as part of, or married into, the larger trading community in the region. Although white men served in the most prominent positions of the company, the boatmen, clerks, and traders most often came from French–Indian lineages. Alexander, Leon, and Eloy Bourassa, three descendants of a prominent fur trading family of the eighteenth century, worked for the company in the late 1810s. Years after the death of her husband Joseph, Madeline la Framboise, the daughter of Jean Baptiste Marcot and Thimotee, an

---

7 Robert Simerwell to Rev. C. M. Fuller, December 11, 1828, roll 1124, RSP; Isaac McCoy, *History of Baptist Indian Missions* (Washington, DC, 1840); George Schultz, *An Indian Canaan: Isaac McCoy and the Vision of an Indian State* (Norman, OK, 1972).
8 Anthony F. C. Wallace, *The Long Bitter Trail: Andrew Jackson and the Indians* (New York, 1993), 30–72; Helen Hornbeck Tanner (Ed.), *Atlas of Great Lakes Indian History* (Norman, OK, 1987), 155–161.

Ottawa woman, worked as a trader for the AFC, and she was joined, in later years, by her sons. The existence of the other kinship networks such as the Bertrands, Langlades, Burnetts, and Grignons made it almost impossible to trade with any measure of success without somehow working within these intertwined circles of influence and familial ties. And the surnames soon appeared throughout the documented rolls of Potawatomi bands in the region. Therefore, even as the Scotch-Irish Ewing brothers attempted to establish a niche through political relationships with local officials, they also used more customary measures. Both for love and for business reasons, George married Harriet Bourie, a young woman who belonged to a prominent French-Canadian trading family based in Fort Wayne, Indiana. The brothers also hired Pierre Navarre, a French-Canadian trader married to Keshewaquay, a member of the St. Joseph Potawatomi band, to sell their goods in southern Michigan.[9]

Depending on the perspective of the reporter, the interconnected Potawatomi and trader communities helped or hindered negotiations over removal. Although some outside observers criticized the roles often played by traders, such disapproval did not always take into account the nature of kinship relations and obligations. Joseph Bertrand, Sr., a trader located at St. Joseph's in southern Michigan, came under fire in the late 1820s and early 1830s for his efforts to obstruct a number of land cession and removal treaties. Robert Simerwell, who had assumed control of the Carey Mission, chastised the trader for using "every lawful and I might say unlawful measure . . . to keep the poor Indians where they are." In a similar vein, Isaac McCoy reported that a few traders in southern Michigan had persuaded several Potawatomis to tell American officials that they did not want to move. Although they were very mindful of their economic stakes, these men were not outsiders who twisted the minds of Indians who otherwise would have chosen to move west. Bertrand, the son of Laurent Bertrand and a mixed descent woman named Marie Theresa Dulignon, arrived in the St. Joseph River valley in the early 1800s and married Mouto, a Potawatomi woman. Mouto, baptized as Madeline, was the daughter of the headman Topinebee, a relationship that gave her

[9] Paul Chrysler Phillips, *The Fur Trade Volume II* (Norman, OK, 1961), 118–168; "American Fur Company Employees – 1818–1819," *Wisconsin Historical Collections Vol. XII* (1892): 154–169; "American Fur Company Invoices – 1821–1822," *Wisconsin Historical Collections Vol. XI* (1892): 370–379; Susan Sleeper-Smith, *Indian Women and French Men: Rethinking Cultural Encounter in the Western Great Lakes* (Amherst, 2001), 151–154; Robert A. Trennert, Jr., *Indian Traders on the Middle Border: The House of Ewing, 1827–1854* (Lincoln, 1981), 24–34.

husband Joseph significant standing in the local Indian population. By the
1830s, Bertrand had a distinct history with the Potawatomis at St. Joseph,
and although some missionaries accused him of defrauding the Indians,
the Indians themselves still trusted the trader. High prices or not, Bertrand
served as a conduit for the goods they wanted. The trader also understood
the reciprocity involved in his business and familial relationship with the
Potawatomis, as demonstrated by his decisions to give the Indians corn
and flour in times of need.[10]

However, removal in the Great Lakes was not only about these external
forces. There was no single Potawatomi relocation west, in part because
of diffuse Potawatomi settlements and localized leadership structures. In
1830, more than thirty different Potawatomi villages dotted the landscape
from the mouth of the St. Joseph River on the eastern side of Lake Michigan to the mouth of the Root River on the opposite shore. Significant
populations of Potawatomis also thrived in southern Michigan along the
Kalamazoo River and its tributaries as well as in northern Indiana along
the Tippecanoe and Wabash rivers. And although outsiders grouped them
all under one tribal heading, the Potawatomi leadership operated on much
more of a local level, which meant that treaty commissioners had to meet
with a number of leaders and councils to perform the tasks assigned by
the federal government. Of the more than forty treaties signed between
1830 and 1840 in the southern Great Lakes region, almost half of those
involved members of the Potawatomi bands living in the swath of villages
that stretched from Detroit to the western shores of Lake Michigan.[11]

One consequence of this dispersed leadership was the ability of well-
placed individuals within different Potawatomi bands to influence treaty
negotiations irrespective of traditional authority. In the early 1800s, the
United Band of Ottawas, Ojibwas, and Potawatomis resided west and

[10] Robert Simerwell to Rev. S. H. Cane, December 20, 1830, roll 1124, RSP; Isaac McCoy
to Eaton, SOW, March 2, 1831, roll 610, IMP; Sleeper-Smith, *Indian Women and French
Men*, 93–95; Wilbur M. Cunningham, *Land of Four Flags: An Early History of the St.
Joseph Valley* (Grand Rapids, 1961), 101–110.

[11] Tanner, *Atlas of Great Lakes Indian History*, 134; *Indian Affairs*, II, 353–356, 367–370,
372–375, 428–431, 457–459. For descriptions of Potawatomi leadership structures, see
James A. Clifton, *A Place of Refuge for All Time: Migration of the American Potawatomi
into Upper Canada 1830–1850* (Ottawa, Canada, 1975), 10–14; Thomas G. Conway,
"Potawatomi Politics," *Journal of the Illinois State Historical Society*, 65(Winter 1972):
395–418; James A. Clifton, "Potawatomi Leadership Roles: On Okama and Other Influential Personages," *Papers of the 6th Algonquian Conference* (1975): 42–99; David
Baerris, "Chieftainship Among the Potawatomi," *The Wisconsin Archaeologist*, LIV
(September 1973): 114–134.

southwest of Chicago. Although they were related to and friendly with the Potawatomis living in northern Indiana and southern Michigan Territory, the United Band lived as a distinct polity and therefore did not act for all Potawatomis in the region. Under the auspices of a treaty signed in July 1829 at Prairie du Chien, representatives of this community ceded large portions of land in northern Illinois, stretching from Lake Michigan to the Mississippi River. The treaty had detractors among the Potawatomis, and they wanted their voices heard. Chosequong, Nauntay, and three other United Band members expressed great outrage with the thirty-four men whose marks were affixed to that document, and they traveled to St. Louis to register their protest with Superintendent of Indian Affairs William Clark. "The foolish people who pretended to sell it, had no right to it," Nauntay declared. "My name is not on the treaty which sold our land." In fact, none of the men who sat down with Clark that day had signed the treaty. Among the names of those who did, two stood out from the rest – Soukamok and Cheecheepinquay. Also known as Billy Caldwell and Alexander Robinson, respectively, these two men played an important part in this treaty and many of those that followed.[12]

Caldwell's and Robinson's involvement in a series of treaties in the late 1820s and early 1830s illustrated the ways in which individuals of mixed descent assumed crucial roles within some Potawatomi communities as the level of interaction between the Indians and the American government grew. The two men came from slightly different backgrounds. Robinson was born to a Scottish trader and an Ottawa woman. He entered the fur trade in southern Michigan in the late 1700s, and in 1826 married Catherine Chevalier, the mixed descent daughter of a chief of the United Band

---

[12] Record of talks between Potawatomis and William Clark, SIA, November 2, 4, 5, 1831, OIA-LR, roll 642; *Indian Affairs, II*, 297–300. The names of these two men are spelled with great variation throughout the historical records. Billy Caldwell is also referred to as Sakanosh and Saukonock. Sakanosh is the foundation for the other two variants, and according to Clifton it means "English-speaking Canadian." See James A. Clifton, "Personal and Ethnic Identity on the Great Lakes Frontier: The Case of Billy Caldwell, Anglo-Canadian," *Ethnohistory*, 25(Winter 1978): 69–94. Robinson's Indian name was at times spelled Chichibinway. For a list of some of these variations, see the index of James A. Clifton, *The Prairie People: Continuity and Change in Potawatomi Indian Culture, 1665–1965*(Lawrence, KS, 1977). For the historical background of the United Band, see Rev. Jedidiah Morse, *A Report to the Secretary of War of the United States on Indian Affairs* (New Haven, 1822), appendix 141–143; Donald L. Fixico, "The Alliance of the Three Fires in Trade and War, 1630–1812," *The Michigan Historical Review*, 20(Fall 1994): 1–23; Benjamin Ramirez-Shkwegnaabi, "The Dynamics of American Indian Diplomacy in the Great Lakes Region," *American Indian Culture and Research Journal*, 27(Winter 2003): 53–77.

named François Chevalier and an active participant in the longstanding French–Indian kinship network. Three years later, Robinson appeared on the treaty as a headman, seemingly assuming the position once held by his wife's late father. He shared the designation of chief on the 1829 treaty with Caldwell, the son and namesake of William Caldwell, a British officer, and a Mohawk woman. As a result of his schooling in Detroit in the late 1700s, Caldwell spoke and wrote English and French, a skill that made him invaluable to traders and agents alike. In the early 1800s, he worked as a trader, both independently and for Robert and Thomas Forsyth, who operated primarily out of Chicago. Caldwell also established ties with the Potawatomi settlements on the St. Joseph River by marrying La Nanette, the daughter of Wabinema, or White Sturgeon. Both his background and his connections to the pro-British Potawatomis led him into the British Indian Service during the War of 1812, for which he earned the title of Captain. After the war, he focused on the fur trade, and his ties to prominent Chicagoans like the Forsyths gained him an appointment as justice of the peace in Chicago in the late 1820s. Although his Potawatomi wife died prior to the War of 1812, the British–Mohawk intermediary also remained a known and trusted entity among some circles of the United Band. But this relationship did not necessarily explain why his signature appeared on the 1829 treaty as a chief. From all reports, he owed his promotion to the manipulations of Alexander Wolcott, the Indian agent in Chicago. Wolcott had worked out a deal with the Forsyths, and in an effort to gain more influence in the treaty negotiations, he managed to have both Robinson and Caldwell officially recognized by the American government as chiefs. In exchange for their signatures, both men received land grants near the Rock River in northern Illinois.[13]

Not only did Nauntay's protest prove ineffective against the 1829 treaty, but it also could not prevent another accord two years later in 1833. This agreement, negotiated on the outskirts of Chicago, once again showcased the influence of intermediaries. Caldwell's signature appeared after only the principal man Topinebee's signature on the 1833 accord, and once

[13] James Dowd, *Built Like A Bear* (Fairfield, WA, 1979), 28–30. Dowd refers to François Chevalier as a chief of the "Three Fires," another term used to describe the United Band. The mark of François joined many others of the United Band on an 1821 treaty at Chicago. See *Indian Affairs*, II, 198–201, 297–300, 402–415. For more information regarding the history of the Chevalier name in the southern Michigan trading community, see Sleeper-Smith, *Indian Women and French Men*, 38–53; R. David Edmunds, *The Potawatomis: Keepers of the Fire* (Norman, OK, 1978), 172–173, 198, 228; Clifton, *The Prairie People*, 228, 230–232, 322–323; Clifton, "The Case of Billy Caldwell," 75–79.

again he was rewarded for his efforts. The mixed descent leader not only received $5,000 to pay off trading debts but he also garnered a lifetime personal annuity of $400. Robinson's name followed Caldwell's on the signature page, and, like his colleague, he received a one-time payment of $5,000 and a lifetime annuity of $300. These two men were far from the only individuals who profited from the mischief at work in this treaty. Indeed, the list of beneficiaries appeared to include every trader who ever worked in the region. But as two of the first three signatories on the accord, these men had a higher profile. U.S. officials discarded Caldwell shortly after this treaty because they no longer needed his skills and connections. He, in turn, gave his loyalties fully to the Potawatomis with whom he had traded and intermarried. When these emigrants traveled west in 1836, he traveled with them.[14]

The intricate world of cooperation and intrigue that surrounded the councils at Chicago and other locales throughout the Great Lakes mattered because the Indian Removal Act stated that eastern Indians had a choice whether or not they wanted to sign a treaty, cede their lands, and relocate west. Of course, this notion of choice had far more weight in theory than in practice. For most Potawatomis, the primary issue remained whether or not they had the autonomy or power to exercise this right without interference. In 1833, Kikito's band of Prairie Potawatomis requested removal, an appeal that resulted in a series of errors that substantially undermined the entire relocation. Five years later, Menominee's band fought a fraudulent treaty and struggled to retain their settlements on the Yellow River in northern Indiana. More than eight hundred Yellow River Potawatomis marched west at gunpoint and their forced removal depended almost entirely on the actions of state officials and the relative inaction of the federal government. In the 1830s, then, even contrasting choices revealed the overwhelming influence of local power structures on Potatatomi removals.

After the War of 1812, the non-Indian population in the southern Great Lakes region increased dramatically, although the numbers tell less about the impact of population growth on the Indians' way of life than do the specific locations of white settlement. Census statistics for Illinois from 1820 to 1830 illustrate both the explosion in the state and the settlement

---

[14] Chiefs of the United Nation to Edwin James, February 18, 1838, OIA-LR, roll 215; Major John Dougherty to George Maguire, acting SIA, January 29, 1839, OIA-LR, roll 215; Captain J. Gantt to Major Joshua Pilcher, SIA, September 27, 1839, OIA-LR, roll 215; For more on the 1833 treaty, see Clifton, *The Prairie People*, 238–244; Edmunds, *The Potawatomis*, 247–250.

patterns in the region, as the total population rose from 55,211 to 157,445. Out of the nineteen counties organized in Illinois in 1820, two years after statehood, only ten contained non-Indian populations of more than two thousand. In 1830, thirty-two of the forty-nine counties shared that distinction, and eight of those topped five thousand. However, straight comparisons of numbers and counties fail to highlight those areas most affected by the demographic changes. During the first decades of the nineteenth century, non-Indians in Illinois had largely confined their settlements to the southern river valleys. In 1820 a distinct line stretched across the state from St. Louis on the western border to Vincennes, Indiana, on the eastern border. The lands south of that invisible boundary, less than one-third of the state's total area, encompassed 34,377 people, just over 62 percent of the population. Not surprisingly, the white settlers congregated primarily along the Ohio and Mississippi rivers and left much of the northern part of the state to the Potawatomis, Kickapoos, Sauks, Mesquakies, and Ho-Chunks. By 1830 that line no longer existed. White settlement had pushed northward and five counties containing nearly forty-four thousand people spread along the southern banks of the Illinois River as it wound its way across the northern third of the state. Meanwhile, white miners had entered the lead region in the northwestern section of Illinois displacing the Ho-Chunks and Sauks from their villages along the Mississippi River. This advance of white settlement in Illinois, aided in part by treaties negotiated in the 1820s, placed further pressure on the approximately 7,300 Indians who lived on the decreasing sections of land south of Lake Michigan and along the Wisconsin border. The conflicts that did arise in the late 1820s occurred mostly in the northwest, where Ho-Chunks protested the actions of miners who pursued their work regardless of treaty boundaries. White settlers in Illinois were poised to take advantage of the next series of accords they hoped would follow passage of the Indian Removal Act.[15]

The final push of settlement into the northwestern region in the early 1830s resulted in violence that affected Indian communities in Illinois and Indiana. In the summer of 1832, the conflict between Black Hawk's band of Sauks and Mesquakies and the Illinois militia created an environment

---

[15] Federal census records accessed at the website for the University of Virginia Library's Geospatial and Statistical Data Center, http://fisher.lib.virginia.edu/collections/stats/histcensus/ (Accessed May 25, 2006); Indian population statistics from Tanner, *Atlas of Great Lakes Indian History*, 139–241. For the lead rush and conflicts in northwestern Illinois, see Lucy Eldersveld Murphy, *A Gathering of Rivers: Indians, Metis, and Mining in the Western Great Lakes, 1737–1832* (Lincoln, NE, 2000), 101–133.

of mutual suspicion that led some Indian groups to declare their willingness to move west. Nearly one thousand Sauk and Mesquakie followers of Black Hawk left their settlements on the western bank of the Mississippi in April 1832 and crossed the river heading east. The men, women, and children of this so-called British Band appeared intent on returning to Saukenuk, an ancestral village located on the eastern side. Less than a year earlier, they had retreated from this same region to escape a force of fourteen hundred militiamen sent to clear the ceded territory for white settlement. Because of these recent events, Illinois settlers and local officials viewed the return of the Sauks and Mesquakies as an invasion and act of war. It did not matter that the Sauk women carried bags of seed-corn for planting and that in the first five weeks of their return the Indians showed no violent intentions. Over a period of three months, Illinois militiamen and U.S. soldiers chased the Indians away from Saukenuk and pursued them throughout northern Illinois and the southern Wisconsin Territory. After several smaller skirmishes, the pursuit finally ended on the banks of the Bad Axe River north of Prairie du Chien on August 2. A combined assault of troops on the shore and artillery on riverboats decimated the warriors who turned to fight as well as the women and children who entered the river hoping to escape. More than two-thirds of Black Hawk's band died, and American forces soon had Black Hawk in custody.[16]

For the length of the conflict, Americans throughout the Great Lakes region feared not only Black Hawk's band, but also the possibility of a larger Indian uprising. Even though few Indians answered the Sauk leader's call for assistance, their mere presence in the region placed them under suspicion. Settler anxiety was not limited to Illinois and Wisconsin Territory. In Indiana, Governor Noble informed William Marshall, the Indian agent at Logansport, that "suspicions were entertained and avowed by frontier inhabitants that the young men of the Potawattomie tribe had mysteriously disappeared from the nation, and that the old men appeared unwilling to account for their absence." Based on his experience and knowledge as a former Indian agent, Indiana Senator John Tipton made an effort to reassure citizens and politicians alike. "Some fears...have been entertained of the Indians, within our own State, joining the war party," he noted. But his acquaintance with the Potawatomis gave him no

---

[16] For more comprehensive discussions of the Black Hawk War and the events leading up to it, see Tanner, *Atlas of Great Lakes Indian History*, 151–154; William Hagan, *The Sac and Fox Indians* (Norman, OK, 1980), 123–191; Kerry A. Trask, *Black Hawk: The Battle for the Heart of America* (New York, 2006).

reason to believe those rumors. "They will," Tipton countered, "if desired, join us against the hostile tribes." Despite the Senator's assurances and no outward signs of a developing militant Indian alliance, American settlers remained tense.[17]

Following the destruction of Black Hawk's band at Bad Axe, the pressure on local Indian populations only increased and government officials moved quickly to negotiate more land cession treaties. In a series of councils held in late October 1832 along the Tippecanoe River, Jonathan Jennings, John W. Davis, and Marks Crume signed three different accords with Potawatomi bands. The combined land cessions gave to the United States significant portions of territory along southern Lake Michigan from Illinois to southern Michigan Territory and included much of the Potawatomi lands in northern Indiana. Although these three treaties limited the Potawatomis to smaller land grants throughout the region, only one of them even mentioned removal.[18]

For Kikito's band of Prairie Potawatomis then living near the shores of Lake Michigan in northern Illinois, the environment created by the Black Hawk War had an impact beyond these treaties. Although Kikito did not support or aid the Sauks, some Potawatomis had, and a general air of distrust and hostility permeated interactions between the Indians and white settlers during and after the conflict. Throughout the month of July, as the state militia pursued the elusive band of Sauks and Mesquakies, other white men wreaked havoc on the Potawatomi villages in northern Illinois. It was the height of the growing season and the timing proved devastating for those Indians who had crops in the ground. "During the late Sac difficulties," one Potawatomi headman reported, "the white people destroyed all [our] corn and the game had left the Country." Faced with fields of burnt crops and a decreasing animal population, it became clear that holding on to land in Illinois most likely meant risking starvation. Kikito and his band faced a difficult choice. They wanted to stay and had not lifted a weapon in the recent conflict. However, it appeared that their peaceful intentions would not improve their situation. Rather than remain on their land and risk further hostilities, this band of more than two hundred Potawatomis left Illinois. Although they intended to move west, their journey began in an eastward direction as they made the shorter trip to the Indian agency at Logansport. From their temporary

[17] William Marshall to G. B. Porter, July 6, 1832, OIA-LR, roll 354; William Marshall to Lewis Cass, June 5, 1832, OIA-LR, roll 354; Tipton to his Constituents, June 19, 1832, in *JTP*, II, 632–636.

[18] *Indian Affairs*, II, 353–355, 367–370, 372–375.

encampment fifteen miles west of the agency Kikito informed agent William Marshall that his people would be ready to move to the western territories with the arrival of spring, or "as soon as the grass is sufficiently high for their horses to subsist on."[19]

Marshall greeted Kikito's request with enthusiasm. The wishes of the Potawatomis appeared easy to fulfill, particularly because their only substantial requests were for a few horses and provisions for the journey. As an added benefit, their presence near Logansport modeled desirable behavior for other Indians in the area. "The Chiefs and their whole band are strictly pious," Marshall relayed to his superiors, "and [they] totally abstain from all kinds of intoxicating liquors, nor will they suffer any one who drinks, to remain with them." From the agent's perspective, Kikito would have a positive impact on the local Indian populace and would persuade others to remove with him. With the assistance of his trusted interpreter, Luther Rice, Marshall also believed that the removal could be affected at a minimal expense.[20]

While Marshall thought through the ramifications of Kikito's request, Luther Rice maneuvered his way into a bargaining position. Rice, also known as Naoquet, was one of many young Potawatomi men educated by Baptist missionaries at the Carey Mission School in southern Michigan in the early 1820s. Rice was a practicing Christian as a result of his time at the mission school. He also served as an interpreter for the U.S. government in 1832 and 1833 at the treaty councils on the Tippecanoe River and in Chicago, respectively. By the time Kikito's band arrived in Indiana, Luther Rice had already established himself as a trusted intermediary. William Marshall made it clear that he had faith in the "good pious man" employed as his interpreter. At the same time, Kikito and other Potawatomi leaders knew how valuable a reliable go-between could be in negotiations with American officials. Standing above it all, Rice knew his talents were in demand, and in the spring of 1833 a bidding war began for his services.[21]

---

[19] William Marshall to G. B. Gordon, February 25, 1833, OIA-LR, roll 354; R. David Edmunds, "The Prairie Potawatomi Removal of 1833," *The Indiana Magazine of History*, 68(September 1972): 240–253. Edmunds uses the spelling of Quiquito, Clifton uses Kikito, and Indian agent letters often spell the headman's name Quaquatah. Because present-day writings in Potawatomi do not use "q," I use Kikito. For information on the Potawatomi language, see the Online Dictionary at http://www.kansasheritage.org/PBP/books/dicto/d_frame.html (Accessed May 26, 2006).

[20] William Marshall to G. B. Gordon, February 25, 1833, OIA-LR, roll 354; William Marshall to Elbert Herring, March 11, 1833, OIA-LR, roll 361.

[21] *Indian Affairs*, II, 277, 369, 404, 411; William Marshall to G. B. Gordon, February 25, 1833, OIA-LR, roll 354.

FIGURE 1. Noah-quet. Known as Rice the Interpreter. A Half Breed Indian Sketched – 1837 by George Winter. (Courtesy of Tippecanoe County Historical Association, Lafayette, IN.)

Kikito's efforts to enlist Rice on behalf of his band were matched by those of a Potawatomi band from the Wabash River. Kikito approached the young interpreter first, extending a generous offer shortly after arriving in Indiana in December 1832. Taking into consideration the money that would soon be available from a treaty, the Potawatomi headman proposed a salary of $1,000 per year if Rice journeyed west with and conducted business for Kikito's band. Kikito knew that Rice's skills would prove invaluable during the course of the emigration, to say nothing of the assistance he could provide as the Potawatomis settled in the West. Although the money was tempting, Rice would not accept this proposal until he knew if the Potawatomis on the Wabash could match the offer. The multiple requests for his services had strengthened his bargaining position. "I do not think these Indians [the Wabash Potawatomis] will let me go though I have not seen the principal chiefs," the young man asserted, "but them that I have seen declared that they would do as much as other Indians will before they would let me leave them." Rice said little about the bidding war in the months that followed. As of March 1833, however, he continued to discuss the possibility that he might venture west with Kikito's band.[22]

While Rice pondered his offer, Kikito continued to talk to U.S. officials at Logansport. Along with Marshall, the Potawatomi headman spoke to Colonel Abel C. Pepper, whom Secretary of War Lewis Cass had appointed as the superintendent for any emigrations that resulted from treaties signed in the early 1830s. Pepper earned $2,000 annually to soothe Indian concerns and arrange all the details necessary for a smooth journey west. Kikito first met Pepper in late March when the agent arrived at Logansport. By this time, the Potawatomi band numbered thirty-five families embracing more than two hundred and fifty individuals. Kikito informed Pepper that he and his people wanted to relocate and expected government assistance under the auspices of the fifth article of the treaty they had signed the previous fall. It was an interesting request, particularly because the referenced treaty did not have a fifth article. Not one to be daunted by such technicalities, especially when confronted by a cooperative removal, Pepper proceeded with his preparations. He worried that Kikito's band "will attempt to go to the country west of the Mississippi without the aid of Government" if federal agents did not move quickly. This would result in great suffering, "if they do not entirely fail to accomplish the journey." However, Pepper's comments reflected more than anxiety over the Potawatomis' future by expressing his concern that such suffering might make other Indian bands resistant to the idea of removal. Pepper

[22] Luther Rice to Robert Simerwell, August 9, 1832, roll 1125, RSP; Luther Rice to Robert Simerwell, December 3, 1832, roll 1125, RSP; Luther Rice to Mrs. F. G. Simerwell, March 7, 1833, roll 1125, RSP.

successfully recruited Luther Rice as interpreter, a somewhat surprising turn of events based on the young man's earlier negotiations. Rice never explained why he accepted employment with Pepper instead of Kikito, and as one of his first tasks, he organized a Potawatomi delegation to inspect the lands selected for their relocation.[23]

As word spread of a western emigration supported and supplied by government provisions, small parties of Kickapoos, Weas, and some Potawatomis from the Wabash River joined Kikito's band. By May, approximately four hundred Indians were encamped near Logansport. The Kickapoos mingled easily with Kikito's people, and their presence revealed an explanation for the Potawatomi leader's desire to move west that he had not shared with Marshall or Pepper. Many of the Kickapoos belonged to a band led by the brother of Kenekuk, the Kickapoo Prophet. Once a castout due to a murder committed while he was drunk, Kenekuk had become an influential leader among his people in the 1820s based primarily on teachings that incorporated elements of both Christianity and native practices. This syncretic faith, developed after a dramatic conversion experience, used prayer sticks and Christian devotions. But Kenekuk's doctrine also stressed temperance and land retention. His teachings simultaneously alienated members of his own tribe, including most of the Prairie band of Kickapoos, and attracted non-Kickapoos like Kikito. Kenekuk and his people had already settled in eastern Kansas following the 1832 treaty of Castor Hill. The Prophet's presence in the West now served as a beacon to both his brother's band of Kickapoos and Kikito's band of Potawatomis.[24]

As spring turned to summer, however, a series of problems tested the Indians' desire and willingness to cooperate with Pepper. The influx of nearly two hundred additional Indians caught the government employees unprepared, and they worried that the provisions would soon run

---

[23] Lewis Cass to Colonel Abel C. Pepper, March 6, 1833, in Senate Document No. 512, 23rd Congress, 1st Session, Serial No. 245, 341–342; A. C. Pepper to General George Gibson, April 11, 1833, ibid., 796–797; A. C. Pepper to Gen. George Gibson, May 7, 1833, ibid., 798; J. H. Hook to Col. A. C. Pepper, May 16, 1833, ibid., 256–257; A. C. Pepper to A. C. Pepper to Robert Simerwell, April 11, 1833, roll 1125, RSP; *Indian Affairs, II*, 353–355, 367–370. The treaty that did contain a fifth article and a reference to government assistance for removal was signed only six days after the one that included Kikito and was signed by Potawatomis of the Wabash villages.

[24] A. C. Pepper to Robert Simerwell, April 11, 1833, roll 1125, RSP; Robert Simerwell to Lucius Bolles, June 28 1833, roll 1125, RSP; Cummins to Henry Harvey, SIA, March 25, 1844, OIA-LR, roll 302; Joseph B. Herring, *Kenekuk, The Kickapoo Prophet* (Lawrence, KS, 1988).

out. At Pepper's suggestion, Kikito and his people left their encampments by Logansport and dispersed throughout the region. They were now responsible for their own subsistence. As Potawatomi men and women roamed through central Indiana in search of food, Pepper, Rice, and four Potawatomis left the state to scout potential locations in the western territories. They did not depart until late June, and when they learned of a cholera outbreak in St. Louis, quickly turned back without seeing a blade of grass west of the Mississippi. By early July the Indians who had once gathered at Logansport saw little reason to reconvene at their old camps. The news of disease in St. Louis did not help the cause, but the overall delays had the most serious effect. If the Indians had left in March, they would have completed their journey in time to plant at least some corn before summer began. By leaving in late July they would miss the growing season and face a long winter of dependence on government supplies. Pepper, bedridden from a fever, could not convince the Indians that removal remained in their best interests. Only one hundred and forty-five Indians, mostly Potawatomis of Kikito's band, remained near the agency at the end of July. Traveling by steamboat from Alton, Illinois, to Fort Leavenworth, this diminished party completed the journey before the end of August. Out of the more than four hundred Indians who had gathered in Logansport in the spring, fewer than seventy stepped off the boat at its final destination in the West.[25]

Their arrival showcased the same problems – expansion and inefficiency – that had respectively encouraged and hampered the removal process. The land hunger of American settlers did not disappear on the other side of the Mississippi, and Kikito quickly discovered that Missouri citizens had their eyes on territory once designated for the Potawatomis. "We have been told that the white people want the land on the Platte [River]," Kikito informed President Jackson in 1835. "If we were to settle on Missouri [River] above them perhaps they would wish to extend their settlements there also." Over two years had passed since the Potawatomi headman and his people had made their way to eastern Kansas. In the interim, their population had swelled because of those who relocated separately, and Kikito's band now numbered four hundred and forty-four individuals. But continued government indecision had kept them

[25] A. C. Pepper to Robert Simerwell, April 11, 1833, roll 1125, RSP; Robert Simerwell to Rev. Lucius Bolles, April 11, 1833, roll 1125, RSP; Robert Simerwell to Rev. Lucius Bolles, June 28, 1833, roll 1125, RSP; Diary entry of Robert Simerwell, June 14, 1833, roll 1126.1, RSP; Muster Roll of a Company of Pottawatomie Indians, undated, OIA-LR, roll 300; Edmunds, "The Prairie Potawatomi Removal of 1833," 246–252.

homeless. "If you will allow us to settle on the Osage river instead of the land high up the Missouri, we should be glad to hear you say so soon," Kikito chided, "for we are very anxious to get on to our own lands." Since the winter of 1832, the Potawatomi headman had a clear understanding of what he and his people needed. When he turned to the U.S. government for assistance, he found few men willing or able to facilitate those plans.[26]

Kikito's relocation reflected the push of American expansion, the pull of the Kickapoo Prophet, and the incompetence of the federal government. Menominee's removal, on the other hand, showcased the Indiana state government's ability and desire to use force in the absence of federal authority and action. The treaties and removals of the early and mid-1830s gradually emptied the northern regions of the state of its Potawatomi population. Yet, several communities resisted any talk of relocation. Menominee's band on the Yellow River remained adamant and American officials appeared somewhat reluctant to contest the Indians' position. Although the U.S. Senate did not hesitate to ratify the fraudulent treaty that sparked this removal, federal involvement in the process did not extend beyond the independent actions of Abel C. Pepper, who retained his post as the supervisor of emigrations in Indiana. Instead, the enforcement of the 1836 agreement's removal provisions became the passion of state officials. When tensions over land claims and possession flared between Menominee's people and local settlers, the Indiana government took direct action. Rather than federal conductors and U.S. soldiers, it was Senator John Tipton and one hundred armed Indiana citizens who forced the Potawatomis to march along the Trail of Death in the fall of 1838.

The U.S. government's handling of Billy Caldwell illustrated the usefulness of negotiating treaties through pliant and influential individuals connected with the participating tribe. For the Yellow River Potawatomis, the treaty that extinguished their land claims came about through a less subtle but no less effective approach. In Menominee, government agents faced a determined Indian headman who relied on both federal assurances and missionary support to hold onto a relatively small portion of land near Twin Lakes, southwest of present-day South Bend. Treaty commissioner Pepper therefore chose to negotiate only with those Indians willing to

---

[26] Quihquehtah to the President of the United States, November 20, 1835, OIA-LR, roll 355. Troubles regarding the Platte River region, the Potawatomis, and the state of Missouri continued into the late 1830s. For an analysis of these events, see R. David Edmunds, "Potawatomis in the Platte Country: An Indian Removal Incomplete," *Missouri Historical Review,* 68(July 1974), 375–392.

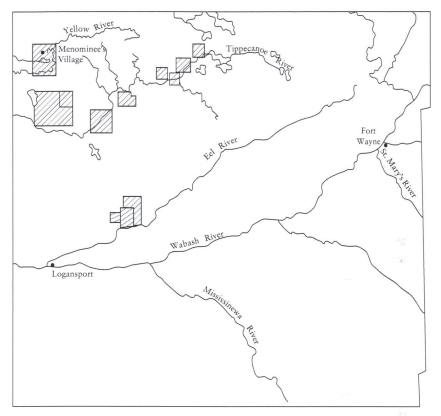

MAP 3. Potawatomi Land Cessions in Indiana, 1832–1836. Based on Map 20 in Charles C. Royce (Comp.), *Indian Land Cessions in the United States.*

sign away their lands. Through an ample use of alcohol and a variety of bribes, Pepper obtained signatures that gave away land grants established by prior treaties and agreed to removal within two years.[27]

Menominee did not think that he needed to worry about losing his reserve in Indiana and therefore paid little attention to Pepper's machinations. A 1832 treaty had set aside a reservation of twenty-two sections for the bands of Menominee, Notawkah, Muckkahtahmoway, and Peepinohwaw. And even after Pepper had negotiated five different treaties with the Potawatomi bands along the Turkey Creek Prairie and Tippecanoe River, the Yellow River Potawatomi headmen remained confident in the position laid out in a letter written by Secretary of War Lewis Cass on

[27] *Indian Affairs*, II, 462–463.

January 9, 1836. The letter stated, "We [the Potawatomis] have obtained from our Great Father the President of the U.S. the special favor of remaining undisturbed upon our reserve as long as we shall wish to remain there." Because the Potawatomis, "most sincere desire is to remain there forever," Menominee and Muckaktahmoway requested that Commissioner of Indian Affairs Elbert Herring authorize the Jesuit priest Louis Deseille to establish a school on the reserve. Deseille, although he was not convinced that the Potawatomis would be able to remain in Indiana, had also received assurances from Commissary General George Gibson that Menominee's band would not be forced from their lands by the federal government. As of April 14, therefore, Menominee and the Yellow River Potawatomis remained confident in the fact that they would not have to cede their lands.[28]

Menominee's confidence also grew from an established stance that he and his followers held on white settlement and Indian removal. His statement to Secretary of War Lewis Cass in 1837 that the Yellow River Potawatomis wanted "to become subjects of the laws of the State," did not reflect a last-minute change of heart or an act of desperation. Years earlier Menominee had made clear his intentions to adapt to American expansion peacefully by accepting and promoting Christianity and western-style farming. From his perspective, these changes would allow the Potawatomis to weather the calls for removal. In 1821, while he was in his early thirties, the Potawatomi leader had visited Reverend Isaac McCoy at the latter's mission at Fort Wayne. The Baptist missionary gladly assisted Menominee's efforts to become a preacher, especially because the young Indian stated that the Great Spirit had called him to give up the same practices McCoy decried. Over the next two decades the Potawatomi preacher spoke out against alcohol, theft, and murder and encouraged conversion to Christianity and dependence on agriculture. When McCoy became an outspoken advocate of removal in the late 1820s, Menominee distanced himself from the Baptists and turned to Catholicism and Deseille. The Jesuit established a mission at Twin Lakes in 1834 at the Potawatomi's request and in August of that year he baptized the Indian headman. Menominee and his teachings gradually attracted a following on the Yellow River and in 1838 his village encompassed approximately one hundred households. Men, women, and children worked together in the fields as the community followed the goals laid out by their leader.

---

[28] *Indian Affairs, II*, 367–369, 450, 457–459; Menominee and Muckkaktahmoway to Mr. Elbert Herring, April 14, 1836, OIA-LR, roll 355; Irving McKee, *The Trail of Death: Letters of Benjamin Marie Petit* (Indianapolis, 1941), 21–22.

By the fall of 1838 the village had nearly one hundred and sixty acres under cultivation in individual and communal plots. "We have worked very hard on the said land," Menominee explained in a letter to President Martin Van Buren, "and were resolved to have it divided amongst us and live as white people."[29]

Yet, on August 5, 1836, Pepper concluded a treaty that ceded all twenty-two sections of land granted the Potawatomis in 1832. Long troubled by the fact that the missionaries supported the Indians' interest in staying in Indiana, Pepper found himself stymied by the unexpected assurances granted by Lewis Cass and George Gibson. The treaty commissioner visited the Yellow River settlement in the early spring to talk to the Potawatomis about land cessions and removal. In response, Menominee sent a few men to inform Pepper of the government's position as stated in Cass's letter. This message did not sit well with the government agent. According to the Potawatomis Pepper angrily, and rather arrogantly, declared that "this was all good for nothing that he Col Pepper was the President of all the Indians that if we would not give up our Lands he would call 2,000 soldiers from Detroit, drive us off, etc." Pepper, unprepared and somewhat unglued, departed in frustration. He returned in early August, however, and called for another council, naming a meeting place nearly twenty miles away from the Yellow River settlements. Menominee did not respond to the summons and, as the council commenced, he and his kinsmen worked in their fields. It took them by surprise when settlers invaded their lands only days later. "The white people was running through our reservation," the stunned Potawatomis complained, "putting preemption claims and told us that they were informed by Col. Pepper that our reserve was sold." The treaty commissioner had found a way to deal with the resistance. The marks of Peepinohwaw, Notawkah, and Muckahtahmoway appeared on the treaty. Menominee's name was glaring in its absence.[30]

---

[29] Menominee and others to Lewis Cass, November 15, 1836, OIA-LR, roll 355; Shirley Willard, "Chief Menominee," in Shirley Willard and Susan Campbell, writers and eds., *Potawatomi Trail of Death: 1838 Removal from Indiana to Kansas* (Rochester, IN, 2003), 320–331; Menominee and Muckahtahmoway to Mr. Elbert Herring, April 14, 1836, OIA-LR, roll 355; Appraisement of Corn in Indian Fields, September 1, 1838, *JTP, III,* 683–684; Menominee, Muckahtahmoway, Peepinowah, Wihgama, to Great Father, April 6, 1837, OIA-LR, roll 355.

[30] *Indian Affairs, II,* 367–369, 462–463; Louis Deseille to Abel C. Pepper, March 21, 1836, *JTP, III,* 246–247; Abel C. Pepper to John Tipton, April 16, 1836, ibid., 259–260; Menominee and others to Lewis Cass, November 15, 1836, OIA-LR, roll 355; Abel C. Pepper to John Tipton, August 8, 1836, *JTP, III,* 301–302; George W. Ewing and Cyrus Taber to John Tipton, August 21, 1836, ibid., 304–305.

Menominee and his band refused to recognize the land cessions and accused Pepper of fraud. The marks of Notawkah, Muckahtahmoway, and Peepinohwaw may have appeared on the treaty, but the three men stated they had "never signed any paper whatever during the whole year." Alert to the tricks used by those interested in gaining land cessions, they had not even put their marks on paper to receive annuities in previous months. "We have preferred to abandon our small part of Ten Dollars then to expose ourselves of being cheated out of our rights," they explained, "consequently if our names are seen in any paper they are false signers." Menominee disputed the treaty regardless of the signatures. In his opinion the negotiations in August 1836 had not included the proper headmen of the Yellow River community. Menominee trusted that "they [the Great Father and the Government] will never Sanction Such unjust and Shameful deed." Similar accusations from Father Deseille raised the specter of Pepper's use of alcohol to obtain the necessary signatures.[31]

Letters supporting the treaty commissioner dismissed allegations of fraud, but these letters came from local traders like George and William Ewing who had a vested interest both in treaty annuities and land speculation in the region. Six years earlier William had argued against removal, admitting that he viewed it as "impracticable," and suggested that they be allowed to remain, "as their increased annuity will be of material benefit in the first settleing [sic] of our country and there is yet room for all." His brother had been less diplomatic. "It is madness," George declared, "to suppose that we can make money in the daily transactions of business with the whites here." Now the Ewings championed the decision to remove the Potawatomis. Their change of heart coincided with the sizeable debts accrued by local Indians in the first half of the decade. As the non-Indian settlements grew in northern Indiana and undermined native subsistence patterns, the Indians bought more and more goods on credit. Traders like the Ewings who once resisted the idea of removal now encouraged the push for treaties with the knowledge that such agreements offered the best opportunities to receive payments for their ballooning claims.[32]

Menominee's band fought relocation for two years while Pepper and Indiana officials increased the pressure. The Potawatomis continued to

---

[31] Menominee et al. to John Tipton, *JTP, III*, 312–313; Menominee and others to Lewis Cass, November 15, 1836, OIA-LR, roll 355; Menominee, Markahtahmowah, Pepenowah, and Wikgoma to Lewis Cass, undated, OIA-LR, roll 355; Pepinawaw, Markaktahmah, and Wikkoma to the President of the United States, May 15, 1837, OIA-LR, roll 355.

[32] William G. Ewing to John Tipton, February 3, 1830, in *JTP, II*, 244–246; George W. Ewing to John Tipton, June 5, 1830, ibid., 284–286; George W. Ewing and Cyrus Taber to John Tipton, *JTP, III*, 304–305; Trennert, *Indian Traders*, 53–54.

find support from their Catholic missionaries, although Pepper worked diligently to counteract the efforts made by the Jesuits on the Indians' behalf. In a pointed letter addressed to Father Deseille, the removal superintendent harped on the missionary's conduct. Having ascertained that Deseille had advised Menominee to resist the government's wishes, it became Pepper's "unpleasant public duty to request you [Deseille] to exhibit...any evidence in your possession of your citizenship of the United States." Whether a citizen or not, Deseille would be prosecuted under the applicable sections of the 1834 Trade and Intercourse Act. The Jesuit submitted to Pepper's authority, left the reserve, and died shortly thereafter in September 1837. His replacement, a young French priest by the name of Benjamin Marie Petit, arrived in October. Petit had legal training to supplement his theological studies and he attacked the 1836 treaty as "a thing as illegal as possible." To aid the cause, Petit wrote a memorial for Menominee to deliver to the President arguing the Indians' case against removal. But the Potawatomis' trip to Washington only brought further frustration. President Van Buren refused to hear their protests and the federal government did not take any action. Back in Indiana, local officials did not relent and the Potawatomis' dissatisfaction grew. At a council near Logansport, an Indian, most likely Menominee, interrupted the interpreter, grabbed Pepper's hand, and declared, "Look here, Father; our lands belong to us. We shall keep them; we do not wish to talk to you any more." Although he later apologized for the outburst, he did not alter his stance on the treaty or removal. Even when Senator John Tipton made a special visit to encourage the Potawatomis' compliance and to threaten them with force, the Indians refused to concede. As these councils continued to fail, Pepper expressed his hopes to deceive the Potawatomis further by concealing the government's willingness to pay their annuities in Indiana. "If they shall be told that their annuity is now ready for them and will be paid here," he reasoned, "I feel quite confident they will not remove this year." Pepper read the situation well, for Menominee resisted well into 1838.[33]

This unwillingness to concede victory to Pepper's machinations and to submit to government threats led to conflict; and violence provided the perfect rationale for Indiana's elected leaders who wanted the Potawatomis off state lands. Because of the terms of the treaty, local citizens continued to assert preemption claims along the Yellow River. Over

[33] A. C. Pepper to Rev. J. Deseille, May 16, 1837, OIA-LR, roll 361; Petit to Bishop Brute, November 27, 1837, in McKee, "The Trail of Death," 35–39; Petit to Bishop Brute, December 9, 1837, ibid., 40–47; Benjamin Marie Petit to Bishop Brute, July 26, 1838, ibid., 81–87; Petit to Abel C. Pepper, July 31, 1838, ibid., 87n; A. C. Pepper to C. A. Harris, August 4, 1837, OIA-LR, roll 361.

the course of one week in the middle of August 1838, tensions flared in a fiery display of hostility. In response to an Indian attack on one settler's cabin, arsonists torched at least ten Indian homes. When the situation threatened to deteriorate further, Indiana citizens found relief in the form of military intervention. Events unfolded quickly in the weeks following the fiery outbreak. In late August, Governor David Wallace authorized Senator Tipton to enroll one hundred men in a voluntary militia. Tipton then used the element of surprise to capture a large number of the Potawatomis who had reported to the Catholic chapel on the reserve at the apparent request of the priest. Before the Indians became aware of the soldiers' presence, the armed force surrounded the building. The armed men did not allow the Potawatomis to leave the area and placed their leaders, Menominee, Black Wolf, Peepinohwaw, and Notawkah, under even closer restrictions. Militiamen spread throughout the reserve to bring to the chapel as many of the Potawatomis as they could find. "In vain," one native woman later told her grandson, "the Indians prayed to be let to return to their homes. Instead of being given their liberty, some several hundred horses and ponies were captured, to be used in transporting the Indians away from the valley." As of September 4, Tipton had forcibly enrolled approximately eight hundred men, women, and children. Over the next two months the Indiana militia marched the Indians to their new lands along the Osage River just west of Missouri. Unseasonably oppressive heat and scarcity of water plagued the emigrants, but disease did the most damage. Early on in the journey, a reported three hundred Indians suffered from illness, and by the end approximately forty-three Potawatomis had died. Fewer than seven hundred Indians reached the Osage River, with those unaccounted for most likely having escaped from their military escorts to find refuge in Michigan or in the Wisconsin Territory.[34]

---

[34] Letters covering the events leading up to and including the removal found in *JTP, III*, 679–758; "Journal of an Emigrating Party of Pottawattomie Indians, 1838," *Indiana Magazine of History*, 21 (December 1925): 315–336. The grandmother's story is presented in Patrick Minges (Ed.), *Black Indian Slave Narratives* (Winston-Salem, NC, 2004), 3–5. Additional accounts of the forced removal in Clifton, *The Prairie People*, 296–300; Louise Barry, *The Beginning of the West: Annals of the Kansas Gateway to the American West, 1540–1854* (Topeka, 1972), 358–359; *Grandfather, Tell Me a Story: An Oral History Project Conducted by the Citizen Band Potawatomi Tribe of Oklahoma and Funded by the National Endowment for the Humanities* (Privately Published, 1984), ix; Rev. Joseph Murphy, O. S. B., *Potawatomi of the West: Origins of the Citizen Band*, edited by Patricia Sulcer Barrett (Shawnee, OK, 1988), 64–65; Sarah E. Cooke and Rachel B. Ramadhyani, comps., *Indians and a Changing Frontier: The Art of George Winter* (Indianapolis, 1993), 99–107.

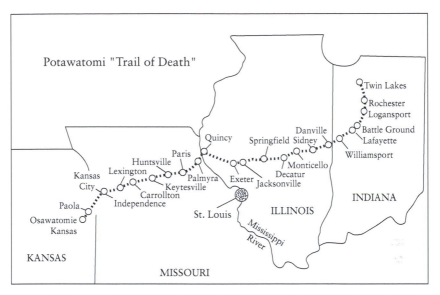

MAP 4. Potawatomi Trail of Death. Based on a map by Tom Hamilton, Fulton County Historical Society, Rochester, Indiana.

The Trail of Death left both devastation and separation in its wake. Among the dead from the journey were at least twenty-eight children, a tremendous loss for such a small community. Death did not claim only the lives of those in the larger detachment. Smaller parties of the sick who had been left behind stretched out behind the main emigrant train, and although some of them caught up to the removal party, others never recovered and were buried along the road. And as this forced removal separated the Potawatomis from their homes in Indiana, its suddenness also broke up families. Tipton's militia did not capture all of the Potawatomis on the Yellow River because some individuals managed to hide from and escape their pursuers. Although it was presented in the romanticized autobiography of Simon Pokagon, the story of the Potawatomi woman Kobunda mirrored the experience of families divided in the aftermath of the militia's surprise attack. Hearing that white men dressed in blue had surrounded her husband and other Potawatomis, "tied [them] together with big strings like ponies" and planned on capturing the rest, Kobunda quickly left her home and headed north to live among the Ottawas in Michigan. Not all family separations occurred so abruptly. Prior treaties with the Potawatomis had established education funds that primarily supported the studies of their youth at boarding schools. Months after Tipton

FIGURE 2. [*Emigration Scene*] *Observed 1838* by George Winter. A note on the sketch states, "Sept The Emigration 1838 It was in October 1838 on Sunday that the Emigration rested in a grove near a clear stream of water named Eel River after the 2d days march Here Bishop Brute preached to the converted Pottawattamies." (Courtesy of Tippecanoe County Historical Association, Lafayette, IN.)

conducted Menominee's band away from the Yellow River villages, several young Potawatomi men returned to northern Indiana. Because of their attendance at the Choctaw Academy in Kentucky, they were unaware of the removal, and instead of finding their homes they found only white settlers. They turned to the government agent at Logansport and requested that the government help them reunite with their families.[35]

Although they never criticized the outcome, senior administrators of Indian affairs in the nation's capital had trouble understanding the sequence of events that led to this particular removal. Specifically, federal officials revealed their ignorance of local circumstances when they

[35] "Journal of an Emigrating Party of Pottawattomie Indians, 1838," 315–336; Dwight L. Smith (Ed.), "Jacob Hull's Detachment of the Potawatomi Emigration of 1838," *Indiana Magazine of History,* 45 (Sept. 1949), 285–288. Kobunda's story is from Simon Pokagon, *O-Gi-Maw-Kwe Mit-I-Gwa-Ki (Queen of the Woods)* (Barrien Springs, MI, 1972), 79–83; Grant Foreman, *Last Trek of the Indians* (Chicago, 1946), 110–111; *Indian Affairs, II,* 294–297; Samuel Milroy to T. Hartley Crawford, October 23, 1839, OIA-LR, roll 361.

tried to uncover the truth about the proceedings of August and September 1838 in Tipton's records. In his reports to the Secretary of War, Tipton downplayed any military aspects of the emigration. Although Governor Wallace had authorized the enlistment of a militia to prevent any possible problems, the Senator never used these volunteers as initially intended. "I found I could collect & remove the Indians without the aid of a military force, in any way," Tipton was pleased to report. Pepper shared in this deception and endorsed records that listed the one hundred and seventy-six paid armed volunteers as collecting agents, conductors, and assistant conductors. The most revealing job description, shared by the majority of the volunteers, read simply "Collecting Indians." Although Commissioner of Indian Affairs T. Hartley Crawford seemingly saw through this charade, his statements were revealing. Summarizing one of Tipton's reports, Crawford stated that the Senator had raised a volunteer military force and removed the Potawatomis "without any previous knowledge or concurrence of the [War] Department." Yet the Commissioner sought the truth to resolve issues of payment, not to prescribe terms of punishment. He had no intention of disciplining Tipton for using force in effecting the Potawatomi removal.[36]

The misery of the Yellow River Band of Potawatomis on the Trail of Death took place at the same time that thousands of Cherokees left their homelands in Georgia and marched west along the Trail of Tears. Although these parallel forced removals appeared to mark the culmination of federal policy, indications remained that not all movements occurred by the decree of state or federal officials. In the days after the main body of Potawatomis arrived at their final destination on the Osage River, stragglers trickled into the encampment. In one instance, a wagon containing six Potawatomis arrived in the evening of November 5. Andrew Fuller and his family of five pulled into the Potawatomi camp shortly after government agents had distributed beef and corn to the weary survivors. The Fullers had left their homes in southern Michigan weeks earlier and had made the western journey without government supervision or supplies. Instead, they had decided to move west to live among the other Potawatomis and paid for the expedition themselves. The images of this independent migration and the coerced removal could not be much different. Indeed, the very contrast emphasizes the fact that removal and

---

[36] Tipton to Joel R. Poinsett, January 28, 1839, *JTP, III*, 805–806; Statement of Agents and others, employed, January 20, 1839, OIA-LR, roll 361; T. Hartley Crawford to Hon. J. R. Poinsett, May 13, 1839, OIA-LR, 361.

relocation continued to mean different things for the Indian residents of the southern Great Lakes region.[37]

In the context of the forced removal of Menomiee's band, the emigration of Andrew Fuller and his family might appear to be no more than an abnormality. However, the river journey of Levi Konkapot and the Stockbridges, Munsees, and Delawares took place in the fall of 1839, a year after the Potawatomis and Cherokees marched west. Their journey illustrated that Fuller's migration was not an aberration. More important, the complex story behind this voyage from Wisconsin Territory to eastern Kansas demonstrated that customary native frameworks of kinship still supported the westward movements of Indian peoples years after the passage of removal legislation.

The boatloads of Indians that reached St. Louis in November 1839 surprised federal officials in St. Louis. Superintendent of Indian Affairs Joshua Pilcher knew that U.S. Treaty Commissioner Albert Gallup had concluded a treaty on September 3 with the Stockbridges and Munsees in Wisconsin Territory. Pilcher was also aware that the accord provided for the relocation of eighty out of the three hundred and forty-two members of that northern community. The treaty even listed the twenty-six families who consented to the land cession and relocation. Consequently, Pilcher did not understand why the Indians disembarked in St. Louis in far greater numbers than anticipated. Instead of eighty, Pilcher and his clerks counted one hundred and sixty-nine men, women, and children who had journeyed by boat down the Mississippi. Perhaps because of their surprise the officials in St. Louis initially miscounted, and a muster roll sent to the Indian Department months later had a corrected tally of one hundred and eighty. Of that number, only sixty-nine names matched those listed in the treaty negotiated by Gallup.[38]

The confusion shared by Pilcher and his colleagues in the Indian Department revealed their ignorance of the ties connecting the Stockbridges, Munsees, and Delawares. In particular, federal officials had not realized that the Indians were responding to an invitation from the Delaware headmen on the Kansas reserve. "We were in a friendly and kind manner invited here," Gideon Williams, a Munsee headman, explained years later. "They [the Delawares in Kansas] told us that we would again be welcome to all their privileges agreeable to our ancient relationship

---

[37] *Journal of an Emigrating Party of Pottawattomie Indians, 1838*, 335.

[38] *Indian Affairs, II*, 529–531; T. Hartley Crawford, CIA to Poinsett, Secretary of War, July 1, 1840, vol. 1, *RCA*; Joshua Pilcher to T. Hartley Crawford, February 27, 1840, OIA-LR, roll 301.

and confederacy." According to Williams, the ancient confederation mentioned by the Delawares included seven tribes, namely the Munsees, Delawares, Mohicans, Nanticokes, and three others. Over time, the colonization of the British and the expansion of the United States had created a geographic separation among most members of that confederation. But, "repeated efforts have been made by the head men of this people now bearing the name Delaware tribe to invite the scattered remnants of our said confederated tribes, in order that they might be united again as a nation and be settled together in one place or Country." That effort by the western Delawares served as the impetus for the journey from Wisconsin Territory.[39]

But Williams's comments only scratched the surface of the history behind the 1839 relocation, and a much more complicated narrative lies below. That narrative begins in New England. The Stockbridges were Mahican, Wappinger, and Housatonic Indians who had taken on the name of the village they inhabited in the Housatonic Valley in Massachusetts for the better part of the eighteenth century. Encroachments on their land during the American Revolution drove them out of Massachusetts, and the Stockbridges found refuge in New York among the Oneidas in the mid-1780s. Over the next three decades and more the Stockbridges lived in New York and intermarried with another displaced community, the Brothertons. The Brothertons were a small population of Delawares who had remained on a reserve in New Jersey when most of the Delawares had relocated to Pennsylvania. This ethnically diverse community of Stockbridges and Brothertons subsequently left New York for Wisconsin Territory in 1822 to escape the settler invasion of Oneida County.[40]

The Munsee designation did not appear in historical records until 1727, at which time it was used to describe the Indian bands living in northern New Jersey and northeastern Pennsylvania. Although the name Munsee once had distinguished either the dialect they spoke or the lands they called home, over the course of the eighteenth century the Munsees had become a separate political entity as well. The Munsee-Delawares of the early 1700s gradually transitioned into the Munsee Indians before the American

---

[39] Gideon Williams et al. to Millard Fillmore, January 15, 1851, OIA-LR, roll 303.

[40] Austin E. Quinney to Governor Dodge, March 20, 1838, in *TP, XXVII*, 969–970; Oberly, *A Nation of Statesmen*, 3–9; Patrick Frazier, *The Mohicans of Stockbridge* (Lincoln, 1992); Colin G. Calloway, *The American Revolution in Indian Country: Crisis and Diversity in Native American Communities* (New York, 1995), 85–107; Herbert Kraft, *The Lenape: Archaeology, History, and Ethnography* (Newark, 1986), 229–232; C. A. Weslager, *The Delaware Indians: A History* (New Brunswick, NJ, 1972), 44–45, 273–275.

Revolution. By the mid-1700s most Delawares and Munsees resided in the Ohio Valley, and many within this community had developed close relationships with the Moravians, living as converts in settlements separate from the Indian villages. But these peaceful settlements were not protected from the backcountry violence of the American Revolution. In 1782, the Moravian settlement at Gnaddenhutten on the Tuscarawas River suffered a devastating attack at the hands of American militia under the leadership of Lieutenant-Colonel David Williamson. Williamson and his men systematically killed ninety men, women, and children.[41]

In the massacre's aftermath, the remaining Moravian Indians left the Ohio Valley and established a new home on the Thames River in Canada at a settlement named Fairfield. Although many of the Indians were content to remain in Canada, the missionary David Zeisberger led a group back to Ohio where he and the other Moravians founded a new mission at Goshen. But American settlements in the region grew exponentially after the War of 1812, and the Ohio Delawares signed a treaty in 1818 that set the stage for their removal west. The greater part of the Munsee population did not want to remove. They stayed in Ohio and, in 1823, signed an agreement with Lewis Cass by which they returned to Canada and the rebuilt settlement of New Fairfield. Under this accord the United States agreed to pay these Indians an annuity or, if they so desired, to give them a land grant of twenty-four thousand acres in the western territories. It was while they were living in New Fairfield that the Canadian Delawares and Munsees received the invitation from the Delaware headmen in the West. "Many of us were living and enjoying ourselves happy on our own land in the said Upper Canada," the Munsees explained. "They [the Kansas Delawares] told us that we would be welcome to all their privileges if we would only come and join them in their country." In all, approximately seventy-five Indians left Canada and traveled directly to the western territories, but more than one hundred stopped among the Stockbridges because they lacked the means to continue the journey.[42]

[41] Weslager, *The Delaware Indians*, 44–45, 273–275; Kraft, *The Lenape*, xvii, 232–239; Linda Sabathy-Judd (Ed. and Transl.), *Moravians in Upper Canada: The Diary of the Indian Mission of Fairfield on the Thames, 1792–1813* (Toronto, 1999), xx, xxv, 229, 276.

[42] T. Hartley Crawford to Poinsett, SOW, July 1, 1840, vol. 1, RCA; David Zeisberger Smith to Luke Lea, CIA, August 11, 1851, OIA-LR, roll 364; John Jacobsen to Alexander H. H. Stuart, May 24, 1852, OIA-LR, roll 364; Joseph Romig to George Martin, Secretary of the Kansas State Historical Society, May 27, 1910, Indian Files – Chippewa and Munsee, Box 6, KSHS; Morse, *A Report to the Secretary of War*, appendix 109–118; Weslager, *The Delaware Indians*, 273–275, 315–317; Articles of Agreement, November 8,

The final move of these Canadian Delawares and Munsees from Green Bay to Kansas in the fall of 1839 attested to more than just this complex kinship network that connected disparate communities across hundreds of miles. It also illustrated how eastern Indians supplemented those relationships with the system developed by federal treaties and policies. The Delawares and Munsees who had temporarily halted their journey on the shores of Lake Winnebago were aware of government treaty provisions that paid the expenses of similar removals and sought to benefit from these precedents and the resolutions of their 1823 agreement. From 1837 until the fall of 1839, the Canadian Indians waited for the government to provide the necessities for the final step of their journey to Fort Leavenworth. In the end, they refused to wait any longer.[43]

Unfortunately, the reunion of these communities on the Delaware lands north of the Kansas River turned out to be more problematic than productive. But the conflicts reflected the problems caused in part by the geographic strain of removal and did not invalidate the networks that had brought the Indians west. When the Stockbridges and Munsees met the Delawares in council shortly after their journey, all seemed well. The groups "renewed their ancient Covenant of relationship to each other," John Newcom reported, and the Delawares then "directed our people to go and settle on their land near Fort Leavenworth." But it seemed that the Delawares rapidly grew unhappy with the presence of the Stockbridges and tensions rose between the two communities. Munsee families had a more direct problem. The Delaware Council sold the piece of land originally designated for the Canadian emigrants to the Wyandots who removed from Ohio in 1843. In the decade that followed, the Munsees struggled to find a secure home within the boundaries of the Delaware reserve.[44]

The 1830s proved to be devastating for the Indian residents of the Great Lakes region. The demographic explosion made it nearly impossible to avoid substantial land cessions and relocation. In the worst-case scenarios,

---

1823, OIA-LR, roll 601; Rich W. Cummins to T. Hartley Crawford, February 12, 1839, OIA-LR, roll 301; Gideon Williams et al. to Zachary Taylor, March 15, 1849, OIA-LR, roll 303. The settlement of New Fairfield was built on the opposite bank of the Thames from the old Fairfield village that had been destroyed during the War of 1812. See Tanner, *Atlas of Great Lakes Indian History*, 126.

[43] Commissioner Crawford to the Secretary of War, July 1, 1840, *TP, XXVIII*, 200.

[44] John Newcom et al. to Zachary Taylor, February 19, 1849, OIA-LR, roll 303. For the Munsee complaints, see Gideon Williams et al. to Zachary Taylor, March 15, 1849, OIA-LR, roll 303.

like that of the Yellow River Band of Potawatomis, the situation resulted in a forced removal during which death and disease struck without mercy. But the harsh realities of the Trail of Death, for all that it displayed the will and desire of local governments and settlers to remove the eastern Indians, did not portray the only experience.

Indian removal in the Great Lakes region highlighted the power of state and local interests over federal authority. Stories of federal ineffectiveness, state initiative, trader influence, and native kinship relations weaken the image of the Great Father sweeping the eastern lands clean of defeated Indian peoples. Pointing to this diminished federal presence does not erase the horrors created by forced removals. Whether at the hands of the state militia or the U.S. military, the Indian men, women, children who died on their western passages remained lost to their families, and the dislocation of the western journey left an eternal imprint on the lives of their communities. However, in the western territories, removed Indians shared space with those who traveled independently – families and bands who avoided a journey at gunpoint. Native networks still supported Indian movements, and the complexities of these ancient relationships were nowhere more evident than in the emigration of the Stockbridges, Delawares, and Munsees in the fall of 1839.

PART TWO

BECOMING BORDER INDIANS

T HE WESTERN BORDER OF MISSOURI PLAYS A PROMINENT ROLE IN
the history of American expansion west of the Mississippi in the
1840s. In towns such as Independence, young families, dreamy-eyed
prospectors, and countless others gathered provisions and garnered the
courage to cross the state line and head to the fertile valleys of Oregon,
the teeming gold mines of northern California, and other points west.
On the other side of that boundary rested a vast open prairie, a daunting
mountain pass, and a final destination. Most hoped that they were up to
the task, and many were perhaps a bit wary of the Cheyenne, Arapaho,
and other Plains Indians whose path they might cross.

Yet, less than a hundred miles into their journey, most wagon trains
had seen or dealt with more Indians than they would encounter during
their entire trip. Many had to pay Wyandot or Potawatomi ferrymen
for passage over the waterways that fed into the Kansas and Missouri
rivers. At times, they purchased supplies from the Shawnee and Delaware
farmers who raised surplus amounts of oats, wheat, and corn. Of course,
the passage of the wagon trains every spring also affected the Indians
living along the border. Oxen and horses trespassed onto Shawnee and
Delaware fields, and the travelers carried with them the pathogens that
led to frequent cholera and smallpox outbreaks throughout the region.

Shawnees, Delawares, Wyandots, and Potawatomis lived on the western border of Missouri from the late 1820s to the 1860s. Their experiences during that period have been pushed to the margins of history for
a much longer time. Though exiled from their former homes in the Great
Lakes, these Indian communities did not disappear when they crossed
the Mississippi. Indeed, for the Shawnees, Delawares, Potawatomis, and
Wyandots in the West, their new homes were not meant to be temporary,
and the treaties that arranged for relocation and settlement did not have

an expiration date. These Indians spent the better part of the 1830s and 1840s coming to terms with their new lives in the West. On a daily basis, native men and women worked to create a stable existence by intertwining old customs with new opportunities. They gradually adjusted to life on the border and made efforts to build better relationships with both their Indian neighbors and the Missourians who lived only miles away. And as the dawn of the 1850s carried with it the reality of renewed American expansion, the leaders of these communities tried to prepare for what that new invasion might mean for them and their people.

All three chapters in this section cover roughly the same chronological period and examine critical transitions among the eastern Indian communities on the border. They begin prior to or during the removal era and end in the early 1850s on the eve of the Kansas-Nebraska Act. Every act of persistence, as well as every adaptation, reflected the pressures of the Shawnee, Delaware, Wyandot, and Potawatomi lives prior to 1854 and laid the groundwork for their responses to the events that followed. It was a struggle, as every year increased both the security in their new lives and the presence of American settlers and travelers. Nevertheless, the actions of these four native communities over the course of three decades illustrate an important and gradual transition – Indian exiles and emigrants became border residents and integral participants in life along the western Missouri state line.

3

Borderline Subsistence and Western Adaptations

Early in the nineteenth century, testimony from western explorations fueled the initial misperception of the lands bounded by the western Missouri border, the Rocky Mountains, and the Missouri River as the "Great American Desert." Out of all of those reports, the one written by Lieutenant Zebulon Pike following his 1806–1807 expeditions best captured and illustrated this view. In his account of the "untimbered country" lying between the waters of the Missouri, Mississippi, and the Pacific Ocean, the military officer offered a less than inviting picture of the lands he had traversed. His investigations had found "a barren soil, parched and dried up for eight months of the year," and the sights convinced him that "these vast plains of the Western Hemisphere may become, in time, equally celebrated with the sandy deserts of Africa." From Pike's perspective, perhaps the only positive aspect of this country lay in the natural boundary to American settlement its desolation would provide. American citizens would halt their march at the Missouri and Mississippi rivers, he concluded, and would be content to "leave the prairies, incapable of cultivation, to the wandering and uncivilized aborigines of the country."[1]

Nearly five decades after Pike's expedition, in the summer of 1854, a New York publication, the *Genesee Farmer*, published an article titled, "The Agricultural Qualities of Nebraska." The article encompassed excerpts from a letter written by William Walker. Walker discussed a wide variety of topics, including the soil, climate, roads, and other environmental aspects of the region that includes present-day Nebraska and Kansas

---

[1] Pike's quotation from Elliott Coues (Ed.), *The Expeditions of Zebulon Montgomery Pike* (2 vols., New York, 1987), II, 525. For a summary of the persistence of the myth of the Great American Desert, see "Early Explorations and Expeditions," in William G. Cutler, *History of Kansas* (Chicago, 1883); Martyn J. Bowden, in David J. Wishart (Ed.), *Encyclopedia of the Great Plains* (Lincoln, 2004), 389.

and rested well within the boundaries of Pike's Great American Desert. "I have no hesitation in affirming that there can be no country found to surpass it in the production of corn, wheat, and oats," Walker proclaimed. "I think I never eat as luscious peaches in my life as my neighbors and I have raised." Though he could not speak in similarly "rapturous terms" of the southern portion of the territory, he still believed that "There can be no better country for raising livestock." Walker proceeded to describe the climate as "about the same as in the northern part of Ohio, except the winters are not so long, and the summers are longer and warmer." This last comparison made sense because the letter first appeared in a Cleveland newspaper. More important, however, Walker had grown up and lived part of his adult life in northern Ohio. He was a former chief of the Wyandot Indians and one of nearly seven hundred who relocated west of Missouri in 1843 following a failed effort to resist removal.[2]

Pike and Walker, only two of the multitude who tried to describe the region, presented opposite extremes of the land to which the U.S. government removed thousands of eastern Indians in the 1830s and 1840s. Their contrasting descriptions undoubtedly raise questions of credibility and each man could be criticized for shortcomings or bias in his reporting. At the very least, both appeared to err on the side of exaggeration. But in the context of Indian removal, Walker's assessment assumes far greater importance than Pike's. Ten years after he left Ohio and relocated west of Missouri, Walker strove to market the wonders of a land he and other eastern Indians now called home. He wrote glowingly of fruit trees and raising livestock and presented an image of settled lands just awaiting the arrival of more emigrants. The Nebraska Territory of Walker's letter was an idyllic place where removed Indians flourished and waited for the next wave of American farmers to join them in the fertile prairie grasslands. Although Walker's pristine picture does not seem believable, his description of an agriculturally bountiful country is not necessarily a complete fabrication.[3]

In the decades after removal, few Indians in Kansas would have shared Walker's idealistic description. But although they did not live in a world of overflowing bounty, most eastern Indians by 1854 had established a relatively stable existence and created a new home along the western Missouri border. In an environment already complicated by forced relocations and multiple migrations, these groups faced obstacles that hindered

---

[2] "Agricultural Qualities of Nebraska," *The Genesee Farmer*, July 1854.
[3] Ibid.

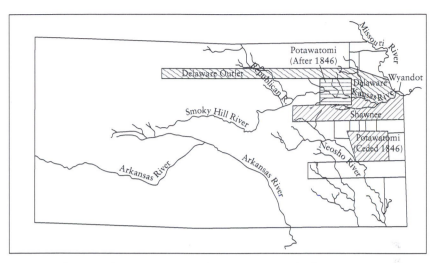

MAP 5. Indian Lands in Kansas. Based on Map 27 in Charles C. Royce (Comp.), *Indian Land Cessions in the United States.*

their ability to conduct daily affairs in the western territories. The eastern prairie-plains differed in ecology and climate; the Indians were not entirely familiar with these rhythms of life. At the same time, government support in the form of agricultural tools and annuities seldom met promised levels or native expectations. In response to these varied problems and realities, the Indians grounded their subsistence in eastern Kansas by intertwining familiar tasks of daily life and adapting to the developing regional economy. For most native men and women living in eastern Kansas, there was no time to write letters extolling the virtues or bemoaning the hardships of their new homes. It remained more important to focus on the daily tasks of living and all the hard work it entailed. This ongoing process of survival and adaptation, accompanied by varying degrees of success, marked a gradual but significant transition for these communities – from exiles and emigrants to border Indians.

Removed Indians in eastern Kansas confronted a new environment under conditions that initially hampered their ability to adapt and survive. According to treaty obligations, the U.S. government provided provisions for the first year, although that material support was often inadequate at best. As a result, the Indians established a sustainable existence by relying primarily on prior experience and available resources. Success depended on two important factors – their knowledge of the physical environment and their ability to recreate prior subsistence patterns or develop new ones. Despite the disruptions caused by the removal process, many Indian groups acclimatized to their new homes within a short period of time. Although few groups thrived, by the early 1850s many communities had developed a solid foundation in eastern Kansas that relied in part on customary patterns of agriculture and hunting.

Before the physical relocation occurred, eastern Indians confronted the prospect of living in a place few had seen, much less knew well. Pike's report did not circulate widely and the Indians relied on other individuals for information. Available descriptions of the western territories seldom came through unbiased sources. Reverend Isaac McCoy, the Baptist missionary turned removal promoter, highly recommended the western lands in an effort to convince both eastern Indians and Americans that the region was well-suited to the needs of relocated tribes. McCoy went on a number of exploratory expeditions in the late 1820s and the 1830s with delegations of eastern Indians charged with choosing a spot for their relocation. As opposed to Pike and other early explorers, McCoy traversed much of the western territory and had personal encounters with prairie fires and dysentery to prove it. In the journals from two of those journeys, he made notes on water supplies, animal populations, and timber. Apparently, prior reports had not done justice to the land. "The country we have explored, I am ready [to] pronounce excellent," McCoy declared. Although he acknowledged a relative deficiency in timber, he gently chided previous accounts and noted that the region "has been reported to be more scarce of wood and water than is the fact." McCoy did not overlook negative characteristics. He mentioned that the streams would most likely disappear during the dry season and that the timber grew almost exclusively along those same waterways. Nevertheless, his travels led him to conclude that well-organized settlement plans would allow the Indians to prosper.[4]

But what McCoy brushed aside, the Indians found much more problematic. In his report to Superintendent of Indian Affairs William Clark, McCoy mentioned briefly that the Potawatomis and Ottawas in his exploration party did not like the fact that there were few, if any, sugar trees in the region. This was by no means a small problem and, indeed, many participants in later expeditions noted with similar concern the absence

---

[4] Lela Barnes (Ed.), "Journal of Isaac McCoy for the Exploring Expedition of 1828," *Kansas Historical Quarterly*, 5(August 1936): 227–269; Lela Barnes (Ed.), "Journal of Isaac McCoy for the Exploring Expedition of 1830," *Kansas Historical Quarterly*, 5(November 1936): 339–377.

of desirable resources. The Wyandots who examined lands just west of the Missouri state border in 1831 found a great deal to disparage. At the time, the area later known as the Platte Purchase was still outside of Missouri's boundaries. In this land on the west side of the Platte River William Walker and the other four Wyandot delegates saw little to please them. They had been told that maple trees, whose sap they used to make sugar, grew in abundance. This was not the case. Nor was it a minor concern. "This article [sugar], we are all well aware," the delegates reminded their community back in Ohio, "is one of the principal commodities of commerce with our nation." The nearly complete absence of such trees was only the first problem, since it was also clear that the timber that did grow in the region was both scarce and "of that description generally that is of no great use to an agricultural community." Furthermore, the "steep, broken, and uneven" lands would hinder cultivation and regardless of latitude the climate was noticeably colder. The critical assessment continued as the Wyandots attacked almost every aspect of the land. They reported that even the hunters in their community would be disappointed. Although the region contained a sizeable animal population, especially of bears, the Wyandots knew that their able hunters would soon lower those numbers considerably. They predicted that "in three years time they [the bears] would be as scarce as they now are upon our reservation." As far as the Wyandot delegates were concerned, neither hunters nor farmers would find much to please them west of the Mississippi.[5]

The respective agendas of McCoy and the Wyandot delegation colored their reports. For McCoy, relocation and removal was a foregone conclusion. The question was not if the land was desirable, but how the land could best be used to increase its suitability. Even as he traveled the region he looked for appropriate sites for the capital of the Indian Territory he envisioned. But at the time of their exploration in 1831, the Wyandots did not want to leave Ohio and did not see removal as inevitable. And as a result of the overwhelmingly critical report, government agents accused the Wyandot delegation, and William Walker in particular, of sabotaging the expedition and lying to the Wyandot chiefs in an effort to bolster resistance to removal. The accusation did not miss the target completely. It could be argued that the Wyandots had made up their minds to

[5] Barnes, "Journal of Isaac McCoy for the Exploring Expedition of 1828," 265; J. Orin Oliphant (Ed.), "The Report of the Wyandot Exploring Delegation, 1831," *Kansas Historical Quarterly*, *15* (August 1947): 248–262; Joseph T. Manzo, "Emigrant Indian Objections to Kansas Residence," *Kansas History*, 4 (1981): 247–254.

dislike the region and, therefore, made no effort to see anything good in the country.[6]

Prejudicial reporting aside, substantial differences existed between the western environment and that which the eastern Indians left behind. Stands of white oak, hickory, American beech, sugar maple, elm, and ash predominated in the deciduous forests in the Great Lakes region. Grasslands comprised significant areas of central and northern Illinois, though stands of oak and hickory distinguished this environment from the bluestem prairies of the central Plains. These diverse growths of timber provided raw materials beyond the sap that Indian women made into sugar. The elm provided wood and bark for lodges, the oak bore acorns that supplemented diets, and all manner of timber fueled cooking fires. Local forests also provided the wood and bark for canoes, although the use of horses as transportation and beasts of burden decreased the importance of water transport among many groups by the late 1700s. In contrast, deciduous forest in the Missouri border region was limited to the strips that hugged the riverbanks. McCoy spoke highly of oak, hickory, walnut, and ash, while the Wyandots described the red elm, mulberry, cottonwood, and other trees as "useless." The limited forests contained different varieties of oak, but cottonwood trees were the most abundant. Instead of woodlands comparable to those in the Great Lakes region, grasslands were the dominant vegetation in present-day eastern Kansas, and approximately 97 percent of the region at the time could be described as prairie, or treeless grasslands.[7]

Following close behind these concerns over the natural environment were those regarding the climate, especially as it related to the health of the Indians. The subject of temperature extremes came up repeatedly. According to the Wyandots, everything they learned led them to believe that the winters in this region were much colder and the summers hotter.

---

[6] For accusations against Wyandot delegation, see Oliphant, "The Report of the Wyandot Exploring Delegation, 1831," 248–253, 258–262.

[7] Barnes, "Journal of Isaac McCoy for the Exploring Expedition of 1828," 247, 264–265; Gordon G. Whitney, *From Coastal Wilderness to Fruited Plain: A History of Environmental Change in Temperate North America 1500 to the Present* (New York, 1994), 76–85; Huber Self, *Environment and Man in Kansas: A Geographical Analysis* (Lawrence, 1978), 66–70; Helen Hornbeck Tanner (Ed.), *Atlas of Great Lakes Indian History* (Norman, 1987), 13–23; William Jones, "Ethnography of the Fox Indians," *Bulletin of the Smithsonian Institution Bureau of American Ethnology,* 125(1939): 50–54; James A. Clifton, *The Prairie People: Continuity and Change in Potawatomi Indian Culture, 1665–1965* (Lawrence, 1977), 128–129; Oliphant, "The Report of the Wyandot Exploring Delegation, 1831," 254; Manzo, "Emigrant Indian Objections to Kansas Residence," 246–254.

A broad comparison of climates between the southern Great Lakes and the area encompassed by Iowa, Missouri, and Kansas, does not present significant differences. Both regions have a maritime climate, and Indiana or Ohio winters undoubtedly match those in Kansas when it comes to temperatures and snowfall. Perhaps the most striking differences are that the mostly treeless grasslands offer little natural protection from the elements and that the plains are more susceptible to drought. Yet, the list of commonalities cannot erase the fact that relocation resulted in a disturbing number of deaths. Many individuals contracted diseases prior to removal or during the journey, but the climate of the plains compounded the sickness. No party escaped death under these circumstances, as both the timing and the length of western migrations affected the health of native travelers. Upon arrival in the West, the eastern Indians faced unfamiliar conditions and an unstable subsistence. For the Wyandots, the mild winter of 1843–1844 did not dramatically lessen the impact. Their late arrival meant that most spent the winter months in temporary shelters. In the first three months, sixty Wyandots died from a variety of fevers and illnesses caused by a combination of exposure and the unfamiliar climate. Sickness usually claims the weak, and, in this case, the majority of these deaths were the youngest children out of the population of nearly seven hundred. The high mortality rate upon arrival dealt a harsh blow to the Wyandots, and they were not the only community to suffer.[8]

The connections between weather patterns and geographic attributes of the prairie likewise shaped the Indians' agricultural pursuits. The lands encompassed by southern Michigan, Ohio, and Indiana served as the former home for the Wyandots, Shawnees, and Delawares. Based on the consistent periods of rain during the growing season, that region also served as a superior environment for corn, a staple crop among the Indian

---

[8] Oliphant, "The Report of the Wyandot Exploring Delegation, 1831," 254; Manzo, "Emigrant Indians Objections to Kansas Residence," 252; *United States Map Book Environmental Atlas* (Cambridge, MA, 1992), 14–17; Self, *Environment and Man in Kansas*, 51–65; Wilbur J. Garret (Ed.), *Historical Atlas of the United States* (Washington, DC, 1988), 10–15; Thomas Mosely, Jr. to D. D. Mitchell, SIA, September 18, 1851, OIA-LR, roll 364; Affidavit, July 28 & 31, 1843, WNP; Robert Emmett Smith, Jr., "The Wyandot Indians, 1843–1876" (Ph.D. Dissertation, Oklahoma State University, 1973), 66–72; Reverend James Wheeler to Rev. E. R. Ames, October 27, 1843, in "Letters from the Indian Missions in Kansas," *Collections of the Kansas State Historical Society*, 16(1923–1925): 227–271. The Delaware and Munsee Moravian community lost 140 out of a population of 250 in the first ten years after removal. See David Zeisberger Smith to Luke Lea, August 11, 1851, OIA-LR, roll 364.

communities. When they moved west of the Mississippi, the native men and women who maintained the gardens and fields encountered a much less reliable growing season. Their new homes rested on the eastern edge of the Great Plains, and they now had a new climate to manage, one dependent on both geography and assorted air masses. Northern winds bring drier and colder air from Canada, southern ones carry warmth and moisture from the Gulf of Mexico, and the moist air from the Pacific Ocean dries out and warms up as it passes over the Rockies. The timing and strength of these various airflows plays a significant role in the weather in the region. Meanwhile, the distance of eastern Kansas from large bodies of water means that temperatures have the potential for extreme fluctuations throughout the year. Annual precipitation can vary dramatically as well, and droughts are not abnormal. These precipitation patterns also directly impact the streams typical to the prairie plains region. Other than the Missouri, Canadian, and Pecos rivers, most of these waterways lie above the ground water level. They serve mostly to drain the countryside and do not receive water from sources other than the seasonal precipitation or melted mountain snows. Consequently, when the snowmelt and strong spring rains coincide, severe flooding hits the region. Once the rains pass and the snows dissipate, many of the streambeds dry up.[9]

The Indians who moved west had only surface knowledge of this new environment, and they entered the region with varying levels of agricultural dependency and expertise. Most native communities in the Great Lakes region prior to removal relied on a mixture of animal and plant life to survive. Except for the climate found in northern Minnesota and northern Michigan, the climate in the Great Lakes region produced advantageous conditions for agriculture, with upwards of one hundred and forty frost-free growing days per year. Beans, pumpkins, and corn predominated in the small areas cultivated primarily by Indian women. The increased number of missionaries and federal agencies in the Ohio Valley in the 1800s further affected native subsistence. Although the Delawares on the White River in Indiana and the Maykujay Shawnees at Wapakoneta in Ohio had different attitudes toward the missionaries who lived and

[9] Bret Wallach, "Physical Environment," in Wishart, *Encyclopedia of the Great Plains*, 613–618; Daniel J. Leathers, "Climate," in ibid., 624–625; Whitney, *From Coastal Wilderness to Fruited Plain*, 49–51; James C. Malin, *History and Ecology: Studies of the Grassland*, edited by Robert P. Swierenga (Lincoln, 1984), 44–45. Malin uses these characteristics of the Plains streams to argue that flooding on the plains was not caused by deforestation, but by naturally occurring factors.

worked among them, both communities developed subsistence patterns that helped their transition to life in the West.[10]

The Delawares in Indiana largely survived on customary practices in the first two decades immediately preceding their relocation. Although the Moravians had an established mission among the Delaware settlements on the White River from 1801–1806, the missionariess' efforts to affect a transition to agricultural dependency did not achieve the desired results. Delaware women continued to tend to the small plots of corn and beans that provided their families with stores of food to supplement the turkey, deer, and bear meat brought in by the men who hunted from mid-autumn through late spring. Most residents of the Delawares' towns continued to participate in the annual corn dances and rituals held every spring before planting and every fall at the harvest. February and March remained a time for making sugar from the tree sap that flowed freely as mild temperatures returned to the region. What needs they could not fulfill through their combined labors, the Delawares obtained through barter or purchase from local settlers, traders, and missionaries. Men sold bear grease, and women exchanged the baskets and brooms they had made. The skins gathered during the annual hunts also provided cash for necessary provisions or alcohol, a notoriously popular trade item. Although a deer skin usually sold for one dollar to traders, a bear skin could fetch as much as two dollars. Both men and women participated in this trade because both contributed their labor to the final product. And although they did not possess them in large numbers, the Delawares raised hogs and cattle to the extent that they could sometimes sell surplus animals to missionaries. The Delawares in Indiana recognized the signs of declining game populations and accepted the new technologies brought by Euro-American traders and settlers. But, in the early nineteenth century, they did not stray far from their customary practices.[11]

Black Hoof's band of Maykujay Shawnees at Wapakoneta made a more concerted effort to prioritize agriculture in their seasonal round, and the endeavor created significant changes within some segments of the Ohio Shawnee community. In 1807, Black Hoof and the nearly five hundred Wapakoneta Shawnees welcomed the services of a Quaker missionary

---

[10] Tanner, *Atlas of Great Lakes Indian History*, 18–23; R. David Edmunds, *The Shawnee Prophet* (Lincoln, NE, 1983), 16–20.

[11] Lawrence Henry Gipson (Ed.), *The Moravian Indian Mission on White River* (Indianapolis, 1938), 104, 142, 190–191, 213–214, 278–281, 341, 347, 598–599.

named William Kirk, who assisted their efforts to erect fences and use customarily Anglo farming methods. Although Black Hoof grew discouraged when the federal government dismissed Kirk in 1808 due to alleged financial improprieties, many Shawnees continued to fence their fields and raise livestock. Even as other Ohio Shawnees subsisted on practices very similar to the Delawares, the Wapakoneta Shawnees continued to move further from traditional subsistence patterns. By the 1820s, Indian farmers consistently used the gristmill located south of Wapakoneta. The land showed signs of increased agricultural efforts at Lewistown as well. One illustrative practice on the rise was the construction of rail fences to delineate and protect the fields of corn, beans, and other crops. Plows appeared in the fields alongside the more commonly used wooden and metal hoes. Big Snake, one of the principal men at Wapakoneta, lived in a log house that looked out over nearly ten acres of cleared land enclosed by a fence consisting of approximately eighteen hundred rails. His neighbor, Nenepemeshequa or Cornstalk, could list an even more impressive inventory that included two log houses beside a field fenced by more than twenty-seven hundred rails, a small orchard of apple trees, and a large quantity of hogs.[12]

Yet in this transition to a more westernized style of agriculture, the Ohio Shawnees had not abandoned past practices completely. Cornstalk's material goods included three ten-gallon sugar kettles, a sure sign that his family traveled to their sugar camps in the colder months. Just as important, if not more so, Shawnee women continued to play prominent roles in the agricultural practices of the Ohio communities. Women and children tended the fields, even as some of these women showed signs of change. In some cases, the women's property rivaled or surpassed that of the more established men in the community. Niemche and her family of four worked two fields enclosed by more than three thousand rails while maintaining twenty apple trees and thirty hogs. Nor was she an exception. The Shawnee women at Wapakoneta maintained their customary roles even as the community as a whole adopted new practices. Rails meant fenced fields, plows meant a more substantial working of the lands, and large numbers of domestic poultry, cattle, and hogs displayed a more marked absorption of American agriculture. Similar to the Delawares in Indiana,

[12] Notes Regarding Shawnee Property, OIA-LR, roll 749; An Enumeration of the Shawanees who have Emigrated West of the Mississippi, since the Treaties of Greenville and Rapids of Miami, April 15, 1830, OIA-LR, roll 300; Henry Harvey, _History of the Shawnee Indians, From the Year 1681 to 1854, Inclusive_ (New York, 1971), 146–151.

however, the Wapakoneta Shawnees had not given up their former way of life.[13]

This reliance on and familiarity with mixed subsistence patterns would prove important during the trying times that followed removal. The western environment and the delinquent delivery of promised agricultural tools hindered the Indians' ability to support their families, especially when they moved in larger numbers. Relocation had also forced many Indians to leave behind substantial assets, a circumstance compounded by the loss of horses and other animals on the journey west. During those initial years, in the late 1820s and early 1830s, members of Indian communities on the Missouri border complained that the government had failed to provide numerous items guaranteed by treaties. It did not help that emigrant parties often arrived at their new homes in the late fall – too late to prepare fields for the following year. As a result, they required the government's assistance, if only to obtain enough food to survive the winter. The Delawares, under Chief Anderson (or Kikthawenund), moved from southwestern Missouri to lands north of the Kansas River in early November of 1830 with the understanding that the government would meet its treaty obligations. They were generally pleased with their new environment. "The land is good," stated Kikthawenund, "and also the wood and water, but the game is scarce." And the Delawares needed provisions. At a minimum, they expected the government to furnish salted meats and corn at their initial encampments. Inefficient, and for some reason unprepared, William Clark could only send them minimal provisions to sustain them through the winter months. These circumstances only compounded the initial dislocation, and Indians usually relied on government resources upon their arrival in the West.[14]

Although it took time and significant effort, the eastern Indians adjusted to the western environment. The Wapakoneta Shawnees arrived at their final destination in December 1832 and settled about eight miles west of the mouth of the Kansas River. "As respects our new country," Joseph

[13] Notes Regarding Shawnee Property, OIA-LR, roll 749; An Enumeration of the Shawanees who have Emigrated West of the Mississippi, since the Treaties of Greenville and Rapids of Miami, April 15, 1830, OIA-LR, roll 300; Erminie Wheeler Voegelin, "The Place of Agriculture in the Subsistence Economy of the Shawnee," *Papers of the Michigan Academy of Science, Arts, and Letters*, 26–27(1941): 513–520.

[14] Notes Regarding Shawnee Property, OIA-LR, roll 749; Richard Graham to William Clark, June 1, 1828, RGP; Money advanced by Richard Graham for Shawnee provisions, April–May, 1828, RGP; Richard Cummins to William Clark, November 4, 1830, OIA-LR, roll 300; Senate Document No. 512, 23rd Congress, 1st Session, Serial No. 245, 599; William Clark to SOW Eaton, January 7, 1831, TFP.

Barnett wrote, "I have seen better and worse." Barnett also noted the absence of wild game and its impact on any Shawnee hunters. "They have come to a country where they must work." The Shawnee settlements showed evidence of that effort by summer. They planted corn and beans, and many built small cabins and fences around their fields. In that first season, their fields still only produced a minimal subsistence, and the Hog Creek Shawnees, who arrived in the late fall of that same year, survived the winter only through provisions contributed by the federal government and Quaker missionaries.[15]

By the late 1830s, the neighboring Shawnee and the Delaware communities showed signs of establishing a more secure and sustainable subsistence. In the fall of 1838, the settlement of just over one thousand Delaware Indians in northeastern Kansas cultivated approximately fifteen hundred acres of corn, beans, peas, pumpkins, and potatoes. Yet, although this produce and the presence of cattle and hogs appeared to indicate a more sedentary lifestyle, parties of Delaware men continued to hunt. Groups of anywhere from ten to twenty-five took advantage of their reserve's western outlet and traveled as far as the Rocky Mountains in pursuit of beaver skins. In the burgeoning local economy along the Missouri border, a single individual could earn up to $1,000 for his efforts. Meanwhile, the nearly one thousand Shawnees showed similar signs of matching previous agricultural outputs. This reserve on the south side of the Kansas River now encompassed the Missouri Shawnees who had ceded their Cape Girardeau grant in 1825 as well as the parties of Shawnees from Wapakoneta and Hog Creek. Neither the Missouri nor the Ohio Shawnees had established anything resembling a village. Instead, families settled throughout the reserve, concentrating primarily in the northeast corner, the area closest to the Missouri border. Fort Leavenworth agent Richard Cummins praised the fields that accompanied these scattered settlements and eagerly reported the success of familiar corn, bean, and pumpkin crops alongside new additions such as wheat and oats.[16]

[15] "Letter from a Shawnee Indian," *The Friend: a Religious and Literary Journal*, March 23, 1833; John D. Lang and Samuel Taylor, Jr., *Report of a Visit to Some of the Tribes of Indians Located West of the Mississippi River* (New York, 1843), 13–15; Harvey, *History of the Shawnee Indians*, 234–236; Rodney Staab, "Farmsteads of the Kansas Shawnee," *The Kansas Anthropologist*, 14(1, 1993): 13–27.

[16] Richard Cummins to C. A. Harris, CIA, September 25, 1838, OIA-LR, roll 301; Lang and Taylor, Jr., *Report of a Visit to Some of the Tribes of Indians*, 13–15; Richard Cummins to Joshua Pilcher, October 1839, OIA-LR, roll 752; Staab, "Farmsteads of the Kansas Shawnee," 13–27; *Indian Affairs*, II, 262–264, 304–305.

The 1840s brought equal parts improvement and tragedy to these two communities. In 1842, Cummins reported that the Shawnees had become "an agricultural people" who lived in "comfortable cabins" and raised corn, wheat, oats, pumpkins, beans, peas, and "many other vegetables." Not everyone agreed with the agent's assessment, which may have suffered from inaccuracies or exaggerations. One Shawnee headman, summarizing his new existence in the summer of 1842, observed that "when he lived in Ohio he had a good farm and lived well, but by being removed to this country he had become poor." Others might have taken issue with Cummins's use of the word comfortable to describe the Shawnee homes. Traveler Matthew Field spent the night in Joe Day's two-room cabin in November 1843, and painted a more critical picture of the hospitable but dark, smoky, and cramped quarters of his Shawnee host. Field remembered a small cabin whose most brilliant light during the evening hours came from the flames sprouting from a frying pan filled with grease, rather than comfortable living area. Cummins's similar description of the Delawares' condition in 1842, therefore, leaves room open for interpretation of how well-off the Indians were on the Delaware reserve. Although the agent described their farms as "nearly equal to those of the Shawnees," that may not have been the case for all members of the Delaware community.[17]

Then, in the mid-1840s, the natural environment of Kansas revealed its destructive power and nearly erased the hard work of the previous decade. From their homes throughout the northern and southern Kansas River valley, the Shawnees and Delawares witnessed firsthand the troubles produced by excessive rains. The record of precipitation levels at Fort Leavenworth and Fort Scott indicates that the eastern Indians arrived and settled in eastern Kansas during a period of above-average rainfall. The spring of 1844 played a large role in those statistics. Starting in late April the rain began to fall in torrents. It continued to pour for more than five weeks. Francis Barker at the Shawnee Baptist Mission compared the continuous rainfall and subsequent flooding to "Noah's day," and fellow Baptist missionary Jotham Meeker surmised that the local Indian population would have nothing to live on for at least a full year. Approximately one hundred and seventy-one Shawnees and two hundred and forty Delawares

---

[17] Richard Cummins to D. D. Mitchell, September 12, 1842, OIA-LR, roll 301; Lang and Taylor, Jr., *Report of a Visit to Some of the Tribes of Indians*, 16; Matthew Field, *Prairie and Mountain Sketches*, edited by Kate L. Gregg and John Francis McDermott (Norman, 1957), 11–14.

lost their houses, crops, and animals. Fifty miles to the south, the Ottawas on the Osage River suffered as well. Jotham Meeker acquired provisions from neighboring communities to help the Osage River settlements, while the federal government gathered food for the Shawnees and Delawares. In January 1845, Superintendent of Indian Affairs Thomas H. Harvey purchased and distributed almost fourteen thousand bushels of corn in the flood's aftermath. Although the Osage River overran its banks again in the spring of 1845, the Kansas River remained within its natural confines and spared the Shawnees and Delawares. Only five years later, however, they experienced the opposite extreme. The floods of previous years seemed a distant memory as the skies remained dry from early May into November in 1850. "I have never known so dry a season as we have now had," Meeker wrote resignedly in his diary.[18]

In between these vacillating extremes of weather, the Shawnees and Delawares managed to glean produce from their fields. The statistics gathered from government agents by Henry Rowe Schoolcraft in 1846 and his more detailed census in 1847 together provide insight into the abilities of these two communities to recover and rebuild. Although a comparison of the numbers from these two years illustrates the imperfect nature of census material, it nevertheless provides enough information to draw some important conclusions. The populations of the Shawnee and Delaware communities each hovered around one thousand, with the Shawnee just below and the Delaware above. According to Schoolcraft's research, with the exception of six families, the Shawnees depended primarily on agriculture. Twenty Delaware heads of families provided for their children by hunting and the remaining one hundred and twenty-seven relied on farming. By 1847, the Shawnees had nearly three thousand acres under cultivation and the Delawares just under sixteen hundred. Shawnee fields produced more than fifty-five thousand bushels of corn in 1847, an increase of more than twenty-one thousand from the previous year. The Delawares' yields dropped slightly during the same period, but

---

[18] Francis Barker to Isaac Barker, July 23, 1844, FBP; Mrs. Meeker to Emoline Clough, June 10, 1844, roll 617, JMP; "Sufferings of the Indian West of the Mississippi," *The Friend: A Religious and Literary Journal*, May 3, 1845; Jotham Meeker to Solomon Peck, June 26, 1844, roll 617, JMP; Jotham Meeker to Solomon Peck, November 14, 1844, roll 617, JMP; Louise Barry, *The Beginning of the West: Annals of the Kansas Gateway to the American West, 1540–1854* (Topeka, 1972), 512–517, 533–534; Merlin Paul Lawson, *The Climate of the Great American Desert: Reconstruction of the Climate of Western Interior United States, 1800–1850* (Lincoln, 1974), 84, 100–101. Meeker's diary quoted in Barry, *The Beginning of the West*, 972; ibid, 554; Jotham Meeker to Thomas Harvey, SIA, September 22, 1848, IMSC.

they still harvested more than twenty-six thousand bushels in the latter year. Members of both communities raised horses, cows, sheep, and hogs in relatively prodigious numbers. Despite removal, an unfamiliar land, and environmental extremes, the eastern Indians appeared to have made remarkable progress.[19]

The reported bounty caused Cummins to once again herald the eastern Indians' progress toward "civilization." In September 1848 he confidently declared that "the 'Indian hunter' has disappeared among the border tribes," replaced by the "Indian farmer." Though his nineteen-year tenure at Fort Leavenworth made Cummins more experienced than most agents, his statements proved misleading. Perhaps most important, his proclamation dismissed prior agricultural practices. At the same time, the short census included in his report reflected the questions asked, and, therefore, it provided insight into agricultural production only. The problem occurred even among agents who mentioned seasonal hunting practices. Alfred J. Vaughn, a colleague stationed at the Osage River subagency, noted that the Miamis, Ottawas, and Potawatomis continued to hunt, but he described this activity as no more than a hobby. "Their hunts generally take place (not so much with a view to profit as to a desire for change) after their farming operations have terminated for the years," Vaughn observed, "and the produce of their fields are housed and secured." Neither Cummins nor Vaughan appeared ready to admit the prior agricultural experience of the Indians at their respective agencies. Nor did they want to indicate that hunting held any importance in native subsistence.[20]

It is quite possible that Cummins, Vaughan, and other agents overstated the Indians' harvests to bolster efforts to wean the Indians away from "the chase." Nevertheless, this emphasis on agricultural production misrepresented conditions and practices on the reserves in eastern Kansas. The Delawares, in particular, continued to rely on hunting for food and furs well into the 1840s and 1850s. Annual hunts remained an important element of their subsistence even as their agricultural production

---

[19] Henry Rowe Schoolcraft, *Historical and Statistical Information Respecting the History, Condition, and Prospects of the Indian tribes of the United States* (6 vols., Philadelphia, 1851), I, 488–497, III, 621–628; Census and Statistics of the Shawnees and Delawares for the Year 1846, OIA-LR, roll 302; Alfred Vaughan to William Medill, CIA, October 22, 1846, OIA-LR, roll 643. The reports from Schoolcraft and the two agents also give statistics for the Ottawas, Potawatomies, and Chippewas of the Osage River Agency and the Kickapoos, Stockbridges, and Munsees of the Fort Leavenworth Agency.

[20] Richard Cummins to Henry Harvey, SIA, September 26, 1848, OIA-LR, roll 302; Alfred Vaughan to William Medill, CIA, October 22, 1846, OIA-LR, roll 643.

grew. Each year Delaware hunters joined Kickapoo, Potawatomi, and
Sauk hunters who traveled great distances to obtain food and marketable
peltries. Traders employed by Pierre Chouteau, Jr., and Company in eastern Kansas and Iowa purchased deer, raccoon, otter, wolf, and beaver
skins during the 1830s and late 1840s. From the mid-1830s into the early
1850s, the post maintained by François Chouteau, Cyprien Chouteau,
and James Findlay on the Kansas River in Westport, Missouri, consistently supplied Delaware hunting parties that traveled west primarily in
the pursuit of beaver. In 1847 alone, Delaware hunters brought in approximately thirty-six hundred skins. As their fields lay frozen and useless in
the winter months, the Indians turned to animals for support. Winter
hunts also captured the best furs as animals similarly fought the season's
cold weather.[21]

The prevalence of Delaware hunters hinted at other activities that
Indian agents either failed to address or chose to ignore. Although Cummins, Vaughan, and other officials eagerly reported on native farms, they
infrequently mentioned who worked in the fields. Only a few scattered
comments give insight into the ways that removal and the stress on agriculture may have altered gender roles within Indian communities. Intent
on making the Indians realize the importance of property and other values
of "civilization," William Clark addressed the labor performed by women
early on in his tenure. They "should be assisted in making fences, to which
their own means and strengths are inadequate," he recommended in 1826,
"also in planting orchards and instructed in raising cotton, and in spinning and weaving it into cloth, and making it up into garments." Only a
few years after Clark made his informal proposal, Indian agent Andrew
Hughes promoted a more direct approach by bringing fifteen women
of the Missouri Sauks to receive instruction in spinning and weaving.

---

[21] Laurent Pensoneau to Mr. P. Chouteau, October 27, 1834, CFP; François Chouteau
to Pierre Chouteau, Jr., July 6, 1835, CFP; Account of Messrs. Chouteau and Findlay,
April 23, 1845, CFP; Amount of Sales and Returns made by the Sac and Fox Outfit Since
September 25, 1843, CFP; Packing Account of Furs and Peltries from Pottawatomi Outfit,
April 19, 1848, CFP; Agreement between P. Chouteau, Jr. and W. G. and G. W. Ewing,
October 22, 1847, CFP; P. Chouteau, Jr. and Co. to Major Andrew Drips, February 26,
1852, Andrew Drips Papers, MHS; A. Street to S. P. Sublette, January 6, 1848, Sublette
Papers, MHS; Schoolcraft, *Historical and Statistical Information, I*, 493; Narrative of
Louis Cortambert, 1837, Indian Papers, MHS; "A Buffalo Hunt with the Miamis in
1854," *Transactions of the Kansas State Historical Society, 10*(1907–1908): 402–409;
Harvey L. Carter, "Jim Swanock and the Delaware Hunters," in LeRoy Hafen (Ed.), *The
Mountain Men and the Fur Trade of the Far West* (10 vols., Glendale, CA, 1969), VII,
293–300.

According to Hughes, "Indian civilization need no longer exist in theory." Both men voiced the opinions of American officials and missionaries, to whom Indian progress depended largely on the appropriate duties performed by the men and women.[22]

The silence regarding the specific activities of Delaware and Shawnee men and women in the 1830s and 1840s makes it difficult to draw conclusions about their respective communities. The property left behind by many of the Ohio Shawnees indicated that, prior to removal, both men and women owned property, and women were still largely involved in tending the corn, bean, and pumpkin crops. And although Cummins focused on production in 1846, and paid little attention to gender differences other than references to population and school attendance, Schoolcraft's more comprehensive accounting provides slightly better insight into gender roles. If his 1847 census was accurate, thirty-seven Shawnee women and twenty Delaware women knew how to spin, knit, and weave. Yet, together these women had spun neither flax nor homespun and had knit a grand total of one hundred and fifty-eight stockings over the preceding year. Meanwhile, neither of the women, from either community, who had the skills of a seamstress had produced a single garment of any kind. The evidence suggests that the ten looms and thirty-seven spinning wheels on the two reserves saw little use. Rather than spending time on the so-called domestic arts, Shawnee and Delaware women focused their efforts on agriculture and horticulture. Whether out of necessity or by choice, the native women spent more time outdoors in the fields than indoors at the looms. The Delawares alone boiled nearly five thousand pounds of maple sugar, made almost eight thousand pounds of butter, and gleaned approximately twelve thousand pounds of wild and domestic honey. Although men surely participated in some of this production, women most likely performed the bulk of the labor.[23]

Another element of Schoolcraft's census reveals an important ambiguity regarding his perspective of Indian gender roles. In two neighboring columns, he first tallied the numbers of hunters and warriors, and then he counted the number of "agriculturalists," a distinction drawn between Indians who continued in past pursuits and those who accepted American civilization. According to Schoolcraft, the Shawnees had no warriors or

---

[22] William Clark to James Barbour, SOW, March 1, 1826, OIA-LR, roll 747; Andrew S. Hughes to William Clark, November 14, 1829, OIA-LR, roll 749.

[23] Notes Regarding Shawnee Property, OIA-LR, roll 749; Census and Statistics of the Shawnees and Delawares for the Year 1846, OIA-LR, roll 302; Schoolcraft, *Historical and Statistical Information, I*, 488–497.

hunters, but the Delawares had two hundred, at the very least a reflection of the Delawares' active participation in the western fur trade. However, the very labels used illustrate either Schoolcraft's gender bias or his unwillingness to publicize the numbers of native women who continued to serve as primary caretakers of the fields. As Erminie Voegelin learned from her female Shawnee informants, although Shawnee men may have provided assistance, agriculture remained a female occupation throughout the nineteenth century. Schoolcraft's numbers for the Delawares also imply the continuation of customary gender roles. A variety of combinations or permutations might explain how the one hundred and ninety-six males between the ages of eighteen and sixty comprised both the two hundred hunters and warriors and the one hundred and ninety-eight agriculturalists. But the most logical rationale affirms the presence of Delaware women in the fields. Specific numbers cannot be determined for either the Shawnees or the Delawares. However, the evidence suggests that native subsistence patterns and gender roles did not drastically change in the decades after removal. Native men and women continued to share responsibilities in feeding their families.[24]

In the two decades after their relocation, eastern Indians worked hard to adjust to life in eastern Kansas. Each Shawnee and Delaware left something behind in Ohio and Indiana. The emotional dislocation and injury that resulted from removal deepened the more material losses. Depending on their respective degree of prosperity, individuals and families lost established homes and substantial portions of accumulated material goods. For almost every Indian family, this meant that they began the next chapter of their lives at a disadvantage, dependent largely on the U.S. government and its willingness to fulfill treaty obligations. The unfamiliar, and at times unpredictable, environment of the prairie grasslands in eastern Kansas further hindered their continued efforts to regain their former standard of life. Yet, even with all that stood against them, the Shawnees and Delawares gradually stabilized their lives in the West.

The years of adjustment were also years of transformation. No single moment marks when the transition took place, but, at some point during their time along the Kansas River, the eastern Indians in the West became border Indians. They arrived in different years and under different circumstances, from the emigration of Tenskwatawa's party of Shawnees in the late 1820s to the forced removal of Menominee's band in the late 1830s.

---

[24] Schoolcraft, *Historical and Statistical Information, I,* 488–497; Voegelin, "The Place of Agriculture in the Subsistence Patterns of the Shawnee," 518.

The Wyandots were removed in 1843 and as late as 1851 Potawatomis continued to leave Wisconsin under government force and supervision. Whether they arrived at gunpoint, or under their own volition, however, none of these Indians considered eastern Kansas a resting point or a temporary home. Treaties grounded their legal claim to the lands, and every day they crafted a livelihood in eastern Kansas the Indians made an equally important statement about their intent to stay. The Delawares, Shawnees, and, after 1843, Wyandots lived across the border from the primary departure points for western trade and travel. The Potawatomi reserve, established in 1846, although farther from the border, rested right along the route that became the Oregon Trail. As of the early 1850s, all four communities also lived at a flashpoint for debates over slavery and expansion. First by proximity and second by participation, Indians from these four communities became important elements of border life in general and the border economy specifically. They took advantage of the burgeoning regional economy to augment customary subsistence patterns as the presence of military posts, missionary stations, settlers, and even travelers opened up possibilities for Indian men and women to supplement their agricultural production. Not all of the developments were positive. The alcohol trade thrived along the Missouri state line, traders continued to chase annuities, and wagon trains carried disease along with American pioneers. As the Shawnees, Delawares, Wyandots, and Potawatomis had learned at previous borders, proximity and participation meant hardship as well as opportunity.[25]

Under the respective treaties that turned eastern Kansas into an unorthodox checkerboard of Indian reserves, most eastern Indians obtained lands that had an eastern boundary adjacent to the Missouri state line. Out of these reserves, those of the Shawnees, Delawares, and Wyandots rested closest to the population centers of the towns of Kansas and Westport. Both settlements were founded by traders and were at the center of the border economy. François Chouteau came from St. Louis and established a trading post in 1821 only a few miles below the big bend in the Missouri River. This town of Kansas had a population of only five hundred in 1840, but five times that number by 1853. Westport, also located on the Missouri side of the border, began its history as a

[25] For the Wyandot removal, see Carl G. Klopfenstein, "The Removal of the Wyandots from Ohio," *Ohio Historical Quarterly*, 66(April 1957): 119–136; Frederick A. Norwood, "Strangers in a Strange Land: Removal of the Wyandot Indians," *Methodist History*, 13(April 1975): 45–60; Robert Emmett Smith, Jr., "The Wyandot Indians, 1843–1876" (Ph.D. Dissertation, Oklahoma State University, 1973), 54–62.

trading post as well. John Calvin McCoy, son of the Baptist missionary
Isaac McCoy, built a post only four or five miles south of the town of
Kansas. By the mid-1840s, from its location along the Santa Fe Trail,
Westport competed with Independence as a supply center for American
emigrants heading west. Both the boom of emigration and the growth of
western trade resulted in marked increases in the populations of towns
like Kansas and Westport as well as the surrounding regions. The combined populations of Clay and Jackson counties, located north and south
of the Missouri River, respectively, went from just over eight thousand
in 1830 to more than twenty-four thousand two decades later. On the
other side of the state border, the Indian population did not experience
similar demographic changes. The combined populations of the Shawnee,
Delaware, and Wyandot communities hovered around twenty-five hundred in the 1840s and 1850s. However, the nature of Missouri population
growth and its foundation of trade and travel provided opportunities for
many members of the border Indian communities. Both the Shawnee and
Wyandot lands rested at the confluence of the Missouri and Kansas rivers
and most of the Wyandots lived a short ferry ride from the town of Kansas.
It did not take long for the economic lives of Indians and non-Indians to
overlap and intertwine.[26]

Years of fur trading had long since normalized the practice of swapping
peltries for goods. But the exchange of money or provisions for Indian
surplus produce illustrated that the farms in eastern Kansas could impact
native subsistence in multiple ways. Agricultural production now offered
entry into both cash markets and simple exchange economies in the region,
especially as the non-Indian population increased along the western
Missouri border. Several U.S. military forts of hungry soldiers also stood
at primary entry and travel points in Kansas, and Indian-grown produce
soon became part of the trade network that helped to feed all of the
above populations. Such participation occurred in a variety of ways and
extended beyond the reserves located near the larger Missouri settlements.
The small band of Stockbridge Indians residing on the Delaware reserve
only a few miles south of Fort Leavenworth often sold portions of their
harvest and stock to the men stationed at the fort. These same Stockbridge

[26] Barry, *The Beginning of the West*, 261; Louis O. Honig, *Westport: Gateway to the Early
West* (Kansas City, MO, 1950), 29–36; David Boutros, "Confluence of People and Place:
The Chuteau Posts on the Missouri and Kansas Rivers," *Missouri Historical Review*,
97(October 2002): 1–19. For Missouri census information see http://fisher.lib.virginia.
edu/collections/stats/histcensus/php/start.php?year=V1830 and http://fisher.lib.virginia.
edu/collections/stats/histcensus/php/start.php?year=V1850 (Accessed September 27,
2005).

Indians had subsisted upon their removal on beef that a government contractor purchased from the Delaware Indians. In the early 1840s the Kickapoos settled in northeastern Kansas took advantage of their bountiful fields and local needs by selling their surplus produce to one of their traders, a Mr. Hildreth. And in the years following the construction of Fort Riley close to the Potawatomi Catholic Mission near present-day Topeka, Potawatomis cultivating the land on the upper Kansas River benefited from the immediate demand for corn, potatoes, and oats.[27]

Individuals also entered into the developing service economy. Paid positions with the U.S. government had existed for decades, and both men and women of mixed descent often profited the most from these opportunities. In the councils and treaty negotiations that predated removal in the 1800s, these individuals obtained decent wages for their efforts as interpreters and intermediaries. The number of these government-appointed positions increased dramatically with the establishment of reserves and Indian agencies in the western territories. In 1838 alone, the Fort Leavenworth Agency employed eight different mixed-descent men. Henry Tiblow, a man alternately listed as Delaware and Shawnee, served as the interpreter for the tribes under the agency's jurisdiction, while the other seven worked as assistant blacksmiths. Among those seven were Paschal Fish, Charles Fish, and Nelson Rogers, all products of relations between Anglo-American men taken captive as children and the Shawnee women they later married. At Indian agencies throughout the trans-Mississippi West, men like Tiblow, the Fish brothers, and Rogers performed services as interpreters and as assistant blacksmiths for salaries that by the early 1850s reached up to $400 per year.[28]

---

[27] Richard Cummins to D. D. Mitchell, SIA, September 12, 1842, OIA-LR, roll 301; J. D. Duerink to General John W. Whitfield, August 31, 1853, roll 1296, IMSC; Richard Cummins to CIA, September 15, 1845, roll 1296, IMSC; John B. Luce to T. Hartley Crawford, CIA, November 11, 1840, Indian Files – Shawnees, Box 6, KSHS; Rodney Staab, "How Much Produce Did the Shawnee Farmers Sell to Trail Emigrants?" *Trails Head Tidings*, 5(October 1991): 3–5; Jackson County, Missouri, Abstract of Census of 1840, MHS; Jackson County, Missouri, Abstract of Census of 1850, MHS.

[28] List of Employees for Fort Leavenworth Agency, September 30, 1838, OIA-LR, roll 301; List of Employees for Kansas Agency, September 18, 1851, OIA-LR, roll 364; Rev. J. Spencer, "Chief Blackfish and His White Captive," Indian Papers, MHS. For Indians hired as interpreters see John B. Luce to T. Hartley Crawford, CIA, November 14, 1840, OIA-LR, roll 301; List of Employees for Fort Leavenworth Agency, September 30, 1840, OIA-LR, roll 301; List of Employees for Fort Leavenworth Agency, September 30, 1846, OIA-LR, roll 302; List of Employees for Fort Leavenworth Agency, September 30, 1848, OIA-LR, roll 302; List of Employees for Osage Agency, September 1, 1845, OIA-LR, roll 632.

Although jobs as interpreters or translators appeared to provide the bulk of nontraditional occupations, Shawnees, Delawares, Potawatomis, and Wyandots worked within the border economy in a number of trades. In total, forty-five men and nine women from the four eastern Kansas communities received some manner of payment for their services as translators and interpreters in 1847. But skilled Indians also worked outside of the language-based occupations. Shawnee and Potawatomi carpenters, Delaware silversmiths, and Wyandot shoemakers all participated in local markets either on their reserve or across the border. For the majority of Indians who lacked such training or interest, other opportunities for paid labor could be found among their white neighbors. Shawnee Indians began working on the Missouri side of the border less than a decade after their relocation. Hired on an individual basis by local farmers, they harvested crops, cut logs, and made rails, all to make money to purchase clothes and provisions. One missionary reported in the winter of 1840 that, "It is not uncommon to see them [Indians] employed by the whites as blacksmiths, carpenters, &c." Although this type of employment was usually piecemeal and seasonal at best, it still served the needs of individuals, families, and communities on both sides of the Missouri state line.[29]

Men and women looking for work did not necessarily have to cross any boundary lines to find opportunities for seasonal labor. In the early 1800s in Indiana, Moravian missionaries often depended on the local native populations for food, wood, or other provisions. They were not alone in this reliance and the move west did not alter that dependent relationship. Indeed, many of the first mission buildings in eastern Kansas were constructed with the assistance of Shawnees and Delawares. Perhaps the most prominent employees of these missions were paid native assistants and preachers. These converts, however, made up only a small percentage of those laborers paid by missionaries. The tasks performed by Indian workers, who often went unnamed, did not necessarily provide substantial daily compensation. But, over time, the money earned could make a significant difference. Thomas Wells and his colleagues at the Friends' Shawnee Labor School on the Shawnee reserve had a two-hundred-acre farm adjacent to their mission buildings. Although the Quakers employed

---

[29] Schoolcraft, *Historical and Statistical Information*, I, 447–448, 489; Richard Cummins to Joshua Pilcher, SIA, October 1839, OIA-LR, roll 752; Martha B. Caldwell, comp., *Annals of the Shawnee Methodist Mission and Indian Manual Labor School* (Topeka, 1939), 100.

two farmers annually, they also hired Indians by the month or by the day. At the Ottawa Baptist Mission, an Indian woman by the name of Wahwosenmokwa received anywhere from $1 to $2.28 per month for her services as a cook at various points from 1842 to 1845.[30]

The account book for the Shawnee Methodist Indian Manual Labor School provides the most comprehensive list of Indian employment at local missions. It was the largest mission in eastern Kansas during its years of operation, educating more than one hundred native students in a given year. As an institution founded on the principle of manual labor, it relied on the work of its male and female students, either in the fields or the kitchens. But student labor alone could not fulfill the daily operational needs of the mission. From January 25, 1847 to March 18, 1847, for example, the Methodist missionaries paid local Indians a total of $734.43 "for wood," a necessity that helped maintain warmer living quarters in the mission buildings during harsh winters. But the Indians also supplied lumber for building and farming needs. In the fall of 1844, the Methodists added a saw to their steam mill. Through this mill, the Shawnees, in particular, not only obtained lumber for their own houses and needs, but also earned an income from the sales of the surplus. Although individual Indians found a ready market for wood among the Methodist missionaries during the winter months, their labor did more than just fill these seasonal demands. In the spring and summer, numerous Indians earned money as farm hands, threshing wheat and harvesting corn. In most cases, the superintendent of the mission, Reverend Thomas Johnson, did not list the names of the laborers and simply labeled them as "Indians." Although it was not necessarily abnormal, this impersonal designation may reflect unfamiliarity, which suggests that a variety of Indians participated in the workforce, not only those who may have had some other connection to the mission as converts.[31]

Indians in eastern Kansas also realized some benefits from the presence of American settlers and from the passage of American emigrant

[30] Barry, *The Beginning of the West*, 304–305; *Christian Advocate and Journal*, November 25, 1840; *Christian Advocate and Journal*, May 5, 1841; Thomas Wells to Thomas Moseley, August 14, 1851, roll 1296, IMSC; Account Books for Delaware, Ottawa, Pottawatomie, and Shawnee Baptist Missions, roll 630, JGP; Ioway Mission Account Book, Kansas Collections, University of Kansas. For native assistants see Jotham Meeker to Lucius Bolles, March 11, 1840, roll 617, JMP; J. G. Pratt to Rev. Solomon Peck, April 6, 1842, FBP.

[31] Shawnee Methodist Indian Manual Labor School Account Book, roll 1296, IMSC; William Patton to CIA, October 26, 1846, in Caldwell, *Annals of the Shawnee Methodist Mission*, 182; Barry, *The Beginning of the West*, 529.

wagon trains. A prevalent business in the 1840s entailed charging American travelers for passage across the creeks and rivers that impeded their journey along the various trails that originated in the Missouri border towns. Indian youths and old men charged tolls of anywhere from five to twenty-five cents to cross bridges, and some reported incomes of nearly $400 a year from their efforts. Other individuals who did not live near bridges responded to pioneer needs by providing ferry passage across rivers. Wyandots, Shawnees, Potawatomis, and Delawares all ran small ferries at the various rivers in eastern Kansas that coursed across both their reserves and the popular emigration trails. The Wyandots established one of the earliest ferries in 1843, an operation that consisted of a flatboat that, when pulled using a cable, could carry one wagon and a team to the opposite side of the Kansas River. By 1848, the national ferryman became an elected position within the Wyandot government and the electoral victor earned $100 a year to work at the junction of the Kansas and Missouri rivers. Farther west, near present-day Topeka, at least five different Potawatomis operated ferries and profited from the fact that the Oregon Trail passed through their reserve along the northern banks of the Kansas River. Depending on the flood stage of the river, one of the men, Joseph Ogee, was able to charge anywhere from $1 to $5 for an individual trip. Only a few miles east of the Potawatomi reserve, Paschal and Charles Fish, two Anglo-Shawnee brothers, also operated a ferry on the Kansas River. They benefited not only from emigrant travel but also from the U.S. soldiers that required the Indian flatboats on their way to Mexico in 1846.[32]

Paschal Fish did more than just operate a ferry, however. He took advantage of other traveler needs and by the 1850s transformed his home into an inn. Located approximately ten miles east of present-day Lawrence, his two-story house greeted weary travelers in need of food and a place to rest their heads. Although the creaking cottonwood boards did not always inspire confidence in the stability of the second floor, and competition for the single washbasin and square mirror often delayed

[32] Barry, *The Beginning of the West*, 598, 632, 801, 922–923, 930–931; Legislation of Wyandot Nation, October 2, 1848, WNP; *Journal of a Tour in the "Indian Territory," Performed by order of the Domestic Committee of the Board of Missions of the Protestant Episcopal Church in the Spring of 1844, by their Secretary and General Agent* (New York, 1844), 40; William E. Smith, "The Oregon Trail Through Pottawatomie County," *Kansas Historical Collections,* 27(1926–1928): 454–456; George A. Root, "Ferries in Kansas: Part II – Kansas River," *Kansas Historical Quarterly,* 2(August 1933): 252–254, 264–267; Caldwell, *Annals of the Shawnee Methodist Mission,* 188.

morning preparations, the inn nevertheless received satisfactory evaluations. A hot breakfast, complete with fresh biscuits and coffee, was served, and it sent travelers on their way. Fish also owned a small store and cultivated approximately one hundred acres of corn and thirty acres of oats. Wagon train drivers told visitors stories of this Shawnee man who "don't drink a drop of whiskey" and who sat on his porch with his hat on, "in a ruminating mood." Although these drivers may have tried to make their stories more colorful with such descriptions, it remained clear that informed travelers in the 1850s knew of Paschal Fish and the services he provided.[33]

Yet, Paschal Fish's fame and economic pursuits could not match those of another Shawnee man, Joseph Parks. Indeed, for those Indians who pursued economic gains through either government or private channels, Parks epitomized the heights to which an individual could reach. Reference is often made to Francis Parkman's description in 1846 of Parks's "fine farm" and "considerable number of slaves." Parks, even more so than Paschal Fish, was a well-known regional figure, and Parkman was not the only traveler to comment on the Shawnee's "elegant residence." The wealth accumulated by this Shawnee leader had diverse origins, beginning with land grants and interpreter's wages earned in the 1820s. Parks's childhood connections to then-Michigan Territorial Governor Lewis Cass gained him entrance to work in Indian affairs. The young man, whose exact lineage remains somewhat difficult to trace, has been described as being anywhere from half Shawnee to full white. Nevertheless, his facility with the Shawnee and English languages allowed him to function as an interpreter for most of the 1820s and early 1830s. He received land grants in several treaties made with the Shawnees, and received further compensation from the removal treaty negotiated at Wapakoneta in 1831. According to one estimate, Parks's net worth in 1833 hovered around $5,000 or $6,000. This wealth enabled him to pay off the debts of other Shawnees prior to removal that totaled more than $15,000.[34]

---

[33] Hannah Ropes, *Six Months in Kansas* (Boston, 1856), 39–43; Staab, "Farmsteads of the Kansas Shawnee," 16.

[34] Francis Parkman, *The Oregon Trail* (Garden City, NY, 1945), 20; Barry, *The Beginning of the West*, 974; John McElvain to Elbert Herring, CIA, May 3, 1833, Indian Files – Shawnees, Box 6, KSHS; Notes of Reverend Joab Spencer on Joseph Parks, ibid.; *Indian Affairs*, II, 145–155, 327–334; Richard Cummins to C. A. Harris, November 20, 1838, OIA-LR, roll 301; Shawnee Indians to Governor Lewis Cass, April 7, 1834, OIA-LR, roll 300; Stephen Warren, *The Shawnees and Their Neighbors, 1795–1870* (Urbana, 2005), 131–133. The history of Parks's debated lineage is discussed in more detail in Chapter 5.

His financial fortunes only improved after he crossed the Mississippi River. He built a residence just south of the Kansas River and not far from the town of Westport, a community with which he maintained strong connections over the next two decades. Parks continued to act as an intermediary and served as the official government interpreter for the Shawnees of the Fort Leavenworth Agency for the years 1835, 1836, 1851, and 1852. But federal employment was the least of his economic interests. Parks accumulated land and fared well in real estate transactions. In one emblematic transaction, he purchased a lot in Westport for $35 in 1836 only to sell it several years later for the sum of $360. Into the 1850s, Parks's interest in Westport also included the growing mercantile economy. With partner James Findlay, a resident of Jackson County, Missouri, Parks received an official license to trade from Indian Agent Richard Cummins in the spring of 1838. They soon opened a trading establishment near the Ottawa settlements along the Marais des Cygnes River. Shortly thereafter, the partners supplied provisions for both the Delawares and Shawnees when the Indians received their annuities. Although their partnership did not measure up to some of the larger trading establishments in the region, Parks and Findlay worked together into the early 1840s. Business success also made him a community resource, and Parks remained a critical financial intermediary for his fellow Shawnees until his death in 1859. When he died, his estate listed twenty-three open accounts with fellow tribal members that totaled nearly $16,000.[35]

Finally, Parks built part of his fortune on the labor of African-American slaves. From 1843 to 1846, Parks received the salary for the assistant blacksmith position at Fort Leavenworth Agency. A young man named Stephen performed the actual work. The prominent Shawnee had purchased Stephen when the boy was around eight years old from Henry Rogers, a man of Anglo-Shawnee heritage. Stephen developed a reputation as a good blacksmith, and his labors earned his master extra money until the young man ran away in the summer of 1848. Although Parks

[35] Statement of Disbursements, July 30, 1838, OIA-LR, roll 751; List of Employees for Fort Leavenworth Agency, 1845, OIA-LR, roll 300; Richard Cummins to Thomas Harvey, December 3, 1847, OIA-LR, roll 302; Richard Cummins to D. D. Mitchell, May 31, 1849, OIA-LR, roll 303; Barry, *The Beginning of the West*, 331, 343, 350–351, 595; Adrienne Christopher, "Captain Joseph Parks, Chief of the Shawnee Indians," *The Westport Historical Quarterly*, 5(June, 1969): 13–17; Richard Cummins to T. Hartley Crawford, May 28, 1841, OIA-LR, roll 301; Sugar and Miami Creek Trading Posts Account Books, 1839–1849, KSHS; Inventory of the Joseph Parks Estate, Johnson County Probate Office 1859; Warren, *The Shawnees and Their Neighbors*, 131–134.

followed Stephen and finally caught up to him thirty miles northwest of Chicago, the abolitionist citizens of Illinois enabled the young runaway to escape into Canada. This incident eliminated the blacksmith money from Parks's income, but it did not erase his dependence on slavery. He continued to rely on slaves to maintain a substantial parcel of land he owned adjacent to the Shawnee Methodist Mission. On this farm of almost seven hundred acres, he used a mixture of hired and slave labor to produce food for his family's consumption as well as for sale. At his death, he owned five adult slaves and several children.[36]

Although they were not alone among the border Indian communities in their financial success and regional renown, Joseph Parks and Paschal Fish remained more of the exception than the rule. Parks's estate points to the ability of a well-placed and diligent individual to succeed, but it does not mean that the standard of living in the Indian settlements was at a reasonable level. One of the intended bulwarks of Indian subsistence after removal, annuity payments, had a relatively minimal impact on Indian lives. Mounting debts and increasing trader influence eroded much of the effectiveness annuities might have had among most of the relocated Indians. By extending credit to groups throughout the region in the summer of 1837, the Chouteaus established claims to more than two-thirds of the annuity payments due to the Kickapoos, Shawnees, Delawares, and other border communities. To make matters worse, the Shawnees and Delawares, whose most recent treaties were signed in the late 1820s or early 1830s, did not receive payments comparable to those of other recently removed Indians. In 1843 Shawnee annuities amounted to only $5,000, and the Delawares received only $6,500. Although these totals did not include the value of salt annuities or blacksmith services, the actual cash payments did not amount to much. On a per capita basis, each of the Delawares living in eastern Kansas received $5.74 in 1846. Only a few chiefs benefited substantially from the payments, as Natcoming, Paterson, and Ketchum each received a lifetime annuity payment of more than $100.[37]

---

[36] Richard Cummins to D. D. Mitchell, February 2, 1843, OIA-LR, roll 302; List of Employees for Fort Leavenworth Agency, September 30, 1846, OIA-LR, roll 302; Declaration of Joseph Barnett, January 24, 1850, Indian Files – Shawnees, Box 6, KSHS; Declaration of Derick Bush, September 10, 1848, ibid. Declaration of Charles Findlay, January 11, 1850, ibid. Barry, *The Beginning of the West*, 660, 723, 729.

[37] Estimate of Funds for 1843 for St. Louis Superintendency, September 30, 1842, OIA-LR, roll 753; Census and Statistics of the Delawares, Shawnees, and Kickapoos for the Year 1846, OIA-LR, roll 302; Alfred Vaughan to William Medill, CIA, October 22, 1846, OIA-LR, roll 643; Schoolcraft, *Historical and Statistical Information*, VI, 720.

Based on the cost of provisions, clothing, and other goods in the 1830s and 1840s, annuities supported Indians to a minor extent. Families had to supplement their subsistence with what little amounts they received or had left over after the traders presented and received payment on their claims. Annuity amounts remained static over the years, but prices of goods did not, especially when the traders tacked on their profit margin. One barrel of superfine flour sold for up to $4 in Louisville in the summer of 1833, but listed at $12 only five years later at a Sauk and Mesquakie trading post run by the Chouteaus near Rock Island, Illinois. Similar markups affected other staple goods from salt to pork. Although the cost of cloth goods varied depending on the quality, Ewing, Clymer, and Company, a merchant outfit based in Westport in the 1840s, usually sold cloth blankets for $4 to $5. Meanwhile, a pair of shoes was priced at anywhere from $1 to $3. Irrespective of the fact that the passage of time, cost of transport, and greed of traders played roles in this price increase, Indian consumers had a set amount with which to purchase those goods. Whether buying the basics for their diet, or blankets to keep warm in the winter, the Delawares and Shawnees especially could not stretch their annuities that far.[38]

The lucrative and insidious alcohol trade further undermined the distribution and effectiveness of annuities. Whiskey sellers infested the Missouri state line and annuity payment grounds, and their success epitomized both the traders' commitment to profits and the American government's inability to enforce its laws and administer its borders. Congress passed a number of acts from 1790 to 1834 designed to regulate both federal and private interactions with the Indian peoples throughout the country. The 1834 Trade and Intercourse Act established specific rules for trade as well as for the presence of non-Indians on Indian land. It also decreed that all land west of the Mississippi not included in Missouri, Louisiana, or Arkansas Territory would be considered Indian Country. Similar to its predecessors, however, this legislation barely affected Indian trade in the West. Merchants, agents, and Indians recognized the weakness of both its provisions and its enforcement. Although Section 20 of the act created penalties for the sale, exchange, barter, and introduction of alcohol into Indian Country, barrels of whiskey and other substances made their way across the borders in significant amounts. This trade had existed for years, but the manner in which western-based traders conducted their

[38] Louisville Wholesale Prices Current – June 22, 1833, roll 21, CFP; Account of the Sac and Fox Indians with Pratte, Chouteau, and Co., September 1, 1838, roll 25, CFP; Sugar and Miami Creek Trading Posts Account Books, 1839–1849, KSHS.

business demonstrated the very porous nature of government-delineated boundaries.[39]

In the 1830s, traders like those attached to Pierre Chouteau, Jr., and Company garnered tremendous profits by disregarding both the intercourse law and the boundaries created to enforce it. In one loophole, merchants abused the regulations that permitted them to carry a definite amount of alcohol into Indian Territory as provisions for their hired boatmen. But traders who transported whiskey into Indian Country represented only part of the problem. Those who set up shop within Missouri state limits proved just as harmful. By residing within state boundaries, these independent traders operated outside of federal territorial jurisdiction and, therefore, beyond the rule of Indian agents. Whiskey dominated trade along the western Missouri border in Clay and Jackson Counties as a result of this successful business plan. Indian agents felt powerless. "It appears...so long as the Indians are permitted indiscriminately to pass the state lines into the settlements that no effectual provisions can be made," Richard Cummins noted from his desk at Fort Leavenworth. As a result, "Regulations to prevent the Indians and the whites from crossing the state line without a permit – a passport – seems to me to be highly necessary." Although his suggestion may have grown from a real concern, it also appeared slightly unreasonable. Cummins already had problems monitoring the borders, and installing a passport system would not change that reality.[40]

The pervasiveness of alcohol was blamed for more than just the loss of annuities. An equally prevalent critique held this trade responsible for the

[39] To examine the content of the different acts passed by Congress to regulate the Indian trade from 1790 to 1834, see Francis Paul Prucha (Ed.), *Documents of United States Indian Policy* (Lincoln, 1990), 14–15, 17–21, 33–35, 64–68; Francis Paul Prucha, *American Indian Policy in the Formative Years: The Indian Trade and Intercourse Acts* (Cambridge, MA, 1962). For discussions of the alcohol trade prior to the 1830s, see Peter Mancall, "Men, Women, and Alcohol in Indian Villages in the Great Lakes Region in the Early Republic," *Journal of the Early American Republic*, 15(Fall 1995): 425–448; Peter Mancall, *Deadly Medicine: Indians and Alcohol in Early America* (Ithaca, 1995); William E. Unrau, *White Man's Wicked Water: The Alcohol Trade and Prohibition in Indian Country, 1802–1892* (Lawrence, 1996), 1–39.

[40] Richard Cummins to Elbert Herring, CIA, September 30, 1833, OIA-LR, roll 300; Robert Johnson to Richard Cummins, September 2, 1833, OIA-LR, roll 300; H. L. Ellsworth to Elbert Herring, CIA, OIA-LR, roll 300; William Clark, SIA, to Lewis Cass, SOW, December 30, 1832, OIA-LR, roll 750; Lt. Freeman to William Clark, SIA, December 8, 1832, OIA-LR, roll 750; W. Ruland to William Clark, SIA, January 27, 1831, OIA-LR, roll 362; Jeanne P. Leader, "The Pottawatomies and Alcohol: An Illustration of the Illegal Trade," *Kansas History*, 3(Autumn 1979): 157–165.

decline in Indian health and the loss of life. One Methodist missionary stated that although war and disease had taken its toll on some border Indian communities, "ardent spirits have been chiefly instrumental" in the declining populations. In other words, Indians became sick after binging on whiskey or fought and killed one another in drunken brawls. Because the federal government appeared unable to enforce the intercourse laws, missionaries and Indian leaders often worked together to prevent intoxication from hurting native communities. It was usually a difficult proposition. Missionaries encouraged the formation of temperance societies and made a point of punishing converts who were caught in an intoxicated state. Indian leaders also made organized efforts to discourage the consumption of alcohol. As the Delawares settled into their homes on the Kansas River, their national council set out to combat the "most oppressive" evils that threatened the peace and harmony of their community. Alcohol was their first target. Principal Chief Natcoming and the other members of the council worked with Isaac McCoy and Richard Cummins to adopt strict regulations. The Delawares stated that they took this action not "on account of being angry with those who drink, but because they are sorry for them, and wish to make them, and all around them more happy." Both missionaries and native leaders saw alcohol consumption as a problem. Although neither was able to eliminate its presence, they did work to mitigate its negative effects.[41]

Indeed, far more than alcohol consumption was responsible for the high mortality rates among border Indian communities. Despite successful adaptations to a new environment and relative economic stability, the physical health of Indians remained mixed. Though death had struck often along the journey west, few emigrant parties suffered losses like the Wyandots did so soon after their arrival. After the tragedy of that first winter the Wyandots were able to avoid similar widespread outbreaks and three years later they lost only four people, while as a community they welcomed twelve new lives. But the statistics for the Delawares and Shawnees in that same year were somewhat less encouraging. The Shawnee community had thirty-six births in 1847, only five more than the number of deaths. For the Delawares, the disparity was far greater. The thirty-nine births could not counter the lives of the fifty-six Delawares lost over the

---

[41] *Western Christian Advocate*, April 1, 1842. For the dismissal of converts, see Shawnee Baptist Church Records, FBP; Recording Steward's book for Shawnee Mission, Indian Files – Shawnees, Box 6, KSHS; "Two Minute Books of Kansas Missions in the Forties," *Kansas Historical Quarterly*, 2 (August 1933): 227–250; Declaration of the Delaware Indians, October 1838, roll 612, IMP.

course of the year. One explanation for the Delaware mortality rate rests in the number of Delawares who continued to hunt on the western prairies. A party of fifteen Delawares, including the war chief Captain Shawanock, died at the hands of a Sioux and Cheyenne band on the Smoky Hill River in June 1844. Only three years earlier, fourteen Delawares lost their lives in a similar incident in present-day Iowa. Yet, although Delaware hunters and trappers continued these hazardous pursuits into the 1850s, their deaths do not address all the factors affecting native mortality rates.[42]

The border Indians also suffered because of their location. Environmental factors led to isolated outbreaks of disease early on. After the severe floods of 1844, one settlement of Delawares suffered twenty-seven deaths. But instances of epidemics skyrocketed with the growth of American western emigration in the 1840s. The U.S. government made some early attempts to protect the Indians from disease, and in the fall of 1839 Dr. Joseph Prefontaine of Westport vaccinated hundreds of Delawares, Shawnees, and other border Indians against smallpox. Outbreaks of the disease were to be feared especially in the aftermath of the epidemic that had devastated the Mandan, Arikira, and Hidatsa populations on the Missouri just a few years earlier. But other than this particular effort, the few vaccination attempts after 1839 fell far short of the protection necessary for the thousands of Indians who soon lived at the center of American western expansion. The Oregon Trail, Mexican-American War, and California Gold Rush brought tens of thousands of people to the Missouri border towns of Independence, St. Joseph, Kansas, and Westport. Every wagon train that entered the streets and every steamboat that pulled up to the dock increased the chances of disease.[43]

Consequently, it is not surprising that cholera struck along the Missouri and Kansas River settlements almost annually in the years before Kansas became a territory. Estimates of the number of emigrants and gold-seekers who left from Independence, Westport, and other Missouri towns were regularly in the tens of thousands. In 1852, for example, anywhere from twenty-eight to forty thousand people passed through Fort Kearny, one of the primary stops for emigrants on their western journey. Although some members of the Indian communities benefited from this travel either through selling provisions, charging tolls, or running ferries, everyone felt

---

[42] Schoolcraft, *Historical and Statistical Information*, I, 442, 488; Barry, *The Beginning of the West*, 439, 520.

[43] *The Friend: A religious and Literary Journal*, May 3, 1845; Joseph R. S. Prefontaine, M.D., to Major Joshua Pilcher, September 6, 1839, OIA-LR, roll 752; Barry, *The Beginning of the West*, 380.

the impact of the disease that came hand-in-hand with the wagon trains. From April to August in 1849, cholera hit the Missouri border region with force, claiming the lives of at least six Wyandots and eight Delawares. Although the Shawnees were also affected, it was not clear how many died from the disease. Two years later, cholera returned and killed more than forty Delawares. And in February 1852, before the arrival of spring and one more cholera outbreak, smallpox struck the Delaware reserve.[44]

In the years between removal and American expansion into Kansas Territory, the Shawnees, Delawares, Potawatomis, and Wyandots worked hard to adjust to life along the Missouri state line. Although degrees of participation in the border economy varied, few could escape the effects of living in a region of increasing activity and importance. For better and for worse, the border Indians grounded their western existence by becoming active members of the Missouri border community.

Removal had both an immediate and an enduring impact on eastern Indians in the 1830s and 1840s. The emotional portion of the dislocation can be described but not quantified. It is different with the Indians' material existence. Many native emigrants left behind fields and homes. In some cases, they had to abandon substantial amounts of accumulated property. The journey west created serious health problems and upon arrival at their final destination the Shawnees, Delawares, Potawatomis, and Wyandots often lacked proper housing and adequate provisions. All of the above complicated and hindered their ability to adapt to life in eastern Kansas. Although these legacies of removal remained, the eastern Indians worked hard to overcome the obstacles presented by a new environment.

The transitions that occurred in the two decades after removal, although often difficult to trace, marked significant developments. Most important, by blending together customary practices and the opportunities provided by the regional economy, individuals, families, and communities built a foundation for life west of the Mississippi. Past experience grounded their survival and the willingness to take advantage of border life showcased their adaptations. And as they gradually settled into their new homes, the Shawnees, Delawares, Potawatomis, and Wyandots assumed new positions as border Indians. By the early 1850s, however, they also knew full well the downside of their location. The same market that allowed Indians to sell surplus produce provided the alcohol that invaded native

---

[44] For estimates of western emigrants, see Barry, *The Beginning of the West*, 863, 871, 933, 1078, 1084. For disease outbreaks, see ibid., 829–830, 864, 878, 1010–1011.

communities. The same wagon trains whose toll money supplemented Indian incomes brought diseases and death. In the end, the very border that provided economic opportunities to Indian men and women was also a porous boundary that could not contain the forces of American expansion ready to overwhelm the Indian reserves created by treaty only decades earlier.

4

Eastern Council Fires in the West

In June 1843, more than four thousand Indians from twenty-two different tribes gathered in council at Tahlequah, the capital of the Cherokee Nation west of the Mississippi. Cherokees, Creeks, Delawares, Shawnees, Wyandots, Iowas, Osages, and others filled an encampment that sprawled across the grasslands adjacent to the enclosed council grounds built only a few years earlier. Over the course of several weeks, the delegates ate, socialized, played stick ball, and reaffirmed relationships that in many cases extended back across the Mississippi. Once assembled around the council fire, they discussed peace and the future. In an opening speech made in Creek and translated into English, Roly McIntosh, head chief of the western Creeks, declared the council's intentions in simple terms. "Brothers," he began, "we are met together to renew our forefathers' talk. It was made in the East. It has been brought to the West. Yet every day we assemble here we attend to it as well as we know how." During the next several days, McIntosh and the other delegates did more than renew past relationships. They also considered an accord that would structure their alliance in more specific terms. Eight different resolutions proposed everything from a ban on alcohol to the adjudication of intertribal murder. As a safeguard against future removals the third article declared that no Indian nation in the West would sell any part of its present territory without the consent of the other nations who were party to the agreement. This latter resolution required no explanation. Despite their recent removal experiences, however, only a few delegates assented to the terms and signed the final accord. When the council ended, the delegates returned to their homes. The proposed confederacy never emerged.[1]

[1] Rev. William H. Goode, *Outposts of Zion, with Limnings of Mission Life* (Cincinnati, 1864), 69–75; Grant Foreman, *Advancing the Frontier, 1830–1860* (Norman, 1933), 205–216; Compact of Great Council of 1843, OIA-LR, roll 215.

FIGURE 3. International Indian Council (Held at Talequah, Indian Territory, in 1843) by John Mix Stanley. (Courtesy of the Smithsonian American Art Museum, Gift of the Misses Henry.)

The 1843 council highlighted the persistence of native diplomacy. Delegates worked with the tools and traditions they had carried with them across the Mississippi, and relied on wampum, kinship, ritual, and council fires to help organize life in their new environment. By bringing together so many transplanted Indian communities, the Tahlequah council and others like it recreated a network that once reached from the shores of Lake Michigan to the woodlands of the Gulf Coast and throughout the trans-Appalachian region. Around the rekindled flames the representatives spoke of days past and of alliances that grounded their relationships. In the process, they resisted the attempts of the U.S. government to impose its own authority and structures on inter-Indian affairs.

However, these western councils demonstrated the persistence of more than just diplomatic traditions. They revealed that obstacles to a pan-Indian league also survived the journey across the Mississippi. For the better part of three decades, efforts to use traditional diplomacy in the West met mixed success. The Osages, Pawnees, and other western Indians proved the most intransigent. But the difficulties were not confined to the divide between the removed Indians and their western counterparts. Alliance building among the eastern Indian communities had never happened easily. Even dependable relationships required maintenance over time, a point Roly McIntosh emphasized in his speech at Tahlequah. In the end, the failed confederacies of the 1840s showed weaknesses similar to those of the late eighteenth and early nineteenth centuries. They employed custom and ritual to weave together what were, at times, divergent agendas. And they splintered when traditional practices were no longer enough to bridge those differences.

Ironically, the external threats that helped bring about the councils in the 1840s were the same ones that created fractures within the proposed alliances. For those communities living on the Missouri state line, in particular, every wagon train heading west deepened the reality of American expansion. Just as intrusive and informative were the government proposals first to create a separate Indian territory and then to organize the western territories for settlement. Although it is difficult to know the exact reasoning behind every decision made in reference to the proposed confederacies, by 1854 one point was clear. Rather than depend on traditional alliances, most Indians on the border chose to negotiate the next wave of American expansion in isolation.

Inter-Indian diplomacy in the Great Lakes region from the 1760s onward revealed that confederacies of the past did not guarantee alliances in the present or future. The foundations and rituals of alliance remained the same. Native diplomats used wampum to communicate and open negotiations for peace or war. Kinship terms and relations remained important and eastern Indians preserved the symbolic language of diplomacy. But the confederacies formed in the Great Lakes region from the 1760s to the 1810s were dynamic relationships built upon the changing nature of village politics and formed in response to the fluctuations in imperial rivalries and agendas. As the specific reasons for unified actions changed, the membership and shape of the confederacy changed, and a Shawnee band that allied to fight against American forces in the 1790s did not always do so in the 1800s. Conventional diplomatic practices provided a useful and necessary foundation in a world where the politics of Indian leaders and communities did not always stay the same.

Custom and ritual had always been crucial elements of eastern Indian diplomacy. Relationships were cultivated and maintained through the proper use of material and linguistic elements, what Richard White has termed the "sinews" of diplomacy. In the fall of 1792, a grand council convened at the Glaize, the multiethnic headquarters for Ohio Indian resistance to American expansion in the late eighteenth century. Shawnee and Miami leaders, who had called the council, presented the calumet pipe to each delegate to smoke prior to any speech. Their ritual use of the calumet, a practice whose origins can be traced westward to the Great Plains, had a significance that cannot be overstated. "The respect attached to the peace pipe in Indian diplomacy," Robert Williams writes, "elevated the temporal agreement represented by a treaty to the realm of sacred obligation." By sharing the pipe, all present gave the discussions that followed a divine importance. Belts and strings of wampum were other instruments used to initiate negotiations, finalize agreements, and record history. Shell colors and designs indicated war and peace, while more intricate belts often presented the history between two nations. The very language of diplomacy among eastern Indians also had a distinct importance that traced back to the condolence ceremony of the Iroquois and the Great League of Peace. In opening remarks, native diplomats spoke of wiping the eyes clean and clearing a path, ritualized and crucial actions that prepared the assembled individuals for the work ahead. Also ingrained in this conventional diplomatic language were kinship terms that structured relations among the Indian communities. Kinship helped define mutual obligations, and in councils eastern Indians used the language of kinship to both reaffirm connections and create fictive kin.[2]

Kinship terms structured clearly delineated relationships among eastern Indians. For example, the Shawnees referred to the Delawares as grandfathers and the Wyandots as elder brothers. They most commonly used the term brothers to describe their relations with others, with some considered younger and others older. This relationship implied a level of equality while simultaneously creating special duties. Most eastern Indians

[2] Richard White, *The Middle Ground: Indians, Empires, and Republics in the Great Lakes Region, 1650–1815* (New York, 1991), 20–23, 93; Brigadier General E. A. Cruikshank (Ed.), *The Correspondence of Lieut. Governor John Graves Simcoe* (5 vols., Toronto, 1923), I, 218–229; Donald J. Blakeslee, "The Origin and Spread of the Calumet Ceremony," *American Antiquity*, 46(Oct. 1981): 759–768; Robert A. Williams, Jr., *Linking Arms Together: American Indian Treaty Visions of Law and Peace, 1600–1800* (New York, 1997), 40–61. The foundation of these practices in Iroquois diplomacy is discussed in Daniel K. Richter and James H. Merrell (Eds.), *Beyond the Covenant Chain: The Iroquois and Their Neighbors in Indian North America, 1600–1800* (Syracuse, 1987); Francis Jennings, William Fenton, Mary A. Druke, and David R. Miller (Eds.), *The History and Culture of Iroquois Diplomacy: An Interdisciplinary Guide to the Treaties of the Six Nations and Their League* (Syracuse, 1985); Daniel Richter, *The Ordeal of the Longhouse: The Peoples of the Iroquois League in the Era of European Colonization* (Chapel Hill, 1992), 30–49.

understood that an elder brother would have the responsibility of taking care of and protecting his younger sibling. The Delawares confirmed their status as grandfathers and, in the early 1820s, declared that only the Wyandots and Senecas did not defer to them as such. Accordingly, the Delawares referred to every other tribe as grandchildren. This honored position apparently originated in an agreement reached centuries earlier. "The Delawares...are our Grandfathers," explained the Stockbridge Indian Hendrick Aupaumut, "according to the ancient covenant of their and our ancestors, to which we adhere without any deviation in these near 200 years." Although the designation of grandfather indicated respect and a close relation, it did not necessarily make the Delawares the most powerful or influential when numerous groups met in council. Indeed, the Shawnee Prophet accorded to the Wyandots the greatest influence, most likely in recognition of their status as keepers of the northern fire.[3]

By tending the council fire, the Wyandots had charge of a vital diplomatic and political entity. As another element of diplomacy, fire had a utility far beyond its use in cooking and heating. It could also be a sign of welcome, a burning symbol of hospitality. When describing the Great League of Peace for the Iroquois, Deganawidah had declared that the fire must be kept burning to guide those nations who wanted to follow the way of peace. But the council fire also had political connotations. During the treaty councils at Greenville in 1795, the Miami chief Little Turtle described the boundaries of Miami lands in the Ohio Valley. "My forefather kindled the first fire at Detroit," he explained, "from thence he extended his lines to the Scioto." Little Turtle went on to trace the remaining boundaries, working out from the fire that first defined the Miamis' settlement in the region. Fire could also be a political identifier, as illustrated by the United Band of Potawatomis, Ottawas, and Ojibways, who referred to themselves as the People of the Three Fires. "We three are faithful allies," explained Mashipinashiwish, an Ojibway chief, "and one

---

[3] Hendrick Aupaumut quoted in Daniel G. Brinton, *The Lenape and their Legends: With the Complete Text and Symbols of the Walam Olum* (New York, 1969), 113; Vernon Kinietz and Erminie W. Voegelin (Eds.), *Shawnese Traditions: C. C. Trowbridge's Account* (Ann Arbor, 1939), 9, 55. For descriptions of kinship terms, see C.A. Weslager, *The Delaware Indian Westward Migration* (Wallingford, PA, 1978), 125–126; Rev. Jedidiah Morse, *A Report to the Secretary of War of the United States on Indian Affairs* (New Haven, 1822), appendix, 141–143; Williams, Jr., *Linking Arms Together*, 72–74; Richard White, "The Fictions of Patriarchy," in Frederick Hoxie, Ronald Hoffman, and Peter J. Albert (Eds.), *Native Americans and the Early Republic* (Charlottesville, VA, 1999), 68–69.

of us speaks for the whole, when in council." Although united as one politically, the three maintained distinct identities in their separate fires. This latter imagery translated well in talks with American officials. Over the course of the same council at Greenville, native speakers repeatedly referred to the United States as the Fifteen Fires, for the fifteen states that comprised the Union.[4]

Council fires in the 1700s and early 1800s gathered Indians from all points in the Great Lakes and the Southeast. From the Scioto councils in the late 1760s to Tecumseh's diplomatic tours from 1809 to 1811, Shawnees, Creeks, Cherokees, Miamis, Delawares, Wyandots, and others met often and maintained open lines of communication during some of the most unstable and violent decades of the colonial era. The bridge between the northern and southern Indians was a relatively recent construction because the Cherokees in particular had warred with the Delawares, Wyandots, and Shawnees at different times during the first half of the eighteenth century. The northern confederacy had a longer history with a council fire centered at Brownstown, the Wyandot village just south of Detroit. This Brownstown fire centered an alliance that had always included Wyandots, Delawares, Shawnees, Potawatomis, Ottawas, Miamis, and Ojibways. "You know that we, the seven nations, have always been of one opinion," the Shawnee headman Blue Jacket reminded those present at the Greenville Council. "You know also, that our uncles [Wyandots] have always taken care of the great fire; they being the oldest nation." More than fifty years later Wyandot delegates at a council held on the Delaware reserve in Kansas affirmed that relationship. James Washington and John Hicks stated that among these seven tribes peaceful relations had existed "from time immemorial" and they had once held all of their hunting territories in common. Although these descriptions of eternal peace and shared hunting grounds had an air of diplomatic hyperbole, they were rooted in a solid legacy. Conflicts had occurred in the past, but the Brownstown fire helped stabilize relations among these communities for decades, if not centuries.[5]

4 Williams, Jr., *Linking Arms Together*, 96–97; Kinietz and Voegelin, *Shawnese Traditions*, 55–57; Minutes of a Treaty with the Indian Tribes...at Greenville, in *ASPIA*, I, 564–583; Donald L. Fixico, "The Alliance of the Three Fires in Trade and War, 1630–1812," *Michigan Historical Review*, 20(Fall 1994): 1–23.

5 Gregory Evans Dowd, *A Spirited Resistance: The North American Indian Struggle for Unity, 1745–1815* (Baltimore, 1992), 42–44; Helen Hornbeck Tanner, "The Glaize in 1792: A Composite Indian Community," *Ethnohistory*, 25(Winter 1978): 15–39; Emma Helen Blair (Ed.), *The Indian Tribes of the Upper Mississippi Valley and Region of the*

Although founded on historical relationships, these alliances were also products of specific cultural, political, and geographic contexts. Conflict and migration in the Ohio Valley affected the composition of the regional native population and thus altered the makeup of alliances over time. The confederacies were drawn from the people at hand, and over the course of the early 1700s bands of Shawnees, Delawares, and Wyandots migrated to the region and settled alongside the Miamis and others who lived along the rivers that coursed through present-day western Pennsylvania, southern Michigan, Ohio, and Indiana. At times the population of these multiethnic villages was as varied as the politics. "The Revolution and the Indian wars that followed," Richard White has explained, "were imperial contests for dominance in the region, but they were also village struggles for power. The particular interests of villages and factions within villages had as much to do with ultimate loyalties as did the imperial rivalry between the United States and Britain." More to the point, although Indians of similar sentiments usually lived near each other, proximity did not always lead to unity.[6]

Shawnee participation in the confederacies of the 1790s and 1800s exemplified these fluctuations. The Shawnees actively defended their country north of the Ohio River during and after the 1760s. At the Glaize in the early 1790s, which Helen Hornbeck Tanner has described as "the headquarters for the militant Indian confederacy," the Shawnees were among those who took the lead. When Messquakeno, or Painted Pole, the Shawnee speaker, opened the council held in September 1792, he noted that, "I am one of those appointed by the unanimous choice of the Delawares, Shawanoes, Miamies, Chippaways, Ottawas, Hurons, Munseys . . . and all the Western Confederacy who are now going to speak

---

Great Lakes (Lincoln, 1996), II, 188–190; John Sugden, "Tecumseh's Travels Revisited," *Indiana Magazine of History* 96(June 2000): 151–168; John Sugden, "Early Pan-Indianism: Tecumseh's Tour of the Indian Country," *American Indian Quarterly,* 10(Fall 1986): 273–304; Henry R. Schoolcraft, *Notes on the Iroquois* (East Lansing, 2002), 157–165; Minutes of a Treaty with the Indian Tribes . . . at Greenville, *ASPIA, I,* 573; Journal of the Proceedings of the Great Council October 10–14, 1848, WNP.

6 White, *The Middle Ground,* 367; James H. Merrell, *Into the American Woods: Negotiators on the Pennsylvania Frontier* (New York, 1999); Tanner, "The Glaize in 1792," 15–39; Helen Hornbeck Tanner (Ed.), *Atlas of Great Lakes Indian History* (Norman, 1987), 29–83. For additional insight into the complicated world of the Ohio Valley in the late eighteenth and early nineteenth centuries, see Dowd, *A Spirited Resistance*; Gregory Evans Dowd, *War Under Heaven: Pontiac, The Indian Nations and The British Empire* (Baltimore, 2002); Randolph C. Downes, *Council Fires on the Upper Ohio: A Narrative of Indian Affairs in the Upper Ohio Valley until 1795* (Pittsburgh, 1940); R. David Edmunds, *The Shawnee Prophet* (Lincoln, 1983).

to you." Blue Jacket, Snake, and Captain Johnny all had towns in the vicinity of the Glaize in 1792, and of the three Shawnee leaders, Blue Jacket was one of the most involved in this confederacy. He had carried the calumet and speeches of alliance to the Indians farther west in the months leading up to the Glaize council, and he was the principal war chief among the Shawnees. After the final defeat of this military alliance at the hands of General Anthony Wayne in 1794 and the signing of the Treaty of Greenville in 1795, Blue Jacket moved north. Leaving behind the settlements in Ohio, Blue Jacket and his band established a town south of Detroit, where he lived until the outbreak of the War of 1812. Black Hoof, another prominent Shawnee leader during the confederacies of the 1790s, abandoned the cause of military resistance after the Greenville Treaty. In the 1800s, he led Shawnee opposition to Tenskwatawa when the Shawnee Prophet continued the military resistance against the United States.[7]

Military defeats and negotiated treaties ended the efforts of most Indian confederacies formed during the late eighteenth and early nineteenth centuries and centered in the Great Lakes region. But although these defeats often scattered the structures of each particular alliance, the diplomatic tradition continued as a reliable means for shaping and stabilizing the world in which they lived. Ritual, language, and kinship remained both important and useful. When military resistance ended east of the Mississippi and the bands of Delawares, Shawnees, Potawatomis, and Wyandots headed west, they carried the history and rituals of these relationships with them.[8]

Two obstacles complicated the initial transfer of these diplomatic traditions to the western territories. First, the eastern Indians eventually settled on lands once claimed by longer established western tribes like the Kansas, Pawnees, and Osages. On the one hand, this hostility helped forge the defensive alliances of Cherokees, Shawnees, and Delawares in the 1810s and 1820s. But in the 1830s, and after, the hostilities tended to be more isolated. For the Delawares in particular, the location of their reserve and

---

[7] Dowd, *A Spirited Resistance*, 103–109; Tanner, "The Glaize in 1792"; "Indian Council at the Glaize, 1792," in Cruikshank, *The Correspondence of Lieut. Governor John Graves Simcoe, I*, 219; Tanner, *Atlas of Great Lakes Indian History*, 87–91; Sugden, *Blue Jacket: Warrior of the Shawnees* (Lincoln, 2000); Edmunds, *The Shawnee Prophet*, 15–21.

[8] For the military defeats of these confederacies, see Dowd, *A Spirited Resistance*, 90–115, 183–190; White, *The Middle Ground*, 454–468; Edmunds, *The Shawnee Prophet*; Daniel K. Richter, *Facing East from Indian Country: A Native History of Early America* (Cambridge, MA, 2001), 223–235.

their continued reliance on hunting for food and trade meant that the
traditions of inter-Indian diplomacy were often pushed aside by the practices of intertribal warfare. The presence and actions of federal officials
presented a second obstacle to the geographic transfer of customary practices. Indian agents had orders to mediate inter-Indian relations, and their
interference seldom improved the situation, at least from the perspective
of the Indians themselves. Whereas Spanish officials had once attempted
to use the eastern Indians as both a buffer and a militia, American agents
in the nineteenth century hoped to avoid conflict and advocated peace.
But the band of Delawares under the leadership of Chief Anderson, or
Kikthawenund, had trouble securing a peaceful resolution. To counter
the violence arising from competition over animals and disagreements
over boundaries, the Delawares used all available resources, supplement-
ing customary diplomatic practices with the efforts of federal agents in
the region. More often than not, they had more faith in their established
practices.[9]

American treaty commissioners negotiated several land cessions with
western tribes in the early nineteenth century. They hoped that at the very
least these accords would defuse tensions created during and after the
years of Spanish governance. Commissioners began with the Osages, who
at the time of the Louisiana Purchase laid claim to a territory that spanned
present-day Missouri, southeastern Kansas, Oklahoma, and northwestern
Arkansas. They had acquired much of their domain by conquest, and
had controlled the flow of goods between other western Indians and the
Spanish, British, and French traders. But the Osages had also split into
three primary bands in the eighteenth century, and these gradual divisions
along with their connections to the Chouteaus made it easier for the United
States to negotiate only with those willing to cede land. Over the course of
three treaties, held in 1808, 1818, and 1825, respectively, willing leaders
signed away almost the entirety of the Osage territory. Only a day after
the Osages signed the 1825 treaty, White Plume and other headmen of the
Kansas put their marks on a similar accord. In this agreement, the Kansas
gave up claims to all lands lying within the state of Missouri, as well as
those that encompassed most of northeastern Kansas. The four primary
Pawnee bands, the Grand, the Tappaye, the Loups, and the Republicans,

---

[9] For a discussion of the defensive alliance of the Delawares, Shawnees, and Cherokees, see
Chapter 1, as well as Stephen Warren, *The Shawnees and Their Neighbors, 1795–1870*
(Urbana, 2005), 85–96.

whose range included much of present-day Nebraska, did not cede any land until 1833.[10]

The influx of Indian and American settlers undermined the federal government's expectations of neatly bounded territories in the West. In the late 1700s, hunting and war parties from the Delawares and Osages clashed near the Cape Girardeau villages just west of the Mississippi River. Instead of decreasing the violence, the passage of time and the negotiation of treaties only changed the venue for conflict. American settlements in Missouri extended further into the interior, which in turn forced the Delawares and Shawnees closer to the Osages. Trouble flared any time Delaware hunters encountered their Osage counterparts in southwestern Missouri. The Osages disputed treaty resolutions and declared that they had not ceded hunting rights, a claim that only increased their ill will toward the Delawares and the hundreds of Shawnees and Cherokees who moved in advance of white settlers. Just as problematic was the fact that boundaries drawn on paper were far less visible in reality. The Osages "could not see the invisible line running from Fort Osage on the Missouri River to the Arkansas," Osage historian John Joseph Matthews explains, "any better than the Cherokees and free men hunters could see it." Shawnee and Delaware eyes did not serve them any better when it came to those same treaty lines.[11]

As the violence continued, Delaware and Osage leaders made an attempt to augment the government accords with a separate agreement. In June 1822, less than a year after leaving Indiana, Kikthawenund's band of several hundred Delawares participated in a council intended to quell the hostilities. The recent emigrants had encamped just south of the Jack's Fork River, only a short distance from the other Delaware villages on the Current River. Kikthawenund and other Delaware leaders worked with representatives from the Big and Little Osage bands to establish regulations to govern the competition over hunting grounds in the Ozarks. In the end, they turned to the U.S. government and, more specifically, to Superintendent of Indian Affairs William Clark. According to their final agreement, Clark had the authority to arbitrate any subsequent claims

---

[10] Willard H. Rollings, *The Osage: An Ethnohistorical Study of Hegemony on the Prairie-Plains* (Columbia, MO, 1992), 68, 215–254; *Indian Affairs*, II, 95–99, 167–168, 217–225, 416–418.

[11] Lynn Morrow, "Trader William Gillis and Delaware Migration in Southern Missouri," *Missouri Historical Review*, 75(January 1981): 147–167; John Joseph Matthews, *The Osages: Children of the Middle Waters* (Norman, 1961), 420.

made by the Delawares and Osages against each other. Three years later, headmen from both communities affirmed that "differences have unhappily arisen" and required restitution.[12]

Neither the nominal authority of Clark nor the paper authority of the treaties halted the conflicts between the Delawares and the Osages. By the mid-1820s, approximately twenty-five hundred Delawares lived in the Ozark region. Kikthawenund had assumed the position of principal chief among the combined Delaware bands, and he had moved with his people to the James and White rivers in southwestern Missouri. This westward migration of thousands of Indians, including Shawnees and Cherokees, placed an even greater strain on the deer, beaver, and buffalo populations in a region once hunted primarily by the Osages. The declining game only made the violence worse. Then in September 1825, someone killed Kikthawenund's son, and Delaware hunters reported seeing the dead man's horse in an Osage village. This damning evidence initiated a cycle of violence that resulted in the deaths of at least eight more Delawares and six Osages over the next eight months. The dead included men, women, and children. As spring arrived Kikthawenund and his people made a final decision. They prepared for war. When subagent John Campbell visited Kikthawenund's village in May, he found an assemblage of local Indians discussing a possible alliance against the Osages. Weeks earlier, five Delaware hunters had died at the hands of fifty Osages. Most important, however, Kikthawenund no longer led the Delawares. He stated that the "War Captains and Young Men had become so clamorous, that he could no longer restrain them." Preparations now belonged to these men, who were "determined to carry on the war." As a civil leader, Kikthawenund's voice now receded to the background. Although Campbell believed he had convinced the Delaware war leaders to stay peaceful for the moment, he had little confidence that their patience would last.[13]

In the weeks that followed, it became clear that the decision for war and the ascension of the war chiefs reflected the Delawares' growing frustration with the U.S. government's failure to bring peace to the region. Although the Osages wanted American officials to mediate the conflict, the

---

[12] Delaware chiefs, Big and Little Osage chiefs to William Clark, June 7, 1825, OIA-LR, roll 631; William Clark to Secretary of War, March 27, 1825, OIA-LR, roll 747; Osage agent to William Clark, March 14, 1825, OIA-LR, roll 747.

[13] Morrow, "Trader William Gillis," 151–157; Pierre Menard to William Clark, February 15, 1824, RGP; Statement of Chief Anderson, May 29, 1826, OIA-LR, roll 300; Richard Graham to William Clark, May 29, 1826, OIA-LR, roll 747; John Campbell to Col. M. Arbuckle, May 24, 1826, OIA-LR, roll 300.

Delawares no longer saw a reason for outside arbitration. Killbuck, one of the Delaware war chiefs, declared that he "regretted to [the] Interference of his G. Father, that if they had been left alone, they would have had peace w/the Osages before this." He expressed a common belief. Many of the Delawares had no desire to comply with government requests simply to settle with the Osages, and others stated in council that they had agreed previously to treat with the Osages only to please the federal government. "The idea of throwing United States troops between them and the Osages was treated lightly," observed Thomas Johnston at Cantonment Gibson, "not . . . from any contempt they had of Government, but they had taken a Stand – had made choice of two evils, reckless of consequences." What Johnston labeled as evil, the Delawares viewed as a viable alternative. For the previous 8 months, and for years before that, they had attempted to work with American officials and restrained their desire for war. Now they had decided to solve the problem away from American councils. Although they respected the power held by the U.S. government and its representatives, the Delawares still believed that their difficulties would be more adequately handled within their own framework. More than that, they believed federal efforts had only confused and lengthened the hostilities. Despite the rumblings, the Delawares did not launch an all-out war against the Osages in 1826. Neither did they reach a settlement, which meant sporadic violence continued to present problems for both communities.[14]

When the Delawares agreed to relocate from their villages in southwest Missouri to a reserve north of the Kansas River in 1829, they did not escape the battles over territory. The very nature of the Indian settlements in eastern Kansas in the 1830s fostered antagonism. Borders established by removal treaties transformed the region into a veritable patchwork quilt on contemporary maps, and incidents of theft and intimidation abounded as the western Indians refused to stand aside while outsiders took over their lands. Residents of the Peoria, Piankeshaw, and Wea villages on the Osage River complained that parties of Kansas Indians stole their tools and that the Osages "would not let our women gather pecans . . . they drove them away, and told them that the land was theirs." The actions of the Osages in particular proved problematic for the Delaware and

---

[14] William Clark to SOW Barbour, June 11, 1826, OIA-LR, roll 747; Richard Graham to William Clark, May 29, 1826, OIA-LR, roll 747; Thomas Johnston to Colonel Arbuckle, June 7, 1826, OIA-LR, roll 300; R. S. Callaway to Major Chouteau, December 24, 1840, OIA-LR, roll 301; C. A. Weslager, *The Delaware Indians: A History* (New Brunswick, NJ, 1972), 363–366.

Shawnee hunters still involved in the fur trade. In 1831 alone, members of the Big and Little Osage bands stole beaver and otter skins from a party of Delawares emigrating to Kansas and took a number of horses, beaver traps, and assorted furs from both Delaware and Shawnee settlements. Despite the long history between the Osages and the eastern Indians, Agent P. L. Chouteau concluded that opportunity, not hostility, explained the thefts. In other words, because Osages, Delawares, Shawnees, Kickapoos, Creeks, and Cherokees had settled in such close quarters, some amount of conflict was to be expected.[15]

Although simple proximity may partially explain the conflicts, the battle over hunting grounds remained the prominent reason for hostilities. And for Delaware residents of the Kansas reserve, problems with the Pawnees quickly overshadowed any lingering hostility toward the Osages. The Delawares' 1829 treaty established a hunting outlet extending westward from their reservation in eastern Kansas, which consisted of a tract of land ten miles wide and approximately two hundred miles long. Treaty commissioners crafted the outlet to allow the Delawares access to better hunting on the western plains. But the scarcity of game in the region often forced Delaware hunters to venture beyond the prescribed boundaries and north into the Platte River valley. Both the outlet and these intrusions into the Platte River region bothered the Pawnees, and they complained to their agent about the Delaware trespasses. They also delivered a more forceful response to unwanted intrusions. In the winter of 1829, Pawnees killed three Delaware hunters on the Republican River north of the present Kansas–Nebraska border. Although the Pawnees claimed they did not know the tribal identity of the hunters, many Delawares viewed the deaths as a direct act of hostility. Kikthawenund appealed to U.S. officials in an attempt to calm the waters, but the death of two young Delaware men at the hands of Pawnee hunters early in 1831 made that job more difficult.[16]

As the situation worsened, Kikthawenund took the initiative and made the first gesture of peace. In April 1831, the Delaware principal chief requested Indian agent John Dougherty to contact the Pawnees. More specifically, he gave the agent wampum and a message that the Delawares wanted "to cultivate and maintain with them the most strict and friendly

---

[15] Senate Document No. 512, 23rd Congress, 1st Session, Serial No. 245, 115; P. L. Chouteau to Captain Pryor, March 12, 1831, OIA-LR, roll 631; P. L. Chouteau to William Clark, SIA, April 6, 1831, OIA-LR, roll 631; P. L. Chouteau to brother, April 30, 1831, CFP; *Indian Affairs*, II, 167–168, 217–225.

[16] *Indian Affairs*, II, 304–305; John Dougherty to Gen. William Clark, July 22, 1831, OIA-LR, roll 300.

intercourse." By using Dougherty, as opposed to a Delaware messenger, Kikthawenund hoped to avoid any further misunderstandings or violence. He had every expectation that the agent would understand the gravity of the task. As of late July, however, the wampum remained in Dougherty's possession and the message of peace had not been delivered. Although he tried to explain this delay to his superiors, Dougherty had a more difficult time explaining his inaction to Suwaunock, Kikthawenund's son. Suwaunock visited Cantonment Leavenworth in July with forty other Delawares. The assembled party spoke to the agent and expressed their dislike of the Pawnees. Knowing that his efforts only slightly appeased the Delaware delegation, Dougherty finally delivered the wampum in early October, catching the Pawnees in their villages between the summer and fall hunts. They accepted the Delaware message of peace in good faith. Through Dougherty, the Pawnee headmen told the Delawares "that they would hold fast the wampum Anderson [Kikthawenund] had sent them, until he, or some of his people should call at their village." Unfortunately, Kikthawenund would not be the one to visit the Pawnees. Around the same time Dougherty delivered the wampum, the Delaware principal chief, who was in his eighties, died in his home on the Kansas reserve.[17]

Despite the exchange of wampum, and perhaps because of Kikthawenund's death, negotiations between the Delawares and Pawnees fell apart over the next 9 months. Before Dougherty returned from the Pawnee village, Suwaunock left the Kansas reserve with several other Delawares on a trapping expedition that took them through the disputed country north of the outlet. They encountered a party of Pawnees, and three Delawares died in the subsequent battle. One of those killed was Poushees, or The Cat, a Delaware headman and another one of Kikthawenund's sons. Suwaunock returned to the Kansas reserve with a renewed hatred for the Pawnees and a disdain for negotiation. Captain Patterson had succeeded Kikthawenund as principal chief, and he and the other civil leaders argued for restraint. They visited Richard Cummins at his agency at the end of February 1832 and requested that Cummins send out a call to council to the Osages, Kansas, Pawnees, and other Indian tribes in the region. The Delawares wanted to ensure that "the Different Nations may have a proper

---

[17] John Dougherty to General William Clark, July 22, 1831, OIA-LR, roll 300; John Dougherty to Major Cummins, October 21, 1831, Indian Papers, Box 2, MHS; John Dougherty to Major Cummins, November 10, 1831, ibid; J. P. Cabanne to Pierre Chouteau, Jr., September 18, 1831, roll 18, CFP; John Dougherty to Gen. William Clark, November 9, 1831, OIA-LR, roll 300.

understanding with each other." Suwaunock had other plans. The son of the man who had sent wampum to the Pawnees in 1831 led a war party north in June 1832 and destroyed the Grand Pawnee village on the Republican River. Not only did the Delawares kill the Pawnees not out hunting, but they also burned every lodge to the ground. "I found it [the Pawnee village] filled with lodges," Suwaunock later boasted. "I left it a heap of ashes." This devastating blow attracted the full attention of the U.S. government. Shortly thereafter, Indian Commissioner Henry L. Ellsworth negotiated a truce between the two tribes. Then, in an agreement intended to end all disputes over hunting territories, the Pawnees ceded all claims to lands south of the Platte River in 1833. Despite these two agreements, Delaware and Pawnee hunting parties skirmished often in the years that followed.[18]

The Delawares fought with the Osages, Pawnees, Otoes, and Dakota Sioux well into the 1840s. But they never abandoned familiar notions of diplomacy. From the Delaware perspective, especially Suwaunock's, American officials seldom proved effective in their assumed roles as mediators, protectors, and disciplinarians. For Kikthawenund's band, therefore, the native framework for peace and war proved more reliable. The desire for a general council in 1832 revealed that the Delaware civil leaders, despite the failures in the past, still believed peaceful negotiations and the traditional tools of Indian diplomacy had authority and utility west of the Mississippi. But other Delaware leaders did not hesitate to use force. Suwaunock described the Delaware position succinctly in the summer of 1840. It had been a year since his people first sought justice for the death of two Delaware men at the hands of Otoe hunters and their patience had worn thin. The Delawares would wait a little longer "to see if he [the Secretary of War] will make the Otoes settle the difficulty," the war chief informed Richard Cummins, "and if that is not done they will then take satisfaction in their own way." This statement summarized the Delaware strategy for interactions with the western Indians. Although American

---

[18] John Dougherty to Major Cummins, October 21, 1831, Indian Papers, Box 2, MHS; John Dougherty to Major Cummins, November 10, 1831, ibid.; John Dougherty to Gen. William Clark, November 9, 1831, OIA-LR, roll 300; Richard Cummins to Gen. William Clark, March 1, 1832, OIA-LR, roll 300; William Clark to SOW, April 24, 1832, OIA-LR, roll 300; Major Dougherty to William Clark, SIA, June 8, 1836, OIA-LR, roll 215. Suwaunock made his statement in a council attended by John Treat Irving. See John Treat Irving, *Indian Sketches Taken During an Expedition to the Pawnee Tribes [1833]*, edited by John Francis McDermott (Norman, 1955), 247. A description of the council can be found in ibid., 241–250; Weslager, *The Delaware Indians*, 377–378; *Indian Affairs, II*, 304–305, 416–418.

officials served a purpose in inter-Indian relations, they were subordinate to customary Delaware practices.[19]

Kikthawenund's band of Delawares played a prominent role in inter-Indian affairs of the 1820s and early 1830s because they, along with the Missouri Shawnees and Western Cherokees, crossed the Mississippi River before other eastern Indian communities. By the late 1830s, however, that situation and the direction of inter-Indian diplomacy had changed. Less than a decade after the passage of the Indian Removal Act, nearly ten thousand eastern Indians had relocated to the western territories from their homes in the Great Lakes region. In contrast to the late eighteenth century, the settlements of these eastern transplants now rested along the western borders of Missouri and Arkansas Territory. Using the legacy of their former alliances as a foundation, eastern Indians attempted to recover from the dislocation caused by removal. Together, it seemed, the Delawares, Shawnees, Cherokees, Creeks, and others would work through their problems and organize their lives within a familiar framework.

Yet each attempt to unite the interests of these border communities foundered as the threat of American expansion into the western territories became more palpable. Conflict with western Indians remained a concern. Shortly after removal, however, most eastern Indians recognized the need to prepare for the next wave of American settlers and treaty commissioners. Indeed, the various calls to organize the Indian lands west of the Missouri border in the 1840s and 1850s only confirmed what thousands of Americans heading to California and Oregon had suggested – Indian reserves west of the Mississippi would soon come under attack. It was a common threat that ultimately failed to generate a united response. Although the instruments of traditional diplomacy consistently brought border Indians to the council grounds, they were not strong enough to keep them there.

The first calls for an inter-Indian peace council originated from the southeastern Indians living just north of the confluence of the Canadian and Arkansas rivers in present-day eastern Oklahoma. Before the Trail of Tears brought John Ross and the bulk of the eastern Cherokee population west of the Mississippi, the Western Cherokees, or Old Settlers, invited representatives from the unified band of Shawnees and Senecas,

---

[19] Richard Cummins to Major Joshua Pilcher, August 30, 1840, OIA-LR, roll 301. For conflicts with the Sioux, see Richard Cummins to Thomas H. Harvey, August 1, 1844, OIA-LR, roll 302; J. C. Fremont to Hon. Wm. Wilkins, August 28, 1844, OIA-LR, roll 302.

the Senecas, the Creeks, and the Quapaws in the fall of 1837 to attend the
annual council held at the official Cherokee council grounds at Tahlequah.
The Quapaws received the invitation primarily due to their proximity to
the new Cherokee homeland, while the other groups were not only neighbors but also shared prior diplomatic ties. This initial meeting did not have
an expansive agenda but merely confirmed the existing friendly relations
among the participants. Its success led to another council the following
fall. This time the Cherokees sent the summons as far as four hundred
miles to the north to the reserves along the Missouri border. None of the
longer-established western tribes received an invitation. As had been the
case in 1837, the Cherokees wanted to reestablish the connections built
on the eastern side of the Mississippi. The western tribes did not share
that history. Moreover, they had shown a distinct hostility toward the
emigrants. Therefore, a council called to reconfirm old friendships would
neither require nor necessarily welcome their participation. The troubled
relations between the removed Indians and the western nations also made
it less likely that Osage, Kansas, or Pawnee leaders would want to venture
into the heart of the emigrant settlements.[20]

Although these two councils depended on conventional symbolism and
ritual to unite the border Indians, the Cherokee and Creek leadership
believed that this western confederacy required a hierarchy based on more
than kinship. They chose to create several leadership positions to be filled
through elections. John Looney, who had only recently ascended to principal chief of the Western Cherokees at the death of John Jolly, thus became
the nominal head of this nascent league. In his new position, he possessed
the league's wampum as well as the authority to call the members of the
league into council. The three subordinate leadership positions also went
to leading men from these two southeastern nations. The Creek headman Roly McIntosh was elected the second chief, while a Cherokee man
named Young Wolf was elected to office of speaker. Finally, Joseph Vann
assumed the position of war chief with the authority to call and lead the
warriors of this new confederacy.[21]

[20] Isaac McCoy, *History of Baptist Indian Missions* (Washington, DC, 1840), 544–545; Isaac
McCoy to C. A. Harris, CIA, September 6, 1838, roll 612, IMP; Foreman, *Advancing the
Frontier*,198–200; David LaVere, *Contrary Neighbors: Southern Plains and Removed
Indians in Indian Territory* (Norman, 2000), 93–94.
[21] Gaston Litton, "The Principal Chiefs of the Cherokee Nation," *Chronicles of Oklahoma*,
15(September 1937): 253–270; Grant Foreman (Ed.), *A Traveler in Indian Territory:
The Journal of Ethan Allen Hitchcock* (Norman, 1996), 69–70; Foreman, *Advancing
the Frontier*, 195–196; LaVere, *Contrary Neighbors*, 93–94; Angie Debo, *The Road to*

Whether because of the election of a war chief, or just the fear of this gathering of multiple Indian nations, several American military officials in the region expressed serious concerns about the possible hidden agendas of the 1838 council. Indeed, Tennessee's *Nashville Banner* printed accusations from Major Mason at Fort Leavenworth and Major General Gaines at St. Louis that the Indians met to organize a militant alliance "preparatory to striking a simultaneous blow upon the settlements of Arkansas and Missouri from Red River to the upper Mississippi." The council attendees acted quickly and addressed a letter to General Arbuckle, the Cherokee agent General Stokes, and the Creek agent Colonel Logan in which they worked to defuse the situation. To counter any alarms over a possible Indian uprising, the Indians asserted that they "met in general Council for the purpose of renewing the friendship once existing among our forefathers."[22]

The misguided accusations of military officials, however, should not necessarily be written off as paranoia. Some Indians had similar fears. Among the Delawares and Shawnees, the decision to travel to Tahlequah for the council was hampered by concerns about Cherokee ambitions. Headmen within the two communities along the Kansas River initially thought that the Cherokees had dubious intentions. To complicate matters further, more than eighty Delaware and Shawnee men from the Kansas River reserves had served recently with the U.S. Army in Florida. Less than a decade after their removal to eastern Kansas these men had joined in the military's attempts to drive the Seminole Indians from the southern swamps. Now the Delaware and Shawnee leadership feared an awkward or tense reunion with any relocated Seminoles who might attend the council. The possibility particularly concerned the Shawnees, because their men under Joseph Parks had convinced the Seminole leader Onselmatche, or Jumper, to surrender in December 1837 and then conducted the Seminole band to Fort Gardiner. Consequently, neither tribe sent representatives to Tahlequah. The Delaware and Shawnee delegates who were in attendance

---

Disappearance: A History of the Creek Indians (Norman, 1941), 134. Although Ethan Allen Hitchcock, LaVere, and Debo state that this council occurred in 1839, the records make it clear that it took place in September 1838. It is also important to note that this Joseph Vann was not "Rich" Joe Vann who had become a wealthy landholder and slaveowner in Georgia by the mid-1830s.

[22] McCoy, *History of Baptist Indian Missions*, 544–546; LaVere, *Contrary Neighbors*, 49–50, 93–94; Foreman, *Advancing the Frontier*, 195–200. Foreman also notes that Major John Ridge of the Cherokees went so far as to visit the offices of the *Louisville Banner* to chide those responsible for printing such accusations.

in 1838 were members of the bands then living along the Canadian River as opposed to those residing on the Kansas.[23]

Isaac McCoy had advised the Kansas River Shawnees and Delawares to attend the 1838 council. It "accorded with the scheme which the Government had proposed in relation to the organization of the territory," he stated. In advising the Delawares McCoy referred to a pan-Indian territory. It was a dream he had nurtured for the better part of a decade. The removal of the eastern tribes had given the federal government an opportunity to act for the betterment of the Indians, McCoy proclaimed, and "the plan of collecting the tribes into one body, and placing them in this country [west of Missouri and Arkansas] under the circumstances embraced in the Government is precisely what has been prayed for and sought, by numerous Christians, for many years." In 1832, he had submitted a proposal to a government commission then examining the status of federal Indian policy. That commission finally produced a bill in 1834 that envisioned an Indian Territory in which a federally appointed governor would oversee a council of twenty-four elected chiefs in a territory stretching from the Missouri River to Mexico. The House of Representatives did not pass this bill in 1834 and gave the same treatment to the similar versions proposed over the next decade and a half. Few Congressmen shared McCoy's passion for the proposal, and indifference repeatedly killed the legislation in the 1830s. In 1838, one of the few times it even reached the Senate floor, John C. Calhoun and his fellow southerners effectively derailed the bill.[24]

More important, McCoy had trouble gaining widespread support for the idea among the border Indian communities. Indian opposition to the legislation rested on issues of sovereignty and perceptions of western Indians. Although McCoy sold this territorial plan to the Delawares and Shawnees in the late 1830s, the western Cherokees, Creeks, and Choctaws

[23] McCoy, *History of Baptist Indian Missions*, 544–545; Indian delegates to General Arbuckle, General Stokes, and Colonel Logan, September 21, 1838, OIA-LR, roll 82; Edwin C. McReynolds, *The Seminoles* (Norman, 1957), 193, 201.

[24] McCoy, *History of Baptist Indian Missions*, 438, 545; Foreman, *Advancing the Frontier*, 182–185; Isaac McCoy, *The Annual Register of Indian Affairs In the Western (or Indian) Territory 1835–1838* (Springfield, MO, 1998), 196–200; House Report No. 474, 23rd Congress, 1st Session, Serial No. 263; *The Congressional Globe, 25th Congress, and Session*, 334–336, 345–348; House Report No. 736, 30th Congress, 1st Session, Serial No. 526. Few historians have written about the overall history of these attempts. One of the best summaries is Annie H. Abel, "Proposals for an Indian State, 1778–1878," *Annual Report of the American Historical Association* (1907): 89–104. Another analysis can be found in Foreman, *Advancing the Frontier*, 180–194.

did not buy it. Joseph Vann, John Jolly, John Brown, and John Looney simply declared "that the Cherokee people cannot agree to come under the Government proposed by the Secretary of War." Imbued with the understanding that they never relinquished their status as independent nations, Indian leaders in the 1840s reacted negatively to any plan that would directly compromise their self-governance. The Choctaw representatives, Pierre Juzan, McKenney, and Oakcheah, asserted that they expected American officials to abide by the stipulations of the treaty they had signed in 1830, one of which was "that our Country would never be embraced within any State or Territorial limits." But it was the prominent Choctaw Colonel Peter Pitchlynn who voiced another critical argument against the bill. He explained that the western Indians occupied "different platforms in civilization," a condition that made unified interests and even communication nearly impossible to achieve. The Choctaws did not want to be forced into a political state with the Osages, Wichitas, Pawnees, Comanches, or other western Indians who did not share the same beliefs in agriculture and a settled existence. "We wish simply to be let alone," he explained, "and permitted to pursue the even tenor of our way." Between Pitchlynn's statements and the general opposition in Congress, the legislation never had a chance.[25]

Although it eventually failed, McCoy's proposal was an important reminder to the border Indians. Even as they tried to negotiate relations with the tribes to the west, they could not ignore the developing push from the east. The progress of American expansion and the recent experience with removal suggested that land management required as much attention as peaceful relations. Once again, the southeastern Indians took the lead. The principal chief of the Cherokees, John Ross, and the principal chief of the Creeks, Roly McIntosh, invited all of the local government and military officials to a council scheduled for early June 1843. Their invitations to thirty-six neighboring Indian tribes extended far and wide, and approximately four thousand Indians representing twenty-two different nations attended the council at Tahlequah. Although border delegates

---

[25] Abel, "Proposals for an Indian State," 94–99; Foreman, *Advancing the Frontier*, 184–189. The statement made by the Cherokees is on page 185. For the Choctaw statement against the proposal, see *The Congressional Globe, 25th Congress, 2nd Session*, 334; *Indian Affairs*, II, 310–319; House Report No. 736, 30th Congress, 1st Session, Serial No. 526. For Pitchlynn's address, see House Miscellaneous Document No. 35, 30th Congress, 2nd Session, Serial No. 544. This general attitude of the Cherokees, Creeks, Choctaws, and Chickasaws toward the Osages and other western nations is discussed in more detail in LaVere, *Contrary Neighbors*.

predominated, representatives from the Osages, Wichitas, and Iowas also attended the lengthy sessions. "The assemblage presented a motley appearance," remarked visitor Reverend William H. Goode, "exhibiting every age, phase, and condition of Indian life of both sexes." Goode and other observers especially noted the differences between the members of the western, "uncivilized" nations, and those of the border nations who dressed more like the whites.[26]

In addition to negotiating the critical aspects of life on the prairie-plains, the council provided an opportunity to socialize on a grand scale. This gathering of representatives from twenty-two different Indian nations created an encampment approximately two miles square and brought together peoples not entirely familiar with each other. The Osage and Iowa delegations kept to themselves for the most part, except for the one evening when the Iowas paraded around the entire encampment, singing, dancing, and playing cane flutes in a salute to their fellow attendees. Over the course of the four weeks that the council lasted, the encampment created a unique social scene, as hundreds of tepees and lodges provided numerous opportunities for interaction. Large groups of men participated in ball games, and most nights produced dances in different parts of the camp. For many of the border Indian delegations in particular, this unique gathering presented an opportunity to catch up with acquaintances and see relatives who had married into another community. The fact that this council was the fourth of its kind in six years contributed to the social atmosphere. As a result of this more relaxed environment, the formal proceedings did not begin until a full two weeks after the day set for opening remarks.[27]

When the talks finally began the Indians only reluctantly abandoned their informal exchanges. Unwilling to cease their socializing entirely, most delegates ignored the initial summons to council in the morning of the first day and grudgingly accepted the afternoon call. Upon their arrival at the center of the council grounds they found benches arranged in concentric semicircles around a table on which rested ceremonial pipes and strands of wampum. One by one the delegates took their seats, and the Delawares, as the grandfathers, assumed the primary position. With so many peoples and languages represented, the pace of the council

---

[26] Louise Barry, *The Beginning of the West: Annals of the Kansas Gateway to the American West, 1540–1854* (Topeka, 1972), 485; P. M. Butler to T. Hartley Crawford, CIA, June 21, 1843, OIA-LR, roll 87; Goode, *Outposts of Zion*, 68–70.

[27] Goode, *Outposts of Zion*, 68–70, 79–80; Foreman, *Advancing the Frontier*, 205–212.

depended in large part on the ability to communicate. In some cases, the tribal languages had enough in common to enable conversation with relative ease. But translators played an important role. Each speaker required eight different interpreters, slowing the process for speaker and listener alike. With each oration translated nine different times after an initial translation into English, men such as Reverend Goode found it relatively easy to take notes, and his observations provide insight into the proceedings.[28]

John Ross, the head chief of the Cherokee nation at Tahlequah and, therefore, the host of the council, addressed the council first. Roly McIntosh followed Ross, and their speeches shared a theme with the previous meetings. Ross, approximately fifty years old and a relatively small man, had weathered an arduous removal from Georgia that had claimed the life of his wife and thousands of his people. In the four years he had lived west of the Mississippi, the Cherokee leader had also struggled for control of the Cherokee Nation with both the Old Settlers and the Treaty Party. On this day at Tahlequah, he took no chances with extemporaneous speech and addressed the assemblage from a manuscript written out in English. Following a brief review of the past peaceful relations among the Indian peoples in attendance, he elaborated on the purpose of the present council. "Brothers," the Cherokee chief intoned, "it is for renewing in the West the ancient talk of our forefathers, and of perpetuating forever the old pipe of peace, and of extending them from nation to nation, and of adopting such international laws as may redress the wrongs done by the people of our respective nations to each other." Following this initial explanation that laid the foundation for the proceedings, Ross impressed upon the delegates the importance of their talks. "Let us . . . so act that the peace which existed between our forefathers may be pursued, and that we may always live as members of the same family."[29]

McIntosh rose to his feet as the Cherokee leader sat down. Younger than Ross, the Creek headman did not speak English and relied on his nephew for translation. Like his Cherokee counterpart, McIntosh spoke of renewing the council fires in the West and referred to the shared desire of the assembled Indians to raise their children in peace. He also described the council as an attempt "to make the path of our forefathers, that it may extend from one door to the other . . . that it may be kept clean." In

[28] Goode, *Outposts of Zion*, 71; Foreman, *Advancing the Frontier*, 207–208.
[29] Goode, *Outposts of Zion*, 74; William G. McLoughlin, *After the Trail of Tears: The Cherokees' Struggle for Sovereignty, 1839–1880* (Chapel Hill, 1993), 7–33.

using these words, the headman used metaphors that most of his audience understood. When they had lived east of the Mississippi, numerous trails had enabled war parties, travelers, and messengers of peace to journey hundreds of miles between settlements. Now, as it had in all prior councils, a clean path represented open communications among the attendees, and thus made it easier for the delegates to accomplish their goals. Due to the difficult nature of the interpretation process, the speeches by Ross, McIntosh, and an unnamed Chickasaw Indian took up the entire afternoon session, after which the delegates dispersed to their respective encampments spread around the council grounds.[30]

A few days later, the second chief of the Cherokees, Major George Lowery, rose in the council and elaborated on the subjects addressed on the first day. Lowery, described by Goode as an "aged and venerable-looking man," had the most comprehensive understanding among the Cherokees of wampum as an instrument of inter-Indian communication and diplomacy. Like McIntosh, Lowery used familiar language as he spoke. Rather than focusing on the path of peace, however, the elderly Cherokee told the history of the council fire. In his speech, he referred to the very first endeavor made by Indian nations to create widespread peace. The effort had its foundation in the warfare between the Senecas and the Cherokees centuries earlier. Initiated by the Senecas, these first peace councils wove together Cherokees, Senecas, Shawnees, Wyandots, and Osages. As the delegates sat and listened, Lowery spoke of the fire lit for the original council, a fire meant to light the way for all the tribes. For the purposes of the 1843 gathering, however, the fire represented the eternal flame that had first sparked years before. According to Lowery, a Shawnee messenger of peace had carried this first fire to the Cherokees, declaring that "this fire is for all the different tribes to see by.... This fire is not to be extinguished so long as time lasts...when you kindle this fire it will be seen rising up toward the heavens. I will see it and know it; I am your oldest brother." By evoking this image, Lowery reminded the delegates of meetings that had brought the eastern Indians together since that time. The Cherokee elder did not recite a list of those previous councils. But the delegates did not need his words to recall events like the grand council held at the Glaize during the peak of the Northwestern Confederacy in 1792. Both the content and the imagery of Lowery's talk struck chords

---

[30] Goode, *Outposts of Zion*, 75–76. For a brief discussion of the language regarding opening a path and the path of peace, see Williams, Jr., *Linking Arms Together*, 85–87.

with those in attendance, and his story provided a foundation for the work done in the days that followed.[31]

If the observations of men like Reverend Goode served as the only remaining records for the 1843 council, the story would end with Lowery's speech. The council had "no definite object in view," the Methodist minister wrote. Moreover, he added, "it seemed probable that this vast body ... would disperse without having done anything." The only benefit he saw emerging from such a council was that the "ruder" tribes might learn something from those who were "semicivilized." Although Goode enjoyed the people-watching aspect of the assemblage and recorded several speeches, his time spent in Tahlequah resulted in several erroneous conclusions. Perhaps he had a point in reporting that the council did not result in any concrete accomplishments. After all, when Goode published his observations twenty years later, he could not speak of an existing pan-Indian association. However, he inaccurately presumed that the council had no definite objective. Other documents point to specific ideas and goals coming out of the gathering held at Tahlequah in June and July 1843.[32]

Apparently unnoticed or ignored by Reverend Goode, the council participants also discussed ways to expand the framework of the loose confederacy constructed in 1838. Five years earlier they had elected officers. Now they proposed an eight-point accord that would bind this league of Indian nations. Rather than the result of consensus or discussion, however, the resolutions in this agreement appeared to be the product of Cherokee and Creek collaboration. The first article of the compact stated that "Peace and friendship shall forever be maintained between the parties," and the second article declared, "Revenge shall not be cherished nor retaliation practiced for offences committed by individuals." Both of these statements went over familiar ground. Three of the next five resolutions elaborated on these subjects and detailed appropriate punishments for an individual of any of the consenting tribes who committed a crime beyond the boundaries of his own nation. The last article resolved that no member of a consenting tribe should introduce alcohol onto Indian lands. But perhaps the most notable statement arrived in the third resolution, which dealt solely with land ownership. To aid in the development of agricultural habits and to prevent any possibility of future removals, the party consenting

---

[31] Foreman, *Advancing the Frontier*, 210–211; Dowd, *A Spirited Resistance*, 103–105.
[32] Goode, *Outposts of Zion*, 84.

to this compact would "solemnly pledge ourselves to each other that no Nation party to this compact, shall without the consent of all the other parties cede or in any manner alienate to the United States any part of their present Territory." More than any other, this final resolution reflected the most recent events that had resulted in removal. Like the Cherokees, many of the assembled delegates had lived to see their homelands sold or ceded either without their consent or by unrepresentative consent.[33]

Yet the assembled Indians did not give these resolutions their unqualified support. Only representatives of the Cherokees, Creeks, and Osages put their marks on this accord while still on the council grounds. Other delegates refused to sign until they had considered the substance of the compact in more depth. The Ottawas wrote to their friend, the Baptist Missionary Jotham Meeker, because they wanted to know what Meeker thought of the proposal. They also sought the opinions of their chiefs who remained in Michigan. Although the specific responses of Meeker and the eastern headmen remain unknown, we know that the Ottawas did not sign the agreement. Richard Elliot, on the other hand, specifically advised the Council Bluffs' Potawatomis not to sign primarily because of the land sale prohibition. The government agent did not give a rationale for his recommendation, but neither he nor his superiors wanted any obstacles to future Indian land cessions.[34]

Missionaries and agents alone did not influence the decisions made regarding this accord. Each Indian community weighed the advantages and disadvantages of such a pledge, and their hesitation originates from a number of contexts. For the Potawatomis at Council Bluffs, led at the council by the elderly Wabansi, Elliott's advice was not necessarily the deciding factor. These Indians were already under pressure from federal officials to cede their lands in Iowa and unite with the Potawatomis from the Osage River on a new reserve on the Kansas River. From the late 1830s to the mid-1840s, the Potawatomis at the Bluffs refused to recognize anyone's claim but their own to the land. Not even other Potawatomis would have a say. "The people who made the treaty of Chicago [in 1833] are at Council Bluffs," the Bluffs Potawatomis declared, "no other people have a right to sell the lands east of the Missouri." Already reluctant to grant other Potawatomi bands a say in their negotiations, Wabansi and

<hr>

[33] Chiefs and Principal Men of the United Nation of Chippewa, Ottawa and Potawatomy to the President, August 8, 1843, OIA-LR, roll 215; Richard Elliot to T. Hartley Crawford, CIA, August 9, 1843, OIA-LR, roll 215.

[34] Richard Elliot to T. Hartley Crawford, CIA, August 9, 1843, OIA-LR, roll 215; Foreman, *Advancing the Frontier*, 213–214.

the other Potawatomi delegates to the 1843 council had little reason to cede such power to other border Indians. Meanwhile, the Kansas River Delawares and Shawnees already had concerns about the ambitions of their southern neighbors. Therefore, although these two communities sent delegates to Tahlequah in 1843, they had no desire to sign an agreement that bound them tightly to the Cherokees.[35]

But the westward relocation of the Wyandots in 1843 also altered the format of inter-Indian diplomacy west of the Mississippi and revealed some of the divisions in the conceived confederacy of border Indians. When the more than seven hundred Wyandot men, women, and children settled at the confluence of the Kansas and Missouri Rivers, they did so within two months of the conclusion of the Tahlequah council. Because of the various negotiations surrounding their reserve, they settled not only across the river from Westport, Missouri, but also adjacent to the Delaware and Shawnee reserves. And along with their belongings the Wyandots carried with them their status as keepers of the northern council fire. With this relocation, then, the Wyandots brought the embers of the northwestern confederacy and therefore an alternative to the fire tended by the Cherokees and Creeks over the previous six years. Although removal had created similar situations for eastern Indians along the western U.S. border, the Shawnees, Delawares, and other border communities did not necessarily need to broker peaceful relations with the Comanches and Wichitas. Their concerns lay farther north in the prairie grasslands of Kansas, the river valleys of the Platte, and the porous boundaries of Missouri. After 1843, then, the Indians in eastern Kansas took steps to address their particular concerns.[36]

Within a few years of the Wyandot relocation, the efforts to revive the northwestern confederacy began in earnest. And although councils held in 1847 and 1848 included members of some western nations with whom they hoped to settle affairs, other invitations were limited to the members of the original alliance. The first flames of the rekindled northern fire burned in May 1847, when the Delawares on the Kansas River hosted a small council that included the Wyandots, Shawnees, Kickapoos, and

[35] Journal of Council with Potawatomis, November 1845, OIA-TR, roll 4; Th. H. Harvey to T. Hartley Crawford, September 18, 1845, OIA-LR, roll 216; James A. Clifton, *The Prairie People: Continuity and Change in Potawatomi Indian Culture, 1665–1965* (Iowa City, 1998), 329–335; Warren, *The Shawnees and Their Neighbors*, 94.

[36] Robert Emmett Smith, Jr., "The Wyandot Indians, 1843–1876" (Ph.D. Dissertation, Oklahoma State University, 1973), 54–66; Carl G. Klopfenstein, "The Removal of the Wyandots From Ohio," *Ohio Historical Quarterly*, 66(April 1957): 119–136.

Pawnees. The inclusion of the latter represented one more negotiation between the Pawnees and Delawares regarding the diminished hunting territories beyond the Delawares' hunting outlet. But outside of those specific discussions, the border Indians also talked about reestablishing their past alliance. At council's end the participants agreed to convene a more substantial gathering a year later at which they would more formally renew the council fire of the northwestern confederacy. Although decades had passed and their location had changed, these delegates hoped their shared history and renewed bonds would once again unite their interests for the benefit of all.[37]

Over the next year, the messages circulated among the reserves in eastern Kansas, setting Tuesday, October 10, 1848 as the starting date. The Delawares would once again host, led by their principal chief, Captain Ketchum. Wyandot principal chief Francis Hicks, along with James Rankin, William Walker, and John Hicks, made the short journey north, as did Joseph Parks and several Shawnee headmen. These delegates sat alongside representatives from the Potawatomis, Ojibways, Ottawas, Miamis, Kickapoos, Peorias, Sauks and Mesquakies and Kansas. Captain Ketchum told the Shawnee, Wyandot, and Kickapoo delegates at a private conference that they needed to "devise means by which the difficulties arising between the different tribes shall be adjusted and put a stop to horsestealing practiced by the prairie tribes." This gathering would in part teach the Kansas the ways of the northwestern confederacy.[38]

But, although they hoped to develop better relations with the Kansas and Sauks and Mesquakies, the border Indians emphasized that this plan depended on the framework of the confederacy. Indeed, they believed that the explanation of their alliance and the "good feeling and harmony" which had always existed among them would teach the "prairie Indians"

---

[37] William E. Connelley (Ed.), "The Provisional Government of Nebraska Territory and the Journals of William Walker," *Proceedings and Collections of the Nebraska State Historical Society*, Second Series, 3(1899): 200–201; Rev. Joseph Murphy, O.S.B., *Potawatomis of the West: Origins of the Citizen Band*, edited by Patricia Sulcer Barrett (Shawnee, OK, 1988), 171.

[38] Connelley, "The Provisional Government of Nebraska Territory," 200–201, 265; Murphy, *Potawatomis of the West*, 171; Journal of the Proceedings of the Great Council, October 10–14, 1848, WNP. The Shawnees told the Senecas in 1853 that the latter had not been invited to the 1848 council because "they did not belong to the Ancient Confederacy of N. W. Indians, but to the Iroquoise Confederacy; therefore could claim no rights, nor have any voice in it." Connelley, "The Provisional Government of Nebraska Territory," 392.

a lesson in proper conduct and incorporate them into the kinship network. More important, however, the invocation of the northwestern confederacy would reinstate the strong bonds that once held these Indians together during the turbulent period of the late eighteenth century. Therefore, when the council opened on the morning of Friday, October 13, Captain Ketchum cleansed the eyes and ears of the delegates representing eleven nations, "so that they may hear correctly and see plainly all the matters which may be brought to their notice during the council." Once he had "set their hearts in their right places" the Delaware chief distributed the wampum prepared by the Wyandots for the occasion. Both the language and the wampum grounded the discussions that followed. During the next day's deliberations, the Potawatomi delegation took over from Ketchum and told the history of the council fire. No work could be done until these ritualistic elements had been completed. Unfortunately, although the council remained in session until October 18, no record remains of the conversations from the remaining four days.[39]

This gap in the record makes it difficult to know Ketchum's and the other delegates' specific agenda in the fall of 1848. However, if they intended to establish a unified policy regarding land cessions or other concerns, the events of the next six years undermined those plans. On a national scale, the end of the Mexican–American War as well as the discovery of gold in California further increased traffic around and through their reserves. Tens of thousands of emigrants crossed the Missouri state line and turned the prairie grasslands into cluttered highways every spring as they made their way to Oregon. But the Compromise of 1850 may have had the most dramatic impact. This legislation organized the territories of Arizona, Utah, Nevada, and New Mexico, and in so doing appeared to further limit the extent of Indian land on the border. Citizens of Missouri also eyed the organization of this region on their western margin as an important symbol in a larger campaign to protect the institution of slavery. All of these events increased the pressure on Indian communities living along the border, especially those of the Shawnees, Delawares, Wyandots, and Potawatomis whose reserves rested along the more popular travel routes. And by the early 1850s, the U.S. government began to

---

[39] Journal of the Proceedings of the Great Council, October 10–14, 1848, WNP; Connelley, "The Provisional Government of Nebraska Territory," 265–266; Peter Dooyentate Clarke, *Origin and Traditional History of the Wyandotts and Sketches of Other Indian Tribes of North America* (Toronto, 1870), 131–132. Clarke mistakenly states that this council took place in 1846.

make more definite moves to organize the lands just west of Missouri. Even the framework of the Indians' ancient alliance did not have the power to weather these conditions.[40]

One final attempt to hold together the northwestern confederacy illustrated both the weakened power of that alliance as well as the divides that existed within native communities. As Congress edged closer to passing the Kansas-Nebraska Act in 1854, Commissioner of Indian Affairs George Manypenny tried to coax land cessions from the Indian residents of the soon to be Kansas Territory. Manypenny first sent Agent Benjamin Robinson to inform each tribe that it needed to select delegates to negotiate treaties in Washington. When Robinson arrived at the Delaware reserve in the first week of April, he discovered nine tribes in council. In an effort to combat the increasing pressure for land cessions, the border Indians met one last time. More specifically they gathered to act on a proposal similar to the one proposed more than a decade earlier at Tahlequah – a league in which each member would pledge not to sell any land without the consent of the other members. But when Robinson informed the Delawares that they needed to select a delegation, the Delawares did not take long to make their decision. They adjourned the council. This unilateral action raised a substantial outcry among the others in attendance. Tauromee, the Wyandot principal chief, was particularly upset. He firmly believed that the Indians in Kansas needed to resist American expansion. Because the Wyandots maintained the council fire, Tauromee's leadership kept the deliberations alive. Only the Shawnees followed the Delawares' example. But the combined departure of the Delawares and Shawnees made it difficult to continue, especially because they held the two largest pieces of land in the region. Robinson spoke to the remaining council participants on April 4 and told them to select delegates with the authority to negotiate a treaty. On April 11, both the Delaware and Shawnee delegations boarded the *Polar Star* and began their journey to Washington. Representatives from the Miamis and the Kickapoos soon joined them and by year's end, these four members of the northwestern confederacy

[40] For insight into Missouri's western gaze, see Stephen Aron, *American Confluence: The Missouri Frontier from Borderland to Border State* (Bloomington, 2006), 239–243. Wyandot delegates in Washington kept the Indians abreast of discussions in Congress about western expansion. They maintained a consistent presence in the nation's capital from the mid-1840s into the 1850s. See Connelley, "The Provisional Government of Nebraska Territory," 159, 163, 166, 176, 303.

signed treaties ceding hundreds of thousands of acres in eastern Kansas. Early in 1855, the Wyandots followed suit.[41]

The failure of the renewed northwestern confederacy to hinder the American government's negotiations for land in Kansas in 1854 did not compromise the rituals and customs that had structured eastern Indian diplomacy for centuries. As brothers, uncles, and grandfathers, the eastern Indians had lit numerous council fires, shared pipes, and exchanged wampum on both sides of the Mississippi. Nor did the migrations and removals undermine their readiness to trust those diplomatic foundations to regulate their new lives in the western territories. Despite the passage of time and the change in geography, the central tools and ideas of native diplomacy remained intact and important from the councils of the 1830s to those in the 1850s.

Instead, the decisions made by the Wyandots, Delawares, and Shawnees to turn away first from the Cherokees and then from the northern council fire reconfirmed that the strength of those alliances depended on the willingness of their participants to share the same goals. Although removal did not eliminate custom and ritual, it did have an impact on how each individual, band, and nation viewed the expansionist tendencies of the United States and its citizens in the mid-nineteenth century. The Delawares and Shawnees on the Kansas River distrusted Cherokee motivations in the 1830s, and were unwilling to participate in a council that might jeopardize their relationship with the United States. And by the 1850s, as the organization of new territories throughout the West appeared to foreshadow the fate of Indian reserves in eastern Kansas, little reason seemed to exist for Shawnees, Delawares, and others to believe that the renewed northwestern confederacy had the power to resist the next wave of American settlement.

---

[41] B. F. Robinson to George Manypenny, April 22, 1854, OIA-TR, roll 5; Memorial of Delaware Indians, April 3, 1854, OIA-TR, roll 5; Connelley, "The Provisional Government of Nebraska Territory," 400–401; *Indian Affairs, II*, 614–626, 634–636, 641–646, 677–681.

5

Joseph Parks, William Walker,
and the Politics of Change

In the middle of March 1832, William Walker sat down at his desk on the Wyandot reserve at Upper Sandusky, Ohio, and composed a statement regarding the recent treaty council between the Ohio Shawnees and the American government. As per contemporary federal policy, this accord arranged for the removal of the Wapakoneta and Hog Creek bands from Ohio. However, several Shawnee leaders had complaints regarding the conduct of Commissioner James B. Gardiner. Walker, Gardiner's official secretary for that treaty, assured the federal government that he had never seen a treaty "conducted with more patience, fairness and deliberation." Moreover, the Shawnees' interpreter, Joseph Parks, was "highly competent in that capacity" and "is one of the Shawnee tribe and has an equal interest" in the issues at hand. Walker saw nothing amiss in the whole proceedings, and "except for one private council relative to making provisions for a few Shawnees in Michigan," all discussions occurred in an open and honest manner.[1]

Walker's letter fails to illuminate some of the more interesting aspects of that 1831 council. Contrary to his report, the private meeting held to discuss the status and concerns of the Michigan Shawnees was important. Over the next ten years the financial arrangement made for this small group of Shawnees remained a focal point for objections to both the treaty and the actions of Parks as the interpreter. Walker's account also connected two men who became important figures in the lives of their respective communities in the mid-nineteenth century. Born within five years of each other, William Walker and Joseph Parks had many reasons to cross paths in the years that followed. Both men served the U.S. government in various capacities, and both became influential tribal members. Although they

---

[1] Written statement of William Walker, March 14, 1832, OIA-LR, roll 601.

FIGURE 4. Governor William Walker from the Connelley Collection. (Courtesy of the Kansas City, Kansas Public Library.)

did not share the same backgrounds, their economic interests, political influence, and regional importance in the postremoval period set them on parallel journeys. West of the Mississippi, Walker's one-level log home sat on the northern edge of the Wyandot town at the confluence of the Kansas and Missouri rivers, while Parks's "elegant residence" rested just south of the Kansas River on the Shawnee reserve. Each man belonged to the Methodist Episcopal Church and attended religious meetings on a relatively regular basis. Both attained a measure of fame in the border world of Westport and Kansas.

More important than these parallels, however, is the fact that their lives offer a critical perspective on the ongoing transformations within the Wyandot and Shawnee communities. In the late eighteenth and early nineteenth centuries, the American Revolution, the organization of Indian confederacies in the 1790s and 1800s, and the War of 1812 had direct impacts on those two nations. The simultaneous entrance of the United States into the Great Lakes region as a colonial power brought new policies in Indian affairs, and the waves of settlers, soldiers, and missionaries immediately affected the lives of all residents of the Old Northwest. Joseph Parks and William Walker were children of this era and carried with them the legacy of these events. They were members of societies in transition, societies responding to a maelstrom of geographic, demographic, cultural, and political pressures. Severe dislocations split families and communities on many levels as Indians in the Great Lakes region struggled to adapt to a new colonial power.[2]

Parks and Walker were two of the many individuals who represented the changing social and political organization among the removed Indians in the nineteenth century. Leaders of the Indian communities in the 1840s and 1850s were primarily men born in the late 1700s and early 1800s; men who grew up with the United States as the primary colonial power and came of age under the confines of removal. The older generation of men and women who had tried to balance American and British interests from the 1780s to the 1810s was dead, dying, or losing its influence. Even as a new generation took the place of their elders, the nature of leadership changed. Clans and other social divisions continued to provide some structure, but connections to the Anglo-American world began to override hereditary leadership and kinship obligations. For both Shawnees and Wyandots living in eastern Kansas in the 1850s, the leaders and the government structures were different than those of the 1790s. Although Joseph Parks and William Walker were not the only men who gained power during the first half of the nineteenth century, their somewhat parallel ascensions were illustrative of the cultural and political changes underway or nearly complete in their respective communities. Neither man initiated the transformations alone. Both men benefited from the circumstances.

---

[2] For an overview of events during this period, see Richard White, *The Middle Ground: Indians, Empires, and Republics in the Great Lakes Region, 1650–1815* (New York, 1991); Colin G. Calloway, *The American Revolution in Indian Country: Crisis and Diversity in Native American Communities* (New York, 1995), 158–181, 272–291, 315–317; Gregory Evans Dowd, *A Spirited Resistance: The North American Struggle for Unity, 1745–1815* (Baltimore, 1992), 65–147; John Sugden, *Blue Jacket: Warrior of the Shawnees* (Lincoln, 2000); Charles Callender, "Shawnee," in *Handbook of North American Indians*, William C. Sturtevant (Ed.) (17 vols., Washington, DC, 1978), *XV*, 622–635; Elisabeth Tooker, "Wyandot," in ibid., *XV*, 398–406.

The births of Parks and Walker reflect the specific circumstances of British and American westward expansion in the late eighteenth century. Military conflicts and western settlement, especially in the Ohio Valley, brought together white and Indian communities in peaceful and violent ways. As a result of those conditions, each man entered early adulthood in different contexts. Whereas Parks's father married a Shawnee woman following his flight from Pennsylvania, Walker's father married a Wyandot woman years after his capture and subsequent adoption. This mixed descent heritage often led to questions about the origins and tribal membership of the two men. Although Walker had a more apparent claim to status, Parks's actions over time illustrated his attachment to the interests of his band, if not to the larger Shawnee nation. And in the years before their respective relocations to the western territories, each man demonstrated his importance to both Indian and white communities and leaders.

Scholars have tended to shy away from definitive statements regarding the heritage of Joseph Parks. Indeed, most sources are at odds over how many Indian ancestors reside in his family tree and many historians go no further than to say that his veins contained a "strong infusion of white blood." Some documents are mutually contradictory. In a schedule attached to an 1826 treaty with the Potawatomis, commissioners define Parks simply as "an Indian." The 1831 treaty signed at Wapakoneta described Parks as one-quarter Shawnee. Lewis Cass, who had a long history with Parks, went back and forth in his portrayals of the man's heritage. In his 1827 publication on the American and British treatment of the Indians, Cass, then the governor of Michigan Territory, described Parks as an "honest half-Shawnee." Twenty-five years later, Cass was a Senator from Michigan and referred to Parks as a white man taken prisoner by the Indians as a boy and brought up among the Wyandots and Shawnees. According to these statements, Cass had first encountered Parks in 1814 while fulfilling his duties in support of the American cause during the War of 1812. Yet, only seven months later, Cass reverted to the labels used in his earlier writings. In March 1853, Cass stated that Parks was a "half breed" who had married among the Shawnees.[3]

---

[3] *Indian Affairs,* II, 273–277, 331–334; Adrienne Christopher, "Captain Joseph Parks, Chief of the Shawnee Indians," *Westport Historical Quarterly,* 5 (June 1969): 13–17; Fred Lee, "Captain Joseph Parks," *Westport Magazine* (August 1981): 3; *Congressional Globe,* August 5, 1852; *Congressional Globe,* March 3, 1853; Lewis Cass, *Remarks on the Policy and Practice of the United States and Great Britain in Their Treatment of Indians* (Boston, 1827), 67.

A more comprehensive account of Parks's background includes a mixture of the above information and some careful sifting. The story of his origins begins with the Revolutionary War. His father Abiah was a mason in the East Bradford township of Pennsylvania and the grandson of an Irish Quaker who immigrated to the colony in 1724. Abiah was an ardent British Loyalist and showed his colors by arranging for the arrest of an uncle who had a more revolutionary bent. As might be expected, this betrayal made it necessary for Abiah to leave Bradford quickly. For all that his family knew, the young man fled to Canada and never returned. Not until later did they learn that Abiah had settled near Detroit, an important hub for British affairs, trader activity, and Indian settlement. The young expatriate soon became an active member of the Detroit community and worked as a trader and cattle dealer. When he advised an emigrant party of Moravian Munsees and Delawares in 1792 to settle on the Thames River, he also established a trading relationship that continued in the years that followed. Within this same general time frame Abiah began a relationship with a Shawnee woman. At least two sons came from this union – Joseph was born in 1794 and his younger brother William followed some time thereafter. By the early 1800s they lived in Blue Jacket's town located north of the Huron River and south of Detroit, where they mingled with the Wyandots at Brownstown.[4]

Because the name of Abiah's Shawnee wife remains unknown, it is difficult to identify the kinship ties of the boys. Joseph and William had connections to both the Detroit River Shawnees as well as the Hog Creek band in Ohio and, at the very least, traveled between the settlements. Both boys received land grants at Hog Creek in an 1817 treaty whose provisions included the Ohio Shawnees. Fourteen years later, Joseph acted as the government interpreter during negotiations in which the Wapakoneta and Hog Creek Shawnee bands agreed to remove west and ceded the

4 J. Smith Futhey and Gilbert Cope, *History of Chester County, Pennsylvania, with Genealogical and Biographical Sketches* (Philadelphia, 1881), 673; List of individuals reported in June 17, 1778 edition of the Pennsylvania Packet as having joined the British Army. http://www.pa-roots.com/~chester/1778%20-%20joined%20British%20army.htm. (Accessed September 21, 2004.); Fred Coyne Hamil, *The Valley of the Lower Thames, 1640–1850* (Toronto, 1951), 31–32, 38; Linda Sabathy-Judd (Ed. and Trans.), *Moravians in Upper Canada: The Diary of the Indian Mission of Fairfield on the Thames, 1792–1813* (Toronto, 1999), 11, 26, 34, 37, 50, 53, 61, 66–67, 73, 79, 118; Richard W. Cummins to Thomas H. Harvey, March 21, 1848, OIA-LR, roll 302; *Indian Affairs, II*, 145–155; Sugden, *Blue Jacket*, 218–220. Although Sugden does not mention Parks as a resident of the village, Joseph and his brother had a clear connection to the Shawnees living south of Detroit in the early nineteenth century. William and Joseph Parks as well as Blue Jacket's sons identified themselves as the Huron River Shawnees. See Statement of Huron River Shawnees, February 1838, OIA-LR, roll 301.

remainder of their lands in the state. The thirteenth article of that treaty reflects Parks's strong connection to the Ohio Shawnee leaders. In that article, the Shawnee chiefs ask that Parks receive a full section of land "in consideration of his constant friendship and many charitable and valuable services towards the said Shawnees." But the second half of that article also displays both the private conference referred to in Walker's 1832 statement and Parks's influence with federal officials. More specifically, it granted the Huron River Shawnees the proceeds from the sale of one section of land in case they chose to remove. Some headmen later argued that they never agreed to give money to the Huron River band and that Parks had manipulated the process. The issue remained contentious into the late 1830s, although Parks asserted that the money for the Huron River band was provided "by mutual agreement of Col. Gardiner and the Shawnee chiefs party to the treaty." Even though the Huron River Shawnees later relinquished any financial interest resulting from this accord, other Shawnee leaders remained convinced that Parks had taken advantage of his position as interpreter. As with many incidents, the truth remains murky. However, it appears that Parks did his best to provide for the band with which he had healthy relations. He had ties to the Wyandots as well. At some point in the 1810s, Parks married a Wyandot woman named Catherine whose family resided either at Brownstown or at Maguaga. Catherine's father, Ronaess or Racer, was a prominent man among the Michigan Wyandots. This marriage and the resulting familial connections further strengthened the young Shawnee's position among the Indian communities on the Huron River.[5]

Starting at a young age, Parks cultivated other relations that helped him establish an important network outside of Shawnee circles. Later in life, Parks said that he lived in the household of Lewis Cass for several years as a young boy. Cass's public statements, however, assert that he did not meet Joseph until 1814, when Cass was the newly minted governor of the Michigan Territory. The providential encounter most likely occurred on the treaty grounds at Greenville in July of that year, when the Governor tried to undermine the British influence with the Indians in Ohio. Parks and the principal chief Black Hoof were two members of a small group of

---

[5] *Indian Affairs*, II, 145–155, 164, 331–334; Henry Harvey, *History of the Shawnee Indians, From the Year 1681 to 1854, Inclusive* (New York, 1971), 164–168; Affidavit of Joseph Parks, November 20, 1838, OIA-LR, roll 301; Statement of Huron River Shawnees, February 1838, OIA-LR, roll 301; Richard W. Cummins to Hon. T. Hartley Crawford, February 19, 1838, OIA-LR, roll 301; Richard W. Cummins to C. A. Harris, November 20, 1838, OIA-LR, roll 301; Richard Cummins to Thomas H. Harvey, March 21, 1848, OIA-LR, roll 302.

Shawnees who formed an auxiliary military force for Cass in the waning months of the war. They made excursions into Canada against the British and became known among locals as the governor's "pet Indians." Parks's service for Cass did not halt at war's end, however. The young Shawnee man stayed in touch, and, six years later, he joined the Governor and forty others on an expedition that visited Indian tribes and settlements throughout Michigan Territory. For twenty-five days, at the rate of $1 per day, Parks served as an interpreter and guide.[6]

Prior to removal, Parks benefited from his relationship with Cass, and for the remainder of his life he did not stray far from the federal government's payroll. A glance at the treaties signed in the 1820s and early 1830s provides some sense of Parks's affiliation with the American official. In an 1826 agreement negotiated by the territorial governor with the Potawatomis at Chicago, Parks received a grant of one section of land for no apparent reason. In a telling sign, however, Parks's name appeared among a list of influential traders and Potawatomi leaders, suggesting that the young Shawnee's connections had proven rewarding. Cass also tapped Parks to guide the Shawnee Prophet's emigrant party that left Ohio in September 1826. That episode, in which Parks abandoned his charges partway through the journey, was a noticeable low point in his service to the government and the Shawnees. But it did not end his employment opportunities. Five years later, the federal government paid Joseph to be the official interpreter at the 1831 Shawnee treaty. Finally, in 1833, he answered the Ohio Shawnees' request that he conduct them west to settle along the Kansas River.[7]

It is telling that even though the Shawnee leaders may have been upset with Parks, they turned to him for assistance in that 1833 removal. At the time he was nearly forty years old, a veteran of Indian–white relations, and a relatively wealthy man. Just as important, he was a member of a nation undergoing some critical transformations. Black Hoof died in 1830, a significant loss that left the Wapakoneta Shawnees without the

---

[6] George H. Hickman, *The Life of General Lewis Cass, with his Letters and Speeches on various subjects* (Baltimore, 1848), 14; *Congressional Globe*, August 5, 1852, 2077; Henry Schoolcraft, *Narrative Journal of Travels through the Northwestern Regions of the United States*, edited by Mentor L. Williams (East Lansing, MI, 1953), 61n, 510. In the footnotes, Williams identifies Parks as a Shawnee captive, similar to what Cass mentioned in 1852. However, there are enough conflicts throughout the source material with that conclusion to render it highly doubtful, and I argue that Parks is Shawnee through his mother.

[7] *Indian Affairs*, II, 273–277, 331–334. For Parks's involvement with the 1826 and 1833 removals, see Chapter 1.

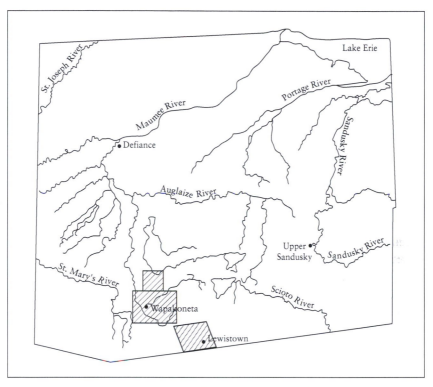

MAP 6. Shawnee Land Cessions in Ohio, 1831–1832. Based on Map 50 in Charles C. Royce (Comp.), *Indian Land Cessions in the United States.*

venerable headman who had led them for decades. On a larger scale, the numerous western emigrations from the 1780s to the 1820s had dispersed the Shawnees and altered the nation's political and social organization. When the Wapakoneta and Hog Creek bands moved west in the early 1830s, they settled in Kansas on lands that American officials assigned to them and the Missouri Shawnees. Treaty commissioners intended to unite the tribe. But this forced reunion led to disagreements about how the tribal government should function. Because of his experience in Ohio, Joseph Parks was well positioned to take advantage of those circumstances.[8]

---

[8] Harvey, *History of the Shawnee Indians*, 185–189; Vernon Kinietz and Ermine W. Voegelin (Eds.), *Shawnese Traditions: C. C. Trowbridge's Account* (Ann Arbor, 1939), 8–15; Thomas Wildcat Alford, *Civilization* as told to Florence Drake (Norman, 1936), 200–203; James H. Howard, *Shawnee!: The Ceremonialism of a Native Indian Tribe and Its Cultural Background* (Athens, OH, 1981), 24–31, 106–110.

William Walker's personal history in the years before the Wyandot removal is easier to follow than that of Joseph Parks. Walker was born about six years after Parks in Wayne County, Michigan, at the Wyandot settlement of Brownstown. His father, also named William, had become a Wyandot through captivity. Abducted by a Delaware hunting party in 1781 in Virginia, the eleven-year-old William was adopted by the Wyandots through the efforts of Adam Brown, another white captive adopted by the Wyandots after Dunmore's War. Catherine Walker, born Catherine Rankin, was a Wyandot woman of mixed descent and a member of the Big Turtle clan. William, Jr., was the third of five sons born to Catherine and William Sr. – John and Isaac were the older brothers and Joel and Matthew the younger. Although less is known definitively about the education of the other four, William attended Worthington Academy run by the Episcopal Bishop Philander Chase in Worthington, Ohio. As a result of his schooling, he could read Greek and Latin, and could read and speak English and French. But it was his extensive knowledge of local Indian languages that brought him work as an interpreter.[9]

William and his brothers learned and benefited from the skills and connections of their parents. Catherine was descended from the Montours, a French-Indian family with a long history in the Great Lakes fur trade. She could allegedly speak a number of languages and, like her maternal ancestors, often served great purposes at inter-Indian councils in the region. William's father also worked as an interpreter, but he mediated relationships between whites and the Wyandots. In the late 1810s those responsibilities expanded when he became the federal subagent for Indian affairs in Ohio. This coincided with the family's move from the Brownstown settlements to Upper Sandusky shortly after the Treaty of Ghent. From here, the younger William made a name for himself in Indian and white communities. His older brother John had already served as an interpreter at several treaties in the early 1800s and fought on the side of the United States in the War of 1812. It is only natural, therefore, that Walker entered into the family profession. Like his father and brother before him, William worked as a paid interpreter at treaties and other councils in the 1820s and 1830s. Government officials viewed Walker as a valuable assistant and noted his influence among the Wyandots.[10]

[9] William E. Connelley (Ed.), "The Provisional Government of Nebraska Territory and the Journals of William Walker," *Proceedings and Collections of the Nebraska State Historical Society*, Second Series, 3(1899), 5–14; *The Wyandotte Herald*, February 19, 1874.

[10] Connelley, "The Provisional Government of Nebraska Territory," 8–11, 25n; Cass, *Remarks on the Policy and Practice*, 67; *The History of Wyandot County, Ohio* (Chicago, 1884), 275–276; *The Wyandotte Herald*, February 19, 1874.

Although Walker had stronger family connections than Parks, he also benefited from timing. In the early 1830s, even as Parks assisted the American government with the relocation of the remaining Shawnees in Ohio, Walker rose within the ranks of the Wyandot leadership. As a result of external pressures, the political and religious customs of the Wyandots had undergone substantial transformations by the 1830s. The conflicts of the late eighteenth century had a direct impact on government structures within the nation, and when the Wyandots moved west of the Mississippi in 1843 they had an elective form of government. Alterations in Wyandot religious practices began later, brought on by the arrival of Methodist missionaries in the late 1810s. Both the changes and their impact on the Indians were interconnected, and Walker's growing authority in the community testified to the results.

Although not the first missionaries among the Wyandots, the Methodists made a lasting impression. Prior to the 1810s, Jesuit missionaries had created the most enduring legacy. The Wyandots in Ohio were only one fragment of the Huron nation first encountered by Jesuits in the 1600s; however, strong symbols and ceremonies of Catholicism remained with them. Learned Catholic hymns, prayers, and rituals could still be heard in the 1800s, especially among the Wyandots living near Detroit. Other denominations, including the Moravians, Quakers, and Presbyterians, all failed to establish a foothold in the decades after the American Revolution. Methodism arrived in 1816 in the person of John Stewart. He was a thirty-year-old man of African and East Indian descent who had recently converted at a camp meeting in Marrieta, Ohio, and had subsequently heard the call to preach in the "wilderness." Following a brief visit at a Delaware village, he stopped at the Walker house in Upper Sandusky, where William Walker, Sr., first believed he was a runaway slave. Once Stewart corrected that initial misunderstanding, he gained the Walker family's support, and both Catherine and William, Jr., became devoted members of the Methodist church and remained so throughout their Ohio tenure. William, Sr., also pointed Stewart in the direction of Jonathan Pointer, a black man who had been adopted by the Wyandots. Pointer would serve as the missionary's interpreter for the next several years.[11]

---

[11] Robert Emmett Smith, Jr., "The Wyandot Indians, 1843–1876" (Ph.D. Dissertation, Oklahoma State University, 1973), 35–38; *The History of Wyandot County, Ohio*, 275–276; Martin W. Walsh, "The 'Heathen Party': Methodist Observation of the Ohio Wyandot," *American Indian Quarterly* (Spring 1992): 189–211; Joseph Mitchell, *The Missionary Pioneer, or a Brief Memoir of the Life, Labours, and Death of John Stewart, (Man of Colour), Founder, Under God of the Mission Among the Wyandotts of Upper Sandusky, Ohio* (New York, 1827), 19–25.

Resistance to Methodism among the larger Wyandot community emerged shortly after Stewart's arrival. The initial protests came from those Wyandots still connected to Catholicism. They argued that the priest stationed at Detroit had declared that only the Catholics proclaimed the truth. This debate came to an end only when, at the Wyandots' request, William Walker, Sr., compared Stewart's Bible to the Catholic's and revealed that the two books differed only in the language in which they were written. Shortly thereafter, several prominent leaders of the Upper Sandusky settlements, including Between-the-Logs, accepted Stewart's preaching. Between-the-Logs appeared most attracted to the Methodists' ideas of sin and salvation as a way of redeeming himself and his community from the alcohol use that had infiltrated their homes. Although other Wyandots may have shared those sentiments, they reacted more adversely to the wholesale changes required by the visiting preacher. Bloody Eyes, the older brother of Between-the-Logs, spoke out against Stewart's rigid stance on abandoning all aspects of traditional Wyandot life. "I do not believe the Great Spirit will punish his red children for dancing, feasting, &c," the Wyandot asserted, "no, we have our public amusements in peace and good will to each other.... Now, where is the great evil you see?" By the early 1820s, a clear distinction formed between the two parties of Wyandots, with Deunquod heading the traditionalists and Between-the-Logs and John Hicks leading the converts. For the next twenty years that the Wyandots remained in Ohio, the Methodist and traditional factions coexisted. The Methodists held a relatively strong position, and two hundred or so of the approximately seven hundred Wyandots belonged to the church in 1843.[12]

Even before Stewart and the Methodist missionaries who followed him began to attack the Wyandots' religious practices, the Indian nation's political structures had undergone more substantial transformations. But the changes in religion and politics became more intertwined in the 1820s. Put simply, over the course of several decades, the Wyandots converted their system of government from a traditional structure that involved women to one loosely based on the American system that to all appearances granted formal powers only to men. By no means did this occur quickly. Indeed, the changes remained incomplete at the time of

[12] *The History of Wyandot County, Ohio*, 276–277; Mitchell, *The Missionary Pioneer*, 24–29; Bloody Eyes quoted in Walsh, "The 'Heathen Party,'" 198–207; Emil Schlup, "The Wyandot Mission," *Ohio Archaeological and Historical Society Publications*, 15(1906): 163–181; Affidavit, July 28 & 31, 1843, WNP.

removal. However, from the end of the eighteenth century to 1843, the Wyandots revised their government, and men like Walker took advantage.

The matrilineal structure of Wyandot society grounded their government prior to the nineteenth century. The main council of the tribe consisted of the councils and chiefs of the twelve different clans of the tribe: Big Turtle, Little Turtle, Mud Turtle, Wolf, Bear, Beaver, Deer, Porcupine, Striped Turtle, Highland Turtle, Snake, and Hawk. Each of the smaller councils had four women and one male chief selected by those four women. Meetings of the clan councils did not have a regular schedule, but occurred when the chief deemed it necessary. Although men filled the offices of chief throughout the structure, the nature of clan leadership meant that women comprised four-fifths of the tribal council. This civil government oversaw a number of aspects of Wyandot society, including personal and property rights. The chief of the Wolf clan served as both herald and sheriff and called the council to order when they met each month on the night of the full moon. Rather than by consensus, the Wyandot council functioned by majority vote taken once each member had a chance to speak. Military affairs, however, fell under the jurisdiction of the military council, which consisted of all the able-bodied men in the tribe.[13]

The first noteworthy changes occurred in the aftermath of military and religious conflicts. General Anthony Wayne's victory over the Indian confederacy in 1794 not only devastated the native alliance but also altered Wyandot practices. The Deer clan, from whom the head chief had been selected formerly, lost so many warriors in the Battle of Fallen Timbers that the council, over the Deer clan's protest, decided to choose future leaders from the Porcupine clan. The splits over Methodism caused a more significant alteration. In 1826, after the death of Deunquod, the principal chief who resisted Christianity, the leading men of the tribe met in council. Rather than accepting the nomination of Deunqod's nephew Sarahas, who shared his uncle's beliefs, these Wyandots decided that they would subsequently choose their leaders through elections held on the first day each year. Reverend James B. Finley, the Methodist minister who observed and noted these events, provided little explanations for the changes. His silence on or ignorance of the roles played by women of the tribe makes it difficult to ascertain their participation in a process that appeared to

[13] William E. Connelley, *Wyandot Folk-Lore* (Topeka, 1899), 25–30; J. W. Powell, "Wyandot Government: A Short Study of Tribal Society," *First Annual Report of the Bureau of Ethnology to the Secretary of the Smithsonian Institution, 1879–1880* (Washington, DC, 1881), 57–69.

undermine their influence in the government. And by the time the Wyandots migrated west of the Mississippi they had a set of written laws. The laws differed in stature. One set up a council of elected leaders and another established a fine for any intoxicated person who rode a horse into another individual's home. Regardless of subject matter, however, the written regulations signaled a departure from custom.[14]

Walker profited from these developments. He was a member of the Big Turtle clan by birth. This clan held an important position in Wyandot society because its members stood first among the twelve in the order of precedence and encampment. Just as the Big Turtle made the Great Island in Wyandot origin stories, the tribal encampment was built around the lodgings of this clan's members. But until Deunquod's death, the principal chief had been the provision of first the Deer and then the Porcupine. William Walker was already an important man in the Wyandot nation. He had worked as an interpreter, as the postmaster for Upper Sandusky, and by the late 1820s as an established merchant. In 1831, he was one of five Wyandots selected by the National Council to inspect the suitability of the lands west of the Mississippi. At the time, U.S. officials viewed Walker as one of the more prominent and influential opponents of removal. Then, in 1836, he was elected principal chief. Although he surely had a voice in Wyandot affairs prior to holding office, this ascension marked a turning point in his authority in Wyandot affairs.[15]

Joseph Parks and William Walker benefited from their respective backgrounds in different ways. A cultivated relationship with Lewis Cass enabled Parks to develop his influence as an interpreter in the Great Lakes even as his kinship ties gave him a place within the Ohio Shawnee community. Meanwhile, Walker relied on the connections of his white father and the clan membership of his French-Wyandot mother to build his position within the white and Indian communities of Ohio. Each man had also shown the ability and desire to serve as a mediator between the

---

[14] Rev. James B. Finley, *The History of the Wyandott Mission at Upper Sandusky, Ohio* (Cincinnati, 1840), 58–59, 377–378; *The History of Wyandot County, Ohio*, 271–272; Amendment to Law, January 22, 1838, WNP.

[15] Connelley, *Wyandot Folk-Lore*, 25–32, 44–45, 70; J. B. Gardiner to Hon. Lewis Cass, September 26, 1831, OIA-LR, roll 601; Abstract of Traders licensed to trade with the Wyandott Indians at Upper Sandusky for the year 1838, OIA-LR, roll 601; Abstract of Traders licensed to trade with the Wyandott Indians at Upper Sandusky for the year 1839, OIA-LR, roll 602; Abstract of Traders licensed to trade with the Wyandott Indians at Upper Sandusky for the year 1840, OIA-LR, roll 602; J. Orin Oliphant (Ed.), "The Report of the Wyandot Exploring Delegation, 1831," *Kansas Historical Quarterly* 3 (August 1947): 248–262; *Indian Affairs*, II, 460–461.

white and Indian communities. It would prove even more valuable in the years after removal.

Although the Shawnees and Wyandots had relocated hundreds of miles from Ohio, they had left behind neither American settlers nor the American government. Instead, they now lived at one of the next focal points of western expansion. But the presence of missionaries, settlers, traders, and federal agents did not disconcert Parks or Walker. Indeed, the two men welcomed the developments that most of their Indian relations viewed as intrusions and invasions. Because of their experience, knowledge, and connections, Parks and Walker became prominent men on the Missouri border. Although their nations struggled at times to handle the onslaught of the 1840s and 1850s, the two men worked hard to rise above the chaos. Parks took advantage of internal Shawnee conflicts and his connections in the nation's capital to gain power. Walker, on the other hand, worked with his brothers and a cohort of like-minded Wyandots to avoid repeating their removal from Ohio.

Shortly after his westward relocation in the fall of 1833, Joseph Parks grounded his already ample economic foundation. He also cemented his good reputation with American officials. Lewis Cass had by then moved on to Washington to serve as Andrew Jackson's Secretary of War, and most officials knew of the relationship between Parks and the new overseer of the Indian Department. "From long acquaintance with him [Parks] the Secretary of War has full confidence in his integrity," observed Commissioner of Indian Affairs Elbert Herring. This understanding trickled down to the lower levels of the administration as well. In the mid-1830s Parks could depend on employment as a government interpreter during the downtimes in his merchant career, in part because he was one of the few men with whom Richard Cummins at Fort Leavenworth was comfortable. Amazingly enough, Parks's relative unfamiliarity with languages other than Shawnee and English did not undermine Cummins's opinion. Yet, it may have been his service in the war against the Seminoles in Florida that forever gave Parks credibility among American officials. In 1837, he led a command of over eighty Shawnees and Delawares to assist the federal government's efforts against the Seminoles. It was during this service that he earned the title of Captain. By the late 1830s, to American officials at least, Captain Parks was a trustworthy man and a reliable intermediary.[16]

---

[16] E. Herring to Col. John McElvain, April 5, 1834, OIA-LR, roll 601. For Parks's economic success in the West, see Chapter 3; B. F. Larned to C. A. Harris, March 12, 1838, OIA-LR, roll 301; Rich Cummins to C. A. Harris, January 29, 1838, OIA-LR, roll 301. For

But the story of his rise from an interpreter at the 1831 treaty to the principal chief at the 1854 accord is as much about the conflicts within the Shawnee community as it is about Joseph Parks. Even as removal separated the Ohio bands from their homes east of the Mississippi it reunited them with those Shawnees who had headed west in the 1780s and 1790s. The difficulties created by this relocation only complicated the larger problem of uniting disparate Indian bands. Debates over the appropriation of land and annuities in the West began not long after the arrival and settlement of the Wapakoneta and Hog Creek Shawnees. At the same time, individuals and bands battled with each other and with missionaries over the roles of Christianity and schools in the lives of the community and the Shawnee children. Although these battles lasted well into the 1850s, they were only one symptom of a more contentious issue – political control. The social and political organizations of years past had fragmented further into the bands and villages of the late eighteenth and early nineteenth centuries. Yet, on the Kansas River reserve, the U.S. government expected the Shawnees to become a nation. The Ohio bands took advantage of their extended contact with U.S. officials and grabbed the leadership reins. And despite criticism from all sides, Joseph Parks, whose economic success and political connections often made him invaluable to both the Ohio and Missouri Shawnees, became the face of the Shawnee nation.[17]

Postremoval debates over land and annuities centered on competing interpretations of the treaties signed in 1825 and 1831. The Cape Girardeau band that had first settled on a Spanish land grant negotiated and signed the 1825 agreement. That accord promised the Shawnees a reserve of fifty square miles west of the Missouri border, a promise that encompassed any of the Ohio Shawnees who emigrated in the future. In the treaty signed by the Wapakoneta and Hog Creek bands in 1831, the federal government guaranteed the approximately four hundred Ohio Shawnees a tract measuring one-hundred thousand acres west of the Missouri border. Although the relevant article stated that this land would be located within the Missouri Shawnee reserve, an additional provision permitted it to be located elsewhere under certain conditions. This situation became much more complicated in May 1844, when the U.S.

Parks and the Shawnees in the efforts against the Seminoles, see Isaac McCoy, *History of Baptist Indian Missions* (Washington, DC, 1840), 544–545; Edwin C. McReynolds, *The Seminoles* (Norman, 1957), 193, 201.

[17] This process of political change before and after removal is also discussed in Stephen Warren, *The Shawnees and Their Neighbors, 1795–1870* (Urbana, 2005).

government issued a title for the entire Western Reserve to the Missouri Shawnees and simultaneously issued a joint right of occupancy to the Ohio Shawnees. Into the 1850s, Shawnee leaders and both houses of Congress argued over who had the proper claim to the reserve, based on those two treaties.[18]

Federal misconceptions about Shawnee society and politics compounded these disagreements. Most treaties failed to recognize the numerous bands that comprised the larger Shawnee community. The Missouri Shawnees, under which designation the Fish, Rogerstown, Apple Creek, and Cape Girardeau bands fell, were not a homogeneous entity with shared political interests. Neither were the Ohio Shawnees, whose membership included the Wapakoneta, Hog Creek, Huron River, and Lewistown bands. Many of these competing interests played out during the relocation to the Kansas River reserve. The Cape Girardeau band believed that government commissioners had misled them about the 1825 treaty and argued that they had never agreed to allow any Ohio Shawnees to settle on the western lands. As a result, a portion of the Shawnees under the leadership of Black Bob did not move to eastern Kansas and instead settled along the White River in Arkansas. Meanwhile, the Rogerstown and Fish bands traveled directly to eastern Kansas, where successive parties of Ohio Shawnees joined them over the next several years. A more complete reunion in 1833 occurred only through intimidation. Black Bob's band still had no desire to move to the Kansas River. "So long a period has elapsed since we [Black Bob band] separated from them [the Ohio Shawnees]," they explained, "that there is now but little of a common feeling of blood and friendship existing between us and them." Attempts at compromise failed, and finally the federal government threatened to use force. By 1833, therefore, except for the Shawnees in Mexican territory and those living with the Senecas along the Cowskin River, the majority of the nation resided on the reserve created by the 1825 treaty.[19]

Mere geographic proximity could not create political unity. The widespread separation of the previous forty years also meant that it was not so simple to return to the customary divisions of the past. Migrations had dispersed members of the five tribal divisions that had once more

---

[18] *Indian Affairs*, II, 262–264, 331–334. For a summation of the issue regarding the title to the Kansas Reserve, see R.W. Thompson to A. S. Loughery, October 3, 1850, OIA-LR, roll 303; *Congressional Globe*, August 5, 1852, and March 3, 1853.

[19] Shawnee Chiefs to President Andrew Jackson, November 20, 1831, in Senate Document No. 512, 23rd Congress, 1st Session, Serial No. 245, 705–706; *American Indian Resource Handbook* (Missouri Lewis and Clark Bicentennial Commission, 2004), 26–27.

fully organized Shawnee society. Even though the Shawnees, who moved
to Missouri in the late 1700s, primarily belonged to the Thawegila division, not all movements had occurred within the context of such frameworks. Having lived apart for so many years, each band resisted merging with another and losing its independence. Years later, the principal
men of the Ohio Shawnees would describe their arrival in the West as
an event that "made the council fires complete." They misrepresented
the situation. The Missouri Shawnees as a whole, and the Black Bob
band in particular, stressed that they maintained hereditary leadership
through the Thawegila, Piqua, and Kispokotha divisions. From the mid-
1830s to the early 1850s, then, the Shawnees lacked a government or
council that reflected the interests of all who lived on the Kansas River
reserve.[20]

One arena in which the Shawnee leaders acted out their differences was
the annuity payments granted by treaties signed over the previous four
decades. The U.S. government seldom had the payments up to date with
the Shawnees' geographic location. In 1838, for example, the Lewistown
Shawnees had to inform William Clark on the whereabouts of their band
members to ensure a proper distribution. The main problem, however,
was that the Ohio Shawnees who relocated in the 1830s received the bulk
of the money and did not believe that any Shawnee who had moved west
during the prior four decades had any claim to it. From their perspective,
the Missouri bands had given up their rights to the Ohio lands when
they moved west without an official treaty. Members of the Fish and
Rogerstown band denounced this interpretation. "When I [Lewis Rogers]
left them [Ohio Shawnees] I left them in possession of a good country
mine as well as theirs," Rogers asserted in 1838. "I have waited to see if
my brothers would ever think of me as I did of them." Especially once
the Ohio bands relocated to the reserve created by the 1825 treaty, the
Missouri bands believed they deserved some of the money. Even those
Ohio Shawnees who relocated in the late 1820s had to fight for their
share of the payments due from the treaties signed in 1795 and 1817.
Cornstalk, who had moved west in 1826, protested that "our brothers
that we left ... have been mad with us for it ever since, and are trying to
do us all the harm they can for it." The debates over the proper payments

[20] Kinietz and Voegelin, *Shawnese Traditions*, 8–15; Alford, *Civilization*, 200–203; Howard,
Shawnee!, 24–31, 106–110; Matthew King, Graham Rodgers, John Perry, Charles
Bluejacket, David Deshane, and Charles Tucker to D. N. Colley, CIA, March 12, 1866,
OIA-LR, roll 814.

and the distribution of moneys persisted into the 1850s, as Shawnees from different bands strove to correct the perceived wrongs.[21]

For the better part of the first three decades they resided on the reserve, the Shawnees also used the Christian missions as a channel for their political struggles. From 1830 to the late 1850s, the Shawnees attempted to control the access and impact of missionaries. Negotiations with the Baptists, Methodists, and Quakers had begun even before the arrival of the Wapakoneta and Hog Creek Shawnees. Unfortunately, at least in the missionaries' eyes, the Shawnees in the West refused to limit themselves to the services of only one denomination. Several headmen welcomed both day and boarding schools, all the while stressing their interest in the services the missionaries provided as opposed to the theology the ministers preached. Although the struggles regarding education and religion did not always involve the larger internal conflicts, such battles more often than not reflected the political divisions on the reserve.[22]

In the summer of 1830, the Methodists and the Baptists answered the call for a missionary among the Shawnees. A Missouri Shawnee chief named Fish spoke to the local Indian Agent, George Vashon, and requested a missionary establishment to educate the children of his band. Fish, also known as William Jackson, was a white man raised among the Shawnees since childhood. He and his band relocated to eastern Kansas from Missouri in 1828, and now wanted a school. Vashon quickly responded to this request and passed along the message to Reverend Jesse Green, the Presiding Elder for the Missouri District of the Methodist Episcopal Church (MEC). As the letter made its way to Green, however, another missionary intruded. Isaac McCoy entered the Shawnee reserve in August 1830 while on a survey expedition for the Delawares. The missionary and his two sons encouraged the Shawnees to accept a Baptist mission. Tenskwatawa, Captain Peter Cornstalk, Captain William Perry, and the other assembled Shawnees appeared pleased with his offer. After the formal council, McCoy also spoke with Fish, at which time the Shawnee headman reiterated his desire for a mission school. But this meeting did not alter his first agreement. Fish's band would have a Methodist school and the Ohio Shawnees would have a Baptist school. In September 1830

[21] James McLean et al. to General William Clark, January 16, 1838, OIA-LR, roll 301; Lewis Rogers et al. to C. A. Harris, March 6, 1838, OIA-LR, roll 301; Statements in Council, April 10, 1830, OIA-LR, roll 300; Warren, *The Shawnees and Their Neighbors*, 143–148. For the texts of the Shawnee treaties from 1795 to 1832 that include annuities, see, *Indian Affairs*, II, 39–45, 77–78, 145–155, 162–163, 262–264, 327–334, 383–385.

[22] Harvey, *History of the Shawnee Indians*, 138–152.

the Methodists organized their mission and appointed Thomas Johnson as
its supervisor. Johnston Lykins, McCoy's son-in-law, crossed the Mississippi in July 1831 and commenced construction on the Baptist mission.[23]

During the 1830s and 1840s, the two denominations traded verbal
jabs. The Methodists initially criticized the Baptist practice of teaching in
Shawnee as opposed to English. They quickly changed their minds when
the Shawnee council decided that they wanted to adopt the written
Shawnee developed by Jotham Meeker, a Baptist missionary and skilled
printer. When the Methodists established a Manual Labor School in 1839
that housed the Indian students, the practice split the Baptist ranks. Lykins
and McCoy supported the idea and Meeker and Robert Simerwell fought
it. From the reports sent by the Methodist missionary Thomas Johnson,
the school was an unmitigated success, with a student population of more
than one hundred students after only a few years. Such numbers made
both the Methodists and the government who supported their efforts
look good, which in turn increased the tension in eastern Kansas, as
both the Baptists and the Quakers felt neglected and overshadowed. Then
in 1842, the Baptists and Methodists went to battle over the standards
used to accept an Indian conversion, and accusations flew over "stolen"
converts.[24]

But these arguments between the Baptists and Methodists were pointless because most Shawnees did not dwell on theological differences.
Shawnee parents saw an opportunity for their children to learn to read,
write, and gain skills that would give them an advantage in future interactions with American citizens and society. As a result, they protested when
any missionary appeared to stray. In May 1833, John Perry, William Perry,
and Peter Cornstalk complained to William Clark about the Methodists.
Rather than dwelling on issues of religion, these Shawnee leaders criticized
Thomas Johnson for meddling in their affairs. Not only did he constantly

---

[23] Isaac McCoy, *History of Baptist Indian Missions*, 403–405; Isaac McCoy to Lucius Bolles,
December 1, 1830, roll 610, IMP; Isaac McCoy to Philanthropists, December 1, 1831,
roll 610, IMP; Martha B. Caldwell (Comp.), *Annals of the Shawnee Methodist Mission
and the Indian Manual Labor School* (Topeka, 1939), 6, 16; Wade C. Barclay, *History of
Methodist Missions* (4 vols., New York, 1973), II, 176–177; J. J. Lutz, "The Methodist
Missions among the Indian Tribes in Kansas," *Kansas State Historical Collections*,
9(1905–1906): 160–230; Kevin Abing, "A Holy Battleground: Methodist, Baptist, and
Quaker Missionaries Among Shawnee Indians, 1830–1844," *Kansas History*, 21(2),
(1998): 118–123. Although Abing asserts that Fish and William Jackson were two different men, they were in fact one and the same person.

[24] For a more detailed description of the numerous fights between these two denominations,
see Abing, "A Holy Battleground," 123–131.

harass them about visiting McCoy's mission, but he also "cultivated too much of our land and builds too many houses and cuts too much of our timber." Because these men were Wapakoneta Shawnees, their protest most likely had an element of politics involved. They even made it clear that although they had given leave to Johnson to set up a school for Fish's band, they did not want him "to meddle himself with our people." Yet, the Shawnees' displeasure extended to the Baptists as well. At two different points in 1834 the tribal council requested that the government remove all missionaries from their lands. Isaac McCoy questioned this decision, and he implied that white men in the vicinity unduly influenced the Shawnees against the missionaries. Putting aside his differences with his religious adversaries, McCoy insisted that the majority of the western Shawnees accepted and desired the Baptists and the Methodists.[25]

By blaming Shawnee complaints on outside meddlers, McCoy ignored both the content of the Indians' initial requests and the missionaries' initial failure to follow through on their promises. When Fish spoke to Agent Vashon in the summer of 1830, he asked for a mission to educate the children. The Shawnee chief's son, Paschal, already had some schooling, and the headman wanted the other children in his band to learn as well. Although other Shawnee leaders did not take the same initiative as Fish, they acceded to the missionary presence, and some welcomed the educational opportunity for their children. When the first missionary schools had problems, therefore, the Indians found good reason to complain. The Methodist mission had to shut down twice in its first two years of operation because of smallpox outbreaks. Similarly, a comment made in a report on the Baptist Missions in Indian Country in 1835 suggests that the Baptist school for the Shawnees was just as inconsistent, if not more so. The report noted that Robert Simerwell held the post at the Shawnee mission, "so school was taught at present." Because Simerwell also worked with the Potawatomis, the amount of energy devoted to the Indians' schooling remains unclear. At the very least, the missionary could not bestow his full attention to the education of the Shawnee children.[26]

---

[25] Shawnee Indians to William Clark, May 26, 1833, OIA-LR, roll 300; Isaac McCoy to Elbert Herring, CIA, January 19, 1835, roll 611, IMP; Abing, "A Holy Battleground," 124–125.

[26] Thomas Johnson to SOW, August 16, 1833, Indian Files – Shawnees, Box 6, KSHS; Caldwell, *Annals, 6,* 13–14; Unknown to Richard Cummins, September 10, 1835, roll 611, IMP. For other reports on the missions, see Rev. Jerome C. Berryman, "A Circuit Rider's Frontier Experiences," *Collections of the Kansas State Historical Society,* 16(1923–1925): 177–226; Rev. William Johnson and Other Missionaries, "Letters from the Indian Missions in Kansas," in ibid., 227–271.

Many of these early disputes regarding the missionaries originated from one segment of the Shawnee population. Because they received the bulk of the annuities and had a longer relationship with U.S. officials, the principal men of the Wapakoneta band were usually described as "the Shawnee Council," a reference that appeared to make them the spokesmen for the entire reserve. And the Wapakoneta Shawnees had little use for the Methodists and Baptists. Although William Perry and Cornstalk accepted the Baptist offer in 1830, even McCoy had to admit that they consented "through courtesy," and not from "a desire really to enjoy the advantages of education." As demonstrated by their verbal assaults against the Methodists, however, the Wapakonetas did not single out the Baptists. The Shawnees even stepped up their attacks when their principal speaker, Wayweleapy, joined the Methodist Church shortly after removal. John Perry and the other leaders immediately expelled him from their council and declared he could only return if he renounced his new religion. Wayweleapy refused. In an extended attempt to hurt the Methodists, the Wapakonetas then capitalized on their control of the annuities and offered any Missouri Shawnee who renounced Christianity the opportunity to participate in the payments. Although not a complete success, the tactic did gain some converts.[27]

But the Wapakonetas' most significant move against the Methodists and Baptists came when leaders encouraged the Quakers to establish a school on the reserve. Removal did not end the relationship that had started with Black Hoof in 1807, and Henry Harvey visited the Shawnees in the summer of 1833 to check in on his former charges. The Friends still wanted to work with the Shawnees. Two years later, Harvey and Simon Hadley talked to the Wapakoneta council and arranged for the construction of a school. The Shawnees praised this arrangement. "Our old grandfathers when they first met the Quakers took them by the hand," Perry and his colleagues explained, "and ever since then we have lived together in friendship." In large part this friendship was built on the fact that, contrary to the Baptists and the Methodists, the Quakers did not coerce change in the Indians' way of life. For this reason the Wapakoneta band did more than just welcome their old friends to the reserve. "We the chiefs are determined to give our children up first," they declared, "so that it will encourage our people to send and encourage the school." Eight

[27] McCoy, *History of Baptist Indian Missions*, 403–405; Isaac McCoy to Lucius Bolles, December 1, 1830, roll 610, IMP; *Western Christian Advocate*, March 31, 1837.

years later a total of thirty-four Shawnee children attended the Quaker manual labor school.[28]

Despite their best efforts, John Perry and the Wapakoneta council did not have the power to enforce their ideas onto either the missionaries or their fellow Shawnees. When Joseph Parks and the Hog Creek band arrived in 1833, they did not follow the wishes of the Wapakoneta council. Parks gave some attention to McCoy and the Baptists but showed more interest in Johnson and the Methodists. By the early 1840s, even some members of the Wapakoneta band affiliated themselves with the Methodists and sent their children to the Manual Labor School. Twenty-seven Shawnees attended regularly during the school's first year in 1839. Over the next decade, the number rose only slightly, reaching thirty-six in 1851. Four years later, according to Johnson's records, the attendance of Shawnee children reached eighty-seven. These affiliations extended beyond the children and into the participation and conversion of adults. Although Fish died in October 1834, his sons Paschal and Charles followed the wishes of their father. Paschal served as a class leader at the mission meetings by 1838, exhorted in public the following year, and became a licensed preacher in 1843. Lewis and William Rogers joined Paschal at the meetings in the late 1830s and early 1840s, which meant that the Rogerstown band also had a presence. The Rogerses were sons of Lewis Rogers, a white captive, and the daughter of the Shawnee chief Blackfish. The two boys and their brothers had gone to a Methodist school in Kentucky, which no doubt influenced their affiliation. Meanwhile, Waywaleapy continued to participate in the Methodist meetings and even spoke during religious services. Although Methodist Shawnees were still a significant minority, their participation illustrated the ability of Johnson and his colleagues to transcend tribal politics.[29]

---

[28] R. David Edmunds, "'A Watchful Safeguard to Our Habitations': Black Hoof and the Loyal Shawnees," in Frederick Hoxie, Ronald Hoffman, and Peter J. Albert (Eds.), *Native Americans and the Early Republic* (Charlottesville, VA, 1999), 162–199; Harvey, *History of the Shawnee Indians*, 234–236; Speech of the Chiefs, May 25, 1835, OIA-LR, roll 302; The Annual Report of Friends Shawnee School for Indian Children, October 8, 1842, OIA-LR, roll 301.

[29] Stephen Warren, "Between Villages and Nations: The Emergence of Shawnee Nationalism, 1800–1870" (Ph.D. Dissertation, Indiana University, 2000), 185–195; *Western Christian Advocate*, January 2, 1835, March 31, 1837, July 19, 1839, July 30, 1841; Report from Shawnee Indian Manual Labor School, August 15, 1842, OIA-LR, roll 301; Annual Report of Indian Manual Labor School, September 15, 1844, OIA-LR, roll 302; Richard Cummins to Thomas Harvey, October 30, 1847, OIA-LR, roll 302; Joab

Although it is true, as Stephen Warren argues, that "the Methodists were the first denomination to significantly break down the division between villagers from Ohio and Missouri," this appearance of unity in the early 1840s ended after only a few years. According to the scattered Methodist records, the adult Shawnees who attended meetings after the summer of 1846 were primarily members of the Hog Creek and Huron River bands. One significant reason for this change rested in the Methodist connection to slavery. Native students were not the only individuals who lived at the Shawnee Manual Labor School. Although the location was far north of the boundary line established by the Missouri Compromise of 1820, Thomas Johnson owned a number of slaves. The labor provided by the students as part of their curriculum did not take care of all the necessary tasks, and these slaves worked both in the kitchens and the fields. Johnson also made additions to this population during his tenure and purchased at least four slaves in the 1850s. In addition, the MEC split in 1845 into a northern and a southern division, neither side willing to compromise. Without hesitation, Thomas Johnson affiliated himself and the school with the southern faction.[30]

The rift in the church revived the divisions within the Shawnee Methodists. By the following year Shawnees with antislavery leanings began to keep their children out of the Manual Labor School. Then in 1849, approximately eighty-five Shawnees petitioned the MEC North to send them a preacher so that they could continue to hold services. Reverend Thomas Markham's arrival brought a quick response. Indian Agent Luke Lea notified the minister that the Shawnee Council wanted the northern preacher off the reserve. Because his preaching was calculated

Spencer, "Chief Blackfish and His White Captive," *Christian Advocate*, October 28, 1910; Thomas Johnson to Major R. C. Miller, September 30, 1855, Doc. 37 in *ARCIA*; Recording Steward's Book for Shawnee Mission, Indian Files – Shawnees, Box 6, KSHS.
[30] Warren, "Between Villages and Nations," 193–194; Recording Steward's Book for Shawnee Mission, Indian Files – Shawnees, Box 6, KSHS; Ed Blair, *History of Johnson County, Kansas* (Lawrence, 1915), 37–38; *New York Daily Tribune*, December 16, 1854; Caldwell, *Annals*, 76, 86, 95. For the split within the Methodist Episcopal Church in 1845, see Barclay, *History of Methodist Missions*, 102–111; John R. McKivigan, "The Sectional Division of the Methodist and Baptist Denominations as Measures of Northern Antislavery Sentiment," in John R. McKivigan and Mitchell Snay (Eds.), *Religion and the Antebellum Debate over Slavery* (Athens, GA, 1998), 343–363. The Baptists also split in 1845 over slavery, but the lack of a central governing structure similar to that of the Methodists made for a less dramatic separation that did not exhibit the same bitter debates or divisions among those present in Indian Territory. See McKivigan and Snay, 349–351; Rev. S. Peck to John G. Pratt, November 15, 1842, FBP; Rev. S. Peck to Isaac McCoy, September 27, 1845, roll 614, IMP.

"to divide and distract their nation," it was necessary for him to leave. Markham's supporters countered quickly. In a communication to Commissioner of Indian Affairs Orlando Brown, Paschal Fish, Charles Fish, and William Rogers railed against Johnson's stance and argued that Lea overstepped the authority of his office. "We as an independent people chose to remain in the old church," they declared. More important, the Fish brothers and Rogers declared that the Shawnee council had gone too far. They asked that the Shawnee chiefs be informed, "that this [religious affiliation] is a matter over which they have no right to control." This attack against the Shawnee council hardened the battle lines.[31]

As demonstrated by the protest addressed to Commissioner Brown, the struggles between the northern and southern Methodist factions could not escape politics. In 1850, as in the 1830s, members of the Ohio bands dominated the council recognized as the tribal government by the United States. But, although the Ohio Shawnees remained the dominant presence, the composition of the council had changed. John Perry served as the head of this council and principal chief for most of the 1830s until his death in 1845. Into the 1840s, in fact, the Wapakoneta band comprised the majority of the council. Then, in the mid-1840s, death claimed several members of the council. Henry Clay (or Nolesimo) and Waywaleapy passed away around the same time as John Perry. The deaths of these entrenched leaders opened the door to both a new generation and a new way of conducting business. Other members of the Wapakoneta band, including at least two sons of Black Hoof, continued to hold positions on the council. However, the Hog Creek and Huron River Shawnees slowly infiltrated the circles of power.[32]

Joseph Parks was perfectly positioned to assume a more influential position as the elder and influential Wapakoneta headmen passed away. No Shawnee was more capable at the time of filling the power vacuum. Starting in the early 1840s, he reaped the rewards of his connections to American officials. Although he was still criticized by some Wapakonetas

[31] Richard Cummins to Thomas Harvey, January 16, 1849, OIA-LR, roll 303; Luke Lea to Rev. Mr. Markham, March 20, 1850, OIA-LR, roll 303; Shawnee Indians to Orlando Brown, April 22, 1850, OIA-LR, roll 303.

[32] Shawnee chiefs to unknown, February 7, 1835, OIA-LR, roll 300; Shawnee annuity request, August 30, 1836, OIA-LR, roll 300; Shawnee chiefs to D. D. Mitchell, June 20, 1842, OIA-LR, roll 302; Shawnee chiefs to T. Hartley Crawford, March 30, 1844, OIA-LR, roll 302; Louise Barry, *The Beginning of the West: Annals of the Kansas Gateway to the American West, 1540–1854* (Topeka, 1972), 566; Declaration of power of Attorney by Shawnee Chiefs, December 10, 1852, OIA-LR, roll 364.

for his work at the 1831 treaty, his influence in Washington could not be ignored. As a result, between 1842 and 1849 Parks made three different visits to Washington to lobby on behalf of the Shawnees regarding annuity and land issues. Then, in 1844, his stock rose further. By March of that year Parks had become the third-ranking chief in the Shawnee council, ahead of even Black Hoof's son, Young Black Hoof. The next month Parks traveled to Washington, D.C., carrying two different letters. In the first missive, the Shawnee council appointed him to investigate when the Wapakoneta and Hog Creek bands might receive a patent-in-fee-simple to the one hundred thousand acres promised them in the 1831 accord. Parks also held a letter from several Missouri Shawnees. Its contents affirmed the ways in which his status as a broker rose above political divides. "We the undersigned Chiefs of the Shawanees who were parties to the Treaty Concluded at St. Louis on the 7th day of November 1825 are concerned that all the provisions of the Treaty have never been complied with," Lewis Rogers, William Rogers, Mayahwathkuck, and Mathahpaskah explained. Because they had not received an answer to their repeated queries, they now took advantage of the opportunity to have "our friend Joseph Parks" obtain a response in the American capital.[33]

Significant structural changes paralleled this personnel shift, although these changes were not without dispute. The power struggle heightened in reaction to the western expansion of the United States. Control of the tribal government was especially important to Parks and the Ohio Shawnees, who feared that, without official title to any land on the reserve, they might be left with nothing. Change began with slight alterations in the decision-making process. At a council held during their annuity payments in December 1848, the Shawnees held a vote when an extended discussion on the chiefs' individual payments did not result in consensus. Many Shawnees, including all of the women present, chose not to participate. Agent Cummins proposed the vote, a departure from the norm and a possible reason why those Shawnees abstained. Yet, nearly one hundred and twenty Indians did cast their votes and abided by the results. In this way, matters of national concern appeared to move beyond the tribal council. Three years later the Shawnees adopted a republican form of government, a move that heralded a more substantial transformation.

[33] Richard Cummins to T. Hartley Crawford, February 2, 1842, OIA-LR, roll 301; Shawnee chiefs and councilors to T. H. Crawford, March 30, 1844, OIA-LR, roll 302; Missouri Shawnee chiefs to T. Hartley Crawford, March 30, 1844, OIA-LR, roll 302; Luke Lea to D. D. Mitchell, November 23, 1849, OIA-LR, roll 303.

This new governing structure contained seven elected officials: a head chief, a second chief, and five council members. Elections took place every autumn and consisted of public declarations by each voter for their candidate. More than a decade after this modification, Charles Bluejacket remembered that the Shawnees "by unanimous consent adopted a republican form of Government under which they lived contented and satisfied." Bluejacket had a selective memory. A delegation of Shawnees, including Black Bob, protested to U.S. officials only a few years after the change. Rather than welcoming an elective government, Black Bob and his supporters believed that the old hereditary chief would best represent the tribe's interests. These men not only opposed the new government, but also declared "that a majority of their nation are with them and would rejoice at an order from their Great father putting an end to the present Government of their nation and restoring their old form of Government." The political divisions on the reserve remained unhealed.[34]

Black Bob and other like-minded Shawnees also found fault with the amount of power granted to Joseph Parks. Parks became the first elected chief in 1852 and over the next two years came under fire for appearing to promote a new treaty with U.S. officials. But his position at the head of a new republican government recognized by the United States made the new chief difficult to depose or even oppose. Knowing that they lacked the power to initiate change from within, a delegation of six Shawnees visited the Kansas Agency in October 1853. Thomas Captain and Charles Bluejacket joined the familiar leading men of the Missouri bands, Charles Fish, Paschal Fish, Henry Rogers, and William Rogers, in protesting the future plans of their principal chief. They had heard that Parks was preparing to hire a frequent business partner of his, a lawyer named Richard W. Thompson, to draw up a treaty to send to the Commissioner of Indian Affairs. From all appearances, their complaints went unanswered. Indeed, it helped the U.S. government to have the Shawnee principal chief amenable to a treaty at a time when American expansion had become both desired and unavoidable.[35]

---

[34] Richard Cummings to Thomas H. Harvey, January 13, 1849, OIA-LR, roll 303; B. J. Newsom to A. M. Robinson, SIA, September 5, 1860, OIA-LR, roll 811; James B. Abbott to William Dole, CIA, April 6, 1863, OIA-LR, roll 813; Charles Bluejacket to D. N. Cooley, CIA, November 30, 1865, OIA-LR, roll 814; B. F. Robinson to Colonel A. Cumming, SIA, March 31, 1855, OIA-LR, roll 364; Callender, "Shawnee," 627–628; Howard, *Shawnee!*, 106–112.

[35] B. F. Robinson to Albert Cumming, October 14, 1853, OIA-LR, roll 364.

As the Shawnees faced the prospect of an organized Kansas Territory in 1854, they remained as divided as they had been when they first arrived on the reserve. The nearly three decades between removal and the organization of Kansas had proved difficult, as a number of Shawnee leaders struggled for power. But the more things had changed, the more they had stayed the same. The Ohio Shawnees had retained their position of influence, although no longer through the hereditary leadership of men like Black Hoof, Cornstalk, John Perry, or their descendants. Now the leadership rested in the hands of Joseph Parks, a man who had the external connections to make him valuable and enough community influence to make him powerful.

Contrary to Parks, William Walker was already well-established in the circles of Wyandot leadership at the time of his nation's removal from Ohio. But he reached new heights in the West. On July 26, 1853, a small group of Wyandots, white traders, and government employees met at the Wyandot Council House and named Walker the provisional governor for the newly organized Nebraska Territory, which would include all of the lands on which the eastern Indians resided. It was a local movement fueled in part by outside interests who hoped to preempt the organization of the region by the federal government. More important, the movement included a number of Wyandot men driven by the interconnected motives of benefiting from American expansion and avoiding one more removal. Along with William Walker and his younger brothers Matthew and Joel, this cohort of Wyandot leaders controlled the nation's government in the 1840s and 1850s. With William in the lead, the Wyandot elite prepared to welcome American settlement.[36]

Discussions about removal and the actual relocation had both produced a struggle within the Ohio Wyandots and set the stage for events in the 1850s. The so-called Pagan party wanted to leave Ohio when white settlements began to surround their reserve. But the Christian party, comprised of Methodist converts, hoped to stay. As Ohio citizens and the state legislature increased the pressure on the Wyandot leadership, the tribal council passed a law criminalizing the sale of the nation's lands without consent. This did not ease the burden. In successive letters to the Governor of Ohio, Joseph Vance, William Walker and the Wyandot leadership wondered whether the citizens of Ohio "positively require our removal to the West?" They already knew the answer to that question.

---

[36] The development and actions of this movement to organize Nebraska Territory is examined in Connelley, "The Provisional Government of Nebraska Territory," 17–42.

"We can only indulge in unavailing regrets, at the idea of being abandoned by our Ohio friends," Walker lamented. Although they disliked the idea, the Wyandot council negotiated and signed a removal treaty in 1842. The situation became more complicated when U.S. officials stated that they could not obtain the promised one hundred forty-eight thousand acres because it had been appropriated to the Miamis and the Six Nations. Instead of finding another open piece of land, the Wyandots used their national funds to purchase a portion of the Delaware Indians' reserve. This, in short, is how the Wyandots came to reside at the confluence of the Kansas and Missouri rivers on thirty-nine sections of land that became more valuable with every year.[37]

The Delaware purchase produced opposition from those who did not believe the leaders had acted in the best interests of the nation. James Rankin, William Walker's maternal uncle and a member of the Legislative Council in the late 1840s, wondered about the paradox involved in the purchase. "The lands bought of the Delawares lies on the Missouri River where our people are exposed to all the vices and frauds of a River trade," he explained. Yet, the Wyandots had left Ohio to move "to a country where there would be fewer snares for our people." Rankin further argued that the Wyandot council made the decision without the consent of the whole nation, a charge that the council refuted. Indian agent Jonathan Phillips agreed with Rankin and reported a hidden motivation behind the purchase. According to Phillips, the Wyandot leaders and "half-breeds" had completed the negotiations with the Delawares "for the object of selling it to the Government in a few years at a great advance." In other words, instead of finding a home for their people, the Wyandot council had made a real estate investment. Phillips, in part, blamed the influence of the Walkers, who "have fattened and got rich among the Indians . . . are the principal advisers of the Chiefs, and wield an influence which it is difficult to keep within proper bounds."[38]

Although he appeared ignorant of the kinship ties, clan membership, and former positions of the Walker family, Phillips did not misrepresent

---

[37] Peter Dooyentate Clarke, *Origin and Traditional History of the Wyandotts, and Sketches of Other Indian Tribes of North America* (Toronto, 1870), 120–121; William Walker to Joseph Vance, July 9, 1837, OIA-LR, roll 601; John Barnett et al. to Joseph Vance, July 29, 1837, OIA-LR, roll 601; *Indian Affairs, II*, 534–537; Jonathan Phillips to Thomas H. Harvey, June 30, 1844, OIA-LR, roll 950; Smith, "The Wyandot Indians," 64–69; Grant Foreman, *The Last Trek of the Indians* (Chicago, 1946), 97–98, 194.

[38] James Rankin to William Wilkins, Upper Sandusky, May 12, 1844, OIA-LR, roll 950; James Washington et al. to Friends, June 4, 1846, OIA-LR, roll 950; Jonathan Phillips to Thomas H. Harvey, June 30, 1844, OIA-LR, roll 950.

their influence. The Walkers were powerful. Silas Armstrong, another Wyandot leader, referred to William and his younger brothers Matthew and Joel at different times as "the Walker tribe." By the late 1840s, the three brothers relied on a combination of social, economic, and political interests to wield tremendous clout in the region. Both Matthew and Joel had mercantile interests in Missouri, and Joel had a partnership with Hiram Northrup and William Chick in Westport. All three Walker brothers oversaw diverse real estate interests worth hundreds, if not thousands, of dollars, whether they rented buildings on the reserve or earned money by leasing land they owned in Cass County, Missouri. The three men also held a variety of appointed and elected positions in the years after removal. The Wyandots elected both William and Matthew to the Legislative Council in 1850, and William proceeded to win reelection two out of the next three years. At different points, Matthew received appointments to survey the boundaries of the Delaware purchase and to assist in the revision of the national constitution. The Walker brothers maintained strong connections to the white and Indian communities, and they wanted to forge a more formidable relationship between those two worlds on the Missouri border.[39]

Their efforts occurred during a period of transition as the Wyandots mixed new developments with old procedures. Between 1846 and 1851, the Wyandots overhauled their written constitution at least three times. By the end of this extended process, the government encompassed a principal chief, an executive council, a legislative committee, and a supreme court. Of these four elements, only the judges on the court were not elected. Prior practices did not completely disappear, however, and although women did not participate in the revisions of the constitutions and did not hold any position in the new governments, they still voted at the National Councils. The annual elections also coincided with the Green Corn Ceremony, a traditional feast that continued after removal. This ceremony, which had parallels among many of the eastern Indian nations, marks the time when sweet corn can be harvested and eaten. Although the traditions differed

---

[39] Silas Armstrong to J. M. Armstrong, March 6, 1846, WNP; Silas Armstrong to J. M. Armstrong, March 10, 1846, WNP; Census Return of Families in the Missouri Branch of the Wyandot Tribe of Indians, 1847, OIA-LR, roll 950; Connelley, "The Provisional Government of Nebraska Territory," 196–197, 246, 281, 301, 304n, 313, 330, 355, 366, 392; Perl W. Morgan (Ed. and Comp.), *History of Wyandotte County, Kansas and Its People* (Chicago, 1911); Washington Henry Chick, "A Journey to Missouri in 1822," *State Centennial Souvenir Number and Program, 1821–1921, Missouri Centennial*, 1(October 3, 1921): 97–104.

from community to community, the celebration also emphasized religious renewal and thanksgiving. The Wyandots also held a ceremony during which clan names were bestowed and clan chiefs symbolically ratified any adoptions.[40]

Yet, the legislation considered and passed by the elected Wyandot leadership in the 1840s and 1850s indicated more substantial alterations of customary practices. The Council dealt with a wide range of issues. Bills prohibiting adultery, erecting jails, and outlawing ardent spirits shared time with resolutions making it illegal for a single family to own more than two dogs. Although the origins of canine ownership regulation may prove difficult to trace, the catalysts for other legislation are more apparent. The influence of Christianity undoubtedly led to the passage of laws punishing "Sabbath breaking" in the early 1850s. Meanwhile, the prevailing interest in private property contributed to the passage of no fewer than four different acts defining lawful fences and protecting enclosures between November 20, 1848 and February 10, 1853. Similar legislation prohibited cutting timber as a way "to prevent others from using" this rare and valuable resource. A closer reading of the council minutes reveals more pervasive cultural change. On the first day of 1852, the Wyandot Council passed a resolution proposing "the preservation so far as possible the language and intent of the wampum in possession of the Wyandott nation." The language of the resolution implied that the very purpose of this ancient instrument of communication and record keeping was no longer common knowledge. Another resolution passed the following week confirmed this problem. The Council voted "to adopt some plan of arrangement as to the laws, so as to make it easy to reference and also to preserve them." By the early 1850s, time-honored methods of regulating Wyandot politics and society could not encompass the myriad resolutions dealing with adultery, fence construction, dog ownership, and other concerns.[41]

The focus of this legislation also highlighted the composition of the Wyandot Nation. Hundreds of Wyandots died during the wars of the

---

[40] Wyandot Constitution, November 1847, WNP; Wyandot Constitution, 1851, WNP; Affidavit of John D. Brown, January 20, 1870, vol. 2, RCA; William E. Connelley, "The Provisional Government of Nebraska Territory," 2–3, 165n, 191, 216, 258, 296, 331, 355, 385; Lilian Walker Hale, "Some Reminiscences of the Wyandottes," *State Centennial Souvenir Number and Program, 1821–1921, Missouri Centennial,* 1(October 3, 1921): 119–121; Connelley, *Wyandot Folk-lore,* 33–35; Tooker, "Wyandot," 402; Dean R. Snow, *The Iroquois* (Cambridge, MA, 1994), 134.

[41] Minutes of Wyandot Council, November 14, 1848–April 21, 1854, Quapaw Agency, roll 14, OSHS.

eighteenth century, and the subsequent influx of adopted captives gradually increased European influences. The surnames of the Wyandot
elite – Armstrong, Zane, Brown, Walker, Hicks – descended from Euro-
American men adopted into the nation in the 1700s. Marriages between
whites and Wyandots, a trend even more prevalent in the 1840s and 1850s,
further intertwined the two societies in the nineteenth century. Intermarriage did not include only white men and Wyandot women, although this
did occur. Indeed, Joel and Matthew Walker married two sisters, Mary
Ann and Lydia Ladd, who were the daughters of a Rhode Island native
by the name of John W. Ladd. The presence of slavery proved to be a
particularly contentious element blamed on the influx of Euro-American
values. Although only a few Wyandots owned slaves, including William
Walker and Francis Hicks, some leaders labeled it a foreign practice and
wanted it outlawed. John M. Armstrong and George I. Clark, men of
mixed descent and former and future elected members of the Wyandot
government, argued that slavery went against ancient Wyandot customs
regarding adoption and tribal membership. These struggles over slavery
in the late 1840s did have connections to the divisions in the Methodist
Church, but they were also grounded in the debates over Wyandot
customs.[42]

In the early 1850s, however, discussions of cultural norms were overshadowed by the efforts of the Wyandot elite to welcome American
expansion to eastern Kansas. On March 15, 1853, the Council considered a petition in which several Wyandots requested "the passage of a
law admitting white people to come in as lessees or tenants in this territory." Although the council records do not mention the names of the
men who proposed this resolution, the events of 1852 and 1853 made its
supporters obvious. The Wyandots "warmly favored the occupation by
white people of the vacant lands and ultimate organization of the territory," William Walker wrote some years later. Indeed, because they were

---

[42] For brief biographies of the various families, see Connelley, "The Provisional Government
of Nebraska Territory," 5–11, 47n, 160n, 179n; Paul Armstrong Youngman, *Heritage of
the Wyandots, and "The Armstrong Story"* (Privately published, 1975). The Wyandot
debates over slavery, like those of the Shawnees, were intertwined with the split within
the MEC. For more on the Wyandots' struggle in the late 1840s, see Lucy B. Armstrong,
Wyandotte History, Indian Files – Wyandots, KSHS; Connelley, "The Provisional Government of Nebraska Territory," 174, 260, 266–268, 271, 278; Wyandottes to American
Congress, October 27, 1848, Lucy Armstrong Papers, Indian Files – Wyandots, KSHS;
Lutz, "The Methodist Missions," 215–225; Smith, Jr., *The Wyandot Indians*, 87–90;
Affidavit of William Walker, January 16, 1861, WNP; Dacotah to Mr. Editor, December
19, 1848, WNP; James Gurley to Thomas Ewing, June 15, 1849, roll 632, JGP.

well aware of the expansionist pressures at work on the Missouri border and in Washington, "the Wyandotts and such whites as were within their [tribe] took the initiatory step, by holding an election for a Delegate to Congress in the fall of 1852." Five of the then-current thirteen elected officials in the Wyandot government and a number of past officeholders participated in this election held at the Wyandot Council House. Also in attendance were several white men with either family or business connections to the Wyandots. Abelard Guthrie, an Ohioan married to a Wyandot woman named Nancy Quindaro Brown, won the delegate election. When Congress rejected the proposal the Wyandots did not relent and held another meeting. This session focused more on the construction of a railroad through Kansas, a matter detailed in the proposal's first seven resolutions. But, the eighth resolution had a slightly different message. "While we earnestly desire to see this territory organized, and become the home of the white man," it read, "we as earnestly disclaim all intention or desire to infringe upon the rights of the Indians holding lands within the boundaries of said territory." Even as it promoted the railroad, this 1853 proposal also encouraged a more integrated settlement pattern for whites and Indians. In addition, three of the newly elected officials were Wyandots: William Walker was Governor, former Wyandot chief George I. Clark was secretary, and Matthew Walker was one of the councilmen.[43]

The participation of William Walker and other Wyandot leaders said a great deal about the beliefs of the Wyandot elite as they faced the next phase of American westward expansion. Rather than relocate, they were prepared to stay in Kansas and live next to American settlers. Walker, a regular contributor to newspapers during his lifetime, wrote a short article in 1854 praising the soil, roads, and water in the region. His descriptions, such as "there can be no better country for raising live stock," were designed to encourage settlement in Kansas. And although the passage of the Kansas-Nebraska Act in 1854 meant that American expansion would not occur on the terms set out in the Wyandots' 1853 proposal, it did not mean they had to or wanted to leave. In 1855, six Wyandots signed the treaty that dissolved the Wyandot tribal relations and laid out a plan to allot their reserve. Any Indian who chose an allotment would become a

---

[43] Minutes of Wyandot Council, November 14, 1848–April 21, 1854, Quapaw Agency, roll 14, OSHS; Connelley, "The Provisional Government of Nebraska Territory," 25–28, 43–46, 58, 340, 354–355; William E. Connelley, "The First Provisional Constitution of Kansas," *Collections of the Kansas State Historical Society,* 6(1897–1900): 97–113.

citizen of the United States and would remain on a tract carved out of the Wyandot lands. Of those six who agreed to the final terms, five – Tauromee, Silas Armstrong, George I. Clark, Joel Walker, and Matthew Mudeater – had been actively involved in the effort to organize Kansas Territory.[44]

As products of circumstance and initiative, William Walker and Joseph Parks represented well the men who held power in border Indian communities by the 1850s. They came of age when the United States gained ascendancy over the remaining colonial powers in North America. The death of established leaders like Black Hoof and John Perry left cracks in the leadership even as the increased cultural intrusions of traders, missionaries, and settlers began to leave their mark on the intertwined worlds of native religion and politics. But, although they did not instigate these events, Walker and Parks were positioned to benefit from them. Both began their careers as professional intermediaries, paid to bridge the language barrier between white and Indian communities. Although their paths diverged slightly in the years that followed, Parks and Walker gained influence because of their ability and desire to negotiate the complicated relationship between their respective communities and the growing entity called the United States. And as they faced the organization of Kansas Territory in 1854, each man appeared ready to welcome, not resist, American expansion.

---

[44] Connelley, "The Provisional Government of Nebraska Territory," 24–27, 33–35; "Agricultural Qualities of Nebraska," *The Genesee Farmer*, July 1854; *Indian Affairs*, II, 677–681.

PART THREE

FROM KANSAS TO EXILE

From 1854 onward, both the idea and the reality of Kansas Territory were flashpoints in American politics and the national experience. Thousands of American citizens made the territory their passionate cause and both houses of Congress held heated debates over Bleeding Kansas. Lawrence burned, John Brown stained his hands with the blood of alleged proslavery men, and Senator Charles Sumner of Massachusetts received a life-altering and brutal beating at the hands of South Carolina Congressman Preston Brooks. For better or for worse, President James Buchanan's legacy has long been tainted by the way he handled the controversial Lecompton Constitution. Indeed, the brief and fiery history of Kansas Territory has even overshadowed the early history of Kansas as a state.

But these territorial years are far more than a turning point in a debate over the inevitability of the Civil War. The seven years that Kansas was a territory and its first decade of statehood proved to be critical for Indian residents of the region. The Kansas-Nebraska Act illegally opened up millions of acres that were still owned by Indians to settlement. Border ruffians and antislavery forces battled over territory on which Shawnees, Delawares, Wyandots, and Potawatomis still lived. Popular sovereignty and slavery were unmistakable aspects of this strife, but they shared the stage with a more concrete battle over the physical landscape of the prairie plains.

Although the Indians residing along the Missouri border were not necessarily surprised by these events, they shared similar fates. The Delawares initially placed their trust in the American government but turned to allotment when they discovered that neither federal nor territorial officials would protect their boundaries from land-hungry settlers. Meanwhile, a select group of Wyandot leaders anticipated the national push to organize the region and, in the 1850s, battled each other and the federal government to control their fates. Yet, this foresight could not prevent fraud, and it only created further divisions within the community. By the time Kansas had become a state, both Wyandots and Delawares had suffered from the moves made by their respective leaders.

Although the events of the territorial years have often overshadowed the first decade of statehood, it was the transition in governance that further complicated Indian hopes to maintain a presence in the region. In a nation battling, in part, over states' rights, the entrance of Kansas into the Union marked a substantial change for all Indians, including the Shawnees and Potawatomis. The internal power struggles within the Shawnee and Potawatomi communities showed marked similarities to those of the Wyandots and Delawares. They faced ambitious local interests that filled the vacuum left in the absence of federal authority. But perhaps most important, they confronted an organized state government intent on flexing its rights, particularly in the realm of taxation.

6

Subtraction through Division

Delawares, Wyandots, and the Struggle
for Kansas Territory

In 1912, John Kayrahoo, a seventy-two-year-old Wyandot resident of Oklahoma, told a story about the historical relationship between whites and Indians. Prior to contact, when the Wyandots and Delawares were the first and second nations respectively in an Indian confederacy, the Wyandots instructed the Delawares to prevent anyone from landing on their shores. But when the Wyandots traveled westward, the Delawares befriended the whites who arrived by boat from a land across the Atlantic Ocean. Shortly thereafter, the white men asked to purchase some land. Once the Delawares agreed, the whites used trickery to obtain more than the Indians planned on selling. Deceived and unsure of the proper response, the Delawares sent for the Wyandots in the West. The Wyandots returned and expressed surprise at the large number of white men in the region. They also learned of the land sale from the Delawares. "The Wyandot," related Kayrahoo, "spoke in these terms, 'So it is, and so shall it always be! The white fellow shall always undermine the Indian until he has taken away from him his last thing.'"[1]

Conflict followed as the Indians defended their lands from the invaders. The Wyandots and Delawares united with several other tribes but lost the war. "After a compact had been reached, the white chief spoke to the Wyandot chief, saying 'Hereafter all the lands that I have purchased from the Delaware shall be mine and I will proceed to occupy them. We shall forever be friends and we must not refer to the past war between us. We shall, moreover, be your guardians and look after your business.' The

---

[1] C. M. Barbeau, *Huron and Wyandot Mythology, with an Appendix Containing Earlier Published Records* (Ottawa, 1915), 268–270. In Kayrahoo's story, the whites asked for land, but only as much as a cow hide could encompass. They then turned the hide into a long string with which they were able to enclose a far larger amount of land than that envisioned by the Delawares.

meaning of this was that the Indians now had fallen under the conqueror's government." With his story at an end, Kayrahoo presented Barbeau with the lesson the Wyandots had learned and carried with them in the centuries that followed. "The old-time saying has long been handed down among us," he explained, "that we must adopt the white man's way, because we are now in his clutches."[2]

Kayrahoo's story described the first contact with the Europeans. But the lessons he offered were just as applicable to the experiences of the Delawares and Wyandots in Kansas Territory. Kayrahoo was a teenager when the 1854 Kansas-Nebraska Act initiated an assault on Indian land ownership west of the Missouri border. Thousands of settlers crossed the state line into the newly organized territory and marked off claims although not a single acre was available for sale. For the first several years after the Kansas-Nebraska Act passed Congress, not a single acre was legally open even to preemption. And although American politicians proclaimed the glory brought by expansion and participants in the slavery debates went to extraordinary lengths to control the territory, Indian agents decried the impact on Indians under their jurisdiction. In 1854 Commissioner of Indian Affairs George Manypenny reminded both politicians and settlers that "the Kansas-Nebraska Act . . . does not, as has been occasionally claimed, countenance any intrusions whatever upon the Indian lands within these territories." Yet, the settler incursions and apparent lack of security offered by the federal government undermined these very principles. Indeed, from the organization of the territory to the beginning of the Civil War divisions within the U.S. government allowed for and even encouraged settlers and speculators to establish illegal claims on Indian lands.[3]

Yet even as the divisions within the federal government allowed settlers to run rampant in eastern Kansas, conflicts within many Indian

[2] Barbeau, *Huron and Wyandot Mythology*, 268–270.
[3] George Manypenny to R. McClelland, Secretary of the Interior, September 22, 1855, vol. 3, *RCA*. Paul Wallace Gates was one of the first historians to point out the illegitimacy of the land rush in Kansas following the Kansas-Nebraska Act. See Gates, *Fifty Million Acres: Conflicts over Kansas Land Policy, 1854–1890* (Ithaca, 1954); Paul Wallace Gates, "Land and Credit Problems in Underdeveloped Kansas," *Kansas Historical Quarterly*, 31(Spring 1965): 41–61; Annie Heloise Abel, "Indian Reservations in Kansas and the Extinguishment of Their Title," *Transactions of the Kansas State Historical Society*, 8(1903–1904): 72–109; H. Craig Miner and William E. Unrau, *The End of Indian Kansas: A Study of Cultural Revolution, 1854–1871* (Lawrence, 1978); Joseph B. Herring, *The Enduring Indians of Kansas: A Century and a Half of Acculturation* (Lawrence, 1990).

communities also facilitated the dispossession. Nearly a year after the Delawares signed a land cession treaty in 1854, members of the Wyandot Nation placed their marks on an accord that not only allotted their reserve but also initiated a progression toward American citizenship and the legal dissolution of the tribe. In the ensuing struggle, members of the Wyandot community battled over access to government officials and control over the future of and membership in the Wyandot Nation. Although still a battle over land, the Wyandot struggles in the 1850s were also contests over citizenship and tribal identity. And these struggles centered on the issue raised by Kayrahoo in 1912 – whether or not to adopt fully the "white man's way."

From the inception of Kansas Territory in 1854 to the formation of the state of Kansas seven years later, squatters, agents, Delawares, and Wyandots struggled over land. Although national headlines focused on the fiery contest over slavery, local interests placed land ownership at center stage. By the early 1860s, both the Delawares and the Wyandots had suffered substantially from American policies. More specifically, most Delawares and Wyandots had lost or were on the verge of losing their land as the Civil War came to a close. Their respective paths to dispossession shared common elements. The treaties of 1854 and 1860 served as bookends for a six-year period on the Delaware lands that saw the absence of government protection ruin the reserve once held in common. But the subsequent institution of allotment occurred with the acquiescence of the Delaware Council. Just to the east at the confluence of the Kansas and Missouri Rivers, a small faction of Wyandot elites campaigned more explicitly for land in severalty and citizenship for members of the Wyandot Nation. In each case, federal indifference and the influence of a powerful minority both increased the land loss already in motion and created social and political divides that fractured the Delaware and Wyandot communities in Kansas.

The nine Delaware men authorized by their tribal council to negotiate and sign the 1854 treaty agreed to terms that drastically decreased the amount of Delaware-owned land in eastern Kansas. Prior to the negotiation, their reserve extended west from the Missouri border north of the Kansas River and encompassed approximately two million acres. In the 1854 accord, the Delawares ceded over one million acres and retained a diminished reserve ten miles wide and approximately forty miles long. The federal government would survey the ceded land so that it could then be divided and sold at a public auction, with the proceeds from the sale going to the Delawares. This treaty also provided for the future division of the remaining Delaware lands, then held in common, into individual plots if the Indians so desired. Eighteen total articles included other elements more typical of these agreements, including the distribution of $10,000 in annuities to the five Delaware chiefs – Captain Ketchum, Sarcoxie, Secondyne, Neconhecon, and Kockatowha – for their "long and faithful services." And in the fourteenth article, the treaty stated that "they[the Delawares] will at all times, as far as they are able, comply with the law in such cases made and provided, as they will expect to be protected and their rights vindicated by it, when they are injured." In their homes on the diminished reserve, however, the Delawares could not escape the troubles that beset the region. Divisions within the government eliminated protections for Indian lands in the chaos of Kansas Territory. And divisions within the Delaware community facilitated the invasion that led to dispossession in the early 1860s.[4]

Problems arose as soon as American citizens crossed the Missouri border at the announcement of the 1854 Kansas-Nebraska Act. Missourians had lobbied to open the territory for years, their patience long since worn thin by government inaction. "The more restless, and lawless portion of the frontier inhabitants will take the matter into their own hands," Superintendent of Indian Affairs David Mitchell warned late in 1852, "and settle the country in their own way: using the rifle as an argument quite satisfactory to themselves." But Congressional action did not avoid the violence Mitchell had feared. With the institution of popular sovereignty, Stephen Douglas and his Congressional colleagues opened the door to a bitter contest between proslavery and antislavery forces in the region. Border ruffians crossed the Missouri state line to promote slavery's cause, and the founders of the New England Emigrant Aid Company aimed to make Kansas a free state by sending twenty thousand northern supporters to the territory each year. The resulting regional clashes spilled the blood of American citizens and wreaked havoc with the Indian settlements on the border. Sheer numbers also made a difference. In the six years after the organization of the territory over one hundred thousand Americans entered the lands west of the Missouri state line.[5]

---

[4] Memorial of Delaware Indians, April 3, 1854, OIA-TR, roll 5; *Indian Affairs, II*, 614–618.

[5] D. D. Mitchell to Thomas Moseley, Jr., November 14, 1852, OIA-LR, roll 364; Herring, *The Enduring Indians of Kansas*, 48–49; Gates, *Fifty Million Acres*, 2–8; David M. Potter, *The Impending Crisis, 1848–1861*, completed and edited by Don E. Fehrenbacher (New York, 1976), 199–201; James M. McPherson, *Battle Cry of Freedom: The Civil War Era* (New York, 1988), 145–153; Stephen Aron, *American Confluence: The Missouri Frontier from Borderland to Border State* (Bloomington, 2006), 233–243.

From 1854 to 1858, the Delawares in Kansas struggled in vain against this onslaught. Although the U.S. Attorney General ruled that treaty land was not subject to preemption and that the federal government must protect it until the public auction, the non-Indian population on the reserve increased rapidly. As early as August 1854, only a few weeks after the ratification of their treaty, the Delaware council issued a declaration to squatters: "that all settlements on the lands ceded . . . by treaty dated at Washington May 6, 1854, is in violation of said treaty and that we in no wise have or will consent to such settlement, and if persisted in by our white brethren we shall appeal to our great father the President of the US for protection." Both this proclamation and subsequent petitions reflected the lack of notable violent resistance to the settler invasion. Incidents of theft or individual conflicts may have occurred, but such acts were more conspicuous in their absence. Much to their misfortune, the Delawares chose to rely on the promises of government protection. Repeated proclamations and letters sent to President Franklin Pierce had little if any affect on the settlers who wanted to both take possession of the land and harvest the timber. By March of the following year, an official census listed the number of non-Indian settlers within the boundaries of the Delaware reserve and the ceded lands at almost twelve hundred. In the newly founded town of Leavenworth, located two and a half miles below the fort of the same name, approximately two hundred inhabitants had already constructed over forty buildings. Although poorly built, the buildings announced the intentions of speculators eager to establish claims in anticipation of profits from future sales. Between the spring of 1855 and the fall of 1856, the number of inhabitants of the Leavenworth town site grew to almost twenty-five hundred men, women, and children. This figure more than doubled that of the Delawares, who in the 1850s numbered just over one thousand.[6]

As the size of Leavenworth and other sites increased, the ineffectiveness of government policy became more apparent. Squatters even laid claim and asserted rights to lands within the boundaries of the common reserve not ceded in the 1854 treaty. Both the Delawares and the Indian

[6] Declaration of Delaware Indians, August 1854, OIA-LR, roll 364; Delaware Indians to President Pierce, December 1854, OIA-LR, roll 364; B. F. Robinson to George Manypenny, December 12, 1854, OIA-LR, roll 364; B. F. Robinson to George Manypenny, March 2, 1855, OIA-LR, roll 364; George Manypenny, to George C. Whiting, October 20, 1854, vol. 1, RCAKC; Declaration of President Franklin Pierce, August 14, 1856, Indian Files – Delaware, Box 6, KSHS; Petition of Citizens of Leavenworth City to President Pierce, September 18, 1856, ibid.

agents assigned to protect them complained about these intrusions and received ineffective responses. In the spring of 1857, the Delaware council informed Superintendent of Indian Affairs Alfred Cummings that settlers had trespassed throughout the Indians' assigned reserve, making claims and cutting down trees. Permissive, or at the very least, passive, territorial courts abetted the timber theft. In the fall of 1859, Judge Petitt of the First District Court of Kansas Territory ruled that no law existed "to prevent white persons taking timber off of Indian Reserves in Kansas." In the absence of explicit legislation, Kansas judges ruled that they had no legal grounds on which to punish timber theft. As a result, most trees on the Delaware reserve fed the sawmills non-Indians erected along the waterways west of the Missouri border. Petitt's ruling further undermined the authority of Indian agents already hampered by a weak federal policy. To decrease the potential for violence, the Office of Indian Affairs required its agents first to give public notice to all trespassers, ordering them to leave. If that step failed to remove the intruders, the agents then served written notices on those who disobeyed the public declaration. As a last resort and only upon higher orders, the agent could attempt to use military force to clear the lands. The policy possessed little bite on paper and even less in reality.[7]

When the Delaware Agent Benjamin Robinson responded to Indian grievances in the fall of 1857, he encountered obstacles at every stage. Robinson groused about the government policy, hinted at the lack of support from the territorial legal system, and complained that without any military involvement he had no reason to expect compliance from settlers. Shortly thereafter Commissioner of Indian Affairs James Denver answered Robinson's entreaties and gave the agent authority to remove all the intruders from the Delaware lands. Robinson not only had a mandate to call on the soldiers stationed at Fort Leavenworth to remove the intruders but he also had authority to prosecute the settlers and to burn all of their improvements. This removal process did not go smoothly, however, because many of the military officers stationed at Fort Leavenworth had personal investments in the Indian lands. As early as October 1854 reports circulated throughout the territory that many of the Fort's officers had been among the first speculators. In fact, some of the soldiers had as much at stake as the settlers whose claims dotted the landscape and at least two commissioned majors had financial interests in the town

---

[7] William E. Murphy to SIA, January 22, 1860, OIA-LR, roll 682; B. F. Robinson to A. M. Robinson, December 6, 1858, OIA-LR, roll 275; Delaware Indians to unknown, March 2, 1857, vol. 3, *RCA*.

FIGURE 5. Lawrence, Kansas Territory, c. 1856. (Courtesy of the Kansas State Historical Society.)

of Leavenworth. Although Secretary of War Jefferson Davis attempted to discredit such rumors, all signs pointed to the military's involvement in the territory's land rush.[8]

Many other agents shared Robinson's frustration, for the men who filled the political offices in Kansas showed little concern for the rights of Indians. Like most other settlers, these men viewed the removal of Indians from Kansas as necessary and wanted to be among the first to secure sections of land. Andrew Reeder, the governor of Kansas Territory from June 1854 to July 1858, led the charge. During his tenure Reeder speculated in approximately six different townships established on Indian lands. He added to his malfeasance by using public funds to support some of these schemes. Other territorial officials, including two associate justices and the territorial secretary, joined the governor and became partners in speculation. Because the abuse of their positions seldom resulted in more than relatively minor fines, the possible rewards far outweighed any risks. In Reeder's case, removal from office did not occur until 1858. Even then, he was one of a few officials who suffered any serious consequences. The real estate ventures of Kansas politicians like Reeder often reflected the

[8] B. F. Robinson to John Haverty, September 29, 1857, roll 632, JGP; J. W. Denver, CIA, to B. F. Robinson, October 2, 1857, roll 632, JGP; B. F. Robinson to A. Cumming, October 30, 1854, OIA-LR, roll 364; B. F. Robinson to George Manypenny, November 14, 1854, OIA-LR, roll 364; Miner and Unrau, *The End of Indian Kansas*, 109–113.

activities of "Indian Rings." These loose affiliations of agents, territorial officials, traders, and other businessmen, worked in concert to attack further the integrity of treaties and government promises. More specifically, local officials and traders used political connections in the nation's capital to manipulate treaty negotiations, land sales, and other aspects of Indian affairs for personal gain. They focused their efforts not only on Indian lands, but also on the trust funds created by treaties. In the 1860s in particular, these informal associations managed to channel hundreds of thousands of dollars from the Indian trust funds into the bonds and stocks of railroad companies.[9]

By the late 1850s the relentless intrusions and absence of federal protection had taken a heavy toll on the Delaware property and morale. Incidents of theft rose as more settlers entered Kansas, and in March 1858, Robinson recorded official complaints from more than twenty Delawares. Although the details often differed, the most common grievance dealt with stolen horses, a loss that hindered Delaware agricultural efforts as well as mobility. To complicate matters further, the Delawares had incurred sizeable debts with Cyprian Chouteau and other traders with posts on the reserve. A combination of bad weather and low annuities contributed to these financial difficulties. In the summer of 1857, drought hit eastern Kansas and the Delaware corn and other produce withered in the fields. "Our crops are very small," James Secondine reported, "we hope our great father will...see that his red children will not suffer in the winter for the food they could not raise on account of the dry weather." The next summer, however, the weather overcompensated for its previous shortcomings and so much rain fell that the rivers flooded and submerged the Indians' fields cultivated along the banks. Although not all of the Delawares depended solely on agriculture for their subsistence, the combined effects of drought and floods in consecutive years made their calls for government assistance even more persistent. "If there is any of the money arising from the sale of our lands, which has not been invested, say to the amount of one hundred thousand dollars," the Delaware Council stated, "we would like to receive about that amount."[10]

---

[9] Miner and Unrau, *The End of Indian Kansas*, 20–24, 55–80. In pages 55–80, Miner and Unrau discuss numerous examples of fraud involving Indian trust funds as a result of these Indian rings.

[10] Affidavits recorded by B. F. Robinson, March 1858, OIA-LR, roll 275; James Secondine to James W. Denver, August 17, 1857, OIA-LR, roll 274; B. F. Robinson to A. M. Robinson, September 22, 1858, OIA-LR, roll 275; Delaware Council to the President of the United States, October 26, 1858, OIA-LR, roll 275.

The Delawares repeatedly requested this money because they both deserved and needed it. Although squatters had hurt the public land sales dictated by the 1854 treaty, auctions of over five hundred fifty-eight thousand acres had garnered more than one million dollars by the end of the decade. And the Delawares intended this money to pay for both provisions in the lean months to come and debts incurred in previous years. The land cessions in the 1854 accord had forced many Delaware families to relocate to the diminished reserve from the ceded territory. Both the move and the resettlement required money, time, and effort, all of which used up the per capita payouts received by each Delaware from the 1854 treaty. The drought of 1857 and the flooding of 1858 further cut into family accounts. Needing provisions but lacking the necessary funds, Delaware families turned to the traders on the reserve and obtained goods on credit. By February 1861, the combined debt of the Delaware nation totaled $38,168.78 owed to five different merchants. Of this amount, nearly $2,700 was owed to James Ketchum and John Marshall, two Delaware Indians who had become traders during this crisis at the behest of the Delaware Council. And the numbers could have grown considerably had the government not distributed a total of $160,000 in two different per capita payments in the spring and fall of 1857.[11]

Political change within the Delaware community coincided with and fueled the problems created by settlers, traders, and government officials. The first blow came in July 1856 with the death of Captain Ketchum, the principal chief. Ketchum had first been appointed a band chief in 1829 and, through the influence of Superintendent of Indian Affairs Alfred Cummings, was named principal chief in 1851. According to Clinton Weslager, U.S. officials had a say in the selection of Delaware chiefs from that point forward. The events following Ketchum's death as well as the contents of the late chief's written will support that assessment. "I want my nephew Ahlarachech or James Conner to be a chief," Ketchum asserted. "I think he is suitable man to fill the place of chief." Among the Delawares a brother or nephew assumed the chieftancy as opposed to the son of a recently deceased leader. As the son of Ketchum's youngest sister, Mekinges, James had the proper lineage. He and his elder brother John

[11] C. A. Weslager, *The Delaware Indians: A History* (New Brunswick, NJ, 1972), 401–407; Thomas B. Sykes to A. B. Greenwood, February 2, 1861, OIA-LR, roll 275; James Ketchum to William P. Dole, March 3, 1862, OIA-LR, roll 276. For some of the Delaware requests for payments, see James Ketchum to Dr. Robinson, May 2, 1859, OIA-LR, roll 275; John Conner et al. to unknown, June 9, 1860, OIA-LR, roll 275; John Conner et al. to CIA, August 5, 1862, OIA-LR, roll 276.

were products of a union between the American trader William Conner and Mekinges that occurred prior to the Delaware removal from Indiana. While the Delaware relocations of the early nineteenth century brought James to Kansas, John traveled with a separate band of Delawares and settled in Texas, where he lived and worked primarily as a U.S. interpreter for almost thirty years. Contrary to Captain Ketchum's wishes, however, James declined the position. Convinced that most Delawares would oppose him as principal chief, he nominated his brother John, who accepted. The Department of Indian Affairs, based on the recommendation of the Delaware agent, approved this decision. John Conner became the new principal chief of the Delawares in Kansas.[12]

Under John Conner's leadership, the Delaware Council advanced a proposal that failed to meet the needs or desires of the nation as a whole. In two different letters to President Buchanan in 1858, the leadership described the status of the Delawares in Kansas Territory. The Council admitted that internal divisions existed. On the one hand there were those who "do not pay that attention to agriculture necessary to support them." But although this portion of the community did not want to change, the rest of the nation felt differently. "Many of us have adopted the manners and customs of our white brothers," the Delawares explained. "We have in many instances large farms fenced and under cultivation, we have good houses, have our children educated, and notwithstanding this have nothing we can call our own." Driven by a desire to secure property and ensure a future in Kansas, Conner and the Delaware Council asked the federal government to act on the eleventh article of their 1854 treaty, an article that proposed allotment. By dividing up the reserve and becoming individual landowners, the Delaware Council reasoned, they would also

---

[12] Will of Captain Ketchum and Statement of James Conner, October 20, 1856, OIA-LR, roll 275; Statement of John R. Bazlon, June 1, 1857, OIA-LR, roll 275; B. F. Robinson to A. M. Robinson, May 8, 1858, OIA-LR, roll 275; Weslager, *The Delaware Indians*, 387–390; John Lauriz Larson and David G. Vanderstel, "Agent of Empire: William Conner on the Indiana Frontier, 1800–1855," *Indiana Magazine of History*, LXXX(December 1984): 301–328. For Delaware practices regarding leadership, see Richard C. Adams, *Legends of the Delaware Indians and Picture Writing*, edited by Deborah Nichols (Syracuse, 1997), xviii–xix; Leslie A. White (Ed.), *Lewis Henry Morgan: The Indian Journals, 1859–1862* (Ann Arbor, 1959), 52–55. According to the Delaware responses to then-Michigan Territorial Governor Lewis Cass's questionnaire in 1821, the position of chief did not pass along strict matrilineal lines. If a chief died, his brother was entitled to the position. If the chief had no brother, then a nephew on the mother's side would become chief. See C. A. Weslager, *The Delaware Indian Westward Migration: With the Texts of Two Manuscripts (1821–1822) Responding to General Lewis Cass's Inquiries about Lenape Culture and Language* (Wallingford, PA, 1978), 91.

come under territorial law and would have greater recourse against any further transgressions of American settlers.[13]

This request for allotment was premature. Although Conner and the Council believed it would best serve their nation, few Delawares shared their optimism. Perhaps the largest impediment to allotment was the fact that the division of the reserve would require each Delaware to remain in Kansas and would hinder relocation. This held little appeal for most Delawares. In the months before their delegates negotiated the 1860 treaty, the Delaware Council convened several times away from the prying eyes and ears of U.S. officials. As they sat in council, the Delawares debated their options, focusing on whether they should remain in Kansas and "if they could find elsewhere, a country anything as good as this." Upon polling the nation, the leaders found only ten to fifteen Delawares opposed to a land sale and relocation. This talk of removal centered on two possible regions. One was the Rockies and the Far West, a choice that made sense not only because of the history of migrations among the Delawares but also because councilors like Black Beaver knew the western territories well from a life time of trading, scouting, and trapping. The Delawares also considered relocation south to Indian Territory. Within a short distance they might find land, and based on their relationship with other Indian nations on the border, hospitality.[14]

But even as most Delawares pushed their leaders to consider land cession and removal, dissidents within a more acculturated section of the community aired their opinions. These men protested their lack of representation and advocated change. Charles Journeycake, a licensed Baptist minister and a member of the Delaware delegation that signed the 1854 treaty, led this faction. He and four others addressed a letter to Commissioner of Indian Affairs William Dole requesting that the federal government name "one of our enlightened, sober men" to a position of authority. Six reasons grounded this request, and most attacked the established

---

[13] *Indian Affairs, II*, 614–618; Delaware Council to President Buchanan, 1858, Roll 632, JGP; John Conner et al. to their great father the President of the United States, October 26, 1858, OIA-LR, roll 275.

[14] Thomas B. Sykes to Hon. A. M. Robinson, February 10, 1860, OIA-LR, roll 275; Thomas B. Sykes to Hon. A. B. Greenwood, March 12, 1860, OIA-LR, roll 275; Weslager, *The Delaware Indians*, 408, 416–417. For Delaware participation in the Rocky Mountain Fur trade, see Harvey L. Carter, "Jim Swanock and the Delaware Hunters," in LeRoy R. Hafen (Ed.), *The Mountain Men and the Fur Trade of the Far West* (10 vols., Glendale, CA, 1969), VII, 293–300. For Delaware participation in an expedition of John C. Fremont, see John C. Fremont to unknown, September 16, 1853, OIA–LR, roll 274.

Delaware leadership. According to these five progressive Delawares, their more traditional colleagues still viewed hunting as a viable means of subsistence and displayed a willingness to sell lands for money. Unfortunately, this mindset made relocation appear to be a viable option. "Old men seeking to perpetuate past customs are willing to move," they wrote, "whenever these long cherished ways are invaded and their end sought for." Journeycake and his colleagues refrained from mentioning specific names, but concluded their letter by painting a dire picture. "If our business be left either to the Chiefs, or Council, as it is now organized, then is there nothing for us to expect but submition[*sic*], and the future is only sure to reveal fearful ruin to all we hold most dear." For the moment, and despite the ominous tone, this appeal went unanswered.[15]

However, the treaty signed on May 30, 1860 may have appeased the Journeycake faction even as it ignored the opinions garnered in the recent councils. It occurred under dubious circumstances, as Sykes negotiated the treaty on the reserve without any other U.S. officials present. Reverend John Pratt, the Baptist missionary on the Delaware reserve, hoped that something could be done to prevent its ratification, and accused Sykes of plying Conner and the others with alcohol. Bribes in the form of land grants and payments of $15,000 each further eased negotiations with the Delaware leaders. John Conner, Sarcoxie, Kockatowha, and Neconhecon each received plots ranging from 320 to 640 acres "in consideration of... long and faithful services." With this extralegal assistance Sykes set in motion the allotment of the remaining Delaware lands and gave the Leavenworth, Pawnee, and Western Railroad (LP&W) the first right to purchase any and all of the unallotted acreage. This portion of the treaty signaled the successful manipulations of Thomas Ewing, Jr., Andrew Isaacs, and other men who orchestrated this coup for the LP&W. Isaacs built his reputation while serving as the Attorney General for Kansas Territory in the late 1850s when he protected the rights of squatters on Indian lands. Ewing, Jr., later the Chief Justice of the Kansas Supreme Court, was the son of a former Secretary of the Interior. He had also partnered on several real estate deals with William T. Sherman, the soon to be infamous Union General whose brother John represented Ohio in Congress. The local and national influence wielded by these two

---

[15] Harry M. Roark, *Charles Journeycake: Indian Statesman and Christian Leader* (Dallas, 1970), 26–29; Charles Journeycake et al. to W. B. Dole, no date, OIA-LR, roll 275 (This letter marked received October 15, 1861, but based on the content this letter was written substantially earlier); Weslager, *The Delaware Indians*, 387–391; Lynette Perry and Manny Skolnick, *Keeper of the Delaware Dolls* (Lincoln, 1999), 29–30.

men, as well as the resources of their partners, individuals such as banker William H. Russell, made the LP&W a powerful force. Indeed, Ewing, Jr. and Isaacs had promised parcels of land to a number of men in the nation's capital and elsewhere if the treaty fulfilled the wishes of their railroad company.[16]

The circumstances of the negotiations and the content of the treaty brought a mixed reaction from the Delawares. One of the more prominent critics of the accord, a Delaware councilor named Captain Fall Leaf, declared that the chiefs were old men who made treaties "for their own benefit and not for the tribe." Agent Fielding Johnson dismissed this dissatisfaction, but Fall Leaf had a valid complaint. By the summer of 1861, John Conner, Sarcoxie, and Neconhecon had all sold their respective land grants from the 1860 treaty. It had not taken them long. Other Delaware protests targeted allotment. A petition sent to President Buchanan in October 1860 allegedly signed by fifty Delawares accused Sykes of distributing alcohol and proclaimed that the Delawares would treat all surveyors as intruders. "We are willing to make a treaty," the petition concluded, "but such a one and such a way as T.B. Sykes forms treaties we will never accede." But shortly thereafter a statement by the Delaware Council brought the petition into question. Captain Neconhecon, whose name appeared both on the treaty and the petition, stated that his name was forged on the latter because he had been on a buffalo hunt at the time he was alleged to have signed the document. Sykes speculated that the fraudulent petition was the work of Missouri businessmen hoping to undermine the LP&W's venture.[17]

The interests of settlers and the railroads conflicted in the treaty's aftermath and, in the absence of any significant federal presence, overrode the minimal protection given Delaware lands. Most notably, the LP&W failed

---

[16] *Indian Affairs, II*, 803–807. Kockatowha is sometimes referred to as Rockatowha in treaties and other government documents; Gates, *Fifty Million Acres*, 109–122; Weslager, *The Delaware Indians*, 413–414; David G. Taylor, "Thomas Ewing, Jr., and the Origins of the Kansas Pacific Railway Company," *Kansas Historical Quarterly*, 42(Summer 1976): 155–179; Alfred Gray to Hon. Geo. W. Patterson, June 18, 1860, Alfred Gray Collection, #361, Box 1, Folder Correspondence 1855–1879, KSHS.

[17] Captain Fall Leaf to William Dole, September 15, 1863, vol. 6, *RCA*; Fielding Johnson to unknown, vol. 6, *RCA*; *Indian Affairs, II*, 803–807; Petition of Delawares to the Honorable James Buchanan, October 10, 1860, OIA-LR, roll 275; Thomas B. Sykes to Hon. A. B. Greenwood, November 2, 1860, OIA-LR, roll 275. For other protests against the treaty, see Charles Robinson to Hon. Caleb B. Smith, July 2, 1861, OIA-LR, roll 275; Alfred Gray to Hon. Geo. W. Patterson, June 18, 1860, Alfred Gray Collection, #361, Box 1, Folder Correspondence 1855–1879, KSHS.

to follow the treaty resolution stating that they would not receive patents to any land until the Secretary of the Interior had verified the construction of the proposed twenty-five-mile track along the western boundary of the Delaware reserve. Because the company, which in 1863 became the Union Pacific, Eastern Division, apparently made no move to pay for the lands or to lay a single track, squatters quickly laid claim to most of the railroad grants. In an ironic twist, these settlers soon shared the brunt of the railroad's faulty business practices. Well aware of the imminent expiration of their contract, the UPED used as much of the timber on the lands as possible. Men connected to the railroad even set up a lumber company to cut wood throughout the Delaware lands and sold this bounty primarily for home construction. By 1866, more than ten sawmills operated in the region, most if not all with financial ties to John Perry, the president of the UPED, and James Lane, a Kansas Senator.[18]

The Journeycake faction also received its wish when Charles became an assistant chief and the head of the Turkey division. It signified a substantial change – Charles by descent belonged to the Wolf division – and was the final crack in the traditional system of Delaware governance. In early April 1861, Kockatowha, the Turkey chief, died. Three months later, the Delawares had not replaced him in office. However, the new Delaware Agent Fielding Johnson argued that Charles Journeycake should assume the title. The agent described Journeycake as "one of the most intelligent Indians belonging to the tribe, honest and upright in his dealings." If made chief, Journeycake "would look after and protect the interest of the people and particularly the industrial and moral interests of the tribe." Perhaps most important, however, this appointment would ease the relationship between U.S. officials and the Delawares. Johnson closed his argument in this vein, leaving his superiors with the image of what might happen if "some ignorant savage belonging to the tribe" filled the vacancy. In October, at a council called by Johnson for this purpose, the Delawares confirmed the promotion of Charles Journeycake to the position of chief.[19]

---

[18] Fielding Johnson to William Dole, CIA, May 1, 1862, vol. 6, *RCA*; Kansas citizens to Secretary of the Interior, January 31, 1863, vol. 6, *RCA*; John G. Pratt to unknown, December 5, 1865, roll 633, JGP. For an analysis of the years following the treaty, see Miner and Unrau, *The End of Indian Kansas*, 28–40; Weslager, *The Delaware Indians*, 403–426.

[19] Fielding Johnson to H. B. Branch, July 5, 1861, OIA-LR, roll 275; Fielding Johnson to H. Branch, October 14, 1861, OIA-LR, roll 275. In her memoir published in 1999, Lynette Perry remarks that rather than a Turkey, Journeycake was the "favorite of the Indian agent," and his promotion resulted in the abandonment of "traditional leadership." See Perry and Skolnick, *Keeper of the Delaware Dolls*, 29.

In late 1861, at the onset of the Civil War, the Delawares' status was far different than seven years before when Congress organized Kansas Territory. Lands once guaranteed "to the said Delaware Nation forever" had been pillaged and preempted, stolen and sold. And the process of allotment had only just begun. Just as important, both the federal government and their own leadership had abandoned the main body of the Delawares. Even as Charles Journeycake demanded representation and gained a position he could not have obtained through traditional channels, most Delawares who had voiced their desire for removal in 1860 were trapped in allotments they did not want and could not sell, on lands that decreased in value with every trespass and timber theft.[20]

Allotment via treaty came to the Wyandots more than five years before the Delawares. On the last day of January 1855, six leaders and delegates of the Wyandot nation signed what could have been their last federal treaty. The accord represented both the culmination of a determined effort and the beginning of a new crisis for the Wyandots as individuals and as a community. Tauromee, or John Hat, and John Hicks put their marks on the page, while Matthew Mudeater, Silas Armstrong, George Clark, and Joel Walker signed their names. When they left the city of Washington behind, the six Wyandots carried word of this agreement and brought news that would forever alter the Wyandot Nation. The opening lines of the first article stated the situation clearly. "The Wyandott Indians," it began, "having become sufficiently advanced in civilization, and being desirous of becoming citizens, it is hereby agreed and stipulated, that their organization, and their relations with the United States as an Indian tribe shall be dissolved and terminated on the ratification of this agreement ... and from and after the date of such ratification, the said Wyandott Indians ... shall be deemed, and are hereby declared, to be citizens of the United States." The remainder of the treaty detailed enactment. Most notably, government surveyors would partition the Wyandot lands and grant each Wyandot an equal portion. This plan for allotment and citizenship, however, was the crowning achievement of only a small group on the Wyandot reserve. Consequently, the 1855 treaty created social, political, and geographic rifts that remained long after Kansas entered the Union.[21]

The American government did not impose the terms of the 1855 treaty on the entire Wyandot Nation. Indeed, the resolutions came five years

---

[20] Quoted from the 1829 Treaty with the Delawares, in *Indian Affairs*, II, 304–305. For limits on the sale of Delaware allotments, see ibid., 803–807.

[21] *Indian Affairs*, II, 677–681.

FIGURE 6. Joel Walker. (Courtesy of the Kansas State Historical Society.)

later than hoped for by the Wyandot elite. The first push came in early
1850, when Francis Hicks, George Clark, and Joel Walker traveled to
Washington to negotiate a new treaty. At the time, Hicks was the elected
principal chief and Clark was one of the elected councilors. Walker served
as secretary to the Wyandot Council. The Council had charged these three
men in November 1849 with the task of negotiating compensation for the

one hundred and forty-eight thousand acres of land promised in the 1842 removal treaty. A portion of this desired money would immediately pay off the remaining $20,000 debt owed the Delawares for the land on which the Wyandots now resided at the confluence of the Missouri and Kansas rivers. The Wyandot Council also hoped its delegates would induce the federal government to locate and assign the thirty-five individual tracts of land promised to certain Wyandots in the fourteenth article of the 1842 agreement.[22]

By mid-January, however, the goals of the delegation had changed dramatically. Although the 1842 treaty remained integral to their mission, Hicks, Clark, and Walker added a new twist. "The United States," they proposed in a statement to Commissioner of Indian Affairs Orlando Brown, "shall stipulate and guarantee the rights of citizenship to the Wyandotts where the foregoing [settlement of land issues] shall have been done." This proposition brought a quick response from the Commissioner. He did not countenance the measure. "This could not be done and they remain where they are," Brown declared, "without breaking down the barrier which has been created to secure to our Indian tribes permanent homes." In other words, granting the Wyandots citizenship would compromise the integrity of all Indian reserves in eastern Kansas. "It would be an entering wedge to the extension of our settlements into the Indian country," he added, "before the Indians generally would be prepared to become citizens themselves." From Brown's perspective, the Indians were simply unprepared. Nor could they endure the onslaught of settlers and the accompanying "evils." Less than two months later, however, the Commissioner switched sides for reasons that remain unclear. By early March he proclaimed that a division of the Wyandot lands would serve as "the most triumphant vindication of the ultimate tendency of our policy to bring the Indians within the actual pale of civilization and Christianity." Brown recommended that the negotiations commence soon. On April 1, the three Wyandot delegates sat down with treaty commissioner Ardavan S. Loughery and worked out an accord that arranged for land payments and Wyandot citizenship.[23]

The only remaining hurdle was ratification, and the treaty encountered opposition on the Wyandot Reserve and in Congress. The Wyandot

[22] Thomas Moseley to Hon. O. Brown, November 18, 1849, OIA-LR, roll 951; *Indian Affairs*, II, 534–537.
[23] F. A. Hicks et al. to Hon. Orlando Brown, January 17, 1850, OIA-LR, roll 951; Orlando Brown to Messrs F. A. Hicks, Geo. I. Clark and Joel Walker, January 26, 1850, OIA-LR, roll 951; Orlando Brown to Hon. Thomas Ewing, March 6, 1850, OIA-LR, roll 951.

Council called a convention for May 7. John M. Armstrong, then a member of the Legislative Committee, presided and William Walker, another Legislative member, acted as secretary. These two men had a long history of mutual animosity and this hostility may have helped set the tone on that first day. Those present could not reach a consensus on any issue except when to adjourn. The Wyandots reconvened on May 14, and from noon, when Armstrong called the convention to order, to five o'clock that evening, those in attendance engaged in a heated debate. After adding two amendments that altered language more than substance, the Wyandots approved the accord by a margin of sixty-three to twenty. "If the President and Senate should confirm our treaty it will certainly be the last," William Walker noted. "As after that event we Wyandotts will become citizens of *Uncle Sam's States*. A truly *new era* in the history of the Wyandott Nation." But controversy marred the vote. In his journal Walker described the debates as "animated," but did not give any details. At the same time, out of the six hundred and six Wyandots in eastern Kansas, one hundred and sixty-seven of whom were men and heads of families, only eighty-three voted. The favorable vote therefore represented the sentiments of a small segment of the community. Based on these numbers, Superintendent of Indian Affairs David Mitchell reported that, "I cannot consider the vote taken as expressing the sense of the majority of the nation." The U.S. Senate may have shared Mitchell's reservations. In September, it ratified the treaty, but with considerable revisions. The final version included only two articles, one that granted the Wyandots $185,000 for the acreage promised in the 1842 treaty and another that promised to pay for the expenses of the delegation. The articles granting citizenship no longer appeared.[24]

Rejection only temporarily halted the efforts of those Wyandots who favored citizenship. On Saturday, May 8, 1852, Principal Chief George Clark presided as the Wyandots debated whether or not to authorize the Council "to take measures for the ratification of that part of the Treaty of

[24] For references to this relationship between Armstrong and Walker, see J. M. Armstrong to Hon. Luke Lea, OIA-LR, roll 951; William E. Connelley (Ed.), "The Provisional Government of Nebraska Territory and the Journals of William Walker," *Proceedings and Collections of the Nebraska State Historical Society*, Second Series, 3(1899): 346–347, Walker quotation on page 309 (emphasis in original); Journal of the Proceedings of the Wyandott Convention, OIA-LR, roll 951; Thomas Moseley, Jr., to D. D. Mitchell, May 23, 1850, OIA-LR, roll 951; D. D. Mitchell to Hon. Orlando Brown, June 6, 1850, OIA-LR, roll 951; *Indian Affairs, II*, 587–588; Thomas Moseley to Hon. Luke Lea, December 2, 1850, OIA-LR, roll 951.

April, 1850, which was suspended by the President and Senate." Opposition to this notion remained. Yet, "after an animated discussion of some four hours," William Walker reported, "a vote was taken and the measure was carried by two thirds majority." The discussions must have been more than animated, especially because many Wyandots still disputed the voting results nearly two decades later. According to John Grey-eyes, an elected member of the Wyandot Legislative Committee in 1852, the voters rejected the proposal "by a very large majority of at least two to one." Jacob Whitecrow, another member of the Legislative Committee in 1852, remembered that a "large majority" voted down the measure. Nevertheless a month after the convention a delegation of three Wyandots appeared in Washington and announced their authority to negotiate with the federal government.[25]

Although their mission had questionable legitimacy, the three men who traveled to Washington were not outlaws. Matthew Mudeater was a young man of thirty-five serving his fifth consecutive year as an elected official. Principal Chief George Clark was the eldest of the three, just shy of fifty and, like Mudeater, had served as an elected member of the Wyandot government since 1848. Joel Walker had traveled to Washington before and rounded out the delegation in his capacity as the Secretary of the Council. Relaying the Wyandots' alleged dissatisfaction with the Senate's treaty alterations, the three men argued that the federal government should reconsider its position and claimed that many Wyandots would make prepared and capable citizens. In addition, present conditions on the Missouri border made it necessary for the Indians to own individual plots to secure their property. The three men also responded directly to points made by critics. They realized that some within the federal government believed that the educated and intelligent would take advantage of the "ignorant and needy." The Wyandot delegates, no strangers to statesmanship, framed their response within a larger context. "Suppose this were true," Clark, Mudeater, and Walker argued, "may we not ask, whether such things are not enacted among the citizens of every state in the Union? There are rich and poor men – owners of the soil and laborers who till it, every where ... These disparities are natural," the Wyandot delegates concluded, "and must and will exist." Clark, Mudeater, and Walker assured Commissioner of Indian Affairs Luke Lea that the more

---

[25] Connelley, "The Provisional Government of Nebraska Territory," 348; Affidavit of John Grey-eyes, January 18, 1870, vol. 2, *RCA*; George Clark et al. to Luke Lea, July 3, 1852, OIA-LR, roll 364; Affidavit of Jacob Whitecrow, January 20, 1870, vol. 2, *RCA*.

advanced Wyandots wanted to protect their less fortunate tribal members. They downplayed concerns over the possible fate of those less able or inclined to prosper as citizens.[26]

Although federal officials rejected the delegations' request, the Wyandot elite refused to drop the issue. The next discussion proved at once the most disputed and the most decisive. President Millard Fillmore had argued in 1852 that not only would the Wyandots lose or sell their lands to white men if they received allotments, but also that citizenship would be useless because the Indian lands were not located within any state. But as evidenced by their involvement in and awareness of the various efforts to organize the western territories, Wyandot leaders knew that Fillmore's argument would soon have no foundation. Several months after the Kansas-Nebraska Act became law, the Wyandot Council called a meeting to revisit allotment and citizenship. Apparently tired of the question and secure in the knowledge of its past defeats, most Wyandots did not attend the council. Those in favor of negotiating a treaty, George Clark, Matthew Mudeater, and Joel Walker, among others, saw their opportunity. They called for a vote. As a veteran of Wyandot politics and an older man just over forty, Jacob Whitecrow refused to yield so easily to a position he strongly opposed. Whitecrow argued that any vote would be illegal and unconstitutional. He was not alone. "A great many others refused to vote," he reported, "as they declared that the paramount law of the tribe would not justify them in so doing as it required fifty to be present when any law affecting the interests of the whole tribe were to be considered." But the men who favored negotiating a treaty pressed their advantage. Although the total number of voters fell somewhere between twenty-eight and thirty-three, the protreaty faction declared victory. It was a crucial moment. Eighty-three Wyandots had voted on May 1850 on this same issue. In the elections held in August 1851, more than one hundred Wyandots had cast ballots. Yet, approximately thirty men authorized the treaty negotiations in 1855. In a clear violation of the laws set forth in their 1851 constitution, a small faction decided the fate of the entire nation.[27]

This time U.S. officials supported the proposal, and the accord signed on January 30, 1855 matched the wishes expressed by previous Wyandot

---

[26] George Clark et al. to Luke Lea, July 3, 1852, OIA-LR, roll 364.

[27] Millard Fillmore to Luke Lea, July 19, 1852, OIA-LR, roll 364; Affidavit of Jacob Whitecrow, January 20, 1870, vol. 2, *RCA*; Affidavit of John D. Brown, January 20, 1870, vol. 2, *RCA*; Affidavit of John Greyeyes, January 18, 1870, vol. 2, *RCA*; Connelley, "The Provisional Government of Nebraska Territory," 330; Robert Emmett Smith, Jr., "The Wyandot Indians, 1843–1876" (Ph.D. Dissertation, Oklahoma State University, 1973), 126–130.

delegations. With the organization of Kansas Territory and the negotiation of an allotment treaty with the Shawnees in 1854, it appeared that prior arguments against both allotment and citizenship no longer mattered. Therefore the Wyandot agreement laid out the process through which the Wyandots would dissolve their tribal affiliation and become American citizens. It also presented the opportunity for any Wyandot to apply "to be temporarily exempted from citizenship and for continued protection and assistance from the United States." However, the treaty did not allow anyone who took that exemption to hold land in common. Every Wyandot man, woman, and child would receive a portion of the land purchased from the Delawares in 1848. Three commissioners, one appointed by the federal government and two chosen by the Wyandot Council, were responsible for creating the lists required to fulfill these terms. Their efforts would categorize more than just citizens and noncitizens. The Wyandots who chose citizenship would also be described as competent or incompetent, with further subsets of orphans, insane persons, and idiots where deemed appropriate.[28]

Events unfolded quickly in eastern Kansas once the Senate ratified the treaty at the end of February. By late July, the proper authorities had selected the three commissioners charged with overseeing the division and allotment of the Wyandot lands. The Wyandot Council chose Lot Coffman and John C. McCoy, and the federal government appointed Benjamin Robinson. McCoy, the son of the late Isaac McCoy and the founder of Westport, Missouri, had prior experience as a surveyor in the region. Coffman had also completed surveys while Robinson was the present Indian agent for the Kansas Agency and, therefore, a familiar face in the region. To enact the terms of the treaty and to get a better count of the Wyandot population, the commissioners first requested two Wyandots, Silas Armstrong and Joel Garrett, to take a complete and accurate census. Their completed census was then submitted to the Wyandot Council, who had the opportunity to add or subtract any names. From that final list the commissioners divided the Wyandots into several groups. When they had completed their assigned tasks, they had lists of the exempt, competent, incompetent, and orphan Wyandots.[29]

---

[28] *Indian Affairs, II*, 618–626, 677–681.

[29] *Indian Affairs, II*, 677–681; Geo. W. Manypenny to Messrs. Robinson, McCoy, and Coffman, November 25, 1856, OIA-LR, roll 952; Louis O. Honig, *Westport: Gateway to the Early West* (Kansas City, MO, 1950), 29–36; John C. McCoy and B. F. Robinson to Hon. G. W. Manypenny, December 8, 1855, OIA-LR, roll 274. Coffman resigned in November 1856 to take a job surveying the Shawnee reserve. The Wyandot Council replaced him with Robert Lawrence. See Smith, Jr., "The Wyandot Indians," 152.

The composition of these multiple lists caused several problems. Debates first started over tribal membership. The Wyandot Council appointed James Bigtree chairman of a committee to review the census completed by Armstrong and Garrett. That committee's report contained twenty-eight names to be removed from the census. Reasons for suspension varied. In one case, Bigtree's committee recommended that Hiram Northrup and his immediate family be stricken from the membership rolls. Northrup, a white Westport merchant, married Margaret Clark, the daughter of Thomas Clark, a leader of the Canadian Wyandots, in 1845. He had also served one term on the Wyandot Legislative Council from 1850 to 1851. Northrup defended his status and claimed that the Council acted not only against the "laws, customs, and usages," but also that they "they have been governed in their decisions by interested motives." He did not elaborate. Bigtree's committee also recommended exclusion based on marriage outside of the community. Lewis Clark's suspension was based not only on his Seneca heritage but also on his union with a black woman. And shortly after the report's submission the Wyandot Council affirmed Bigtree's suggestions and declared that Rosanna Stone and Martha Driver had "forfeited all rights and claims to membership in the Wyandott Nation by uniting with the Senecas." In a similar ruling, the Council declared that Sarah Bigtown had given up her membership by leaving her Wyandot husband and marrying a Munsee Chief named Gordon Gideon.[30]

Although the Wyandot Council expected its decisions to stand, McCoy, Coffman, and Robinson saw it as their obligation to examine each case thoroughly. They believed it necessary to adhere to the eighth article of the treaty, which read in part, "the persons to be included in the apportionment of the lands and money . . . shall be such only as are actual members of the Wyandott Nation, their heirs and legal representatives . . . according to the laws, usages, and customs thereof." The three men had a difficult time. Wyandot "usages and customs," the commissioners explained, "we found in many instances to vary so much as to be of but little service to us in making up our decisions." Nevertheless, they took into account every piece of evidence they thought necessary to make their rulings. The commissioners' final report had a list of five hundred and forty-two names.

---

[30] List of persons suspended from the census, October 10, 1855, OIA-LR, roll 809; Affidavit of H. M. Northrup, October 30, 1855, OIA-LR, roll 809; H. M. Northrup to Maj. Robert C. Miller, October 30, 1855, OIA-LR, roll 809; Minutes of Wyandotte Council, October 24, 1855, Indian Files – Wyandot, Box 6, KSHS. Sarah Bigtown is referred to as Sally Bigtown in the commissioner records.

Included on that list were twenty-three of the twenty-eight individuals noted by Bigtree's committee. McCoy and Robinson knew that their final roll was "not satisfactory to the Council and several other members of the tribe." To no avail, the Wyandot leadership argued that the commissioners were supposed to act merely as "attesting witnesses" to the Council's actions.[31]

A second problem arose regarding the citizenship and exemption lists. Despite their differences of opinion with the Wyandot Council, the commissioners provided Commissioner of Indian Affairs George Manypenny a completed roll in early December 1855. Their records indicated that only forty-six individuals applied for exemption. But the very process of requesting exemptions came under fire, primarily because many Wyandots did not realize that such an option even existed. According to John Grey-eyes the Commissioners chose to accept applications for exemption in October 1855 at a meeting held by the Wyandot Council to deal with some "ordinary business" of the tribe. "There was but very few of the tribe present," Grey-eyes remembered, "as it was not known before that this particular business would be transacted on this particular day." In addition, the Commissioners only kept the list open for two hours. "I know of no other opportunity being given at any other time, neither before nor since," Grey-eyes stated, "for any of the tribe to have their names placed on the temporary suspension list." John D. Brown, a former principal chief, had a similar recollection. Whether absent from the reserve at the time or simply unaware of the meeting, numerous Wyandots missed their chance and complained that the commissioners used fraudulent tactics to keep the exemption list short.[32]

The commissioners' lists had multiple impacts and meanings. Disputes over tribal membership illustrated both the Wyandot Council's desire for control as well as the intent to limit access to the annuities and payouts resulting from the 1855 treaty. Money mattered and many in the Wyandot

---

[31] *Indian Affairs, II*, 677–681; John C. McCoy and B. F. Robinson to Hon. G. W. Manypenny, December 8, 1855, OIA-LR, roll 274; List of those determined to be members of the Wyandot Tribe of Indians, December 8, 1855, OIA-LR, roll 274.

[32] John C. McCoy and B. F. Robinson to Hon. G. W. Manypenny, December 8, 1855, OIA-LR, roll 274; List of those determined to be members of the Wyandot Tribe of Indians, December 8, 1855, OIA-LR, roll 274; List of those persons who have applied . . . to be temporarily exempt, December 8, 1855, OIA-LR, roll 274; Deposition of John W. Greyeyes, January 18, 1870, vol. 2, *RCA*; Affidavit of John D. Brown, January 20, 1870, vol. 2, *RCA*; Affidavit of Russell Garrett, January 18, 1870, vol. 2, *RCA*; Affidavit of Jacob Whitecrow, January 20, 1870, vol. 2, *RCA*; Affidavit of Betsy Porcupine, February 21, 1870, vol. 2, *RCA*.

leadership knew that resources would only stretch so far. But at its foundation, the troubles within the Wyandot Nation after the 1855 treaty
reflected the differing opinions about the importance of the community
as a whole. The driving force behind the treaty was a group of men who
believed both that they could better secure their property with the protection offered by citizenship and that they had a real stake in the future
of Kansas Territory. For those Wyandots who opposed the treaty, eastern Kansas no longer provided a safe home and relocation appeared to
be the best option. Although Kansas and Indian Territory served as the
stage, the federal government's lists served as the media through which
these opposing parties acted out their respective visions of the Wyandots'
future.

The advocacy of citizenship among Wyandot elites was not an empty
gesture. Indeed, the same men who had attempted to organize the
Nebraska Territory prior to the Congressional legislation in 1854 took
an active role in the messy territorial politics of the day. On March 30,
1855, Missourians led by Senator David R. Atchison "made a mockery
of local self-government," crossed the state line, and cast illegal ballots to
elect a territorial legislature favorable to slavery. Matthew Walker, Silas
Armstrong, Isaac Long, Matthew Splitlog, Matthew Mudeater, George
Clark, and at least twenty-nine other members of the Wyandot Nation
cast ballots at a polling station in Lawrence. Six months later, on October
1, the Wyandots returned to the polls when Kansans elected a delegate to
Congress. This time the Wyandot Council House served as a polling station. Of the two hundred and forty-six men who voted in the Wyandotte
Township that day, at least eighteen were Wyandots. Eight days later these
voters elected delegates to the constitutional convention in Lecompton,
and at least twenty-six Wyandots cast ballots in two different precincts in
eastern Kansas. Finally, of the thirty-five men who voted at the Wyandot
Council House in the elections of January 1856, eighteen belonged to the
Wyandot Nation. At no point did they cast their ballots surreptitiously.
According to election guidelines adopted at the State Constitutional Convention held in Topeka in September 1855, qualified voters would be "all
white male inhabitants" of the territory. Yet in their report on the polling
in the Pawnee Precinct for the October 9th election, the three judges noted
that, "the voters were white male inhabitants '(except five, who are members of the Wyandot tribe of Indians).'" In some of the poll books, the
notation "(Wyt.)" was even written next to the name of the individual
voter. Election officials displayed more concern about the participation

of nonresidents than they did about guidelines specifying "white male inhabitants."[33]

Just as important, these Wyandot voters believed that they had an investment in the battles between the Missouri border ruffians and the free-state supporters. The tense divide between pro and antislavery factions on the Wyandot reserve had simmered since first surfacing after the Methodist Episcopal Church (MEC) split in 1845. Starting in 1854, the Wyandots lived in a war zone. White proslavery supporters temporarily established their territorial legislature at the Shawnee Methodist Mission in the summer of 1855, adjacent to the Wyandot reserve. And it may have been a Wyandot messenger who warned the free-state supporters in Lawrence of an impending attack by a force of border ruffians in the winter months of 1855. But a series of fires in the spring of 1856 also unmasked the tensions still lingering within the Wyandot community. Toward the end of March, several Wyandots entered the church building maintained by the anti-slavery MEC North and burned both the Bible and valuable church records. The arsonists delivered a stronger message a few days later when the building itself went up in smoke. Retaliation was swift, and in a matter of hours flames shot from the rooftop of the MEC South church. These two attacks broadened the conflict and, within a few days, fires reduced at least three individual houses to ashes. Agent William Gay blamed the outbreak on outside meddling and the consumption of whiskey provided by a local shop. But more than just whiskey provoked these actions. At least one of the men who lost a house due to the arson, James Armstrong, stood accused of firing the MEC South church. Surprisingly, the violence faded almost as quickly as it had arisen. No specific explanation for this change stands out, although Agent Gay threatened to withhold annuities from anyone involved, which may have quelled the passions to a certain extent.[34]

For most Wyandots, however, the territorial elections and the struggles over slavery were less important than the invasion of thousands of

---

[33] Michael F. Holt, *The Political Crisis of the 1850s* (New York, 1978), 193; "Report of the Special Committee Appointed to Investigate the Troubles in Kansas," House of Representatives Report No. 200, 34th Congress, 1st Session, 408–409, 495–503, 593–594, 615, 686–687, 705–706, 818–819. Names of the Wyandot members can be found in William E. Connelley, "Wyandot and Shawnee Indian Lands in Wyandotte County, Kansas," *Collections of the Kansas State Historical Society,* 15(1923): 103–181.

[34] William Gay to Alfred Cumming, May 3, 1856, OIA-LR, roll 809; Affidavit of William Johnson and John Solomon, February 13, 1862, OIA-LR, roll 812; Smith, Jr., "The Wyandot Indians," 141–145.

American settlers. As might be expected based on proximity alone, the experience of the Wyandots paralleled that of the Delawares in the mid to late 1850s. By the end of 1854, white settlers in eastern Kansas had stolen fifteen hogs from Matilda Hicks, twenty hogs from Noah Zane, and three heifers and a sow from Margaret D. Solomon. And the complaints registered by these three Wyandots represented only a fraction of the animals and other goods lost in the years after Kansas became a territory. This assault consumed Wyandot lands as well as property. "There are at this time trespassers on the Wyandott Lands," Silas Armstrong and Matthew Mudeater protested to Acting Commissioner of Indian Affairs Charles Mix in May 1858, "and who are now occupying the same as they claim by virtue of the 'Preemption Law.' These settlers are destroying timber and otherwise interfering with the rights of the Wyandotts." But due to the 1855 treaty and the legal dissolution of their tribe, the Wyandots no longer had an agent responsible for their protection. Fully aware that the federal government left them without a safety net after the treaty ratification, Armstrong and Mudeater argued for more assistance from local officials.[35]

Rather than stay in Kansas and struggle with white settlers, many Wyandots chose to leave. In the subsequent geographic split, these men and women generally relocated to one of two regions. The few who had maintained ties to relatives in Canada traveled northeast to live in southwestern Ontario. Most journeyed south and settled among friends on the Seneca reserve. In the late 1810s, the Wyandots had granted nearly forty thousand acres of land in Ohio to Senecas who had left their previous homes further east. Now the Wyandots needed their brothers to return the favor. Individual Wyandots like Betsy Porcupine headed south early in 1856. As the pressures in Kansas grew, however, larger numbers followed her lead. In 1857, a Wyandot delegation spoke to the Senecas in Indian Territory about purchasing a portion of the latter's reserve. Although the final arrangement remained incomplete, that summer an emigrant party of Wyandots under the leadership of Matthew Mudeater left Kansas and headed south and settled on the Seneca lands located just west of the meeting point of Arkansas and Missouri. By the fall of 1858, approximately two hundred Wyandots resided on the Seneca lands. They would remain

[35] For the full complaints of Hicks, Zane, Solomon, and numerous other Wyandots, see Senate Executive Document No. 77, 41st Congress, 2nd Session, Serial No. 1406, 1–55; Silas Armstrong and Matthew Mudeater to Hon. Chas. E. Mix, May 11, 1858, OIA-LR, roll 952; Benjamin Newsom to A. M. Robinson, August 24, 1858, in Senate Executive Document No. 1, 35th Congress, 2nd Session, Serial No. 974, 463–464.

there until conflicts created by the Civil War drove them back to Kansas in the early 1860s.[36]

But even those Wyandots who relocated to Indian Territory still had to deal with their allotments from the 1855 treaty, a situation that quickly embroiled them in the complexities of exemption and land sales. According to John Sarahess, many Wyandots who initially chose exemption "went to the Wyandotte Commissioners and requested them to remove their names from the suspension list so as to enable them to sell their lands and enable them to remove to the Seneca Country." These men and women had not realized that remaining an Indian meant that they would not be allowed to sell their allotment. Jacob Whitecrow, speaking from personal experience, stated that this decision was not necessarily a straightforward proposition. As one of the fortunate ones present at the Wyandot Council House in October 1855, Whitecrow had requested a spot on the exemption list. One week later, however, one of the commissioners suggested that Jacob become a citizen so that he could sell his land and move to Indian Territory. "I finally consented but I was always opposed to becoming a citizen," Whitecrow lamented, "had it not been for the advice of the Commissioners aforesaid, I should have continued on the temporary suspension list." Although he felt deceived, Whitecrow at least registered by choice. Others who moved to live with the Senecas, such as Betsy Porcupine, could not say the same. She relocated to Indian Territory unaware that she needed to choose to remain an Indian in the legal sense. Both she and her son John ended up on the citizenship list.[37]

For every Wyandot like Jacob Whitecrow who became a citizen and sold his land somewhat willingly, there were far more like Betsy Porcupine who lost their tribal affiliation as well as their allotment through more

---

[36] Affidavit of Betsy Porcupine, February 21, 1870, vol. 2, *RCA*; Affidavit of John Sarahess, February 21, 1870, vol. 2, *RCA*; Affidavit of Frank Whitewing, February 21, 1870, vol. 2, *RCA*; John W. Grey-eyes to CIA, April 9, 1857, OIA-LR, roll 809; Minutes of Wyandotte Council, February 23, 1858, September 15, 1858, September 22, 1859, Indian Files – Wyandot, Box 6, KSHS; Tauromee et al. to William Dole, December 23, 1862, OIA-LR, roll 812; Andrew J. Dorn to Col. Elias Rector, August 31, 1857, in House of Representatives Executive Document No. 2, 35th Congress, 1st Session, Serial No. 942, 493–495; Andrew J. Dorn to Col. Elias Rector, September 9, 1858, in Senate Executive Document No. 1, 35th Congress, 2nd Session, Serial No. 974, 488–489; Tauromee et al. to Hon. Wm. P. Dole, December 3, 1862, OIA-LR, roll 812; Smith, "The Wyandot Indians," 146–147.

[37] Affidavit of John Sarahess, February 21, 1870, vol. 2, *RCA*; Affidavit of Jacob Whitecrow, January 20, 1870, vol. 2, *RCA*; Affidavit of Betsy Porcupine, February 21, 1870, vol. 2, *RCA*; List of those determined to be members of the Wyandot Tribe of Indians, December 8, 1855, OIA-LR, roll 274.

blatant acts of fraud or deception. Speculation was rampant throughout eastern Kansas in the late 1850s and was not limited to white Americans. Two of the main culprits were the Town Companies of Wyandotte City and Quindaro, both of whose associations included prominent Wyandots. The Wyandotte City Town Company formed in December 1856 when four white men – W. Y. Roberts, Thomas H. Swope, Gaius Jenkins, and John McAlpine – abandoned their previous partners and joined their interests with Isaiah Walker, Joel Walker, and Silas Armstrong. These seven stock-holders proceeded to organize a town within the limits of the former Wyandot reserve at the mouth of the Kansas River. Lot sales began in March 1857 once the government's survey was completed and the Kansas territorial legislature incorporated the town in June 1858. Quindaro, on the other hand, was founded on the west bank of the Missouri River about five miles north of Wyandotte City as a site at which free-state support-ers could enter Kansas. Abelard Guthrie, one of the founders, named the town after his wife, Nancy Quindaro Brown Guthrie. Joel Walker was named one of the town officers in 1857.[38]

For their towns to exist, however, the founders needed to own the land on which those towns were located. And at the time of their found-ing, although the Wyandots owned the land, allotment complicated the efforts of those who wanted large sections. Town organizers needed to acquire the plots one at a time. Therefore, even as the Wyandot commis-sioners allotted the lands to each tribal member the speculators involved in Quindaro and Wyandotte worked to obtain what they could. Many Wyandots shared John Sarahess' observation that, "there was a strong influence brought to bear on the Wyandotte people to sell their lands by the Town Companies of Wyandotte City and Quindaro." Guthrie and his colleagues centered Quindaro around the allotment of one hundred and fifty acres granted to its namesake, and added smaller plots through purchase. Wyandotte City's location, however, made it more difficult to create a compact town center. In an attempt to overcome the presence of individual allotments in the middle of the envisioned bustling town, Silas Armstrong even attempted to defraud and strong-arm his sister-in-law,

---

[38] Affidavit of Robert Robitaille, February 21, 1870, vol. 2, *RCA*; Affidavit of Irwin P. Long, February 16, 1870, *RCA*; Affidavit of John Sarahess, February 21, 1870, vol. 2, *RCA*; Grant W. Harrington, *Historic Spots or Mile-Stones in the progress of Wyandotte County, Kansas* (Merriam, KS, 1935), 238–240; Perl W. Morgan (Ed. and Comp.), *History of Wyandotte County, Kansas and Its People* (2 vols., Chicago, 1911), I, 87–107; Alan W. Farley, "Annals of Quindaro: A Kansas Ghost Town," *Kansas Historical Quarterly*, 22(Winter 1956): 305–320.

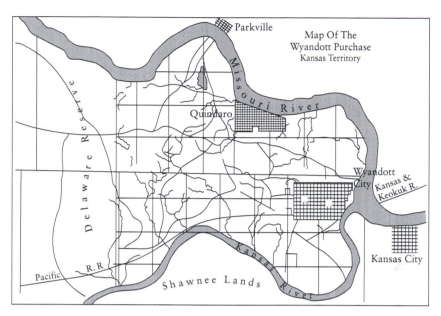

MAP 7. Wyandotte Purchase. Based on map in William E. Connelley (Ed.), "The Provisional Government of Nebraska Territory and the Journals of William Walker," *Proceedings and Collections of the Nebraska State Historical Society*, Second Series, 3(1899).

Lucy B. Armstrong. Lucy's husband, and Silas's brother, John had died in 1852. John, a Wyandot and a licensed attorney in Ohio, and Lucy, the daughter of a Methodist minister, had married in 1838. The two had removed in 1843 and were two of the first to build a home on the land purchased in Kansas. In 1857, however, the Armstrong home and lands stood in the heart of town proposed by Silas and his partners. Silas took action. The Wyandot Commissioners, based in large part on the word of this prominent Wyandot, apportioned the allotments of Lucy and her five children in such a way that Lucy's personal section did not include the house she and her late husband had built. Silas also arranged for the purchase of one his nephew's shares without Lucy's consent. When Lucy protested all of these maneuvers, her brother-in-law presented a solution. If Lucy "would sell a part to the town company he would influence the commissioners to locate the remainder around the house."[39]

---

[39] Affidavit of John Sarahess, February 21, 1870, vol. 2, *RCA*; for similar statements, see Affidavit of Irwin P. Long, February 16, 1870, vol. 2, *RCA*; Affidavit of William Johnson, February 21, 1870, vol. 2, *RCA*. At least fifteen Wyandots received allotments near Nancy Guthrie. See Connelley, "Wyandot and Shawnee Indian Lands," 128–157.

Silas's maneuvers played into another complication that specifically harmed Wyandot widows. For the better part of 1857 and 1858, Lucy and at least nine other women petitioned for the right to be declared competent heads of family. They had to fight John McCoy, who used the foundations of common law to argue that, "orphans in law are those who are fatherless." Such a ruling could prove extremely devastating, for it meant the children's lands were put under guardianship, and made more accessible to speculators both inside and outside of the Wyandot community. Lucy, Matilda Hicks, Hannah Armstrong, and seven others knew the dangers this posed. "We believe," the widows declared, "that the Commissioners are tools for men in our nation, whose object is to get themselves appointed guardians for our children, that they themselves may have the use of their property." These women further argued that because the treaty did not distinguish between male and female it trumped common law. Fortunately for these widows, Commissioner of Indian Affairs James Denver and Secretary of the Interior Jacob Thompson shared this sentiment. Although the Wyandot Commissioners ignored Denver's opinion in 1857, they could not dismiss Thompson's message in June 1858 that the land "should be patented to the head thereof, whether male or female." This firm statement did not end the Wyandots' struggle. But for the widows it at least provided some measure of security.[40]

These small victories could not halt the divisions that split the Wyandot community socially and politically by the 1860s. Although the Civil War chased the Wyandots living in Indian Territory back to Kansas, their

---

For biographical information on the Armstrongs, see Connelley, "The Provisional Government of Nebraska Territory," 261n, 307n; Quotation from Affidavit of Lucy B. Armstrong, January 8, 1858, OIA-LR, roll 952. For further discussions of this dispute, see Lucy B. Armstrong to Charles E. Mix, May 10, 1858, OIA-LR, roll 952; Affidavit of C. Amalia M. Armstrong, September 26, 1857, OIA-LR, roll 952. Quindaro and Wyandotte City were not the only towns to use Wyandot lands as a foundation. For insights into the birth and growth of Lawrence, Topeka, and others, see Homer E. Socolofsky, "Wyandot Floats," *Kansas Historical Quarterly,* 36(Autumn 1970): 241–304.

[40] For the Wyandot Commissioners' stance see Robert J. Lammar to Lucy B. Armstrong, December 2, 1857, OIA-LR, roll 952; J. C. McCoy to Charles E. Mix, February 8, 1858, OIA-LR, roll 952; B. F. Robinson, J. C. McCoy, and William Miller to Charles E. Mix, November 11, 1858, OIA-LR, roll 952. For the widows' position see Lucy B. Armstrong to Messrs. McCoy and Lawrence, November 23, 1857, OIA-LR, roll 952; Lucy B. Armstrong to Messrs. Robinson, McCoy, and Lawrence, January 5, 1858, OIA-LR, roll 952; Lucy B. Armstrong to Hon. C. E. Mix, May 21, 1858, OIA-LR, roll 952; Hannah Armstrong et al. to Hon. Charles E. Mix, September 3, 1858, OIA-LR, roll 952. For the federal government's opinion see James Denver to J. C. McCoy, November 13, 1857, OIA-LR, roll 952; Jacob Thompson to Charles E. Mix, June 5, 1858, OIA-LR, roll 952; Minutes of Wyandotte Council, October 20, 1858, Indian Files – Wyandot, Box 6, KSHS.

return did not reunite the disparate factions. Those who sought to retain their tribal identity by moving south did not believe that the citizen Wyandots had any right to make decisions or participate in negotiations with the federal government. Yet the complications involving the citizenship list as well as the ambitions of the Wyandot elite created a community still hoping to maintain a relationship with the United States. As late as 1865, the "Indian Party" of Wyandots, under the leadership of Tauromee, had to struggle for recognition from the local officials intent on designating Silas Armstrong and the "Citizen Party" as the voice of all Wyandots. Tauromee, one of the few whose name appeared on the exemption list, argued that he and others like him held proper authority that came from their status as noncitizens. Only adoption could return a citizen to the fold, not government decree. "The right to adopt members is as indisputable as any right a tribe can have," Tauromee explained, "and after an Indian becomes a citizen he cannot return to the tribe in any other way." The Wyandots did not want Silas Armstrong and other citizens to return to the fold without tribal consent, if they returned at all.[41]

Although a treaty signed in 1867 granted Tauromee and the Indian Party the authority they desired, it failed to solve the problems created by the 1855 accord. The 1867 agreement carved a home for the Wyandots in Indian Territory out of the Seneca reserve, an act that provided legal basis to an arrangement first negotiated between the two tribes the previous decade. And with this accord the federal government agreed to make Tauromee and his council the final arbiters on which citizen Wyandots, if any, would be adopted back into the Nation. But this treaty could not force a reunion of the two factions. Too much had gone wrong. By 1870, fifteen years after the 1855 accord, only forty or fifty Wyandots remained in Kansas as most had lost their lands through deception, fraud, preemption, and even state taxation. But although landlessness was a common denominator between Citizen and Indian Wyandots, political divides had not healed. John Kayrahoo, Tauromee's successor, requested Commissioner of Indian Affairs Ely Parker to "give notice that no citizen of the US, whether of Wyandotte blood or not, will be allowed to interfere with our affairs without our permission." What the 1855 accord had set in motion could not be settled with yet another federal treaty.[42]

---

[41] John G. Pratt to unknown, December 1, 1865, vol. 6, *RCA*; Wyandotte Council to John G. Pratt, November 24, 1865, vol. 6, *RCA*; Connelley, "Wyandot and Shawnee Lands," 126–127. Perhaps the only extended discussion of these post–1860 disputes and difficulties is in Smith, Jr., "The Wyandot Indians," 173–237.

[42] *Indian Affairs, II*, 960–909; John Kayrahoo to Ely S. Parker, January 26, 1870, vol. 2, *RCA*; Enoch Hoag, SIA, to Ely Parker, June 14, 1870, vol. 2, *RCA*.

By the early 1860s, the future of Indian land ownership in Kansas Territory appeared grim. Treaties established procedures for the transfer of Indian cessions, but the federal government failed to follow through on some of the most basic steps. In the chaos that beset Kansas Territory, George Manypenny and other Indian Affairs employees found that denouncing the settlements as trespassing and condemning speculation as illegal placed them in the distinct and powerless minority. Few government officials expected or wanted expansion to stop at the Missouri border. Settlers like those who established claims in Kansas, Secretary of War Jefferson Davis pointed out to President Franklin Pierce in January 1855, "have uniformly been favored by the govt, and Congress has never failed to follow them with preemption laws, securing to them the narrow limits of their unauthorized settlements." Davis also clearly outlined the reasons for this consistently permissive policy. Rather than "a weak concession to men acting in defiance of law," the federal support of settler intrusions provided "a measure of justice to those who conscious of meditating no injury to the public property and no violation of the spirit of the statutes ... place themselves at the mercy of the govt in expending their toil upon its domain." The Secretary of War's words could not have satisfied those officials hoping to protect Indian lands. But his assessment fit Kansas Territory well. From 1854 to the outbreak of the Civil War, a combination of settler ambition and government permissiveness erased the boundaries of Indian reserves and consumed Indian lands.[43]

For the Wyandots and Delawares, the organization of Kansas Territory proved equally devastating for the integrity of their communities. When John Kayrahoo related to Barbeau the Wyandot old-time saying about adopting "the white man's way," he spoke more than fifty years after the events in Kansas and made no reference to the divisiveness that this idea had fostered within his Nation. But the decision to accept or encourage allotment proved controversial for Wyandots and Delawares alike, as a select group of prominent individuals and leaders made decisions that went against the interests and opinions of the majority in their respective communities. For the Wyandots in particular, the repercussions of those actions echoed in the decades that followed.

[43] Jefferson Davis to President Pierce, January 18, 1855, OIA-LR, roll 364.

7

Power on the Western Front

Shawnee and Potawatomi Indians in Kansas

In 1867, Potawatomi leaders in Kansas signed a treaty that allowed them to select a reservation of thirty miles square in Indian Territory, "without interfering with the locations made for other Indians." But the land they chose, due in part to misunderstandings and conflicts with other treaties, overlapped with acreage claimed by the Absentee Shawnees. And when the Potawatomis relocated to this contested region, the resulting tensions nearly led to violence. "They would select a homesite and erect a cabin," Thomas Wildcat Alford remembered, "then some of our [Shawnee] people would go by night or when the family was away from home, and tear it down." To avoid further controversy, Congress passed a measure in May 1872 titled, "An Act to Provide Homes for the Pottawatomie and Absentee Shawnee Indians in the Indian Territory." Under this legislation, members of both communities were to select allotments from the reservation designated under the 1867 Potawatomi agreement.[1]

These disputes noted by Alford and tackled by Congress were only one aspect of the difficulties faced by both Shawnees and Potawatomis in the 1860s and 1870s. Most significantly the Civil War and American expansion into Kansas led to severe displacement and division. The Potawatomis who relocated to Indian Territory were primarily members of the Citizen Band who had already lost or were in danger of losing their allotments. Meanwhile, the more traditional Prairie Band struggled to hold onto the common land they had obtained through the 1861 treaty. Several distinct Shawnee communities also established new homes throughout the region

---

[1] *Indian Affairs*, II, 970–974; Thomas Wildcat Alford, *Civilization* as told to Florence Drake (Norman, 1936), 70; Rev. Joseph Murphy, O.S.B., *Potawatomi of the West: Origins of The Citizen Band*. Edited by Patricia Sulcer Barrett (Shawnee, OK, 1988), 281–282; *U.S. Statutes at Large, XVII*, 159.

in the early 1870s. Approximately 80 percent of the Black Bob band left Kansas to live among the Absentees. This placed them near, but not with, the Eastern Shawnees, formerly the Lewistown Shawnees, who had separated from the Senecas and retained a small and separate reserve in the northeastern corner of Indian Territory. The Shawnees, who had taken their lands in severalty under the auspices of an 1854 treaty, resided on unoccupied sections of the Cherokee lands.[2]

Two intertwined elements affected these Shawnee and Potawatomi relocations, and they were at once familiar and new. As had been evident during the transition from the Great Lakes to the western territories earlier in the century, movement was inextricably connected to power. Both the Shawnees and the Potawatomis dealt with internal and external struggles for influence in the years during and after the Civil War. Missouri and Ohio Shawnees battled for prominence in negotiations with the federal government, and new connections between wealth and power wrestled with traditional leadership structures. Among the Potawatomis, headmen of disparate bands struggled to maintain autonomy even as American officials pushed for a united Potawatomi polity. And the stakes of these internal battles increased with every passing year. For the Shawnees, settlers and local officials proved most harmful to their existence, while the Potawatomis faced off against the acquisitive strategies of railroad companies. In both instances, the continued absence of a significant federal presence proved more dangerous than advantageous.

Although the location and composition of these power struggles had changed from those of previous decades, the overarching context and ultimate outcome had not. Despite their strength within the Shawnee community, even the powerful, wealthy, and experienced Ohio Shawnees still remained vulnerable to outside forces. Their influence proved no match for that of state officials and settlers who capitalized on the lack of federal authority. Although their distance from the Missouri border initially mitigated the Potawatomis' exposure, the Citizen Band soon faced a similar situation – owning allotments and at the mercy of the railroads and the state government. At the outbreak of the Civil War it was not a foregone conclusion that most Shawnees and Potawatomis would be forced to leave Kansas by the end of the decade. But the efforts of state officials, settlers,

---

[2] *Indian Affairs*, II, 970–974; Murphy, *Potawatomi of the West*, 305–307; *ARCIA 1902*, 277; William E. Smith, "The Oregon Trail Through Potawatomi County," *Kansas Historical Collections*, 28(1926–1928): 453–456; Alford, *Civilization*, 13–15, 70–73; *Indian Affairs*, II, 942–950, 960–969; Articles of Agreement between the Shawnee and Cherokee Indians, June 7, 1869, OIA-LR, roll 817; Stephen Warren, *The Shawnees and Their Neighbors, 1795–1870* (Urbana, 2005), 170–173.

and railroads, as well as the absence of a corrective federal authority, made it extremely difficult for any Shawnees and Potawatomis to alter the course of events.

The treaty the Shawnees signed in May 1854 arranged for the sale of 1.6 million acres, nearly two hundred thousand acres of which were set aside for individual allotments. Black Bob and Long Tail opposed allotment and their bands each received a small reserve to hold in common. The Absentees not residing in Kansas had five years to select allotments. To Joseph Parks, the principal chief and primary negotiator, the treaty represented a victory. It meant that the Shawnees would not have to leave Kansas. Just as important, those Shawnees who accepted allotment could now improve their lives and adjust to life alongside their new American neighbors. "Like a man climbing up hill," Parks had preached during the treaty negotiations, "when on top the people see and follow him. Whites have prospered a long time. Good many on the hill top but many yet at the bottom. It is the best way. The Shawnees are trying to climb that hill – therefore it is [my] wish that [my] people should remain not sell out." The Shawnee chief stood in a unique position of economic security, making it easier to speak of the potential for Shawnee prosperity. It also explained why he signed the treaty.[3]

From the 1850s to the 1860s, political influence and power became intricately connected to wealth within the Shawnees in Kansas. The same men who supported the 1854 agreement, believed in allotment, and led the Shawnees into the 1860s were those who had the most material success. Parks, who died in 1859, was only one of many individuals who hoped to use this combination of wealth and power to make it to the top of the hill. Yet most Shawnees left Kansas and their lands behind by 1870. Dispossession and relocation occurred in part because the federal government negotiated only with the Ohio faction and dismissed other Shawnee voices. Ironically, this empowerment of the Ohio Shawnee Council was the federal government's only effective use of its authority. In most other matters, federal policy proved either weak or pointless. State officials in particular capitalized on this futility and negatively influenced the distribution, sale, and ownership of Indian lands in the 1860s. Even the Ohio Shawnees had to leave Kansas soon after the Civil War ended.

Despite the weakness of the federal government, the Shawnees' relationship with the United States rested at the center of this struggle for control and ownership of Shawnee lands. Leaders of the disparate Shawnee

---

[3] *Indian Affairs*, II, 618–626; Minutes of Council with Shawnee Indians, April 24–26, 1854, OIA-TR, roll 5.

bands battled each other for the right to serve as a voice for their people in federal affairs. And although it played out in the specific context of 1850s and 1860s Kansas, this struggle was as much a continuation of postremoval conflict as it was a reflection of contemporary circumstances. All the while, state officials consistently worked to manipulate or bypass the federal relationship that nominally structured Indian affairs.

Contests over authority among the Shawnees after 1854 were imbalanced. The Shawnees who held their lands in severalty dominated the elected council. Although Ohio Shawnees formed the core of this group, the leadership ranks included men of mixed descent who nominally belonged to the Missouri faction. Graham Rogers, a member of the Council in the 1850s and the elected principal chief in 1865, was one of the more prominent of these Missouri-born Shawnees who accepted allotment and allied with the Ohio faction. He was the son of Lewis Rogers, a white man adopted by the Shawnees in the 1700s, and Parlie Blackfish, the daughter of the Shawnee leader Blackfish. Along with other members of the Shawnee band that once lived at Rogerstown, Graham and his family had settled along the Kansas River in 1828. He and other members of the Rogers band allied with the leading members of the Ohio Shawnees. Blurred membership lines and the need to highlight their claims to authority led these leaders to refer to their administration at times in the mid-1860s as the Council for the United Tribe of Shawnees. Their Shawnee opponents were those who sought to hold their land in common, largely the Black Bobs and Absentees.[4]

Indian agents and federal officials negotiated only with the Council elected by the Ohio Shawnees and encouraged the Black Bob and Absentee Shawnees to unite with their relatives. They refused. "We thought you urged us to unite with the Maquecheh (Ohio Shawnees)," they wrote to Commissioner of Indian Affairs Louis Bogy. "Our people instructed us not to do it and our own views agree with theirs. If you knew how long and how much these people have wronged and opposed us you surely would

---

[4] Charles Bluejacket to D. N. Cooley, November 30, 1865, OIA-LR, roll 814. For information on Rogerstown and Graham Rogers, see John Mack Faragher, "'More Motley than Mackinaw': From Ethnic Mixture to Ethnic Cleansing on the Frontier of the Lower Missouri, 1783–1833," in Andrew R. L. Cayton and Fredrika J. Teute (Eds.), *Contact Points: American Frontiers from the Mohawk Valley to the Mississippi, 1750–1830* (Chapel Hill, 1998), 304–326. The prospect of allotment had prompted some controversy within the Absentee community, as some chose to select individual plots. The majority of Absentees, however, rejected land in severalty. See, Warren, *The Shawnees and Their Neighbors*, 78–79, 97.

FIGURE 7. Portrait (Front) of Wa-Wa-Si-Mo, called Graham Rogers. (Courtesy of the National Anthropological Archives, Smithsonian Institution.)

not ask us to do a thing so injurious to our people." Both the statement and the use of "Maquecheh" testified to the deep divide still measured by the eighteenth-century split. The Black Bob and Absentee Shawnees in particular still viewed politics through the lens of these older divisions, and despite the federal government's efforts, they refused to relinquish their distinctive identities. The Shawnee Council's continued participation in treaty negotiations with federal officials during the course of the Civil War further fueled this discontent. Both the Black Bob and Absentee Shawnees disputed the right of the Ohio faction to control the lands in Kansas, especially since the 1825 treaty that established the Western Reserve bore the marks of Missouri Shawnees.[5]

---

[5] Paschal Fish et al. to Hon. Louis V. Bogy, February 12, 1867, OIA-LR, roll 815; Warren, *The Shawnees and Their Neighbors*, 159–168. For further references to these Shawnee divisions and connections, see Vernon Kinietz and Erminie W. Voegelin (Eds.), *Shawnese Traditions: C. C. Trowbridge's Account* (Ann Arbor, June 1939); Alford,

But these clashes in the 1860s added a twist to those of previous decades when the Black Bob band capitalized on the wartime emigration of the Absentee Shawnees. Stephen Warren has asserted that, "the Civil War inadvertently contributed to parity between the Shawnee rivals." This parity existed more in numbers than in influence, but it provided a notable challenge to Ohio Shawnee dominance. In 1861, the Confederacy sent Albert Pike on a diplomatic mission to Indian Territory. Southern sympathizers, Creek Indians among them, harassed the Absentee Shawnees when the latter refused to ally with the Confederacy. Rather than endure this harassment, the Shawnees left Indian Territory and traveled north to Kansas. Shortly thereafter many young men joined M Company of the Fifteenth Cavalry in the Union Army. By the summer of 1863, the migration of Absentee Shawnees had increased the population of the refugee settlements on the Black Bob lands to more than one hundred and fifty men, women, and children. In the winter of 1864 the community expanded again when five hundred to seven hundred Shawnees fled their homes along the Kansas–Missouri and Kansas–Indian Territory borders.[6]

With this refugee infusion, the more traditional element now had the numbers to oppose the severalty Shawnees. Approximately five hundred and forty Absentees resided in Kansas by the fall of 1863, and together with the Black Bob Shawnees, this mixed band totaled nearly seven hundred and seventy. Early that year, the two Shawnee factions held competing elections for a representative government. Although voting normally took place in the fall, the 1862 elections were postponed to January 1863 because of wartime unrest. But when the Shawnees came together at

Civilization 10–12; James Howard, *Shawnee!: The Ceremonialism of a Native American Tribe and Its Cultural Background* (Athens, OH, 1981), 17–30; Dark Rain Thom, *Kohkumthena's Grandchildren The Shawnee* (Indianapolis, 1994), 172–177. For the protests against the Ohio Shawnees, see Perry Fuller to J. P. Usher, September 15, 1863, OIA-LR, roll 813; Statement of Missouri Shawnees, not dated but received by OIA on August 2, 1866, OIA-LR, roll 814; *Indian Affairs, II*, 262–264.

6 Warren, *The Shawnees and Their Neighbors*, 163–166; James Abbott to H. B. Branch, June 5, 1863, OIA-LR, roll 813; James Abbott to H. B. Branch, SIA, June 1863, OIA-LR, roll 813; Abelard Guthrie to William Dole, September 29, 1864, OIA-LR, roll 813; Paschal Fish to William Dole, January 9, 1865, OIA-LR, roll 814; Alford, *Civilization*, 5–12; Record of Shawnee Company by Samuel Cornatzer, October 14, 1864, roll 1259, JBA; Annie Heloise Abel, *The American Indian in the Civil War, 1862–1865* (Lincoln, 1992); Edmund J. Danziger, Jr., "The Office of Indian Affairs and the Problem of Civil War Indian Refugees in Kansas," *Kansas Historical Quarterly*, 35(Autumn 1969): 257–275; Dean Banks, "Civil War Refugees from Indian Territory in the North, 1861–1864," *Chronicles of Oklahoma*, 41(Autumn 1963): 286–298.

DeSoto on January 12, a disagreement arose as to the manner of elections and those who would be allowed to participate. The Black Bob Shawnees' opposition to the republican government was clear from its inception in 1852, when Black Bob argued that as a member of the Chillicothe division and the designated keeper of the sacred pack, he had a more substantial hereditary right to lead the Shawnees. Now the Black Bobs argued that, "all Shawnees that held their land in severalty were citizens, and had no rights in the tribe." In a decisive move, they held a separate election. On January 14 these Missouri Shawnees gathered at Paschal Fish's house and elected Black Bob as head chief and Paschal Fish as assistant chief. In the election report sent to President Abraham Lincoln, this alternate leadership argued their case in simple terms. "Which shall govern," they asked, "the majority or the minority [?]" From their position the proper answer was clear. Yet, neither Lincoln nor any other federal official viewed this election as legitimate and did not alter their relationship with the Ohio Shawnee Council. Nevertheless Paschal Fish continued to assert the rights and authority of the Missouri Shawnees even after Black Bob's death in 1864.[7]

The Ohio Shawnees eagerly cast Paschal Fish as a hypocrite. He not only owned land in severalty, they pointed out, but had also served as an elected member of the Shawnee Council at various times from 1852 to 1860. Fish and his family had accepted allotments under the terms of the 1854 treaty. He had also actively participated in the republican government before his sudden passion for Black Bob's cause. Indeed, the Shawnees elected Paschal Fish as their principal chief in the fall of 1859. However, Fish resigned in disgrace less than a year into his tenure. "A charge was made against him," Charles Bluejacket explained, "of receiving a bribe of one thousand dollars to induce him to pay to certain claimants a large sum of money belonging to the tribe." Apparently the evidence was damning enough to force Fish's resignation. According to Bluejacket, Fish became

---

[7] Perry Fuller to J. P. Usher, September 15, 1863, OIA-LR, roll 813; James B. Abbott to Hon. Wm. P. Dole, April 6, 1863, OIA-LR, roll 813. For reference to Black Bob as the holder of the sacred pack, see Warren, *The Shawnees and Their Neighbors*, 135; W. H. H. Fishback to Abraham Lincoln, January 28, 1863, OIA-LR, roll 813. Population statistics can be difficult to pin down in the source material. The figure of 768 for the Missouri Shawnees is given in Statement of Missouri Shawnees, not dated, but received by OIA on August 2, 1866, OIA-LR, roll 814. Agent James Abbott listed a total of 571 severalty Shawnees in 1866, and based on an 1869 census Stephen Warren gives a number of 770. See Statistics of Farming, etc. at the Shawnee Agency Sept. 1866, JBA; Warren, *The Shawnees and Their Neighbors*, 163–164, 206n; Paschal Fish et al. to Hon. D. N. Cooley, January 4, 1866, OIA-LR, roll 814.

an enemy of the Council from that point forward, and in Black Bob the former headman found a person and a cause to manipulate. Because Fish had attended a missionary school as a child and even became a Methodist preacher, his western education far surpassed that of most in the Black Bob band, and an intermediary role presented opportunities to influence negotiations. Critics of Fish also attacked his association with Abelard Guthrie. Guthrie, the Wyandot by adoption who claimed in the 1860s that he alone was responsible for the organization of Kansas Territory, was often accused in the 1860s of meddling in Shawnee affairs. Charles Bluejacket and others viewed Guthrie as a blowhard and an opportunist taking advantage of dissension to promote a personal agenda.[8]

Consequently, Paschal Fish's leadership may have had the unfortunate consequence of undermining the legitimacy of Missouri Shawnee opposition. At the very least, his participation made it easier for federal officials to ignore the voices of those Shawnees determined to assert traditional rights to leadership. Fish's personal history as a speculator and disgraced principal chief overshadowed the fact that the Missouri Shawnees had long seen themselves as the proper leaders based on the ancient divisions. But it is also likely that the federal government would have held the same position regardless of Fish's participation. Federal officials had consistently revealed a desire to promote "government chiefs" and to create single polities from the multiple bands and villages of Indians who once populated the southern Great Lakes region. Rather than negotiating separately with several leaders, federal agents and commissioners had long advocated centralized native governments with at least nominal authority to make business decisions. Paschal Fish's presence would not necessarily have altered their position.

Yet politics alone did not create divisions among the Shawnees, as disparities in wealth mirrored the power imbalance. The line between prosperity and mere survival had as much to do with the Civil War as with the 1852 government change and the 1854 allotment treaty. Land selection and distribution under the terms of the 1854 accord took several years, and it was not until early 1859 that each Shawnee who chose allotment actually possessed his plot and knew its location and boundaries. Even

[8] Charles Bluejacket to D. N. Cooley, November 30, 1865, OIA-LR, roll 814; Matthew King et al. to D. N. Cooley, March 12, 1866, OIA-LR, roll 814; Rev. William H. Goode, *Outposts of Zion, with Limnings of Mission Life* (Cincinnati, 1864), 295. For statements against Guthrie, see Affidavit of Charles Bluejacket, November 30, 1865, OIA-LR, roll 814; Affidavit of Matthew King, November 30, 1865, OIA-LR, roll 814; Affidavit of Moses Silverheels, November 30, 1865, OIA-LR, roll 814.

then they had to deal with squatters, trespassers, and speculators pushing for land sales. Beginning in 1861, while the armies under Robert E. Lee and multiple Union generals battled on the eastern seaboard, Kansas became a war zone as well as a refuge for thousands of Indians who fled the harassment of Confederates in Indian Territory. Guerilla warfare along the Missouri border damaged Shawnee settlements even as Shawnee families struggled in the absence of the men who had enlisted in the Union Army. In the midst of the chaos, Shawnee individuals and families battled both to hold on to their land and to survive. More often than not they had to choose between the two.[9]

The Black Bob and Absentee Shawnees suffered the most. On September 6, 1862, the Black Bob settlement in northeastern Kansas endured one of the most destructive assaults of the war's early years. Nearly two hundred men, under the command of the Confederate William Quantrill, ransacked the Indians' homes. He swore to kill any man found in a Union military uniform and told the Shawnees he attacked because the Indians furnished soldiers for the northern cause. Although Quantrill and his band killed only one man, they ruined the Black Bob Shawnees. Approximately eighty men, women, and children immediately moved as far west on their reserve as possible and built small shacks for shelter from the impending winter weather. The Absentee Shawnee refugees further strained the resources of this struggling community. At war's end, the mixed settlements of Black Bob and Absentees had difficulty recovering from the combined effects of these crises. Squatters presented a significant obstacle. When the Black Bob Shawnees had moved to the western portion of their reserve after Quantrill's attack, white settlers moved onto the lands to the east. Some squatters were war veterans, men who claimed that treaty cessions and the 1862 Homestead Law gave them the right and the opportunity to stake their claims. The Black Bob Shawnees protested and wanted the settlers removed. But the situation was not resolved quickly and this displacement compromised the Shawnees' ability to sustain their families. Circumstances only worsened after 1865. "I know of my own personal knowledge of about one hundred and eighty seven persons," Paschal Fish reported in 1867, "members of the Black Bob band and Absentee Shawnee Indians who are in a destitute and suffering condition for want both of clothing and subsistence." A September 1866 census illustrated

[9] A. Arnold to George Manypenny, March 23, 1857, OIA-LR, roll 809; Danziger, Jr., "The Office of Indian Affairs and the Problem of Civil War Refugees in Kansas," 257–275; Banks, "Civil War Refugees from Indian Territory in the North," 286–298.

this problem. Of the twenty-six families noted by Agent James Abbott, only seven cultivated even one acre. Only one man, Big Fox, grew something other than corn. All told, the Black Bob Shawnees owned seventeen horses but did not raise any livestock.[10]

Territorial conflicts and wartime violence severely compromised the basic elements of subsistence and survival among the severalty Shawnees as well. Individual Shawnees had filed claims for damages with the federal government in 1860 to receive compensation for losses during the territorial period. The Civil War proved just as destructive. Jane Bobb and Elizabeth Walton requested permission to sell land because they needed money while their respective husbands fought against the Confederacy. Due to her husband's arrest for desertion, Walton required funds to support her three children, all of whom had recently survived a bout of smallpox. Jesse Whitedeer had an even more dramatic story. In the fall of 1864 Confederate "bushwhackers" under the command of Major General Sterling Price took him prisoner during the course of a Missouri raid. The Rebel soldiers shot Whitedeer, cut his throat, and left him to die in a field. Although he miraculously survived the ordeal, he had not fully recovered nearly one year later and needed the money to support his family.[11]

By the latter years of the war, the two hundred-acre allotments granted to each Shawnee had become the most convenient source of money to support families and emigration. Currency provided by the 1854 treaty was paid out in seven annual installments and left the Shawnees with minimal income after 1861. Because border violence made it difficult to farm, the Shawnees needed money for food and clothing. Sales records reflected this trend. From April 1, 1863 to May 24, 1865, the Secretary of the Interior approved at least seventy-five Shawnee deeds of conveyance. But more than that amount changed hands. From June 1862 to July 1865,

[10] James Abbott to H. B. Branch, SIA, September 25, 1862, OIA-LR, roll 812; James Abbott to H. B. Branch, June 5, 1863, OIA-LR, roll 813; James Abbott to H. B. Branch, SIA, June 1863, OIA-LR, roll 813. For a more expansive look at the Civil War period, see Abel, *The American Indian in the Civil War*; William Nichols et al. to D. N. Cooley, December 26, 1865, OIA-LR, roll 814; Paschal Fish and Jim Jacob to Louis V. Bogy, November 12, 1866, OIA-LR, roll 814; Paschal Fish to H. L. Taylor, May 21, 1867, OIA-LR, roll 815; George Dougherty and Charles Bluejacket to Col. H. L. Taylor, June 5, 1867, OIA-LR, roll 815; Statistics of Farming, etc. at the Shawnee Agency Sept. 1866, JBA.

[11] "Depredations Upon the Shawnee Indians," House of Representatives Report No. 300, 36th Congress, 1st Session, Serial No. 1068; James B. Abbott to Hon. Wm. P. Dole, Jan. 7, 1865, OIA-LR, roll 814; J. B. Abbott to Hon. Wm. P. Dole, July 11, 1865, OIA-LR, roll 814; Jas. B. Abbott to Hon. Wm. P. Dole, July 12, 1865, OIA-LR, roll 814; James B. Abbott to Hon. W. P. Dole, June 3, 1865, OIA-LR, roll 814.

Indian agents sent approximately one hundred and forty-four deeds to the Secretary's office. The portions sold ranged from one acre to over three hundred acres, depending on both the seller and the purpose. Nancy McDougal, a Shawnee widow, sold one hundred acres in the summer of 1865 because she "needed the money for her sustenance." James Bone sold one hundred acres because "he has a large family to support has been sick a long time and is now and has been heretofore in need of money to assist in clothing and feeding his children." In the months immediately following the Civil War, at least three Shawnee families sold their entire allotments and moved to the Indian Territory. They had had enough. "Once the Indians get away from there," Samuel Cornatzer, the clerk of the Shawnee Council, observed, "the persons buying their land will never have any trouble from them." The problems in Kansas had grown too burdensome. Many Shawnees wanted to sell their plots, move south, and start anew in Indian Territory.[12]

Twelve years after the Shawnees ceded the bulk of their land in Kansas, few allottees had made it to the top of the hill once described by Joseph Parks. In September 1866, five hundred and seventy-one Shawnees belonged to families that held land in severalty. These Shawnees worked in fields that produced harvests of wheat, corn, oats, and potatoes, and eighty out of the one hundred and ninety-two households had either cattle or hogs, with forty-seven raising both. Although the overall numbers present an aura of self-sufficiency, concentrated material wealth illustrated clear disparities. More than 55 percent of the 3,652 acres in cultivation belonged to less than 10 percent of the Shawnee households, creating what might be termed a "cultivating elite." Those same Shawnee households owned just over 46 percent of both the cattle and hogs raised to supplement the harvests from the fields. Meanwhile, approximately 32 percent of the Shawnee households had no discernible agricultural produce and roughly the same number did not own a horse, much less a hog or cow.[13]

Among these severalty Shawnees, wealth reinforced leadership and leadership reinforced wealth. Parks died in 1859, and years after his death

[12] *Indian Affairs*, II, 618–626. The notices of deed applications and approvals from which I compiled these numbers can be found in OIA-LR, rolls 812–814. For Nancy McDougal and James Bone, respectively, see J. B. Abbott to Hon. W. P. Dole, June 2, 1865, OIA-LR, roll 814, frame 112, and J. B. Abbott to Hon. W. P. Dole, June 2, 1865, OIA-LR, roll 814, frame 117; Samuel Cornatzer to D. N. Cooley, July 10, 1866, OIA-LR, roll 814.

[13] Statistics of Farming, etc. at the Shawnee Agency Sept. 1866, JBA; *Indian Affairs*, II, 618–626. Members of the Long Tail Band, who had also received a reserve in common in the 1854 treaty, gave up that reserve for allotments in the late 1850s.

FIGURE 8. Portrait (Front) of Kalui, called Charles Blue Jacket. (Courtesy of the National Anthropological Archives, Smithsonian Institution.)

the Kansas judicial system mediated disputes over the vast amounts of real estate the Shawnee leader left behind. His successors in office also fared well. Graham Rogers, the elected principal chief of the Shawnees in 1866, cultivated two hundred acres that produced nearly two thousand bushels of wheat, twenty-five hundred bushels of corn, and twelve hundred bushels of oats. In addition, he was one of only five Shawnees to raise sheep, and his flock of one hundred accounted for over half of the sheep population on Shawnee lands. His predecessor in office, Charles Bluejacket, had half the acreage but concentrated his efforts on sixty hogs and forty cattle. At least five other members of this Shawnee cultivating elite – Matthew King, Charles Tucker, George Dougherty, Dudley Tucker, and Samuel Cornatzer – held positions in the Shawnee government at some point from 1860 to 1865. Cornatzer, a white man adopted by the

Shawnees in 1847, had served as the clerk for the Shawnee Council since 1856. His assets included one hundred and twenty-five cultivated acres, forty-three cattle, and thirty hogs. Isaac Parish was also a white man who appeared on the Shawnee rolls as a result of his marriage and subsequent adoption. His herd of one hundred and twenty hogs more than doubled the closest competitor and he raised wheat, oats, and corn on one hundred and sixty acres. These men and the few others who shared their prosperity profited even as their neighbors lacked the most vital necessities.[14]

The land in Kansas grounded these disparities both figuratively and literally. Even though factionalism and material wealth created problems prior to the organization of Kansas Territory, events in the 1860s proved critical because of how those divisions solidified. As important as the manner of allotment was the speed with which those lands left Shawnee hands and who influenced those exchanges. It is amazing that the Shawnees had property to cultivate by 1866. From 1857, when government surveyors finalized selections among the Kansas Shawnees, to 1866, allotment, warfare, sales, and taxation separated most Shawnees from at least a portion of their original selection. Although numerous factors made the process of dispossession seemingly complex, the actual equation was simple. Conditions in Kansas made it difficult for anyone but the wealthy to hold on to their allotments. Before 1860, land sales occurred primarily at the instigation of prosperous Shawnees. As early as July 1857 local officials reported that, "a number of the principal men of the tribe such as the Chief Joseph Parks, Blue Jacket and others are buying out those that will sell." The key question was whether the federal government would validate such exchanges, and how soon the Office of Indian Affairs would permit sales to white men. Paschal Fish in particular intended to profit from eager and prosperous emigrants. In the winter of 1856–1857, he met three German speculators who traveled from Chicago to Kansas to purchase land on which they might establish a town. After a brief negotiation, the three men arranged to buy a large section at the mouth of the Wakarusa

---

[14] *Catherine Swartzel et al. v. Sally Rogers*, 3 Kan. 374; Statistics of Farming, etc. at the Shawnee Agency Sept. 1866, JBA. For members of Shawnee government, see B. J. Newsom to A. M. Robinson, September 5, 1860, OIA-LR, roll 811; Statement of Charles Bluejacket and Graham Rogers, April 7, 1863, OIA-LR, roll 813; James B. Abbott to Thomas Murphy, January 15, 1866, OIA-LR, roll 814; Statement of Graham Rogers et al., November 19, 1866, OIA-LR, roll 814. For Cornatzer and Parrish background, see Samuel Cornatzer testimony in *Charles Blue-Jacket v. The Commissioners of Johnson County et al.*, 3 Kan. 299; James B. Abbott to Hon. W. P. Dole, June 2, 1865, OIA-LR, roll 814.

River. According to the contract, the town company would survey all of the eight hundred acres purchased from Fish. In a canny business move, however, Fish sold the men only half of the acreage and retained the remaining four hundred acres in alternating sections on the surveyed town site. Then, in February 1858, the Shawnee real estate mogul sent a letter to Commissioner of Indian Affairs James Denver requesting a patent in fee simple for the land he and his family selected under the 1854 treaty. "I propose to sell all or a portion of my lands to a company of men from Chicago, Illinois who intend to build up a town," Fish explained, "and unless you shall favorably regard my request I shall be unable to retain them here and my lands and those of my neighbors will lose the plus value they might acquire by the instance of that town." Yet this communication was nothing more than a formality. The Chicago group settled, built, and populated the town of Eudora, appropriately named after one of Fish's daughters. Following the lead of the Territorial Legislature, Governor Samuel Medary approved Eudora's charter in February 1859. The only hindrance to the town's existence was the fact that Fish still had not received an official deed to his land from the federal government by the summer of 1859.[15]

In Eudora and elsewhere, the federal regulation of land sales lacked strength even as hardship and desperation made money offers increasingly attractive to impoverished Shawnees. In addition, the process of deed certification granted substantial control to the leaders of the Shawnee Council. The federal government hoped to control the exchange of Shawnee lands by retaining the power to administer deeds of conveyance contracted in Kansas. Indeed, the eleventh section of an act passed by Congress and approved in March 1859 set a number of conditions to be met before an Indian could sell off part of his or her allotment. These conditions included a certificate of competency signed by two chiefs of the individual's tribe as well as a certificate from the appropriate Indian Agent. If these and other steps were not fulfilled, the Secretary of the Interior could reject the deed. As illustrated by Paschal Fish, however, federal inaction did not necessarily hinder land transfers. This lax system cut both ways. Land sales helped Shawnees in desperate need of money to purchase food and clothing in the early 1860s. Yet the ease with which deeds were written

---

[15] S. C. Taylor to C. E. Mix, July 17, 1857, OIA-LR, roll 809; C. E. Mix to S. C. Taylor, August 22, 1857, OIA-LR, roll 809; Edward C. Clark to Hon. A. B. Greenwood, January 5, 1859, OIA-LR, roll 811; Paschal Fish to Hon. J. W. Denver, February 1858, OIA-LR, roll 810; C. F. Schowarte to Lewis Cass, July 25, 1859, OIA-LR, roll 810; "Douglas Country: Part 32-Eudora," in William G. Cutler, *History of the State of Kansas* (Chicago, 1883).

and ownership transferred also made it easier for Shawnees to lose their allotments.[16]

The certificates of competency signed by the Shawnee chiefs gave additional influence to allotment advocates and land speculators. Every deed of conveyance sent to the Commissioner of Indian Affairs included several documents. The standard form signed by the chiefs read: "We [blank], the two chiefs of the Shawnee tribe of Indians...certify that [blank] the Grantor mentioned in the accompanying Deed of conveyance is the Identical Individual to whom the land in said deed was originally granted...that [blank] is competent to manage [his] affairs and to dispose of [his] property." For all of the deeds issued from 1862 to 1865, the names of Charles Bluejacket and Graham Rogers filled the first blank on those forms. Although they helped some of the poorer Shawnees obtain much needed funds through these sales, the two chiefs also oversaw a vast exchange of Shawnee allotments during a relatively short period of time.[17]

The value of the acreage as well as the honesty of the exchanges also compromised the sales. Although the Shawnees received more money per acre in private negotiations than they ever did in treaties, undervalued purchases predominated. Jesse Whitedeer received $3 per acre for the eighty acres he sold to Philip Becker in the summer of 1864, while M. Barlow received $5 per acre. But the Shawnees owned valuable territory in eastern Kansas, and their leaders knew that the right conditions could produce higher prices. The Shawnee Council in July 1868 attacked their agent H. L. Taylor for undermining this potential. According to acting first chief Charles Tucker and his councilors, "lands belonging to individual members of said Tribe, which if owned by white men would be worth not less than $10 or $15 per acre, have been sold for much less than its real value." More important, these sales were "approved of and recognized by" Taylor. Agent Taylor was simply the latest agent accused of rapid deed approval. B. J. Newsom and James Abbott also came under fire for profiting from and facilitating land sales in eastern Kansas.[18]

---

[16] "Rules and Regulations to be observed in 'The execution of conveyance of lands...'" in OIA-LR, roll 814.

[17] For the several hundred deeds and accompanying documents that include copies of the form signed by Bluejacket and Rogers, see OIA-LR, rolls 812–814.

[18] Wm. Holmes to Wm. P. Dole, June 17, 1864, OIA-LR, roll 813; Preamble and resolutions adopted by the Shawnee Council in July 1868, OIA-LR, roll 816; Paschal Fish et al. to A. B. Greenwood, March 18, 1860, OIA-LR, roll 811. Abbott was also intricately involved in the fraudulent allotment and sale of Black Bob Shawnee lands in the late 1860s. For a record of the investigation, see Senate Executive Document No. 40, 41st Congress, 2nd Session, Serial No. 1406, 1–210.

Meanwhile, affluent Shawnees sold land for strategic and business purposes. Matthew King, an elected councilor and frequent government-employed interpreter, executed six different deeds from February 2, 1864 to July 12, 1865. In total, he sold approximately six hundred acres. However in September 1866 he still had one hundred acres in cultivation and owned horses, cattle, and hogs. Charles Bluejacket sold three hundred and sixty acres in the summer of 1865 and shared King's prosperous lifestyle. For these two men and others like them, such exchanges were opportunities to make money, not a necessity for survival. "Bluejacket ... is a large farmer," Agent Abbott observed, "intelligent and capable of using to an advantage any money that he may obtain from the sale of his land." Other Shawnees sold their allotments because they did not need the land. Rachel Rogers Journeycake and Melinda Rogers Connor were sisters who had married Delaware men and received land under the Delaware's 1860 accord. These women now wanted "to dispose of their whole Shawnee selections, that they may use the proceeds of the sale for the improvement of their Delaware land." There were many who shared the sisters' idea and sold off a portion of their allotment to raise the capital necessary to cultivate the remainder of their selection.[19]

But even as they requested permission to sell, Rachel Journeycake and Melinda Conner raised a concern shared by all border Indians who owned land in severalty. The two sisters wanted "to have their money invested where it will not be taxed for the support of a State Government in which they have no interest." This proved to be a serious point of contention. Within months of entering the Union as the thirty-fourth state, Kansas, and its incorporated counties, took steps to assess Indian lands for tax purposes. It was both a demonstration of newly gained power as well as a targeted attempt to remove the Indians from the state. In 1865, many land sales in Johnson, Wyandotte, and Douglas Counties, where most of the Shawnees owned property, were closely connected to taxes levied by the respective county governments.[20]

---

[19] Notice of Matthew King's sales can be found in OIA-LR, rolls 813 and 814 on the following dates: February 2, 1864, May 19, 1864, January 22, 1864, September 27, 1864, December 5, 1864, July 12, 1865; J. B. Abbott to Wm. P. Dole, July 12, 1865 OIA-LR, roll 814. For Journeycake and Connor, see J. B. Abbott to Hon. Wm. P. Dole, February 18, 1865, OIA-LR, roll 814; "Delaware Allotments Treaty May 1860" and "Census of the Delaware Tribe of Indians Within The Delaware Agency [Kansas] Taken February 15th One Thousand Eight Hundred Sixty Two," in Fay Louise Smith Arellano (Transcriber), *Delaware Trails: Some Tribal Records, 1842–1907* (Baltimore, 1996), 25–73, 92–118.

[20] J. B. Abbott to Hon. Wm. P. Dole, February 18, 1865, OIA-LR, roll 814.

Taxation first arose in 1859, when Shawneetown decided to assess the lands of all Shawnee Indians lying within the town limits. This settlement, first founded as Gum Springs in August 1857, took action while Kansas was still a territory. The town government informed the Shawnees in the area, including Charles Bluejacket, Eliza Randall, and Margaret Williams that the combined assessment on all Indian lands totaled $500. The Shawnee Council questioned the legality of this action and hired the law firm of Glick, Bartlette, and Glick to investigate. These attorneys were unsure of the town's rights to tax Indian lands and contacted Commissioner of Indian Affairs to see if the 1854 treaty permitted such actions. They wrote with urgency, because the collection deadline was little more than a month away. However, the 1854 treaty said nothing about taxation on individual allotments, which meant that Shawneetown's assessment did not violate the treaty. From the subsequent lack of interest or uproar, the town did not follow through on its threats.[21]

In the 1860s, however, Kansas state officials revived these tax assessments. The allotment accords negotiated from 1854 to 1861 contained wording that ranged from specific to ambiguous. Wyandots with patents in fee simple could only be taxed five years after Kansas became a state, while Potawatomis with patents for their allotments were immediately subject to taxation. Like that of the Delawares, the Shawnee treaty failed to address this issue in specific terms. The Shawnee agreement, instead, included a rather ambiguous article. "Congress may hereafter provide for the issuing," it read, "to such of the Shawnees as may make separate selections, patents for the same, with such guards and restrictions as may seem advisable for their protection therein." What that protection might entail was never explained thoroughly. When Kansas entered the Union in 1861, however, the first section of the Congressional Act declared that, "nothing in the [Kansas] constitution respecting the boundary of said state, shall be construed to impair the rights of person or property now pertaining to the Indians in said Territory, so long as such rights shall remain unextinguished by treaty between the United States and said Indians." In other words, federal authority remained supreme in the regulation of Indian affairs in the state of Kansas.[22]

---

[21] Ed Blair, *History of Johnson County, Kansas* (Lawrence, 1915), 160–161; Glick, Bartlett, and Glick, to CIA, May 7, 1859, OIA-LR, roll 810. For the location of Shawnee allotments in relation to town of Shawnee in the late 1850s, see J. Cooper Stuck Plat Map, JBA; *Indian Affairs*, II, 618–626.

[22] *Indian Affairs*, II, 618–626, 677–681, 803–807, 824–828; Act quoted in Jas. Harlan to Jas. Speed, February 6, 1866, OIA-LR, roll 814.

In the absence of a specific restriction in the Shawnee treaty, however, Kansas state and county officials declared and exercised their right to tax. Beginning in 1861, the authorities in Johnson, Douglas, and Wyandotte Counties assessed the lands of Shawnee Indians. Each county assessed the Shawnee lands at $15 per acre. But the Shawnees refused to believe that such action had legal standing. They sent delegates to Washington who returned with word that the Shawnees should not pay a dime to local officials. Attorneys in the region similarly advised the Shawnees. Some of those Shawnees with the means, including Charles Bluejacket, paid the taxes to avoid any possible fines. Such compliance, however, did not signal acceptance.[23]

Instead, Bluejacket and the Shawnees took their grievance to the Kansas judicial system and in a prolonged fight gained a bittersweet legal victory. In the petition filed against Johnson County, the Shawnees argued that "they never have surrendered to the United States nor to the state of Kansas their national existence and the right to regulate their affairs in their own way." Thus, they had never given the state of Kansas the right to impose taxes. But when their case made it to the Kansas Supreme Court, the Justices disagreed. In the February 1865 decision of *Bluejacket v. Commissioners of Johnson County*, Chief Justice Robert Crozier declared that "the lands are subject to taxation unless exempted specifically by the constitution of this state." Integral to this ruling was the fact that the severalty Shawnees did not hold their lands in a compact fashion and the Court's opinion that this and other practices failed to align with the characteristics of an Indian tribe. "It is difficult to conceive of a national existence without a national domain upon which to maintain it," Crozier wrote. The Shawnees appealed and when the U.S. Supreme Court rendered its decision in May 1867, the Shawnees had their victory. The nine Justices reversed the Kansas ruling. More specifically, Justice David Davis declared in his opinion that, "the action of the political department of the government settles, beyond controversy, that the Shawnees are as yet a distinct people, with a perfect tribal organization." Therefore, "as long as the United States recognizes their national character they are under

---

[23] J. B. Abbott to Thos. Murphy, February 16, 1866, OIA-LR, roll 814. For reference to the Johnson County rates, see James Elliott to Wm. P. Dole, February 10, 1865, OIA-LR, roll 814; Abstract from the Records of the County Treasurer's Office Showing the Taxes Due Wyandott County, Kansas, By the Shawnee Indians Holding their Lands in Severalty from 1860 to 1865 inclusive, OIA-LR, roll 814; Shawnee Indian Lands situated in Douglas County, Kansas Sold for the Tax of 1861–1863, OIA-LR, roll 814; S. M. Cornatzer to Judge Cooley, January 22, 1866, OIA-LR, roll 814.

the protection of treaties and the laws of Congress, and their property is withdrawn from the operation of State laws." The Supreme Court had affirmed the distinct and special relationship between the federal government and Indian nations.[24]

Yet this legal triumph arrived too late for most Kansas Shawnees. As soon as the Kansas Supreme Court announced its decision in February 1865, county officials began to sell deeds to Shawnee allotments for unpaid taxes and interest. In Douglas County alone, the delinquent fees from 1861 to 1863 totaled $5,163.22. And as the U.S. Supreme Court worked through its caseload, Shawnee leaders pressed the government for a speedy resolution. "County officers are selling our lands," Samuel Cornatzer reported early in 1866. "We are waiting in almost painful anxiety to hear from Washington in regard to these abominable taxes." Only six months later, the Shawnees still had not heard any news and conditions remained grim. Matthew King argued that the situation was "Life or Death." If the U.S. Supreme Court upholds the decision, "then by mere technicalities we will be thrown out of our property and reduced to poverty; to poverty what an Idea. When was an Indian ever rich." The fact that these protests came from some of the wealthier Shawnees highlights the precarious position of the less privileged members of their community. In its annual report for 1866, the Office of Indian Affairs reported that most of the Shawnee lands had been sold off as a result of taxes and other debts. With each sale the U.S. Supreme Court decision proved to be more of a moral victory than a tangible one.[25]

The Shawnee Council subsequently moved to sell the remaining lands in Kansas and relocate to Indian Territory. To the consternation and frustration of the Shawnee Council, the U.S. Senate rejected six treaties

---

[24] *Charles Blue-Jacket v. The Commissioners of Johnson County et al.*, 3 Kan. 299; *Re: The Kansas Indians*, 72 U.S. 737. The Blue-Jacket case was decided by the U.S. Supreme Court in conjunction with two similar cases involving the Wea and Miami Indians in Kansas. For a discussion of the larger legal context of court decisions and Indian sovereignty in the nineteenth century, see David E. Wilkins, *American Indian Sovereignty and the U.S. Supreme Court: The Masking of Justice* (Austin, 1997), 19–63; Jill Norgren, *The Cherokee Cases: Two Landmark Federal Decisions in the Fight for Sovereignty* (Norman, 2004).

[25] Shawnee Indian Lands situated in Douglas County, Kansas Sold for the Tax of 1861–1863, OIA-LR, roll 814; S. M. Cornatzer to Judge Cooley, January 22, 1866, OIA-LR, roll 814; Matthew King and Others to D. N. Cooley, July 11, 1866, OIA-LR, roll 814; Paul Wallace Gates, *Fifty Million Acres: Conflicts over Kansas Land Policy, 1854–1890* (Ithaca, 1954), 45–47; ARCIA, 1866, 245–246; John W. Ragsdale, "The Dispossession of the Kansas Shawnee," *University of Missouri-Kansas City Law Review*, 58(Winter 1990): 209–256.

negotiated and signed by Shawnee delegates over the course of the 1860s. "The Government Officers and the Senate," Samuel Cornatzer declared, "while living high and drinking their fine liqueurs think a small matter whether it [treaty negotiated in 1867] is ratified or not while it is almost a matter of life or death with many of us and a matter of great anxiety to us all." The Shawnee leadership wanted to leave Kansas as soon as possible and by the summer of 1868 had already made several trips to Indian Territory to inspect the land and to talk to members of the Cherokee Nation. Finally on June 7, 1869, the Shawnee Council reached an agreement with the Cherokees, whereby the Shawnees would pay the Cherokees approximately $50,000 and would become members of the Cherokee Nation. The severalty Shawnees thus became Cherokee-Shawnees. President Grant approved this agreement on June 9, and the Shawnees arranged the disposal of their Kansas territory. Because of this agreement, the Shawnees, through their former agent and current attorney James Abbott, requested that "the rules and regulations for the conveyance of their lands be so modified as to permit them to dispose of all their lands." By 1871, seven hundred and seventy Shawnees resided within the boundaries of the Cherokee Nation.[26]

Even as they struggled to reach this agreement, the Shawnee Council battled with the Black Bob Shawnees over the latter's thirty-three thousand acre reserve. By 1865, squatters had laid claim to most of that land. Then in 1866, right before his term ended, Shawnee Agent James Abbott issued patents to individual plots on the reserve to sixty-nine Black Bob Shawnees. Most of these plots were promptly sold to persons other than the squatters. The resulting conflicting claims placed the Black Bob band in the middle of a legal battle that lasted into the 1880s. Paschal Fish argued that Abbott had issued fraudulent patents and that the subsequent sales should not be recognized. Further investigation by Kansas officials supported Fish's accusations. "I never applied for a patent to my land," a Shawnee named Wahkachawa testified in July 1869, "nor never authorized any one to do so for me; I am opposed to the issuance of patents." On the same day Wahkachawa registered his complaint, Jim Jacob and

---

[26] Graham Rogers and Charles Tucker to E. S. Parker, January 6, 1870, in Senate Executive Document No. 40, 41st Congress, 2nd Session, Serial No. 1406, 5–6; S. M. Cornatzer to C. E. Mix, June 1, 1868, OIA-LR, roll 816; Matthew King et al. to C. E. Mix, May 9, 1868, OIA-LR, roll 816; Articles of Agreement between the Shawnee and Cherokee Indians, June 7, 1869, OIA-LR, roll 817; J. D. Cox to E. S. Parker, June 10, 1869, OIA-LR, roll 817; Cherokee-Shawnee Census, 1869, MS 1097, KSHS; James A. Abbott to E. S. Parker, July 1, 1869, OIA-LR, roll 817; Shawnee Census of 1871 at http://www.accessgenealogy.com/native/1871shawnee. (Accessed May 24, 2006.)

John Perry informed Justice of the Peace for Johnson County Sherman Kellogg that at least three of the Black Bobs who reportedly requested patents had been dead for years.[27]

Yet Graham Rogers and Charles Tucker, the elected leaders of the Shawnee Council, did not oppose these patents. Arguing instead that both the patents and the land sales should be recognized, Rogers and Tucker observed that every delay in the confirmation of these sales forced the Black Bob Shawnees "to remain another winter, living in mere apologies for shanties, without the ability to procure hardly a pittance of the necessaries of life, where they must suffer with cold and hunger." The two headmen provided an accurate depiction of living conditions in 1869, although they ignored the Black Bob protests against allotment. With their reserve overrun, the Black Bobs planned to leave Kansas. But because they wanted compensation for their lands, the debates over the patents held them hostage. More important, the Black Bob band continued to dispute the authority of Rogers, Tucker, and the Shawnee Council to participate in this process and accused them of acting in concert with federal officials. "We...want you to know," James Jacob and twenty-two other Black Bob and Absentee Shawnees stated in October 1868, "how our people are imposed on and annoyed by Agent Taylor and the late agent, Abbott, through the men they employ, principally severalty Shawnees. These men want to break up our reserve that they may speculate in our lands." Yet both the Superintendent of Indian Affairs and the Secretary of the Interior allowed the sixty-nine sales to stand. When a series of appeals and lawsuits by squatters and other interested parties kept the issue alive, the Black Bob Shawnees chose to leave Kansas without obtaining any satisfactory resolution. Rather than wait for financial closure that might never come, most of the Black Bobs moved to Indian Territory. What money they did receive did not reach them until the 1880s.[28]

[27] *Indian Affairs, II*, 618–626. For appearances of Black Bob Shawnees before the Justice of the Peace, see Senate Executive Document No. 40, 41st Congress, 2nd Session, Serial No. 1406, 182–184. For fraudulent patents see 144–150; Gates, *Fifty Million Acres*, 45–47; *ARCIA 1866*, 245–246.

[28] Graham Rogers and Charles Tucker to E. S. Parker, CIA, January 6, 1870, Senate Executive Document No. 40, 41st Congress, 2nd Session, Serial No. 1406, 5–6. For letters regarding the desire to sell the patents and move to Indian Territory, see 144–150; James Jacob et al. to Charles E. Mix, October 13, 1868, in ibid., 56–57; Enoch Hoag, SIA, to E. S. Parker, CIA, September 17, 1869, ibid., 154–157; *ARCIA 1872*, 37; *ARCIA 1873*, 200; *ARCIA 1875*, 88–89; *ARCIA 1876*, 71; Anna Heloise Abel, "Indian Reservations in Kansas and the Extinguishment of Their Title," *Transactions of the Kansas State Historical Society*, 8(1903–1904): 93–97.

Like that of the Shawnees, the Potawatomi experience in the 1860s was defined largely by two different battles – one for autonomy and one for power. From the time of removal to the 1870s the Prairie Band maintained a consistent stance against incorporation into a single Potawatomi nation. They had no desire or need to unite politically with Potawatomis who did not share their values or vision for the future. At the same time, members of the Citizen Band and a growing number of influential men of mixed descent assumed positions of prominence in Potawatomi politics and diplomacy. Yet neither autonomy nor power protected the Potawatomi bands from the impact of American expansion in Kansas.

The Prairie Band's assertions of autonomy in the 1860s built on decades, if not centuries, of persistence. Their stance had solidified less than twenty years earlier when American officials attempted to unite all Potawatomis on a single reserve on the Kansas River. In the fall of 1845, these Potawatomis resided in and around Council Bluffs, Iowa, less than five hundred miles from their former homes. It had taken just over a decade for the leading edge of American settlement to overtake them. Iowa had become a territory in 1838 and in the fall of 1845 was a little over one year away from statehood. Because of the growth of the non-Indian population in the region, U.S. officials worked constantly to sign land cession treaties. The Council Bluffs Potawatomis had arrived in the spring of 1837 and lived in six different clusters of villages established on different waterways in western part of the territory. Almost all of these Potawatomis were members of what was known as the United Band of Potawatomis, Ottawas, and Ojibways. Although by the late 1830s the composition of this group was almost completely ethnically Potawatomi, the United Band designation referred to a long existent confederation also known as the People of the Three Fires. For much of the eighteenth century, the United Band had lived in northern Illinois and southern Wisconsin. Now residents of Iowa, the nearly two thousand Potawatomis had begun to develop a somewhat stable existence in their western homes.[29]

But from 1837 onward, American officials constantly pressed the United Band to join the other western Potawatomis. This southern Potawatomi community encompassed Indians who formerly lived along the Wabash, Kankakee, Yellow, and St. Joseph rivers in northern Indiana and southern Michigan. Included in this population were survivors of the Trail of

---

[29] James A. Clifton, *The Prairie People: Continuity and Change in Potawatomi Indian Culture, 1665–1965* (Lawrence, KS, 1977), 317–329.

Death as well as other Potawatomis who had relocated between 1833 and 1840. Their new homes rested along the Sugar and Potawatomi creeks, two small tributaries of the Osage River, close to the Missouri state line. By 1840, these scattered settlements contained nearly two thousand men, women, and children. Because of concerns about the future extension of American settlement into the region, American officials wanted the Potawatomis from the Council Bluffs and Osage River agencies to relocate to a new reserve that straddled the Kansas River near present-day Topeka.[30]

Major Thomas H. Harvey, Superintendent of Indian Affairs for the St. Louis Superintendency from 1844 to 1849, explained at least two reasons for the federal government's position in September 1845. "There is no subject connected with the superintendency that I feel more interest in than I do in uniting the Potawatomis in the south country and merging their funds in to one common stock," he asserted. "I should think that I had done the state some service and the Indians a lasting benefit." From Harvey's perspective this would be at once a political and an economic union, one that would simplify future treaty negotiations and annuity distributions.[31]

Extensive council sessions in the summer of 1845 finalized nothing, and negotiations continued in Washington that fall. During those fall meetings, General George Gibson and Major T. P. Andrews, the appointed treaty commissioners, emphasized the need to unite the Potawatomis to create "one grand council fire." But the commissioners also tried to elevate the status of the Potawatomis from the Bluffs. Late in the negotiations, on November 29, the commissioners referred to the Council Bluffs Potawatomis as "the most important Band of the Pottawattomies." "You know that all the Pottawattomies are Brothers," they continued. "But you are the Band and chiefs to go ahead: you do go ahead in all councils, and the others follow you." Gibson and Andrews then grounded this assertion in a helpful analogy. "Your Band is like his [the Great Father's] large

---

[30] Anthony L. Davis to C.A. Harris, November 20, 1837, OIA-LR, roll 642. For the Potawatomi removals, see R. David Edmunds, "The Prairie Potawatomi Removal of 1833," *Indiana Magazine of History*, 68(September 1972): 240–253; R. David Edmunds, "Potawatomis in the Platte Country: An Indian Removal Incomplete," *Missouri Historical Review*, 68(July 1974): 375–392; Irving McKee, *The Trail of Death: Letters of Benjamin Marie Petit* (Indianapolis, 1941); Shirley Willard and Susan Campbell (Eds.), *Potawatomi Trail of Death: 1838 Removal from Indiana to Kansas* (Rochester, IN, 2003).

[31] Th. H. Harvey to T. Hartley Crawford, September 18, 1845, OIA-LR, roll 216; Clifton, *The Prairie People*, 329–335.

States. The Pottawattomies have Smaller Bands like his smaller States. But all ought to be consulted in treating with your Great Father. You should act first, being the great chiefs of the large Band: and the other Bands follow after you."[32]

The commissioners were not necessarily off target. Potawatomi bands and villages had long operated autonomously in a manner consistent with the actions of states in the Union. But the similarities ended there. James Clifton has used the descriptive phrase "segmentary tribal organization" to describe Potawatomi political structures of the seventeenth and eighteenth centuries. In other words, the Potawatomi "tribe" was not a "single, standing, sovereign political entity. It had no centralized governing authority." Rather than an organized alliance of villages under the rule of an overarching hierarchy, the Potawatomi community was a confederation of autonomous bands held together by the bonds of kinship, language, and culture. The flexible nature of this confederation had even contributed to expansion of the Potawatomis' territorial domain in the seventeenth and eighteenth centuries.[33]

The United Band of Potawatomis, Ottawas, and Ojibways illustrated that political development well. Centuries ago these three peoples were one, and they all shared the same language. At some point in the sixteenth century a division occurred, perhaps beginning with separate villages based on clan and kinship. Yet, even as a once-unified people developed along three different paths around three different fires, the political alliance remained. The Potawatomis were the "Younger Brothers" in this relationship, in part because they had a smaller population than the other two. But the Potawatomis also separated over time into three general divisions – the Prairie eventually lived in northern Illinois, the Wabash in northern Indiana, and the St. Joseph in southern Michigan. In each region the village leader, the okama, remained the important political entity. Yet while all remained Potawatomis, the regional distinctions made a

---

[32] Journal of Council with Potawatomis, November 1845, OIA-TR, roll 4. For summer sessions, see Minutes of Council June 1845, OIA-LR, roll 216.

[33] James A. Clifton, *A Place of Refuge for All Time: Migration of the American Potawatomi into Upper Canada 1830–1850* (Ottawa, Canada, 1975), 10–14; Thomas G. Conway, "Potawatomi Politics," *Journal of the Illinois State Historical Society,* 65(Winter 1972): 395–418; James A. Clifton, "Potowatomi Leadership Roles: On Okama and Other Influential Personages," *Papers of the 6th Algonquian Conference* (1975): 42–99; David Baerris, "Chieftainship Among the Potawatomi," *Wisconsin Archaeologist,* LIV(September 1973): 114–134.

difference. In the first several decades of the nineteenth century, the United Band did not refer to those Potawatomis living in Indiana and Michigan. And when U.S. officials negotiated with the United Band, it did not imply that they negotiated with the Potawatomis as a whole.[34]

Consequently, the Potawatomi delegates in Washington in November 1845 evaluated the federal government's agenda from a distinct perspective. The Potawatomis in attendance were headmen from the Bluffs. Wabansi, a man just over eighty years old, was the eldest, a leader who served as the principal negotiator throughout the 1845 meetings. Half Day was the designated speaker in council and had held that position for more than a decade. Of the other Potawatomi men present, only Miamis, who lived in the cluster of villages established along the Nishnobotna River south of Council Bluffs, spoke with any regularity during the course of the negotiations. None of the headmen were new to their position, and each one had been present in Chicago twelve years earlier at the treaty council that resulted in the cession of approximately five million acres of land in northern Illinois and southern Wisconsin.[35]

Little Miami, Shabeni, White Pigeon, three other Potawatomis, and two metis interpreters in a council room in the White House joined Wabansi, Half Day, and Miamis. Together with their Agent, Richard Smith Elliott, they faced Gibson and Andrews. On November 12, Elliott read from a lengthy statement prepared by the Potawatomi delegation the night before. Their most direct critique of the federal government's plan came in the conclusion. "You say that our Great Father wishes to unite all the Pottawatomies. It used to be that we had but one fire but he disturbed us. He put out that fire and scattered the ashes. He cannot collect them; but if he will make a treaty, as we have said, he will see how many fires will burn. We will go to the land we ask [for] and make a fire. This is all we will say." The Potawatomi delegation argued that the Great Father had put out their one fire and scattered the ashes. Indeed, in 1845 in addition

---

[34] Donald L. Fixico, "The Alliance of the Three Fires in Trade and War, 1630–1812," *Michigan Historical Review*, 20(Fall 1994): 1–23; Benjamin Ramirez-Shkwegnaabi, "The Dynamics of American Indian Diplomacy in the Great Lakes Region," *American Indian Culture and Research Journal*, 27(Winter 2003): 53–77.

[35] *Indian Affairs, II*, 402–415; Journal of the Proceedings of a Treaty between the United States and the United Tribes of Pottawottamies, Chippeways, and Ottawas, September 1833, OIA-TR, roll 3; Anselm J. Gershwin, "The Chicago Indian Treaty of 1833," *Journal of the Illinois Historical Society*, 57(Spring 1964): 117–142; Richard Smith Elliott, *Notes Taken in Sixty Years* (St. Louis, 1883), 198–207; Murphy, *Potawatomi of the West*, 49–52.

to those in the West, different bands could be found in southern Ontario, southern Michigan, Wisconsin, and Mexico.[36]

But this fragmentation represented more than geographic distance. Cultural differences and choices had also gradually altered relationships. On the Yellow River in Indiana, Menominee and his band had accepted Jesuit missionaries and built a chapel on their reserve. Members of the St. Joseph bands sent their children to a Baptist mission school. The United Band was less receptive to Christianity, and had frustrated the efforts of Father Pierre Jean De Smet and his Jesuit colleagues in the late 1830s. Just as dramatically, the United Band made a point of excluding the metis members of their population from participating in the political process on the reserve. Only in rare instances was a metis even allowed to speak in council. It was a critical move, especially because the Potawatomis and French had intermixed to a significant extent as a result of alliance and the fur trade. In the 1840s, then, the United Band at Council Bluffs was far more culturally conservative than the Potawatomis at Osage River.[37]

More important, for the 1845 council and the decades that followed, the United Band viewed itself as politically distinct from the Osage River Potawatomis. "The people who made the treaty of Chicago are at Council Bluffs," the Potawatomi delegation's statement read, "no other people have a right to sell the lands east of the Missouri." Their negotiations did not require affirmation or approval from anyone other than the villagers back in Iowa. What transpired in Washington was of no concern to those living on the Osage River. Therefore, despite what other Potawatomis or even federal officials might say to the contrary, the leader of the Osage River Potawatomis, Topinebee, did not have any say in the matter. He was not their principal chief, and "he has never built a fire among us." The United Band did not see him as a relevant figure in their lives in the West.[38]

The Potawatomis from Council Bluffs, known by the late 1840s as the Prairie Band, would not submit to the federal government's view that the

---

[36] Journal of Council with Potawatomis, November 1845, OIA-TR, roll 4; Elliott, *Notes Taken in Sixty Years*, 208–210; Helen Hornbeck Tanner, *Atlas of Great Lakes Indian History* (Norman, 1987), 134; Clifton, *The Prairie People*, 272–311; Clifton, *A Place of Refuge for All Time*, 65–86.

[37] Jerry E. Clark, "Jesuit Impact on Potawatomi Acculturation: A Comparison of Two Villages in the Mid-Plains," *Ethnohistory*, 26(Autumn 1979): 377–395; Murphy, *Potawatomi of the West*, 37–58; Clifton, *The Prairie People*, 317–329.

[38] *Indian Affairs, II*, 402–415; Journal of Council with Potawatomis, November 1845, OIA-TR, roll 4; Topinape et al. to T. Hartley Crawford, December 14, 1843, OIA-LR, roll 642.

Potawatomis were and should be a united tribe. As one delegate stated clearly, "They sold their lands separately and they made their own bargains." But they did see a need to leave Iowa, and by the end of the council the delegates appeared content with the government's offer. Wabansi and the others had no intention of talking to those Potawatomis on the Osage River. Instead, they would sign the treaty, and their Great Father would see how many fires would burn on the Kansas River reserve. They would leave Iowa and relocate to the Kansas River. But the United States should not expect there to be one fire.[39]

Gibson and Andrews wrapped up this 1845 council with a rhetorical flourish that revealed ignorance, optimism, or a combination of the two. "All the Pottawattomie people will again be Brothers. Then, when you are united and living harmoniously together . . . the Great Spirit will look down upon you, we hope, and say, 'these are my good children I will smile on them and make them happy.'" But when anyone, the Great Spirit included, looked down on the Kansas River reserve in the years after this treaty, he did not see harmonious coexistence. The Prairie Band lived on the north side of the river and resisted agricultural dependence and individual land ownership. The villages south of the river encompassed almost exclusively the Osage River Potawatomis, known by then as the Mission Band for their affiliation with Christian missionaries. Although Jesuits from St. Mary's Mission had convinced some members of this band to move north of the river, most stayed south. Settled on the same reserve but separated by the Kansas River, these two bands maintained distinct governments and functioned as separate entities on a day-to-day basis.[40]

Leaders of both bands continued to clarify their respective positions in the decades that followed this geographic union. At two different times in the spring of 1858, the Potawatomis explained why the American government had failed to unite the disparate communities and why it would continue to fail. In a letter to the Superintendent of Indian Affairs, a number of Prairie Band headmen placed the blame for the factions on the federal government. Their statement revealed both a struggle for power and an important transition in the politics on the reserve. "The department has accused this nation of having no head. It is true," the Potawatomis admitted. But the headmen then pointed a finger at the American government. "Who has caused it. Commissioners who acted under the seal of the United States. Within the space of eight days on Tippecanoe River. You

---

[39] Journal of Council with Potawatomis, November 1845, OIA-TR, roll 4.
[40] Ibid.

have created twenty eight chiefs by making Band Reserves and we have many aspiring men who make money their god. They sow the seed of dissention. Thereby disunion oppresses this people." Less than three weeks later, a different delegation of Potawatomis met at the Agency building and addressed a statement to the Commissioner of Indian Affairs, James Denver. "We as Chiefs of our Nation," they acknowledged, "are now fully sensible of the division, discord, and bad feeling that exists within our Nation, amongst our children of the full blood, half breed, and white people intermarried in our nation, and we are pained and regret to see these things, knowing as we do that it operates against us, and against our Children, in our efforts to make an arrangement with the Government to better our condition...we as chiefs intend for the future to unite as brothers." The full statement, although read to the council, did not meet the approbation of the Prairie Band chiefs and they refused to sign it.[41]

Both the letter and the subsequent council highlighted the internal discord on the Potawatomi reserve in the late 1850s. The first communiqué directed its gaze on men who made "money their god," a description that established a connection to the statements made in council to Commissioner Denver. The Potawatomi delegation had focused particularly on individuals of mixed descent. Many of these individuals had long been members of different Potawatomi bands and had participated in the western removals. The foundations and relationships built during the height of the fur trade continued to bring them influence. And they followed the examples of those who had gone before them. The men who worked their way into leadership positions during the 1860s built on the patterns created by men like Billy Caldwell and Alexander Robinson in the 1830s.

The turning point came in 1861. The Potawatomi reserve created in 1846 spread across present-day Jackson and Shawnee Counties, just west of the Delaware and Shawnee lands. From the late 1840s to the 1850s the Potawatomis coexisted out of necessity with the seasonal migrants who journeyed westward along the Oregon Trail, a section of which passed through the reserve. By 1861, however, speculators and railroad executives had set their sights on the Potawatomi lands. The Prairie Band received a portion of the original reserve, 77,358 acres, to hold in common. This diminished reserve, located north of the Kansas River in present-day Jackson County, further hemmed in the Potawatomis. But they had resisted all talk of allotment and this allowed them to maintain their desired way of life.

---

[41] Potawatomi Indians to SIA, April 2, 1858, OIA-LR, roll 681; Memorial of Potawatomi Chiefs, April 19, 1858, OIA-LR, roll 681.

In all, about seven hundred and eighty men, women, and children chose to live on these common lands. Those Potawatomis who chose allotments from the remaining 498,642 acres consisted almost exclusively of the Mission Band, and they numbered approximately fourteen hundred.[42]

Just as Caldwell and Robinson had used the 1829 and 1833 treaties in Chicago to punctuate their entrance into the higher levels of Potawatomi leadership, the men who rose to power in Kansas profited from this 1861 agreement. Joseph LaFramboise had grown up in a French–Indian community in the Milwaukee area, and first established himself among the United Bands in the late 1820s. A contemporary of Caldwell and Robinson, LaFramboise signed the 1833 accord and gained influence with the United Band at Council Bluffs. By 1861 he had become a headman and signed the allotment treaty. The names of Joseph Bertrand, Jude Bourassa, and Joseph Bourassa joined that of LaFramboise. Bertrand was the son of the French trader Joseph Bertrand, Sr., and Madeline, a Potawatomi woman. He had attended the Carey Baptist Mission School in Michigan, and had lived with the Potawatomis ever since. The Bourassas were also alumni of the Carey Mission School, and the school records listed them as Ottawas of mixed descent. These individuals, along with a number of others, assumed more prominent intermediary positions as the years passed, not only because of their importance to the Potawatomis, but also because of their value to federal officials and traders.[43]

Subsequent events more concretely entrenched the status of LaFramboise and his cohort. Before the Senate had even ratified the 1861 treaty, a small delegation of Potawatomis formed a Business Committee "fully empowered to transact all business between the Potawatomi Indians and the government of the US." The committee only nominally represented the Prairie and Mission bands and its membership of six was self-appointed rather than elected. The initial group included Medone B. Beaubien, Joseph N. Bourassa, and Anthony F. Navarre as delegates for the Prairie Band. Beaubien was the son of Jean Baptiste Beaubien and his French–Ottawa wife Josette LaFramboise. As a trader he first connected with the Potawatomis in the late 1820s and moved west to Council Bluffs with the United Band. Beaubien solidified his standing within the metis and Potawatomi communities in 1846 when he married Theresa Hardin LaFramboise, the daughter of Joseph LaFramboise and quite possibly a

---

[42] *Indian Affairs*, II, 824; Clifton, *The Prairie People*, 351–352.
[43] Clifton, *The Prairie People*, 351, 362–369; Murphy, *Potawatomis of the West*, 48, 106–111.

not so distant blood relation. Navarre had a bit more colorful history with the Potawatomis. Born to a French trader and a Potawatomi woman in northern Indiana, Navarre lived briefly with the Potawatomis at Council Bluffs before joining the Mormons' western migration. He returned to the Potawatomis in 1857 as a missionary intent on convincing the Potawatomis to join the Mormons' struggle against the federal government. Navarre soon abandoned this mission and entered into the mercantile business. Members of Prairie Band particularly appreciated Navarre's stand against the American government and their initial support of his leadership reflected that admiration. The Mission Band representatives on the Business Committee had their own interests at stake as well. Benjamin H. Bertrand was the brother of Joseph and an alumnus of the Carey Mission School. Louis Vieux belonged to a metis family from Milwaukee. By the late 1850s, he owned several mills and toll bridges throughout the reserve and had a considerable economic interest in Potawatomi affairs. John Tipton, the third delegate for the Mission band and also metis, had worked for the Potawatomis as an interpreter in the late 1850s.[44]

The title for the Business Committee fit quite well, for the men who comprised it involved themselves primarily in the economics of the community. Indian agent W. W. Ross took a decidedly positive view of this turn of events. "This step has been considered necessary in order to facilitate the transaction of their business," he reported. "Under their old system, in order to do business, no matter of how trivial a nature, a council of the Nation must be called thus consuming much time and often to no purpose. The Department will readily see what difficulty attends the transaction of business with a heterogeneous mass of men and boys without any system of organization." Shortly after its inception, and in the years that followed, however, the Business Committee seldom represented the unified interests of the entire Potawatomi community, and by 1867, even members of the Citizen Band were calling for its termination. "Through some misconception of their prerogatives or from intentional usurpation of power," Wewesay and other headmen protested to Agent Luther Palmer, "they have failed to act in conformity with the wishes of

---

[44] W. W. Ross to William Dole, CIA, March 10, 1862, OIA-LR, roll 683; Testaments of R. A. Kinzie and John D. Lasley, April 15, 1852, OIA-LR, roll 684; William Murphy to Alexander Robinson, SIA, August 22, 1859, OIA-LR, roll 682; William Murphy to Alexander Robinson, SIA, November 25, 1858, OIA-LR, roll 681; L. R. Palmer to D. N. Cooley, CIA, March 27, 1866, OIA-LR, roll 686; Memorial of Potawatomi Chiefs, April 19, 1858, OIA-LR, roll 681; Clifton, *The Prairie People*, 243, 317, 367–371; Murphy, *Potawatomis of the West*, 49.

the Chiefs or the people, and have not thought proper to make reports of any or but few of their proceedings." Just as critical, the American government also ignored the Prairie Band leadership and worked solely with the Business Committee.[45]

Regardless of these developments, all Potawatomis faced the consequences of the 1861 treaty and the desires of railroad companies in Kansas. The combination of allotment and railroad interests was already at work on the Delaware reserve in the machinations of the Leavenworth, Pawnee, and Western Railroad Company (LP&W). But the LP&W did not limit their ambitions and also managed to gain rights to unclaimed Potawatomi lands in the 1861 agreement. This maneuver was not necessarily forced on the Potawatomis. LaFramboise, Bertrand, Bourassa, and their allies recognized the government's unwillingness to protect Indian reserves in Kansas and hoped to profit from the land speculation that would surely follow the treaty. They knew that railroad construction equaled increased real estate prices, and allotment represented the first step toward selling the land.[46]

With the treaty signed and ratified, it appeared that all involved achieved their goals. Over the next five years, commissioners mapped out a total of 152,128 acres in individual plots of land for those individuals. This left almost 350,000 acres from the original Potawatomi reserve for the LP&W. After the Potawatomis chose their individual plots, the company could purchase the lands and construct their railroad. Executives expected significant profits and only had to wait until the completion of allotment to reap the benefits.[47]

Much to the dismay of railroad executives, however, the Potawatomis made intelligent selections. All told, the survey and land distribution took almost five years, lasting from 1862 to 1867. During this time, the Potawatomis' knowledge of the land made trouble for the LP&W in its new incarnation as the Union Pacific, Eastern Division. Edward Wolcott, one of two supervisors appointed by the federal government, observed that the Indians "know the value of land and select personally every tract which is alloted to them." These educated choices prolonged the process and after a year the commissioners still had yet to record the plots of over

---

[45] W. W. Ross to William Dole, CIA, March 10, 1862, OIA-LR, roll 683; Wewesa et al. to L. R. Palmer, June 29, 1867, OIA-LR, roll 687.

[46] Smith, "The Oregon Trail through Potawatomi County," 453–456; Clark, "Jesuit Impact on Potawatomi Acculturation," 382–384; *Indian Affairs, II*, 937–942.

[47] *Indian Affairs, II*, 824; Clifton, *The Prairie People*, 351–352; Edward Wolcott to William Dole, CIA, April 18, 1865, OIA-LR, roll 685.

three hundred out of the fourteen hundred Potawatomis who chose allotment. Although it was detrimental to the railroad's intentions, the delay
had less of an impact than the actual selections had. "The allotments
to the Potawatomis," John Perry, President of the Union Pacific, Eastern
Division(UPED), remarked with some concern, "have been made so as
to embrace all the timber lands upon the streams making the allotments
very irregular and exposing the Indians on all sides to contact with the
whites." But Perry's true distress grew from his observation that many of
the chosen allotments crossed into his railroad's right of way. The UPED
president encouraged Commissioner of Indian Affairs D. N. Cooley to
force all allotments to exist within a compact section.[48]

Perry's interest in having the Potawatomis select allotments in a
compact form illuminated the connections between the railroads and
the federal government. This interplay also had consequences for the
Potawatomis who opted for individual land ownership. Once the commissioners completed the survey, their maps showed that several plots crossed
into the railroad's right of way, just as Perry had feared. The UPED president detested the thought of working around individual allotments and
he was frustrated that most of the timber now grew on unavailable plots.
Perry's subsequent decision to forfeit the right to purchase the unalloted
lands proved a mixed blessing for the Potawatomis. Although the railroad's departure relieved some of the pressure on individuals intending to
retain their plots, it also undermined the plans of those hoping to make
a profit. Fortunately, for the hopeful profiteers at least, Kansas Senator
Samuel C. Pomeroy and the Atchison, Topeka, and Santa Fe Railroad
filled the void and obtained the rights to the unallotted lands in an 1867
treaty. The ease with which another railroad took over the negotiations
demonstrated the overwhelming desire shared by politicians and promot-
ers alike to build the railroad through Kansas. It also suggested that, when
confronted with the combined power of the federal government and the
railroads, the Indians could only hope to delay the intrusion.[49]

But even as the Potawatomis frustrated the UPED's vision of an easy
land transfer, they also faced the intertwined issues of allotment, citizenship, and taxation. Circumstances were similar to those among the
Shawnees. Joseph Bourassa's purchase of an eighty-acre allotment from

---

[48] Edward Wolcott to William Dole, CIA, May 10, 1863, OIA-LR, roll 684; John D. Perry to
D. N. Cooley, CIA, December 11, 1865, OIA-LR, roll 685; H. Craig Miner and William E.
Unrau, *The End of Indian Kansas: A Study of Cultural Revolution, 1854–1871* (Lawrence,
1978), 43–44.
[49] Gates, *Fifty Million Acres*, 132–143; *Indian Affairs*, II, 970–974.

Kacamsa in 1866 was one of many sales within the Potawatomi community. And the Business Committee had the authority to determine the competency of any Potawatomi man or woman to sell their land. But taxation was further complicated by federal missteps. Once a Potawatomi accepted allotment, was deemed competent, and became a citizen, he or she was subject to taxes. Citizenship also entitled each Potawatomi to a payment equal to his or her share of the tribal assets held in trust by the government. But the cash payments did not arrive after the first dispensation of patents in December 1865. Because a large percentage of the Potawatomis needed these funds, significant losses ensued. Louis Vieux, one of several individuals who made a living by running a toll bridge and providing services to travelers, could easily meet his payments without assistance. For the majority of the Potawatomis, however, taxation quickly developed into a tremendous burden. Individuals refused to pay their taxes until they had received their payments from the federal government and the state of Kansas seized and sold the title to their lands.[50]

When the 1867 treaty established a home for members of the Citizen Band in Indian Territory, the Prairie Band retained their reserve established by the 1861 accord. They did not want to move and requested that the tribal funds maintained by the federal government be divided between the two bands. The Prairie Potawatomis depended on the annuities and other government payouts and had no desire to subsidize any members of the Citizen Band who had not yet relocated to Indian Territory. But in their request for a partition of the government payments this more traditional faction of the Potawatomis also moved toward an official separation from the people with whom they believed they had little in common. Based on the history of land losses among the Citizen Band and the continued struggle of the Prairie Indians to eke out a living, most agents viewed the latter's resistance to removal as only temporary. In the fall of 1872, Superintendent of Indian Affairs Enoch Hoag predicted that "the time may not be distant when the Pottawatomies will be reunited on their selected lands in the Indian Territory." Contrary to Hoag's prediction and despite the power and influence of the railroads arrayed against them, the Prairie Band continued to maintain a presence in Jackson County, Kansas.

[50] *Indian Affairs*, II, 824, 916, 970; L. R. Palmer to Thomas Murphy, December 22, 1866, OIA-LR, roll 687; Joseph N. Bourassa to William Dole, December 29, 1867, OIA-LR, roll 688; A. B. Burnett to Ely Parker, CIA, June 26, 1869, OIA-LR, roll 689; Lucius R. Dorling to CIA, October 12, 1869, OIA-LR, roll 689; L. R. Palmer to N. G. Taylor, February 16, 1869, OIA-LR, roll 689; Smith, "The Oregon Trail Through Potawatomi Country," 454–456.

FIGURE 9. Pisehedwin, A Potawatomi, and others in front of his Kansas farm home, 1877. (American Indian Select List, number 9, National Archives and Records Administration.)

They gradually devoted more and more of their acreage to agriculture and raised a large number of animals, horses in particular. Time also eased daily interactions with their neighbors. "Their relations with the white people living contiguous to them are of the kindest nature," observed agent H. C. Linn, "and all difficulties about trespass of stock, &c., are easily settled without resort to law."[51]

But when government agents delivered reports on the Prairie Potawatomis in Kansas, they could not avoid mentioning the "absentee" band members. Agent J. H. Morris counted approximately four hundred and fifteen Indians on the diminished reserve in 1871, a severe drop from

---

[51] Representatives of the Prairie Band of Potawatomi Indians to Major L. R. Palmer, 1869, OIA-LR, roll 689; *Indian Affairs, II,* 824–828, 970–974; Clifton, *The Prairie People,* 386–389; *ARCIA 1871,* 496; *ARCIA 1872,* 226. For dispossession among the Citizen Potawatomis, see L. R. Palmer to Thomas Murphy, SIA, November 11, 1867, OIA-LR, roll 687; A. B. Burnett to Ely Parker, CIA, June 26, 1869, OIA-LR, roll 689; L. R. Palmer to N. G. Taylor, CIA, February 16, 1869, OIA-LR, roll 689; F. A. Walker to Enoch Hoag, September 4, 1872, Quapaw Agency, roll 4, OSHS; Alford, *Civilization,* 70–73, 136; *ARCIA 1879,* 81–84.

the seven hundred and eighty persons named in the roll of 1865. Death was not the primary cause. In that six-year period, nearly one quarter of the Prairie Band left Kansas and joined the Potawatomis living in Wisconsin. The latter group had long avoided removal and followed their seasonal subsistence patterns in and around the unsettled areas of the Wolf and Wisconsin rivers. A federal investigation confirmed that the Potawatomis coexisted peacefully with their non-Indian neighbors. Yet government officials still visited the Wisconsin community in 1873 to convince the almost one hundred and eighty members of the Prairie Band to return. The Potawatomis would not budge. In the absence of government annuities they found employment in the lumber industry and followed more customary practices for subsistence. Because their white employers and neighbors raised few protests about their presence and because they already lived without federal support, these Potawatomis left little room for government influence. If they did not want to move, they did not have to move.[52]

The dispersal of the Shawnees and Potawatomis did not begin in the 1860s. Nor could members of either community blame any one entity for their circumstances. These removals unfolded in ways similar to the movements of prior decades and centuries as a combination of forces, from the federal government to the Kansas state government, pushed aside Indian interests in a scramble for land and money. The passage of time also made this experience unique. Men like Joseph Parks, Graham Rogers, and Charles Bluejacket owned hundreds of acres of land, raised livestock, and made a distinct attempt to work with the forces of American expansion. Their ambitions to get to "the hill top," like those of the Potawatomi Business Committee, often contrasted with the wishes of many they claimed to represent. And their actions and attitudes did little to change the agendas of those who promoted Indian removal from Kansas.

Nor did internal power struggles benefit the winners or losers. The Shawnee government with whom federal officials dealt in the 1860s was also that which surrendered its autonomy to live among the Cherokees. And by the turn of the century Agent Frank A. Thackeray estimated that "the Citizen Band of Potawatomi Indians are scattered through nearly every state of the Union, only about one-half of their number residing upon their allotments in this [Indian] territory." Beginning with their

---

[52] *ARCIA 1871*, 496; W. W. Ross to William Dole, CIA, August 19, 1864, OIA-LR, roll 684; O. H. Lamoreux to CIA, September 30, 1865, OIA-LR, roll 685; Edward Wolcott to William Dole, CIA, April 18, 1865, OIA-LR, roll 685; *ARCIA 1880*, 98.

respective allotment treaties, the Ohio Shawnee Council and the Potawatomi Business Committee had fought for power and gained the ear
of the U.S. government. But it still left them at the mercy of local
interests. Similar problems plagued the Black Bob Shawnees and Prairie
Potawatomis, despite their efforts to maintain a separate existence. In
post-Civil War Kansas, reliance on the federal government equaled dispossession.[53]

[53] *Indian Affairs, II,* 970–974; Warren, *The Shawnees and Their Neighbors,* 170–173;
Murphy, *Potawatomi of the West,* 305–307; *ARCIA 1902,* 277; Smith, "The Oregon Trail
Through Potawatomi County," 453–456; Articles of Agreement between the Shawnee and
Cherokee Indians, June 7, 1869, OIA-LR, roll 817.

Epilogue

Life after Exile

More than one hundred years after Charles Trowbridge sat down in Ohio with Tenskwatawa and Black Hoof to obtain the stories and traditions of the Shawnee Indians, J. R. Carselowey stood outside of the Ketchum residence on Rural Route #3 in Vinita, Oklahoma. It was June 9, 1937, and he had come to talk to the father of the household, Sol, but had encountered a problem. Seventy-six-year-old Sol would not stop plowing his cornfield. He focused his efforts on the dirt first planted by his father in 1881. J. R. was anxious, and wondered aloud whether the young man currently relaxing inside the house could take over for his father so that Carselowey and Ketchum could have some time to talk. Sol's wife had a quick and definitive answer for her impatient guest. As far as her husband was concerned, only one man could plow the fields correctly for the corn crop, and that man was already doing the job. He never gave his sons even the briefest opportunity to mess up the family farm.

When the dedicated farmer finally took a break, J. R. commenced the interview for which he had traveled to Vinita. He wanted to know as much as possible about the history of Sol Ketchum's journey to and time in Oklahoma. This was not an errand of simple curiosity. J. R. was one of one hundred writers sent throughout Oklahoma in the mid-1930s to gather the accounts and anecdotes of the state's earliest settlers. Beginning in 1936, under the auspices of a grant from the Works Progress Administration (WPA), J. R. Carselowey and other writers conducted interviews and collected valuable information under the direction of the venerable scholar Grant Foreman. The resulting collection of more than eleven thousand interviews constitutes what is known as the *Indian Pioneer History Collection*.

It is not clear what questions J. R. asked, or how long the interview lasted, but Sol Ketchum certainly had some interesting tales to tell. While

his plow sat restless in the field, Ketchum sat on his porch and remi-
nisced about his days as a prizefighter in Oklahoma and Kansas City.
Although his boxing anecdotes may have had more thrills, he spent a
sizeable portion of the interview relating stories about his father, Louis
Ketchum. Louis had been born in 1808 in Sandusky, Ohio, and died
ninety-six years later on his allotment in Craig County, Oklahoma. Over
the course of his life, Louis had been a fur trapper, hunter, and farmer.
Sol traced the geographic course of his father's life in a matter-of-fact
manner. "While my father was growing up he lived near Sandusky, Ohio;
from there he moved to White River, near Springfield, Missouri; and from
there to Wyandotte, Kansas. In 1880, he gave up his allotment in Kansas,
went before the National Council at Tahlequah and paid $287.00 per
head for an equal right with the Cherokees." By 1881, Louis Ketchum,
his wife Elizabeth, and their children were living near Louis's two brothers
in Vinita. Indeed, the small town of Ketchum in northeastern Oklahoma,
southeast of Vinita, was named after these three brothers.[1]

There are some significant connections between the remarks made by
Sol Ketchum and the stories told by Tenskwatawa and Black Hoof more
than one hundred years earlier. But perhaps nothing captures the importance of this association better than the simple statement Ketchum made
about his family's journeys. His grandfather, George Ketchum, had been
born in Pennsylvania and died in Oklahoma at the age of one hundred.
During that century, George and his son Louis had participated in at least
three significant relocations and lived through the defining moments of
Delaware history in the nineteenth century. In one sense, their movements
picked up where those described by Black Hoof and Tenskwatawa left off.
The two Shawnees had spoken to Trowbridge at a time when only four
hundred Shawnees remained east of the Mississippi. They had discussed
the migrations of the past and could not predict events of the future. In
the Ketchum family history, then, we trace not only the trajectory of the
Delaware movements but also stay linked to the emigrations discussed by
the two Shawnee leaders. Although separated by time and context, the
Shawnee and Delaware stories and storytellers unveil distinct pieces of
that larger map in motion that helps describe native histories in North
America.

The contrasting intentions of the two interviewers are also revealing. Trowbridge was under orders to collect important ethnographic

---

[1] Interview with Sol C. Ketchum: Volume 50, Roll 17, *Indian Pioneer History Collection*,
Archives and Manuscript Division, OSHS.

information before the Indians, their stories, and their way of life disappeared from the American landscape. Lewis Cass hoped to document the traditions of Indians whom he and many others believed were a part of the nation's past. Foreman and his team of one hundred writers in the 1930s also wanted to capture family histories and traditions before they disappeared. But both the context and the nature of Foreman's process were different. The writers did not visit and talk only to Indians. They interviewed Oklahoma's early settlers and pioneers, and a large proportion happened to be of native descent. Resting within the numerous volumes of the *Indian Pioneer History Collection* are the memories of Cherokee men and women whose parents and grandparents traveled the Trail of Tears as well as those of white men and women whose parents had participated in the land runs of the late nineteenth century. Consequently, the umbrella of this vast enterprise in the mid-1930s encompassed personal experiences that were unique even as they intertwined with larger events and narratives.

Sol Ketchum's story was important because he was a Delaware Indian who remembered how he and his family had first arrived in Indian Territory. He could provide insight into how individual Delawares lived and provided for their families in the years after removal. But the story was also notable because Sol was a colorful and dynamic thread in the tapestry of Oklahoma, a former prizefighter who had apparently lost none of his strength or energy since his days in the ring. He was a member of the Delaware community that had left Kansas, removed to Indian Territory. But he was also a pioneer who, along with the thousands who rushed into the region in the late nineteenth century, had played a role in the early history of the state of Oklahoma.

There are a number of ways to analyze Sol Ketchum's personal and family history within the larger narratives of American Indian history. He was interviewed in 1937, only a few years after the Indian Reorganization Act had officially ended allotment, a policy that had begun in 1887 under the Dawes Act and resulted in the loss of approximately two-thirds of Indian lands in the decades that followed. Ketchum and his family were therefore fortunate because they still owned land on which they could farm. Sol and his family also belonged to the Delaware community who had agreed to live with the Cherokees and, in the process, surrendered their tribal sovereignty. And in the end, Sol and his family were survivors whose experience illustrated the ways in which the Delawares had endured the tragedies of the nineteenth century and persisted into twentieth century.

Yet, where do Sol Ketchum and other Indian pioneers fit into the narrative of American history from the late nineteenth century forward?

Individuals like Ketchum, whether or not they boxed, often appear in local histories in fascinating ways. But even though they were also members of vibrant native communities throughout the country, Delawares, Shawnees, Wyandots, and Potawatomis continued to work from the margins in the 1900s. The example of the Potawatomis is as representative as it is unique in this way. More than a century after their dispossession in Kansas, diverse Potawatomi communities live as federally recognized bands and nations in four different states. Despite the consequences of allotment and the implications of citizenship, the Citizen Band retained rights as an Indian nation based in large part on the treaty they signed in 1867. The Prairie Band overcame years of hardship as well as the renewed assault of allotment under the 1887 Dawes Act and preserved a land base in Kansas. Meanwhile, the descendants of those who returned east of the Mississippi now comprise portions of the Hannahville and Forest County communities in Michigan and Wisconsin, respectively. Modern-day polities of Shawnees and Wyandots also make their homes in Oklahoma and other states in the Union, similar survivors of dispossession and assaults on their sovereignty. The Wyandotte Nation of Oklahoma even regained its sovereignty twenty-two years after the 1956 termination of its tribal status by the federal government.[2]

The contemporary lives of these native communities testify to the impact and the importance of those geographic and political struggles of the nineteenth century. During a period of substantial and invasive American expansion, Potawatomis, Shawnees, Delawares, and Wyandots laid claim to and held onto the lands they could, hoping that the decisions they made would ensure the future of their people. All the while, they negotiated increasingly complex relationships with local, state, and federal officials and searched for the best way to protect their rights, promote their interests, and maintain their communities.

Yet, the enumeration of federally recognized bands and nations in the twenty-first century is more than a simple story of survival and persistence. It is a story that testifies to the complicated and often neglected interweaving of the narratives and experiences that comprise American Indian and U.S. history. From the American Revolution to the Civil War, the United States government and its people created a nation out of what

---

[2] Rev. Joseph Murphy, O.S.B., *Potawatomi of the West: Origins of The Citizen Band*. Edited by Patricia Sulcer Barrett (Shawnee, OK, 1988), 281–283; James A. Clifton, *The Prairie People: Continuity and Change in Potawatomi Indian Culture, 1665–1965* (Lawrence, KS, 1977), 347–444; Stephen Warren, *The Shawnees and Their Neighbors, 1795–1870* (Urbana, 2005), 170–173.

had once been a loose collection of disparate colonies. During that same period of time, American Indian individuals and communities in the trans-Mississippi West fought first to maintain their place on the continent and then to defend the lands and rights that they deemed most important. Circumstances brought the two processes together in a number of significant historical moments, whether it entailed the larger history of western expansion or the more specific elements of slavery debates and the Civil War. Conflicts and compromises blended together in the communal struggles of the Shawnees and in the individual experiences of men like William Walker and Joseph Parks.

Cast as exiles by the developing American nation in the early 1800s, these American Indian individuals and communities established new lives west of the Mississippi River. As native pioneers on the prairie grasslands of eastern Kansas in the mid-nineteenth century, they often battled over whether to counter or encourage the settlement of the thousands of non-Indian pioneers favored by federal, state, and local governments that once again pushed Indians to the geographic and political margins.

Now, as citizens of Indian and American nations in the twenty-first century, Shawnees, Delawares, Wyandots, Potawatomis, and others continue to live with the collective legacy of all of those struggles. Even before the organization of Kansas Territory, members of those four communities in the West tried to figure out how they might coexist with the expanding American nation. Although the passage of time has altered the specific contexts, it has not changed the core of that contest. Most important, they continue to battle over their political position within the United States. Together and separately, the General Allotment Act, the Indian New Deal, the Indian Claims Commission, and Termination affected Indian land ownership over the course of the 1900s. And every swing in federal policy has reaffirmed that land will always play a central role in Indian–U.S. affairs. But it is the debates over native sovereignty and the politics of federal, state, and Indian relations that have become even more prominent since the late 1800s.

And so in the present day, some of the most critical confrontations focus on the process of obtaining federal recognition as an Indian band, tribe, or nation. It is a process that is at once crucial to contemporary politics and is anchored in historical events. The Shawnees who agreed to live with the Cherokees, and thus surrendered their tribal status in 1867, finally gained status as a sovereign nation in 2001. Meanwhile, descendants of the Wyandots who chose allotment and citizenship in 1855 have yet to achieve a similar goal, although they have reestablished a presence in

Kansas. Those respective treaties were not singular events that exclusively altered the course of Shawnee and Wyandot history, just as specific agreements cannot bear sole responsibility for the contemporary status of Delawares and Potawatomis in the United States. Yet, each accord had and has meaning. Treaties open windows into the events and decisions of the past, even as they ground the relationship between American Indians and the federal government in the present. Much like historical narratives, the past, present, and future of these four communities are intertwined.

Index